LATIN
for Christian Schools®

Edith E. Smith

🏛 **BJU Press**
Greenville, South Carolina

This textbook was written by members of the faculty and staff of Bob Jones University. Standing for the "old-time religion" and the absolute authority of the Bible since 1927, Bob Jones University is the world's leading Fundamentalist Christian university. The staff of the University is devoted to educating Christian men and women to be servants of Jesus Christ in all walks of life.

Providing unparalleled academic excellence, Bob Jones University prepares its students through its offering of over one hundred majors, while its fervent spiritual emphasis prepares their minds and hearts for service and devotion to the Lord Jesus Christ.

If you would like more information about the spiritual and academic opportunities available at Bob Jones University, please call
1-800-BJ-AND-ME (1-800-252-6363).
www.bju.edu

NOTE:

The fact that materials produced by other publishers may be referred to in this volume does not constitute an endorsement by Bob Jones University Press of the content or theological position of materials produced by such publishers. The position of the Bob Jones University Press, and the University itself, is well known. Any references and ancillary materials are listed as an aid to the student or the teacher and in an attempt to maintain the accepted academic standards of the publishing industry.

LATIN for Christian Schools®

Edith E. Smith

for Christian Schools is a registered trademark of Bob Jones University Press.

© 1999 Bob Jones University Press
Greenville, South Carolina 29614

Printed in the United States of America
All rights reserved

ISBN 1-57924-216-2

15   14   13   12   11   10   9   8   7   6   5   4   3   2

Table of Contents

Welcome

In this book your teacher is called Mr. Cornelius. After the first two chapters, just call him *Magister* (Teacher). If your teacher is a lady, call her *Magistra Cornelius,* or just *Magistra.* You will learn later why there are two spellings for these words.

If you are the only student, you will read the parts of all the students. That should keep you alert! If you are in a class of fewer than twelve students, your teacher will assign you more than one part or may even ask you to take the role of Magister or Magistra sometimes. Most of your assignments will include the reading of sections of the conversations.

Magister often uses a series of questions to lead you from what you already know to information you are to learn. You will be asked to figure out the answers to the questions. This kind of teaching is called *inductive.*

The *Contents* provides (1) a list of the main points covered in each chapter and (2) a list of the Appendices. In the back of the book are the *Appendices,* the English-to-Latin *Vocābulārium,* the Latin-to-English *Vocābulārium,* and the *Index.* Wait for your teacher to tell you when to use the Appendices and the Vocābulārium. Much of the information included there will confuse you if you try to use it too soon.

In the chapters, you will work at first with short, easy sentences. You will concentrate your attention on nouns, then on adjectives, then on verbs, and finally on pronouns. One main difference between Latin and English is that the Romans put many more endings on words than we do in English. These endings, called *inflections,* are presented gradually to help you understand and memorize them.

The best way to learn another language is to *see it, hear it, say it,* and *write it.* As you read the chapters, you will see, hear, and say Latin sentences. The activities in the Activity Manual provide practice in writing Latin. In the text and in the activities, you will often be asked to answer Latin questions with Latin answers. By doing this, you will probably begin to *think* in Latin. You will be reading some verses from Latin translations of Scripture. Reading Scripture in another language can give you new insights into the meaning of God's Word. You will learn about Roman religion and will see Roman myths in the light of God's Word.

At the end of each chapter is a section called *Essential Information.* This section helps you to prepare for chapter tests and for the chapters that follow. New vocabulary words and important terms that you are to learn are easy to find in the chapters because they are in bold type or in section titles.

Your study of the Latin language will be valuable to you throughout your life.

CAPITULUM I

All your life you have been using Latin words. Some of these are spelled exactly the way the ancient Romans spelled them. Many more have been changed in spelling. You probably have not read any Latin sentences. Now you can learn to read in the language that has greatly influenced the English language and several other languages.

When you started to walk, you took short steps. Little by little you learned to take bigger steps. As you learned to walk, your steps became automatic; you were walking without thinking. Likewise, in the study of Latin, after the short first steps you can soon be reading Latin sentences and whole paragraphs. Like taking longer and longer walks, you will read longer and harder Latin sentences and even paragraphs as you work through this book, chapter by chapter.

FIRST STEPS

Reading a Latin Sentence

Mr. Cornelius: Hic est liber.

Mark: What did you say?

Clement: I think I know. You said, "This is a book."

Mr. Cornelius: Tell us how you figured it out.

Clement: You pointed to a book. Besides, the word *est* sounds a little like the English verb *is.*

Mr. Cornelius: The *-t* ending tells us that the subject is a singular noun or pronoun. The subject in *Hic est liber* is the pronoun *hic.*

Paul: Clement said, "This is *a* book." Where is the word for *a?*

Mr. Cornelius: The Romans didn't have words for *a, an,* and *the,* which in English we call **articles.** At first the lack of these words will seem strange, but you'll soon find yourselves just naturally adding them to make your translations sound right in English.

Let's talk more Latin. Hic est liber meus. Ille est liber tuus.

Gloria: "This is my book. That is your book." I could figure out *ille* and *meus* and *tuus* from where you pointed.

Mr. Cornelius: Excellent.

Gloria: Why are the words for *my* and *your* after the word for *book?*

Mr. Cornelius: The Romans usually put adjectives after the nouns. *Meus* and *tuus* are adjectives in Latin.

Sylvia: How can I ask, "Is that book yours?"

Mr. Cornelius: "Estne liber ille tuus?" The Romans put an **enclitic** on the end of the first word of a question. This enclitic, *-ne,* means "Here comes a question." An enclitic is a short, unaccented word joined to the preceding word. Latin has only a few of them.

The Romans did not use question marks or most of the other punctuation we use. To make our study easier, however, we will use modern punctuation.

Timothy: The verb starts both the Latin and the English questions.

Mr. Cornelius: You're very observant. But not all Latin and English questions begin with verbs.

This book has my name on it. Estne liber hic meus?

Mark: Liber ille est tuus. Or should I say, "Ille est liber tuus?"

Mr. Cornelius: Both are right. *Hic* and *ille* are sometimes pronouns and sometimes adjectives, depending on how they are used. In the English sentence *That book is yours,* the word *that* is an adjective. In *That is your book,* the word *that* is a pronoun.

Quid means "what?" It is an **interrogative pronoun** when it begins a question. The enclitic isn't needed at the end of an interrogative pronoun since the pronoun itself tells us that a question is being introduced. Here's a question for you: Quid est hic?

Timothy: Ille est liber tuus.

Mr. Cornelius: Quid est ille?

Timothy: Hic est liber meus.

Mr. Cornelius: *Stilus* means "pen." Quid est hic?

Victor: Ille est stilus tuus.

Mr. Cornelius: Quid est ille?

Victor: Hic est stilus meus.

Mr. Cornelius: *Hic* or *this* refers to something near, and *ille* or *that* refers to something farther away.

Activity A

(1) Can you correctly pronounce all the words in the Latin sentences you have read? (2) Can you give the English meaning of each Latin sentence you have read?

Pronouncing Latin Words

Flora: The Romans lived a long time ago. How do we know the right way to pronounce Latin words?

Mr. Cornelius: We don't know exactly how they pronounced their words. The few simple rules we follow are based partly on the similar sounds of letters in several languages that developed from ancient Latin. You'll be learning about these **Romance languages** in Chapter 3.

Clara: Who decided what the rules would be?

Mr. Cornelius: People who have used Latin down through the centuries have agreed on some simple rules so that people who use Latin can understand one another no matter what their native language is.

Julia: Are the rules much different from English rules?

Mr. Cornelius: They're much simpler. In English, for example, a vowel (*a, e, i, o,* or *u*) may have several different sounds, but in Latin each vowel always has approximately the same sound. A **long vowel** is held twice as long as a **short vowel.**

Victor: How can you tell long vowels from short ones?

Mr. Cornelius: A **macron** (ˉ) over a vowel tells us that the vowel is long and is to be held twice as long as a short vowel. The first *a* in the English word *aha* sounds like a Latin short *a,* and the second *a* sounds like a Latin long *ā.* A vowel that has no macron over it is short. The macrons in your book are to help you learn which vowels are long. The Romans didn't use macrons.

Clement: How are the other Latin vowels pronounced?

Mr. Cornelius: Here's a chart of all the long and short Latin vowel sounds.

a = first *a* in *aha*

ā = second *a* in *aha* or the *a* in *father*

e = *e* in *let*

ē = *e* in *they*

i = *i* in *it*

ī = approximately the sound of *i* in *machine.*

o = *o* in *obey*

ō = *o* in *home*

u = *u* in *put*—<u>not</u> *u* in *cut*

ū = approximately the sound of *u* in *rude*

Mr. Cornelius: Look back at the sentences you've read so far. Are the vowels long or short?

Gloria: They must be short because they don't have macrons over them.

Mr. Cornelius: You're right. Listen to these sentences and notice the consonant sounds. *Hic est liber. Ille est liber. Quid est stilus?* Here are English equivalents to some Latin consonants, syllable division rules, and an accent rule.

a. Consonants

Any letter that is not a vowel is a consonant.

c = *k* in *book,* not *s* in *city*

s = *s* in *this,* not *s* in *these*

qu = *kw,* as in *quick* (The *u* in this combination is a consonant.)

r should be trilled

Both *l*s in *ille* are pronounced. Latin has no silent conso-nants or vowels.

b. Syllable division

Usually syllables are divided

- between two vowels (me•us, tu•us)
- before a consonant between two vowels (li•ber, sti•lus)
- between any two consonants that do not form a blend (ul•ti•ma, lin•gua)

Every syllable must contain a vowel.

c. Accent

The **ultima** (last syllable) is never accented.

Lydia: Would you pronounce the Latin translation of the book title for us?

Mr. Cornelius: Yes, you've noticed it on the title page with the English title. It is *Lin'•gua La•tī'•na Scho'•līs Chris•ti•ā'•nīs.* Here is more information to help you with the pronunciation.

---

a. Consonant sounds

ch = k + a quick outbreathing, as in *chorus* (The *ch* is not a true blend; instead it is a Latinized spelling of the single Greek letter χ, pronounced *chi.*)

gu = gw in *language,* not *gu* as in *gun* (The *u* in this combination is a consonant.)

b. Accent

The **penult** (next-to-last syllable) is accented when it is long. A syllable is long if it contains a long vowel.

Notice which syllables I accent when I say the Latin translation of the title again. *Lin'•gua La•tī'•na Scho'•līs Chris•ti•ā'•nīs.* Why is the accent on the first syllable in *lingua* and *scholīs?*

Mark: Because the ultima can't be accented.

Mr. Cornelius: Name the syllable that is accented in *Latīna* and *Christiānīs* and tell why the accent is placed there.

Timothy: The next-to-last syllables are accented because they are long. I guess I should call them the penults.

Mr. Cornelius: Yes. The penult is always accented when it contains a long vowel.

Activity B

Understanding the Book Title

Flora: What does the Latin title of this book mean?

Mr. Cornelius: You can probably figure it out with a little help. *Lingua* is a noun that means "language." The meaning of the adjective *Latīna* is obvious. Remember the **position of adjectives.** In Latin they usually come *after* the nouns they modify. How would you say "Lingua Latīna" in English?

Mark: "Latin language." Should I add an article?

Mr. Cornelius:	Try it. Generally if an article sounds right, we should add it.
Mark:	"The Latin language"—sounds right to me. Does *scholīs* mean "school"?
Mr. Cornelius:	Good guess. But it's plural. The Latin word Christiānīs can be either an adjective or a noun. Which do you think it is here?
Mark:	I think it's an adjective because "Christian schools" sounds logical. *Christiānīs* ends in *s* too. Should adjectives have plural endings?
Mr. Cornelius:	Yes, in Latin they do. That's something we'll talk more about in a later chapter.
Timothy:	"The Latin Language Christian Schools." That doesn't sound right. Don't we need to add something? How about "The Latin Language the Christian Schools"—no, that's not right.
Mr. Cornelius:	What word can you supply to make the title sound better?
Victor:	"The Latin Language *in* or *for* Christian Schools." *For* sounds better. May I just add any word to make the English sound right?
Mr. Cornelius:	No, it's not that simple. But you made the right choices when you supplied *for* and omitted the article before "Christian Schools." Later on you will find out why *for* must sometimes be **supplied** to make correct English translations.
Lydia:	Is there a reason that both *Lingua* and *Latīna* end in *a* and both *Scholīs* and *Christiānīs* end in *s?*
Mr. Cornelius:	Yes, there is a reason for the corresponding endings. In each pair of words, the adjective modifies the noun. Let's review. What are the adjectives?
Sylvia:	*Latīna* and *Christiānīs.*
Mr. Cornelius:	That's right. The *-a* endings on *Lingua Latīna* are subject-form endings, but because this is not a sentence, there is no verb. The endings on the words *Scholīs Christiānīs* are actually *-īs,* not just *-s.* Later you will learn when to use the *-īs* inflection. From now on, **inflection** is the term we will always use for a word ending.
	Now, apply your reasoning ability. What can you conclude about adjectives and the nouns they modify?
Rex:	You mean besides the fact that adjectives come after the nouns?

Mr. Cornelius: I'm glad you remembered that. Yes, I mean besides the word order.

Rex: Well, the adjective inflections look the same as the inflections of the nouns they modify.

Mr. Cornelius: For the two sets of words in this title, you've reached the correct conclusion. These adjective inflections are spelled like the noun inflections. Adjectives always agree with the nouns they modify, but the inflections will not always be spelled the same. In *liber meus* the noun and adjective agree even though they don't have the same inflections. Don't worry. That will be cleared up as you go along. A noun with any words that modify it is called a **noun phrase.** How many noun phrases are in the translation of the book title?

Mark: Two. *Lingua Latīna* and *Scholīs Christiānīs.*

Mr. Cornelius: Very good. Watch for noun phrases in the sentences we will be working with from now on.

Can you (1) pronounce the translation of the Latin title of this book correctly and (2) give the English meaning of the title?

Tracing the Word Latin *to Its Origin*

Latium, where Rome began

Alps

Po R.

ETRUSCANS

Tiber R.

CORSICA

Rome

LATIUM

SARDINIA

SICILY

Mediterranean Sea

Flora: Where did the word *Latin* come from? *French* comes from *France*, and *German* comes from *Germany.* But what country is Latin named for?

Mr. Cornelius: The word *Latin* comes from *Latium,* a small district in central Italy. Today it is called Latium or *Lazio.* The people in Latium were called **Latins.** They were speaking Latin several centuries before Christ was born—before there was a country called Italy.

Victor: I thought Rome was the name of that country.

Mr. Cornelius: **Rome** is a city, but down through the centuries the word *Rome* has referred to more than just the city. Rome became the strongest city in ancient Latium. She then gained control over the whole peninsula that we know as Italy and was eventually the capital of a huge empire.

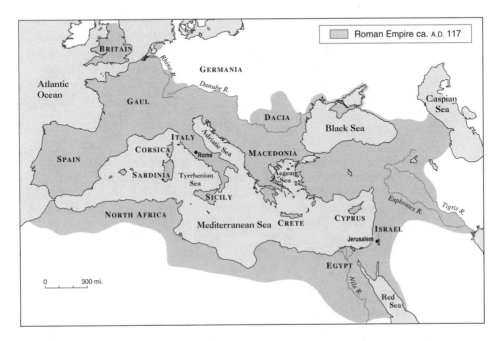

Mark: You mean the **Roman Empire.**

Mr. Cornelius: That's right. The whole empire is often referred to as Rome. Even though Latium was a very small part of the Roman Empire, the language of the whole empire was always called Latin.

Rex: I've heard French and Spanish called Romance languages. Does *Romance* come from *Roman?*

Mr. Cornelius: Good thinking, Rex. You're right.

 Can you (1) give the origin of the word *Latin,* and (2) explain two ways that the word *Rome* is used?

Using Context to Translate Understood Subjects

Mr. Cornelius: Because the **verb inflection** -*t* means that the subject is a singular noun or pronoun, a Latin sentence can be written without a noun or pronoun subject. The pronoun **subject is understood.** Let me illustrate.

> Hic est liber.
> Quid est hic?
> Est liber.

Please translate these sentences.

Gloria: "This is a book. What is this? It is a book."

Mr. Cornelius: You just naturally supplied *it* as the subject of *est*. If I had said in Latin "Bill is my brother. Who is Bill?" you would have said, *"He* is your brother." The context tells you what pronoun to supply. The **context** is the information in the sentence or paragraph that enables you to solve a problem. Sometimes the context is a picture or a situation.

You need some practice with what you have learned.

Activities C, D

 Can you answer a Latin question with an understood subject if the context makes the subject clear?

Saying "Hello" and "Goodbye" in Latin

Mr. Cornelius: When we meet for our next class, let's greet each other in Latin. I will say "Salvēte." You should reply, "Salvē." The *v* is pronounced like the *w* in *way*.

Clara: Why are there two ways to say *hello* in Latin?

Mr. Cornelius: The Latin -*te* inflection is used when we greet more than one person. The -*e* inflection is for just one person.

Paul: How do we say "Goodbye"?

Mr. Cornelius: You say to me, "Valē." And I say to you, "Valēte." After you learn all the noun inflections, you will be able to greet people in Latin calling them by their titles and by their names if their names have Latin origin.

Essential Information

Mr. Cornelius: Each chapter concludes with a section called "Essential Information." The items in bold type in the chapters are "essential information." Be sure that you understand each item.

Essential vocabulary words are in bold type. (In this chapter all the vocabulary words are essential. In later chapters, the lists include a few that are not essential.) Make it a habit to master every essential vocabulary word: the spelling, the meaning, and any other information given. Review them regularly.

Grammar terms

- noun phrase, enclitic, interrogative pronoun
- understood subject, articles, *for* (in book title)
- inflections (endings): noun, adjective, singular and plural, verb

General terms

- Latins, Latium, Romance languages, Rome, Roman Empire

Pronunciation

Vowels

- Compared with the short vowels, the long vowels (those with a macron) take approximately twice as long to say.
- *a* = first *a* in *aha*
- *ā* = second *a* in *aha* or *a* in *father*
- *e* = *e* in *let*
- *ē* = the *e* in *they*
- *i* = *i* in *it*
- *ī* = approximately the sound of *i* in *machine*.
- *o* = *o* in *obey*
- *ō* = *o* in *home*
- *u* = *u* in *put*
- *ū* = approximately the sound of *u* in *rude*

Consonants and consonant blends

- *c* = *k* as in *cat,* not as in *city*
- *s* = *s* as in *this,* not as in *these*
- *ch* = *k* + *a quick outbreathing* as in *Christian,* not *ch* as in *church*
- *gu* = *gw* as in *language,* not *gu* as in *gun*
- qu = *kw* as in *quick* (The *u* is a consonant when combined with *g* or *q*.)
- *r* should be trilled

- *ll*—both letters are pronounced. Latin has no silent letters.
- *v = w* as in *win*

Accent

- The ultima (last syllable) is never accented: *li'•ber, Rō•mā '•nus.*
- The penult (next-to-last syllable) is accented when it is long. It is long if it contains a long vowel.

Syllable division

- Every syllable must contain a vowel.
- Syllables are divided between two vowels: *me•us, tu•us.*
- A single consonant goes with the vowel that follows it: *li•ber, La•tī•nīs*
- Two consonants are divided unless they form a blend.

Translation

- Since Latin does not have articles (words for *the, a, an*) these words should be added to make normal English sentences.
- The word *for* is supplied in the book title.
- An adjective generally follows the noun it modifies.
- The understood subject of a Latin verb can be determined from the context.
- The enclitic *-ne* attached to the first word of a sentence makes the sentence a question.

Activity E

Vocabulary

Nouns
liber, book
lingua, language
scholīs, schools
stilus, stylus, pen, writing instrument

Pronouns
hic, this
ille, that
quid, what?

Adjectives
Latīna, Latin
Christiānīs, Christian
meus, my
tuus, your

Verb
est, is

Enclitic
-ne, indication of a question when attached to first word of a sentence

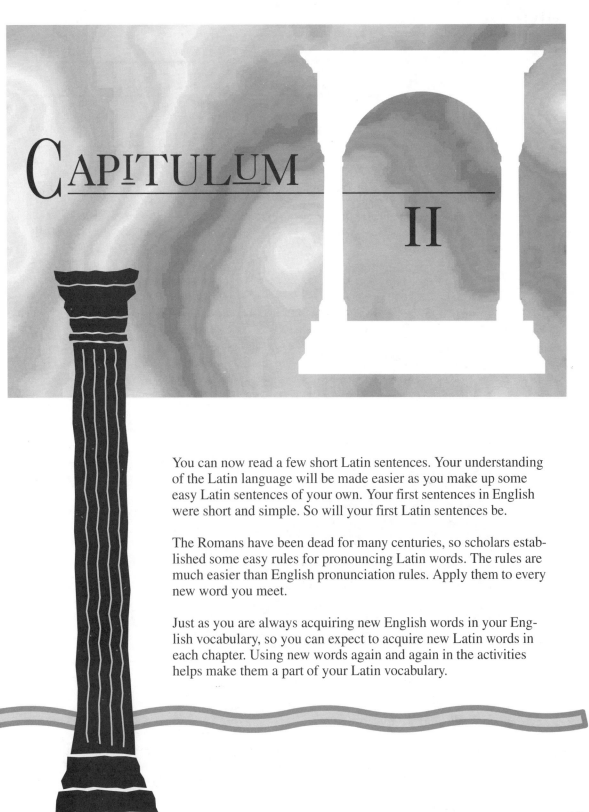

CAPITULUM II

You can now read a few short Latin sentences. Your understanding of the Latin language will be made easier as you make up some easy Latin sentences of your own. Your first sentences in English were short and simple. So will your first Latin sentences be.

The Romans have been dead for many centuries, so scholars established some easy rules for pronouncing Latin words. The rules are much easier than English pronunciation rules. Apply them to every new word you meet.

Just as you are always acquiring new English words in your English vocabulary, so you can expect to acquire new Latin words in each chapter. Using new words again and again in the activities helps make them a part of your Latin vocabulary.

YOUR OWN LATIN SENTENCES

Rex: If we knew more words, maybe we could make up some Latin sentences.

Mr. Cornelius: All right. Here are some nouns and verbs and one adverb. Before you use them, you need to practice pronouncing them.

Building Your Latin Vocabulary

> *ph = p + quick outbreathing* (as in English *pot*). It is <u>not</u> equal to the English letter *f*, as in *elephant*.

Nouns	Adjective
ca′nis, dog	**Rō•mā′nus,** Roman
e•le•phan′tus, elephant	**Adverb**
equ′us, horse	**nōn,** not
fē′les, cat	**Verbs**
lu′pus, wolf	**ca′pit,** catches, seizes
mūs, mouse	**do′cet,** teaches
por′cus, pig	**ha′bet,** has
pu′er, boy	**in•ve′nit,** finds
Pronoun	**pas′cit,** feeds
quis, who	**ti′met,** fears

 Can you (1) correctly pronounce all the words in the list above and (2) give the meaning of each word from memory?

Learning about Latin Sentences

Subjects and predicate nouns

Mr. Cornelius: Before you make up Latin sentences, let me tell you about the Latin inflections of nouns. As you saw in Chapter 1, an **inflection** is a word ending that shows the grammatical use of the word. The inflections of the nouns you just pronounced are used on subjects and predicate nouns.

All the forms listed, both nouns and verbs, are singular. You will learn plural forms in later chapters.

The linking verb *est*

Mr. Cornelius: A complete sentence includes a subject and a predicate. The **predicate** is the verb and any words that may complete the thought.

To start off, I'd like you to make up sentences with the verb *est* and follow the pattern of *Hic est liber.* In sentences like these **a linking verb** connects the **subject** with a **predicate noun.** The subject tells what the sentence is about; the predicate noun renames the subject.

Paul: Hic est puer. Hic est canis. Ille est lupus. That's too easy!

 Can you make up one or two sentences of your own, using the linking verb *est?*

Transitive active verbs and direct objects

Mr. Cornelius: You're ready now for another kind of sentence. All the verbs listed above can have receivers of action, called **direct objects.** A verb that has a direct object is a **transitive active verb.**

To use nouns as direct objects, you must change the inflections. Here are the forms you will use when the nouns are used as direct objects: *canem, elephantum, equum, fēlem, lupum, mūrem, porcum,* and *puerum.* Check the spelling carefully when you use these nouns as direct objects.

Let's begin with the verb *capit.*
A common Latin expression is this:
Elephantus nōn capit mūrem.
Before you write sentences of your
own, look carefully at this sentence.

What do you think *Elephantus
nōn capit mūrem* means?

15

Timothy:	I think it means "An elephant doesn't catch a mouse."
Mr. Cornelius:	That's right. How can you tell that the verb isn't a linking verb?
Lydia:	Well, *mouse* doesn't rename *elephant*.
Mr. Cornelius:	Since *mūrem* isn't a predicate noun, what is it?
Lydia:	It's a direct object. *Mūrem* is in the list of direct object forms. Do all direct objects end in *m?*
Mr. Cornelius:	In the singular most of them do.
Lydia:	Would the direct object form of *lingua* end in *-am?*
Mr. Cornelius:	Yes, that's correct.

Making Up Latin Sentences

Mr. Cornelius:	Now complete the Latin sentences in Activity A by using words chosen from the list on page 14. Then translate the sentences in Activity B.

Activities A, B

Mr. Cornelius:	For more practice, here is another sentence and some pronunciation helps: *An•tō'•ni•us lin'•guam La•tī'•nam do'•cet.*

Syllable division and accent

a. **Syllable division**

  • Put a single consonant with the vowel that follows it: *mū'rem.*

  • Divide between two consonants unless they form a blend. For three consonants, keep together the two that blend.

b. **Consonant blends**

  • Do not separate the consonants when you divide syllables.

  • Example of a blend: *gl = gl* as in *glass.*

c. **Accent**

  • Accent the **antepenult** if the penult is not long. The antepenult is the syllable right before the penult: *An•tō'ni•us.*

antepenult penult ultima

Operas are still performed today in this Roman amphitheater in Verona, Italy.

Mr. Cornelius: Practice reading the sentence until you're sure you can pronounce it right. (The name **Antōnius** in English is either *Antony* or *Anthony.*)

Antōnius linguam Latīnam docet. *(An•tō'ni•us lin'guam La•tī'nam do'cet.)*

Mr. Cornelius: Which does that sentence have—a predicate noun or a direct object?

Gloria: A direct object—*linguam.*

Mr. Cornelius: The **complete direct object** is the direct object with any modifiers it may have. What is the complete direct object in this sentence?

Gloria: *Linguam Latīnam*

Mr. Cornelius: What does the sentence mean in English?

Timothy: "Antony teaches the Latin language."

Mr. Cornelius: That's right. What kind of verb is *teaches* in this sentence?

Victor: Transitive active because it has a direct object.

Mr. Cornelius: Look at the sentences in Activity A. Do you have a direct object inflection for each receiver of action and a predicate noun inflection after each use of *est?*

Activities C, D, E

Can you make up (1) a sentence containing a predicate noun and (2) a sentence containing a direct object?

Discovering Variety in Latin Word Order

Mr. Cornelius: Look at this sentence again. *Elephantus nōn capit mūrem.* Where is the verb?

Clement: It's in the middle of the sentence.

Mr. Cornelius: Transitive active verbs are usually at the end of a Latin sentence, and linking verbs are usually placed where we put them in English sentences. If the author wants to emphasize a word, he puts it at the end. The most emphatic position for a word in Latin or English is the end of a sentence.

Victor: Does that mean that the Romans usually emphasized the verb?

Mr. Cornelius: Yes, and the second most emphatic position is the beginning of the sentence. The author of the Latin sentence we just read showed the contrast between the elephant and the mouse by putting those words at the beginning and the end of the sentence. In Latin an idea can be expressed in several ways, depending on the emphasis the author wants to make:

> *Elephantus nōn capit mūrem.*
> *Mūrem nōn capit elephantus.*
> *Elephantus mūrem nōn capit.*
> *Nōn capit elephantus mūrem.*
> *Nōn capit mūrem elephantus.*

Flora: Then Latin words can be in any order.

Mr. Cornelius: Latin words may be in the usual English word order, but generally they are not. The five sentences I read have the same English meaning. Although great variety is possible in Latin word order, Latin word order is not helter-skelter. You will begin to recognize common patterns of word order as you proceed. For example, *nōn* usually comes right before the verb.

Can you name the part of speech that usually receives the most emphasis in a Latin sentence?

Writing More Original Sentences

Mr. Cornelius: Here are some pronunciation helps to use as you begin using the new words that follow. The new words in the list will help you when you begin to make up some sentences of your own.

---

a. Consonants

g—always hard, as in *gun,* not as in *gem*

b. Consonant blends

bs = ps in *tops* (urbs)

tr = tr in *train* (pa•tri•a)

c. Accent

Accent the penult when it is long. A **long syllable** (1) contains a long vowel, (2) contains a diphthong°, or (3) ends in a consonant. A **short syllable** (1) is followed by another vowel (that is not part of a diphthong°) or (2) is followed by a single consonant.

°Diphthongs are introduced in chapter 4.

Activity F

Nouns	**Verbs**
Mar′cus, Marcus, Mark	**dē•fen′dit,** defends
Quin′tus, Quintus	**dī′cit,** speaks
Rō′ma, Rome	**dī′li•git,** loves
pa′tri•a, country, native land	**dis′cit,** learns
urbs, city	**Adjectives**
	An′gli•ca, English
	Ger•mā′na, German

Word order, a means of achieving emphasis

Mr. Cornelius: Now let me hear you make up some original Latin sentences, using the words above and any words from Chapter 1.

Clara: Marcus Germānam linguam docet.

Mr. Cornelius: Apparently you are emphasizing the adjective *Germānam,* since you put it before the noun it modifies.

Paul: Quintus linguam Anglicam docet.

Gloria: Marcus linguam Latīnam discit.

Clara: Marcus Anglicam linguam discit. I put the adjective before the noun to stress that he is learning the *English* language.

Rex: Marcus linguam Germānam dīcit.

Learning a Language: A Four-Part Process

Mr. Cornelius: You did very well. The best way to learn another language is to **hear** the words, to **see** them, to **say** them, and to **write** them. To understand what is said and written in Latin, you need to listen and read carefully. Then pronouncing and writing accurately will be easier.

In Activity G you will be labeling the parts of sentences. By putting labels on the words, you will notice how the word order can differ from English word order. The Latin inflections are the key to the meanings of sentences.

Activity H asks you to write Latin answers to Latin questions. Try to do this without translating into English.

Activity G, H

Reading Latin Paragraphs

Mr. Cornelius: First, read the paragraphs orally twice in Latin and then in English. One word in the paragraphs is new to you. Because of its use in the sentences, you should be able to deduce what it means.

> Marcus habet fēlem. Fēles canem timet. Mūs fēlem timet. Fēles mūrem capit. Quintus porcum habet. Porcus lupum timet. Antōnius habet equum et° canem. Puer equum et canem pascit. Puer elephantum nōn habet.
> [°and]

Recognizing Latin Sources of English Words

Mr. Cornelius: According to some studies, over three-fourths of the words in an unabridged English dictionary have been borrowed directly or indirectly from Latin and Greek. Of the commonly used English words, more than half have Latin or Greek origins. More are from Latin than from Greek.

Derivatives, Loan Words, and Loan Phrases

Mr. Cornelius: Most of the borrowed words differ from their Latin origins in spelling. In this book if words differ either slightly or considerably from their Latin origins, they are called **derivatives.** If the spelling is exactly the same as their Latin origins, they are called **unaltered loan words** or—to save time—**loan words.** Whole phrases that are borrowed without change are called **loan phrases.**

Sylvia: *Canine* comes from *canis*, and *pork* probably came from *porcus*.

Mr. Cornelius: I'm glad you recognized the shift from the *c* in Latin to the *k* in English.

Clement: *Canine* looks more like *canis* than it sounds like it.

Mr. Cornelius: The main reason is the differences between English and Latin vowel sounds.

The Latin word provides a good clue to the meaning of the English word. Our canine teeth are a little bit like the corresponding teeth of a dog. Canine characteristics, then, are like those of a dog—"doglike," to be brief. Then what must *porcine* mean?

Mark: "Piglike."

Mr. Cornelius: That's right. Of course, the English definition is not that simple.

Mark: Is there an English word *equine* that means "horselike"?

Mr. Cornelius: You're off to a good start at word discovery. You can add *equine* to your English vocabulary and keep enriching your vocabulary through this logical process.

Paul: Our "canine teeth" aren't really much like a dog's teeth.

Mr. Cornelius: It's true that the comparison between a derivative and its Latin origin is sometimes only a suggestion of resemblance. Consider another derivative: *trunk*. The trunk of a human body, like the **truncus** of a tree, is the main part without the limbs. (Note here the change of the *c* to *k,* as in *pork.*)

Timothy: Does *library* come from *liber?*

Mr. Cornelius: It does. Like other derivatives we have talked about, the similarity is more in appearance than in sound because of the difference between English and Latin vowel sounds.

Flora: What about *stylus?*

Mr. Cornelius: Yes, we just changed the *i* to *y.* This change, like the change of *c* to *k,* shows how the uses of letters have changed.

Begin to watch for loan phrases and words. Here are a few that you will understand better as you learn more Latin.

Some common loan phrases and loan words

ante meridiem (A.M.)   video

post meridiem (P.M.)   animal

"Adeste Fideles"   audio

E pluribus unum   data

et cetera (etc.)

terra firma

bona fide

Mr. Cornelius: Here is the Essential Information covered in this chapter. Check each item and be sure you understand it. The vocabulary words that are not in bold type were introduced incidentally. They will not be included in your test for this chapter, but they are listed here as a reminder that you have used them. Most of the words that occur incidentally are found in later chapters as words to be learned.

Let me remind you that each item listed here can be found in the section titles, bold type, or a vocabulary list. You are required to memorize only the vocabulary words in bold type.

Essential Information

Grammar terms
- predicate, linking verb, transitive active verb
- subject, predicate noun, direct object, complete direct object

General terms
- derivative, unaltered loan word or loan word, loan phrase

How to learn another language
- Hear it, see it, say it, write it.

Inflections
- *-t* For verbs to show that the subject is a singular noun or pronoun (The subject may be understood, not written.)
- *-a, -er, -us* For singular subjects and predicate nouns and for adjectives that modify singular subjects and predicate nouns
- *-am, -um, -em* For singular direct objects and for adjectives that modify direct objects

Pronunciation
- Latin has no silent letters.
- a. Consonant
   - *g*—always hard, as in *gun,* not as in *gem*
- b. Consonant blends
   - Consonants that blend are not separated when syllables are divided.
   - *bs = ps* in *tops* (ur**bs**)
   - *gl = gl* in *glass* (An•**gli**•cam)
   - *tr = tr* in *train* (pa•**tri**•a)
   - *ph = p + a quick outbreathing* as in *pot* (elephantus). It is not a true blend; instead, it is the Latinized spelling of a single Greek letter. Another Latin form of a Greek letter is *ch,* as in the word *chorus.*
- c. Syllable division
   - Put a consonant blend with the vowel that follows it: pa•**tri**•a.

- Divide between two consonants unless they form a blend: Mar•cus.

- For three consonants, keep together the two that blend: An•gli•ca.

d. Accent

- When the penult is a **long syllable**, it receives the accent. A syllable is long either if it contains a macron or if it ends with a consonant (Rō•mā′•nus, dē•fen′•dit).

- When the penult is a **short syllable,** accent the antepenult. The **antepenult** is the syllable right before the penult: An•tō′•ni•us.

Translation

Word order

- Generally, transitive active verbs are at the end of the sentence.

- Generally, linking verbs are in the same position as in English sentences.

- Generally, adjectives follow the nouns they modify.

- A word in a position other than the usual position receives emphasis.

- If a question does not begin with an interrogative word, such as a pronoun, the verb is often the first word and ends with the enclitic *-ne.* For example, *Estne liber. . . .* is translated "Is the book. . . ?" rather than "The book is. . . ."

Vocabulary

Activity I

- You are responsible for the words listed on pages 14 and 19 and for these words.

Antōnius, Antony *or* Anthony   **truncus,** trunk

et, and

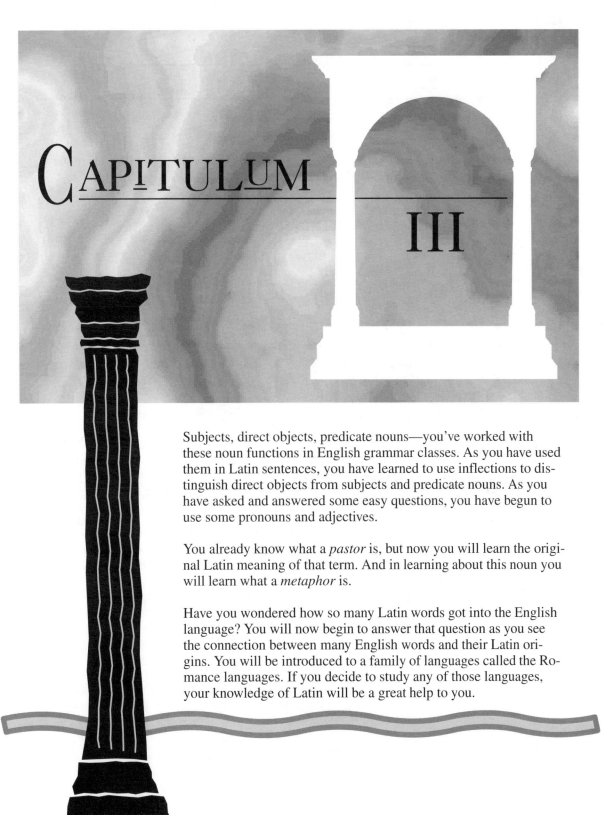

CAPITULUM III

Subjects, direct objects, predicate nouns—you've worked with these noun functions in English grammar classes. As you have used them in Latin sentences, you have learned to use inflections to distinguish direct objects from subjects and predicate nouns. As you have asked and answered some easy questions, you have begun to use some pronouns and adjectives.

You already know what a *pastor* is, but now you will learn the original Latin meaning of that term. And in learning about this noun you will learn what a *metaphor* is.

Have you wondered how so many Latin words got into the English language? You will now begin to answer that question as you see the connection between many English words and their Latin origins. You will be introduced to a family of languages called the Romance languages. If you decide to study any of those languages, your knowledge of Latin will be a great help to you.

NOUNS

Magister: You may call me just Magister. Perhaps you've seen the term *schoolmaster* in your reading. Teachers were called masters or schoolmasters in years gone by. The word *magister* means both "teacher" and "master." In fact, *master* is a derivative of the Latin word **magister.** Another derivative is *mister.* You're more familiar with the abbreviation *Mr.*

Clara: What is the Latin word for *pupil?*

Distinguishing Masculine and Feminine Nouns

Magister: Clara, you are a **discipula;** and Clement, for example, is a **discipulus.** In Latin the difference between many **masculine** and **feminine** nouns is shown by their different inflections. In English very few nouns have inflections that distinguish a feminine form from a corresponding masculine form: for example, *waitress, waiter; hostess, host; Josephine, Joseph; administratrix, administrator; aviatrix, aviator.* In Latin many—but not all—nouns with the inflection *-a* are feminine; and many—but not all—nouns with the *-er* or *-us* inflection are masculine.

Sylvia: If our teacher were a woman, would her name be **Cornelia** instead of **Cornelius**?

Magister: Only if that is her first name. In both Latin and English, *Cornelia* is a first name for girls and women, just as *Cornelius* is for boys and men. In Roman times *Cornelius* was a family name. In America it is both a family name and a given name. If your teacher were a woman with the last name Cornelius, you would call her **Magistra** Cornelius.

Paul: How can we know when *-a* isn't a feminine inflection?

Magister: Other uses for the *-a* inflection will be pointed out when they occur in the chapters. Until you learn otherwise, the nouns you work with that end in *-a* are feminine. Also, for now, the nouns you see that end in *-er* and *-us* are masculine.

Tracing Disciple *to Its Source*

Gloria: Is *disciple* a derivative of *discipula* or *discipulus?*

Magister: Actually it's from both words. In Chapter 2 you used the verb *discit.* These nouns come from that verb. What does it mean?

Lydia: It means "learns."

Magister: What were Jesus' disciples doing when they were with Him for three years?

Clement: They were learning.

Magister: Keep watching for similar connections between nouns and verbs. And use the Latin words you learn to help you understand English derivatives, such as *disciple.*

Activity A

Can you use the correct inflection (ending) on the noun for "pupil" to show whether it is a boy or a girl and for "teacher" to show whether it is a man or a woman?

Pronouncing New Words

Mark: Would you pronounce your name in Latin, please.

Magister: Ma•gis′•ter Cor•nē′li•us. Unlike Latin, in English the letters *-ius* are one unaccented syllable containing a schwa (*yəs*). In Latin class, let's use the Latin pronunciation. Look at the diacritical marks as you pronounce the two words with me: Ma•gis′ter Cor•nē′li•us.

> Latin has no schwa sound. The vowels in the syllables *-li•us* do not blend. Each is pronounced clearly.

Can you correctly pronounce *Magister Cornelius?*

Syllable division and accent

Magister: Your progress will be much faster when you can apply the rules and pronounce Latin words with ease. You may need to check some rules while you are practicing. Check the Essential Information sections of Chapters 1 and 2 if necessary.

If you apply the rules you have learned, the pronunciation practice in Activities B, C, and D should not be difficult.

> The consonants *nc* blend when followed by a third consonant, as in *sanc•tus*.

Activities B, C, D

Answering Latin Questions in Latin

Magister: You can learn to think in Latin by answering Latin questions in Latin without translating into English. Answer these questions in complete sentences. To think of words to use in your answers, you may look at the vocabulary words at the end of Chapters 1 and 2. The last word in question 1 is new, but you can figure it out.

Listen carefully to my pronunciation and try to pronounce the words correctly in your answers.

1. Quid est Italia?
2. Quid est Rōma?
3. Quid magister docet?
4. Quid puer discit?

Can you give Latin answers to the questions you've just read without thinking of the English meanings of the words?

Using the Nominative and Accusative Cases

Magister: In English we use the same form (spelling) of nouns for subjects and direct objects, but we use different forms for some pronouns. For example, *he, she, they,* and *who* are used as subjects; so we say they are in the **subjective case.** *Who will come? He/She/They will come.*

We use *him, her, them,* and *whom* for objects (direct objects, indirect objects, and objects of prepositions); so we say those forms are in the **objective case.** *Whom did you invite? We invited him/her/them.*

The names *subjective* and *objective* are logical for subjects and objects. In Latin, not just pronouns but nouns too have different forms for subjects and objects. And the cases have different names. We'll look at those now.

Magister: In Latin grammar the names of the cases are different. Subjects and predicate nouns are in the **nominative case,** and direct objects are in the **accusative case.** Some of you may use the word *nominative* for English subjects and predicate nouns, but you've probably not heard the term *accusative* before. The Latin nominative and accusative cases also have other uses that you will learn about later.

Here are examples of nouns and one pronoun in their nominative and accusative forms.

Nominative	magist*ra*	magiste*r*	urb*s*
Accusative	magist*ram*	magist*rum*	urb*em*

Nominative	lingu*a*	libe*r*	m*ū*s
Accusative	lingu*am*	libr*um*	mūr*em*

Nominative	stil*us*	can*is*	quis
Accusative	stil*um*	can*em*	que*m*

Compare the words *patria* and *patriam* in these two sentences:

> Italia est patria.
> Marcus patriam dēfendit.

In the first chapter you worked with these phrases: *lingua Latīna, linguam Anglicam,* and *liber meus.*

> Quintus est magister.
> Magister Quintus linguam Latīnam docet.

In the first sentence what case is *magister* and why?

Flora: It's in the nominative case because it's the predicate noun.

Magister: In the second sentence what case is *linguam* and why?

Flora: It's accusative because it's the direct object.

Magister: Why does *Latīnam* end in *-am* instead of *-a*?

Sylvia: It has to be the same case as the noun it describes.

Activities E, F

Can you (1) name the case of a Latin noun from its inflection (ending) and (2) name the function of a noun that has a nominative or accusative ending?

Adjective forms; the predicate adjective

Magister: Often the adjective inflection has the same spelling as the noun inflection of the word it modifies, but not always: *linguam Latīnam* (same, both in the accusative case); *liber meus* (different, both in the nominative case).

A **predicate adjective** is used with a linking verb and describes the subject. It is in the nominative case.

The meaning of any word with the symbol ° is given below the sentence. To know the meaning of any word defined in this way is not required until it occurs later in bold type.

Lingua Latīna nōn est nova.°
[°new]

Complete subject, predicate noun, direct object

A **complete subject,** a **complete predicate noun,** or a **complete direct object** includes any modifiers the noun may have. Any adjective will be in the same case as the noun it modifies.

Spelling variations

Magister tuus est quoque° magister meus.
[°also]
Liber tuus linguam Germānam docet.

Magister: Did you notice that the *e* disappears before the accusative inflection in **magistrum?** In **puerum** the *e* doesn't disappear. You need to notice whether or not the *e* disappears when you work with *-er* words.

 Can you write the accusative form of *puer* and *magister,* spelling each form correctly?

Answering More Latin Questions

Magister: The interrogative pronoun **quis** is the subject form and asks "Who?" **Quem** is the object form and asks "Whom?" *Quis* and *quem* ask questions about persons. **Quid** asks questions about things and is translated "What?" Notice the different forms: *quis* for a subject and *quem* for a direct object. *Quid* is used for both subjects and direct objects.

Here is a statement followed by two questions about it. Timothy, would you please read them.

Timothy: Magister puerum docet.

            Quis puerum docet?
            Quem magister docet?

Magister: Flora, would you translate them, being careful to use the correct pronoun forms.

Flora: "The teacher teaches the boy." "Who teaches the boy?" "Whom does the teacher teach?"

Magister: Your use of *who* for *quis* and *whom* for *quem* was accurate.

Perhaps without noticing the difference between Latin and English, you automatically used the **auxiliary** (helping word) *does* to translate *docet,* putting the subject between the auxiliary and the main verb (Whom *does* the teacher *teach?*)

Rex, would you translate the next two questions, please. You will need to use the auxiliary in one question. Then tell us whether the interrogative pronoun is nominative or accusative case in each question.

            Quid est Rōma?
            Quid Marcus habet?

Rex: "What is Rome?" " What does Marcus have?" In the first question *quid* is nominative, and in the second one it is accusative.

Magister: Well done.

Julia: May we have some more questions to answer?

Magister: Yes, I think you're ready for some. Vincent, you begin by asking me the first question. I will answer in Latin. Then I will ask the other questions for you to answer. Be sure to answer in complete sentences. The inflections show how the words are used in the sentence, so the word order can vary. For each sentence there are two or three possible ways for the words to be arranged.

Remember that in Latin questions that don't begin with an interrogative word, the Latin enclitic -*ne* is used. Often the verb is brought from the end or middle of the sentence to the beginning, and the enclitic is attached to it.

In one sentence you will need to use the nominative case of *mūrem*. It is *mūs*. In sentence 4 the word *pascit* means "feeds."

Accent on -*ne* words

When the enclitic -*ne* is added to a word, the accent is on the new penult, the syllable just before the enclitic, (ha•bet′ne), unless the new penult is short (lin′gua•ne).

---

1. Habetne magister stilum?
2. Quis stilum habet?
3. Quid magister habet?
4. Pascitne magistra canem?
5. Timetne canis magistram?
6. Quem canis dīligit?
7. Capitne mūrem canis?
8. Capitne mūs canem?

Activity G

Can you answer Latin questions indicated by (1) the enclitic -*ne* or (2) the interrogative pronoun?

A METAPHOR

Understanding the Word Pastor

Magister: In many churches the leader is called the *pastor.*

Lydia: In Spanish, *pastor* can mean either "shepherd" or "minister." Does pastor come from *pascit?*

Magister: Excellent observation! Actually, it was the Romans who made the word *pastor* from pascit. In both English and Spanish, the Latin word **pastor** has been borrowed without any spelling change. Nouns that end with *-or* often name a person who does what the verb form means. In this case, a pastor is "one who feeds" (sheep, for example).

Compare the way this noun came from a verb with the way *disciple* (discipulus, discipula) came from *discit.*

> Discipulus linguam Latīnam discit.
>
> Pastor gregem° pascit.
>
> [°flock]

Can you think of an English word that begins with *pas* and has something to do with feeding?

Timothy: A *pasture* is a place to feed animals.

Magister: In the Twenty-third Psalm, the Lord is pictured as a shepherd, who "maketh [us] to lie down in green pastures." To make a comparison, a term that usually refers to one thing (or person) may be used for something (someone) else. For example, God uses the term *shepherd* to refer to Himself because, like a shepherd, He cares for His followers. A comparison without the words "like" or "as" is called a **metaphor.**

Mark: Is *pasture* in this psalm also a metaphor? A shepherd feeds his sheep, and God provides our food.

Magister: You're right. Actually the whole Twenty-third Psalm is a comparison, or a metaphor.

Activity H

 (1) Can you name the verb from which *pastor* came? (2) Can you explain why *pastor* is called a metaphor?

ROMANCE LANGUAGES AND THE ENGLISH LANGUAGE

Seeing the Origin of the Romance Languages

Magister: As the Romance languages developed, many Latin words changed in pronunciation and spelling. The French word for "pasture" is *pâture.* (The circumflex accent over the *a* shows that the *s* was dropped.) And the Spanish word is *pasto.* Here are other words in Italian, Spanish, and French that show the similarities of the Romance languages to Latin.

Latin	*liber,* book	*amīcus,* friend	*Deus,* God
Italian	libro	amico	Dio
Spanish	libro	amigo	Dios
French	livre	ami	Dieu

Clement: Would you explain why Italian, Spanish, and French are called Romance languages?

Magister: Notice the names of countries that were once a part of the **Roman Empire.** The Romans had conquered most of Europe before the time of Christ. The countries marked on your map weren't separate countries in Roman times. After conquering these areas, the Roman soldiers and government officials established permanent camps, and Latin became the dominant language.

Gloria: Why are French and Spanish two different languages if they came from the same language?

Magister: Languages are always changing; and geographic separation naturally causes differences to develop in pronunciation, spelling, and grammar. Think of the Southern, New England, and Western dialects in the United States. If people in these regions did not talk with each other—for example, if these were separate isolated countries—the dialects would eventually become separate languages.

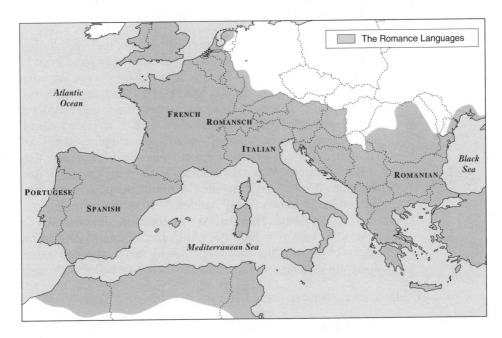

Mark: How many Romance languages are there?

Magister: Six. They are **Italian, French, Spanish, Portuguese, Romanian, and Romansch.**

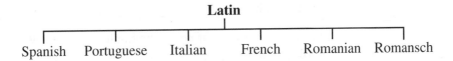

Victor: I've never heard of Romansch.

Magister: It's spoken in a small area of Switzerland and neighboring parts of Italy and Austria. Surprisingly, Switzerland has four national languages: German, French, Italian, and Romansch. Romansch is said to be the closest to ancient Latin of all the Romance languages.

 Can you (1) name three Romance languages and (2) give the word for "God" in each of those languages?

Seeing Latin Influence on English

Julia: Why isn't English a Romance language? The English words *pastor* and *pasture* are like the Spanish and French words.

Magister: English is a Germanic language. This fact may seem puzzling, especially since such a large percent of our words come from Latin. A little history here will help. The **Romans** conquered England and occupied it from about **54 B.C.** to **A.D. 410.** However, the **Celts** there did not begin to speak Latin as many other conquered peoples did. Just a few English words remind us of the Roman occupation. From the Latin word *castra,* "camp," have come such place names as *Lancaster, Chester, Dorchester,* and *Winchester.* These were the sites of Roman camps. When the Romans left Britain, a series of other **invasions** began. First came the **Germanic peoples,** beginning with the **Danes.** Then in **A.D. 449 Angles, Saxons,** and **Jutes** began invading the island. They settled with their families, and the island came to be known as *England,* (Angleland) from the Angles, the largest of the invading tribes. The Anglo-Saxon language became the dominant language on the island, and it is now called Old English.

Paul: Then how did so many Latin words get into the English language?

Magister: **Norsemen** from France invaded England in **A.D. 1066.** That invasion is called the **Norman Conquest** because the invaders came from Normandy, a part of France. The French became the rulers of the island; so naturally their language, derived directly from Latin, had a great influence on the language of the island. At that time a very large influx of Latin-derived words was added to English. *Pasture* is an example of an English word that came to us from Latin through French.

Latin has continued to influence the English language through the centuries, as you will see in future chapters.

Gloria: Why is England also called Britain?

Magister: The people who lived on the island when the Romans invaded were called Britons, and the island was called Britain.

Gloria: So the Angles and Saxons had been there more than six hundred years before the Norman French invaded.

Magister: That's right—they and other Germanic people. Their language became well established as the main language of England in those six hundred years before the Normans invaded in A.D. 1066.

In our discussion I have mentioned four dates: 54 B.C., and A.D. 410, 449, and 1066. This isn't a history course, but these dates can give you an idea of why the English language is a Germanic language enriched by the Latin language.

 Can you (1) name three major invasions of England and (2) give the dates for those invasions?

Rex: What do **B.C.** and **A.D.** mean?

Magister: The abbreviation *B.C.* stands for the words *before Christ* and means "before the date of Christ's birth." The abbreviation *A.D.* stands for **Anno Domini,** "in the year of the Lord," and refers to any year since Christ was born.

Mark: Look, just two Latin words! And it takes six English words to translate them.

Magister: Concise, isn't it? When you learn more Latin grammar, you will see the reason for all the added English words.

Clement: Magister, why do people say that Latin is a dead language?

Magister: Because it's no longer spoken in its ancient form. Actually, it's the Romans who are dead. Their language has outlived them. From our discussion can you tell some ways that Latin still lives?

(Map labels: North Sea, NORMANS, ANGLES, ROMANS, Irish Sea, ANGLES, DANES, BRITAIN, NORMANS, JUTES, ANGLES, ANGLES, ROMANS, SAXONS, SAXONS, NORMANS, ANGLES, English Channel, FRANCE)

Julia: In the Romance languages and in the many words from Latin that we have in our language.

Magister: There is also another way. Through the centuries church leaders, scientists, authors, and others continued to write in Latin in order to be understood by people throughout Europe and America. Latin still has many uses today: mottoes, doctors' prescriptions, scientific terms, and so on.

Activity I

Reading a Latin Paragraph

Marcus est amīcus meus. Linguam Germānam dīcit. Magister linguam Germānam et linguam Latīnam docet. Marcus linguam Latīnam discit.

Recognizing Borrowed Words

Magister: Latin word meanings are a guide to thousands of English word meanings. Since you encounter new words every day, the Latin words you are learning will help you keep adding words to your own vocabularies.

An unaltered loan word

Magister: The word *pastor* is a loan word. In Chapter 2 I explained that we are calling English words that came to us with no spelling change *unaltered loan words* or *loan words* for short. In English the meaning of the word *pastor* is a metaphor based on the literal Latin meaning.

Derivatives

Magister: Let's make a list of English words borrowed from the Latin words in Chapters 1 and 2. Cover the list below and, on your own paper, list as many derivatives as you can think of. You may look back through the chapters, but you need not include any that have already been explained in Chapters 1 and 2. When your list is complete, check each word on your list that is also on the list in your book.

amicable, Anglican, Anglicize, annual, bilingual, defend, Deity/deity, deify, disciplinary, discipline, docile, doctor, doctrine,

Germanic, indoctrinate, librarian (*liberal* and *liberty* come from a different Latin word*)*, lingual, linguist, magistrate, patriotic, patriotism, pork, puerile, scholar, school, schoolmaster, suburb, urban

Magister: Check your knowledge of each item in this Essential Information section and review the same final section of Chapters 1 and 2. A good foundation will enable you to proceed with confidence in the chapters that follow.

Essential Information

Grammar terms

- adjective forms, predicate adjective
- complete subject, complete predicate noun, complete direct object
- subjective case, nominative case, objective case, accusative case
- masculine and feminine forms in English
- auxiliary

General terms

- metaphor
- Celtic people
- invasions of Britain: by the Romans, by Germanic tribes (Angles, Saxons, Jutes, and Danes), and by the French (Norman Conquest)
- Roman Empire
- Romance languages: Italian, French, Spanish, Portuguese, Romanian, and Romansch

Abbreviations

- A.D. and B.C.

Dates

- 54 B.C.; A.D. 410, 449, and 1066

Inflections for the nominative and accusative cases

- See case inflections on page 29.

Spelling variations

- pue*rum*
- magist*rum*

Unaltered loan words, loan phrase

- pastor, Anno Domini

Pronunciation

Vowels

- In *Cornelius* the syllables *li•us* are pronounced distinctly, not like the English pronunciation (-*yəs*).

Syllable divisions

- The consonants *nc* blend when followed by a third consonant, as in *sanctus.*

Accent

- When an enclitic is added to a word, the new penult is accented (ha•bet′ne) unless the new penult is short (lin′gua•ne). (A syllable is **long** if it ends with a consonant.)

Translation

Word order

When the first word of a question ends with the enclitic -*ne*, the English auxiliary do/does is often needed in translation. The English subject comes between the auxiliary and the main verb: Does he have the book?

Vocabulary

In activities you will work with new words that are not required for vocabulary tests. Having seen them in context you will find them easier to learn when they do occur as required words in later chapters.

Activities J, K

Nouns

Cornēlia, Cornelia, a feminine name

Cornēlius, Cornelius, a masculine name

Deus, God

Itālia, Italy

amīcus, friend

castra, camp

discipula, pupil (girl)

discipulus, pupil (boy)

grex, gregem, flock

magister, master, teacher

magistra, a mistress, a teacher

pastor, pastōrem, a shepherd

pater, patrem, father

Pronouns (interrogative)

quis, who

quem, whom

Adjective

nova, new

Adverb

quoque, also

Verb

dūcit, leads

Conjunction

aut, or

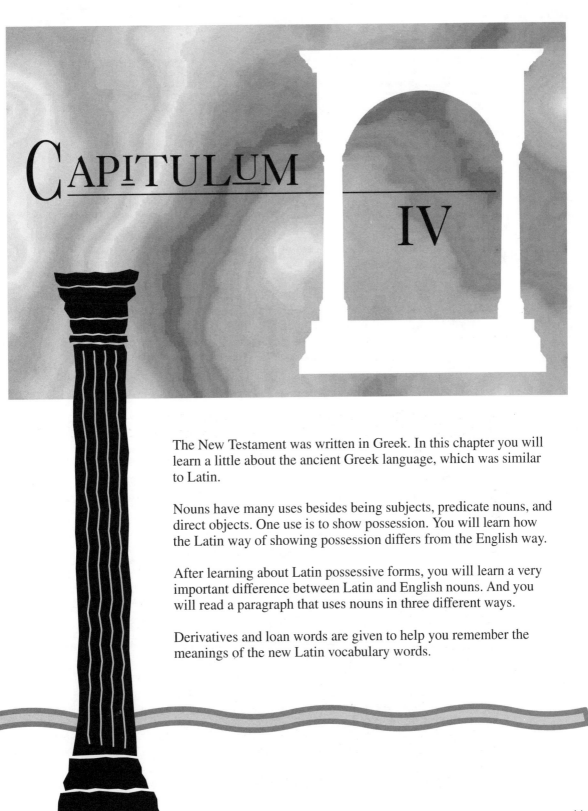

CAPITULUM IV

The New Testament was written in Greek. In this chapter you will learn a little about the ancient Greek language, which was similar to Latin.

Nouns have many uses besides being subjects, predicate nouns, and direct objects. One use is to show possession. You will learn how the Latin way of showing possession differs from the English way.

After learning about Latin possessive forms, you will learn a very important difference between Latin and English nouns. And you will read a paragraph that uses nouns in three different ways.

Derivatives and loan words are given to help you remember the meanings of the new Latin vocabulary words.

ANCIENT LANGUAGES

Rex: I was reading in the Gospel of John, and I have a question about two verses. They are verses 19 and 20 in chapter 19. I'll read them.

> And Pilate wrote a title, and put it on the cross. And the writing was, JESUS OF NAZARETH THE KING OF THE JEWS. This title then read many of the Jews: for the place where Jesus was crucified was nigh to the city: and it was written in Hebrew, and Greek, and Latin.

Why did Pilate write this in three languages?

Magister: In **Hebrew** the Jews could read it; in **Greek** the many non-Jews and some Jews in Jerusalem could read it because Greek was used by many people throughout the Mediterranean area. **Latin** was **Pilate**'s own language. He was the Roman governor of **Judea** and would naturally put the inscription in his own language. So it seems that he wanted everyone to understand what he had written.

Clara: Were there many Romans in Jerusalem?

Magister: Roman soldiers and government officials were in Judea, as they were in all the other Roman provinces.

Can you state the probable reason for each of the three languages chosen by Pilate for the inscription on the cross?

Paul: Are Latin and Hebrew similar?

Magister: No, Hebrew is in a different language family from Latin, Greek, and English. We'll talk more about language families in a later chapter.

Palestine, now called Israel, is in the eastern Mediterranean area; and **Greek** was the main language in that whole region at the time of Christ. The **New Testament,** as you may know, was written in Greek. Latin was the main language in the Roman Empire, including most of western Europe, where eventually the Romance languages developed from it. That's why a knowledge of Latin helps a person in the study of any Romance language.

Clara: Are Latin and Greek very much alike?

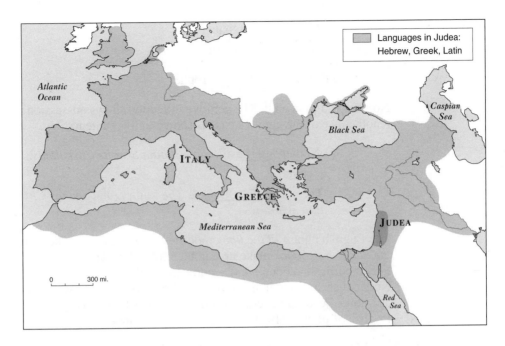

Magister: They have significant similarities. One similarity is the use of case endings—inflections—to show how words are used in a sentence. For example, both languages have a case called the genitive case.

 Can you name (1) the language in which the New Testament was first written, (2) the language spoken throughout the eastern Mediterranean area at the time of Christ, and (3) the main language spoken in western Europe at that time?

NOUNS

Using the Genitive Case

Magister: In Chapter 1 you worked with the phrase *liber tuus,* meaning "your book." In Latin the words meaning "my" and "your" are adjectives that show possession. Now let's talk about **possessive nouns.** For a phrase such as *the boy's book,* the noun for *boy* is made possessive by the **genitive case** inflection: *liber puerī.* Compare these pairs of sentences.

> Puer librum habet.
> Hic est liber puerī.

Quintus stilum habet.

Ille est stilus Quintī.

Victor: Didn't the Romans use the apostrophe?

Magister: No, they didn't need it. The genitive inflection shows possession. Another use of the genitive case is shown in this sentence:

Nōmen° librī est *Lingua Latīna Scholīs Christiānīs.*
[°name]

The name <u>of the book</u> is *The Latin Language for Christian Schools.*

The English phrase *of the book* modifies the noun *name.* The words *the name of the book* make up a noun phrase. Similarly in Latin, *librī* modifies the noun *nōmen,* and *nōmen librī* is a noun phrase. Notice that the noun in the genitive follows the noun it modifies, just as Latin adjectives generally follow the nouns they modify. The English *of* **phrase** always follows the noun it modifies.

Lydia: Could we translate *nōmen librī* "the book's name"?

Magister: You could, but it wouldn't sound as good. We usually use the apostrophe with an *s* for nouns naming persons, and we often use it for nouns naming animals: *the teacher's desk, the elephant's trunk.* For things, we generally use the *of* phrase: *the price of the book.* Notice I said *usually* and *often.* Here are some variations of the general rule: *the trunk of an elephant; a day's work; a student of Mr. Sylvester.*

The genitive case can express several other ideas besides possession, especially when it is translated with the *of* phrase. For example, in the phrase *nōmen librī,* the word *librī* doesn't show possession. Instead, it *specifies* what the word *nōmen* refers to.

 Can you (1) write the nouns *puer* and *Quintus* so that they show possession, (2) use appropriate English translations of nouns in the genitive case, and (3) write in Latin "the name of the book"?

Magister: Before you work more with the genitive case, you need some information about Latin nouns.

Learning About the Five Noun Declensions

Magister: Latin nouns are divided into five groups, called **declensions.** All the words in a declension have the same set of inflections. For example, all first-declension singular nouns have the nominative inflection *-a,* the genitive inflection *-ae,* and the accusative inflection *-am.* When we list the nouns in each declension, we put the genitive case right after the nominative case. Soon you will see the reason for this placement of the genitive case. Below are listed the inflections for these three cases in all five declensions.

Singular Noun Inflections					
Case	**First**	**Second**	**Third**	**Fourth**	**Fifth**
Nominative	-a	-us/-er	(varies)	-us	-ēs
Genitive	*-ae*	*-ī/-iī*	*-is*	*-ūs*	*-ēī/-eī*
Accusative	-am	-um	-em	-um	-em

You will be learning two other cases in later chapters. As we proceed, be sure that you can give the inflection for each case in all five declensions. What similarities do you see that will help you learn these?

Clara: Every accusative ends in *m.* We just have to learn what vowel goes in front of it. The nominative and genitive aren't so easy.

Magister: That's right. But you can soon learn them by working with them in sentences and by spelling them, declension by declension.

Let's begin by spelling them. As I name a case, I want you to give inflections for each declension.

First, give the nominative inflections, declension by declension.

Next, the genitive inflections.

Now, the accusative inflections.

Here is a helpful clue for the accusative forms. A vowel is always short before a final *m,* that is, an *m* that ends a word.

The nominative and genitive inflections are the forms that are given in vocabulary lists. You will be asked to memorize them when you learn word lists.

Diphthong

- The genitive inflection -*ae* is a diphthong. It is pronounced like the *ai* in *aisle*. A diphthong is a blend of two vowels. Like a consonant blend, it is not divided when syllables are divided.

Vowel Before Final *m*

- When the letter *m* is the last letter of a word, any vowel before that *m* is short.

Can you write from memory the correct spelling of the nominative, genitive, and accusative inflections for nouns in each of the five declensions?

Importance of genitive forms

Magister: You need to know both the nominative form and the genitive form of every noun you work with. The genitive form tells you what declension a noun is.

Here are the nouns you have already worked with, grouped according to declension. For fourth- and fifth-declension nouns, the words given are new because you have not had any nouns in those declensions so far. The genitive forms are given in parentheses. If no spelling variations occur in a particular group of nouns, the genitive form is given for only the first noun listed. Notice the two possible genitive forms for *Antōnius* and *Cornēlius*. I'll explain these later in this chapter. You will work with these forms in Activity A.

First declension: discipula (discipulae), lingua, magistra, patria, schola, Cornēlia, Glōria,° Itālia, Rōma
[°a girl's or woman's name]

Second declension:

nouns ending in -*us:* amīcus (amīcī), discipulus, elephantus, equus, lupus, porcus, stilus, truncus, Deus, Marcus, Quintus; Antōnius (Antōniī or Antōnī), Cornēlius (Cornēliī or Cornēlī)

nouns ending in -*er:* liber (librī), magister (magistrī), puer (puerī)

Third declension: canis (canis), mūs (mūris), urbs (urbis)

Fourth declension: manus (manūs),° senātus (senātūs)°
[°hand; °senate]

Fifth declension: spēs° (speī), diēs° (diēī)
[°hope; °day, time]

 Can you state the reason for memorizing the genitive form of Latin nouns?

Genitive case in first declension

Magister: The genitive form is the basis for the accusative form and for the forms of other cases you will learn later. For first-declension nouns, the procedure is very simple. Simply remove the genitive inflection and add the accusative inflection.

Suppose you want to say in Latin, "This is Gloria's book." Can you do that, Rex?

Rex: Hic est Glōriae liber.

Magister: Well done. However, Latin genitive forms usually follow the nouns they modify. Romans would more probably say, "Hic est liber Glōriae."

In the sentence *Cornelia teaches Gloria,* what case is *Gloria*?

Rex: Accusative. That would be *Cornēlia Glōriam docet,* I think.

Magister: That's good. You remembered to put the transitive verb at the end of the sentence, where the Romans usually put their verbs. Their linking verbs are usually placed where we place them in English.

Clara: Are Latin girls' names always in first declension?

Magister: Nearly all Roman girls' names are.

Julia: All the girls in this class have names in the first declension—Lydia, Flora, Clara, Sylvia, Gloria, and I.

Magister: Remarkable! Some classes have girls with names like Mary and Janice and Ruth—names that don't end with *-a.*

Can you write and say in Latin, "This is Gloria's book"?

Genitive case in second declension

Magister: Now we'll use the genitive case of some second-declension nouns. For nouns that have the *-us* nominative inflection, we replace that inflection with the genitive inflection. Timothy, can you say in Latin, "Antonius is a friend of Marcus"? It means the same as saying "Antonius is Marcus's friend."

Timothy: I'll try. "Antōnius est amīcus Marcī."

Magister: Very good. You remembered to put *Marcī* after the noun it modifies. This is the same as the English word order when we use the *of* phrase. Of course, in English a word with an apostrophe precedes the noun it modifies.

Now try saying "Marcus is Antonius's friend." You may use either of the two inflections that are given in the list on page 45.

Sylvia: "Marcus est amīcus Antōniī." Why does the genitive have two spellings?

Magister: For nouns that have an *i* before the *-us* inflection, such as *Antonius,* we may either simply replace the nominative *-us* inflection with the genitive *-ī* inflection or we may omit the *i* that ends the stem. The omission of the *-i* is called elision. **Elision** is the omission of a letter and its sound. This elision in second declension occurs only in the genitive singular form.

amīcus, amīcī, amīcum
fīlius, fīliī (or fīlī), fīlium

Those nouns that end in *-er* are different. We add the genitive and accusative inflections to the end of the nominative form. For some of these nouns, such as *magister,* we drop the *e* before the final *r* for all cases except the nominative.

magister, magistrī, magistrum

Others, such as *puer,* do not drop the *e*.

puer, puerī, puerum

Paul: How can we know whether the *e* is dropped?

Magister: The genitive form tells you. Another help is the spelling of English derivatives. They nearly always indicate the spelling of the genitive form. *Magistrate* doesn't have an *e* before the *r. Puerile* does have an *e* before the *r. Puerile* may be a new word to you. It means "childish, silly"; *puer* means "child, boy." If a person's behavior is puerile, he is acting like a child.

Rex: The girls' names end with *a;* what about boys' names?

Magister: The *-us* inflection of many Roman names disappeared and *c* changed to *k* when the names were Anglicized, that is, when they took English forms. Examples of **Anglicized spelling** include *Marcus,* which became *Mark,* and *Antōnius,* which became *Antony,* or *Anthony.* When *Clementius, Paulus,* and *Timotheus* were Anglicized, they became *Clement, Paul,* and *Timothy.*

 Can you write these nouns in the genitive case: *Marcus, Antōnius* (two ways), *magister,* and *puer?*

- *x = ks* as in *box*
- *th = t + a quick outbreathing*—<u>not</u> as in *this* or *these*

Victor: What about my name and Rex's?

Genitive case in third declension

Magister: They are both in the third declension. Many nouns in third declension have significant spelling differences between the genitive and the nominative cases. You will soon see how important it is that you learn the spelling of both cases. Both spellings are given in all the word lists from now on.

These words, which are used as English names, are examples of how third-declension nouns are listed:

> **victor, victōris,** conqueror
>
> **rēx, rēgis,** ruler, king, prince

Rex: Then Victor's name and mine are loan words.

Meanings of some names

Magister: Yes. In Latin these two words are common nouns, not names, as you can see from their meanings. Perhaps the rest of you would like to know what your names meant in ancient Latin. As far as I can find out, Mark and Julia, your names were just names.

Clara, from a Latin adjective, means "clear, bright."

Clementius, from a Latin adjective, means "kind, merciful."

Flōra, the name of the goddess of flowers and of spring, means "flower, blossom."

Glōria means "glory, fame."

Lydia is the name of an ancient country in Asia Minor.

Paulus means "little, small."

Sylvia, from **silva,** means "forest."

Timotheus, a Latinized Greek name (from *Timotheos*), means "honoring God."

Genitive case in fourth and fifth declensions

We have digressed from our discussion of the genitive case and the five declensions. Fourth- and fifth-declension nouns will be easy to work with. Just learn both the nominative and genitive forms.

The only difference between the nominative and the genitive case of a fourth-declension noun is the short *u* in the nominative case inflection and the long *ū* in the genitive case inflection.

senātus, senātūs, senate

In the fifth declension, if the genitive inflection *-eī/ēī* is preceded by a consonant, the *e* in the inflection is short. If it is preceded by a vowel, the *e* is long.

spēs, speī, hope

diēs, diēī, day, time

 Can you write *spēs* and *diēs* in the genitive case with correct macrons in each?

Magister: Here is a sample word in each declension. The bold type should help you learn the genitive inflections. As you learn the new forms, be sure to review the nominative and accusative inflections. Practice by writing and then pronouncing the three cases of each noun.

• The Latin letter *v* is pronounced like the English letter *w*.

Five Noun Declensions					
Case	**First**	**Second**	**Third**	**Fourth**	**Fifth**
Nominative	vīta, life	equus, horse	rēx, king	manus, hand	diēs, day
Genitive	vitae	equī	rēgis	manūs	diēī
Accusative	vītam	equum	rēgem	manum	diem

Stems of nouns

Magister: Now that you've seen several spelling variations, you can see the importance of knowing how to spell both the nominative form and the genitive form of every noun. The stem of a noun is found in its genitive form.

Rex: *Stem*—that's a strange name for part of a noun.

Magister: It's a metaphor. Compare a noun to a plant. If you remove the leaves and the flower from a plant, what remains?

Lydia: The stem. I see—if we remove an inflection from a noun, the stem is left, the part that is underlined in the lists of cases.

Magister: I need to make your answer a little more specific. If we remove the genitive inflection, the **stem** is left. The genitive case always provides the stem. The nominative singular is the only noun form that may differ a little or much from the spelling of the stem. Notice the change in spelling from the nominative *rēx* to the genitive *rēgis*. The stem is *rēg-*.

Spelling variations of *i-stem* nouns

The second-declension nouns that end in *ius*, such as *Antōnius*, are called **i-stem nouns** because their stems always end with *-i*. Sometimes the genitive form of these nouns is shortened to *-ī* by elision.

 Can you (1) state how to identify the stem of any noun and (2) give the stem of a noun in each of the five declensions?

Derivatives, an aid to spelling genitive forms

Clement: Are there clues to help us remember the genitive in third-declension nouns, like the clues that tell whether to drop the *e* in the second-declension nouns that end in *-er?*

Magister: Again, derivatives are helpful clues. English derivatives come from the stem, which we can always find in the genitive case. Here is an example: from the third-declension noun *rēx, rēgis,* we get the word *regal*. Regal attire is clothing suitable for a king.

In Activity B all the sentences except the first one require genitive forms to translate English nouns either with an apostrophe or with an *of* phrase. Activity C gives more translation practice. Activity D provides more practice with the genitive case. Each phrase has a noun that is modified by another noun with an apostrophe *s* or by an *of* phrase. In Latin the modifier will be in the genitive case. Remember that a noun in the genitive case usually follows the noun it modifies.

> Vowels in prefixes and suffixes do not combine to form diphthongs. Two exceptions to this rule are the pronouns *cui* and *huic,* which you will learn about later.
>
> de<u>us</u>, di<u>ēī</u>

Using Three Cases of Nouns

Magister: Be sure to learn the spelling of the nominative and the genitive form of each new word.

Here is some important information you need as you work with the new words.

> One **macron rule** is as follows: a vowel before a final *r* is almost never long (marked with a macron): in *peccātor,*° the final letter is *r;* but in *peccātōris,* where the *r* is not the final letter, the *o* is long (marked with a macron).
> [°sinner]

Nouns	Adjective
Dominus, Dominī, Lord	**magnus,** great, large
Fīlius, Fīlī or **Fīliī,** Son	**Verb**
peccātor, peccātōris, sinner	**ostendit,** shows
Salvātor, Salvātōris, Savior	
via, viae, way, road	
vīta, vītae, life	

Magister: In Activity E you will need to know the new words as you translate sentences into English.

Activities B, C, D, E

 Can you pronounce correctly each noun in the list above, applying the rules you have studied so far?

The genitive form *cuius*

- The singular interrogative adjective in the genitive case is *cuius.* It is translated "whose, of whom" or "of what." Like other adjectives, it modifies a noun.
- The letters *ui* do not form a diphthong in this word.

The letter *i* between two vowels

- When an *i* is between two vowels, it is a consonant and it is pronounced like a *y.* Therefore *cuius* is pronounced *cuyus.*

Magister: Some nouns can be either common or proper, depending on how they are used. Here are a few examples.

Dominus, the Lord (Christ); **dominus, -ī,** master or lord
Salvātor, the Savior; **salvātor, -ōris,** a savior
Fīlius, Christ; **fīlius, -iī, -ī,** a son
Deus, God; **deus, -ī,** a false god
Rēx, the King of kings; **rēx, rēgis,** a king

Reading Latin Paragraphs

Magister: The two new words in these paragraphs are so much like English words that you should be able to translate them without help.

Patria mea est magna. Nōmen patriae meae est America. Patria mea rēgem nōn habet. Patria mea senātum habet. Italia rēgem nōn habet. Germānia rēgem nōn habet.

Glōria Rōmae antīquae erat magna. Lingua Rōmae antīquae erat lingua Latīna. Lingua Anglica est lingua mea et lingua tua.

Activities F, G, H, and I review pronunciation and translation.

Activities F, G, H, I

Derivatives

Magister: Cover the list below and write as many English derivatives as you can think of from the words presented in this chapter. If you think of any loan words or phrases with unaltered spelling, put them in a separate list. After you have compiled your lists, we'll compare them with the lists here in your book. You will probably have some derivatives that are not listed here.

> *Derivatives:* diary, dominion, dominate, filial, magnate, magnify, magnificent, magistrate, ostensible, puerile, regal, regalia, salvation, senate, senatorial, viaduct, victory, victorious, vital, vitality, vitamin

> *Loan words:* via, victor

Loan Phrases and Unaltered Loan Words

Magister: Here are some common loan words you have learned in this chapter as well as some loan phrases that contain new Latin words. The words you have used are underlined.

The Magna Carta,
A.D. 1215

arbor *vitae*	tree *of life*
et cetera	*and* the other things
Magna Charta / *Magna* Carta	*Great* Charter
per *diem*	for [each] *day*
via	by *way* of
victor	*victor*

The form of *via,* "by way of," is explained in a later chapter. In fact, all of these will be easier to understand when you've learned more about the Latin language. For now, it's good just to recognize that they are Latin contributions to English.

Make sure that you understand all the items listed in this Essential Information section. It is important preparation for future chapters.

Essential Information

Grammar terms

- declension (first, second, third, fourth, fifth)
- genitive case, genitive forms (inflections), possessive nouns, *of* phrase, stems of nouns (genitive forms with inflections removed), *i*-stem nouns, derivatives as an aid in learning genitive forms
- macron rule

General terms

- Greek, Hebrew, Latin
- New Testament, Judea, Pilate
- Anglicized spelling (of derivatives)

Inflections for three cases

- See page 45.

Pronunciation

Consonants

- *v = w* as in *win*
- *x = ks* as in *box*
- *th = t + a quick outbreathing*—<u>not</u> as in *this* or *these*
- *i* between two vowels = a consonant, pronounced like *y.*

Diphthongs

- *ae = ai* as in *aisle*
- *au = ou* as in *out*

Elision

- The singular genitive form of *i*-stem nouns is sometimes shortened: *fīliī* or *fīlī.*

Macron rules

- The *e* in the fifth-declension genitive inflection has a macron when it follows a vowel, as in *diēī.* Compare *speī,* where the *e* does not follow a vowel.

- A vowel is almost never long (marked with a macron) when it precedes a final *r* or *m*.

Syllable division

- Vowels in a diphthong are not divided when syllables are divided, just as consonant blends are not divided.

Translation

Genitive case

- Generally, nouns in the genitive case that name persons are translated with an apostrophe and *s,* and genitive-case nouns that do not name persons are translated with the *of* phrase. Note some exceptions to this rule mentioned in the chapter.

Vocabulary

Activity J

- From the genitive inflections you can tell what declension a noun is: *-ae,* first; *-iī* (or *-ī* when elided), second; *-is,* third; *-ūs,* fourth; *-ēī/-eī,* fifth.
- You are responsible for the words listed on page 53 and for the words in bold type listed below.

Nouns

America, -ae, America
Claudius, -ī/iī, a masculine name
diēs, diēī, day, time
dominus, -ī, lord or master
fīlius, -iī, -ī, son
Glōria, -ae, a feminine name
glōria, -ae, glory, fame
Lucius, -iī, -ī, a masculine name
manus, -ūs, hand
nōmen, -minis, name
pater, -tris, father
Rēx, Rēgis, Christ, the King of kings
rēx, rēgis, king

Salvātor, -ōris, the Savior
salvātor, -ōris, savior, liberator
Secundus, -ī, a masculine name
senātus, -ūs, senate
Tullius, -ī/iī, a masculine name
silva, -ae, woods, forest
spēs, speī, hope
victor, -tōris, conqueror

Pronoun

cuius, (interrogative) whose, of whom, of what

LEGENDA I

Legenda

The Latin word *legenda* is made from the verb *legit,* which means "reads." The -*enda* ending makes the word *legenda* mean "things to be read," or just "to be read."

As you probably already know, the Roman numeral for the number one is *I.* (It can also be written as a lowercase *i.*) The *I* in the title above tells you that this is number one in a series of readings. A Legenda follows each fourth chapter (Chapters 4, 8, and so on). These readings give you practice with what you have learned. Reading and answering questions about the Legendas will help you think in Latin. Try to get the thoughts in your mind without the aid of English words.

In this first Legenda you begin by reading the *Cognitiō,* which is a noun that means "getting to know." You will get acquainted with some children and their teachers. In the last paragraph, the phrase *amīcus meus* is set off by commas because it is an appositive—that is, a noun phrase that renames the noun phrase right before it.

If the meaning of a new word is obvious (if only the ending differs from the English word), the meaning is not given in the margin.

Cognitiō

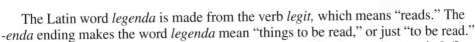

Quintus est puer Anglicus, et Antōnius est puer Germānus. Quintus linguam Anglicam dīcit et legit. Antōnius linguam Germānam dīcit et legit.

Marcus linguam Latīnam docet. Tullia° linguam Latinam discit et Claudia° linguam Latīnam discit. Marcus est magister Christiānus. Deum dīligit.
[°a person's name, °a person's name]

Claudia est fīlia° Marcī et Terentiae.° Claudia diligentiam ostendit. Librum longum legit.
[°daughter, °a person's name]

Ūnus° puer, amīcus meus, canem et equum habet. Nōmen canis est Leo. Nōmen equī est Caesar. Nōmen amīcī meī est Secundus.
[°one]

Think about the names of the people and animals. Try to remember what you have read. Reading "Cognitiō" again, silently or orally, will help you remember what it says.

Dīcenda in Linguā Latīna

The word *dīcenda* means "things to be spoken or said." Give your answers orally or in writing, according to your teacher's instruction. Answer each question with one or two Latin words. Be sure that your noun answers are in the case they would be in if the answer were a complete sentence. In other words, if a noun answer would be the subject in the answer, use the nominative form; and if the noun answer would be the direct object, use the accusative form. Put adjectives in the same case as the nouns they modify.

If necessary, you may look at the paragraphs in order to answer the questions. If you are answering orally, be sure that you understand any corrections of errors before continuing to the next question.

1. Quis est puer Germānus?
2. Quid Quintus dīcit et legit?
3. Quis est magister Tulliae et Claudiae?
4. Quis est fīlia Terentiae?
5. Quid Claudia legit?
6. Quis canem et equum habet?
7. Quid est Leo?
8. Quid est Caesar?

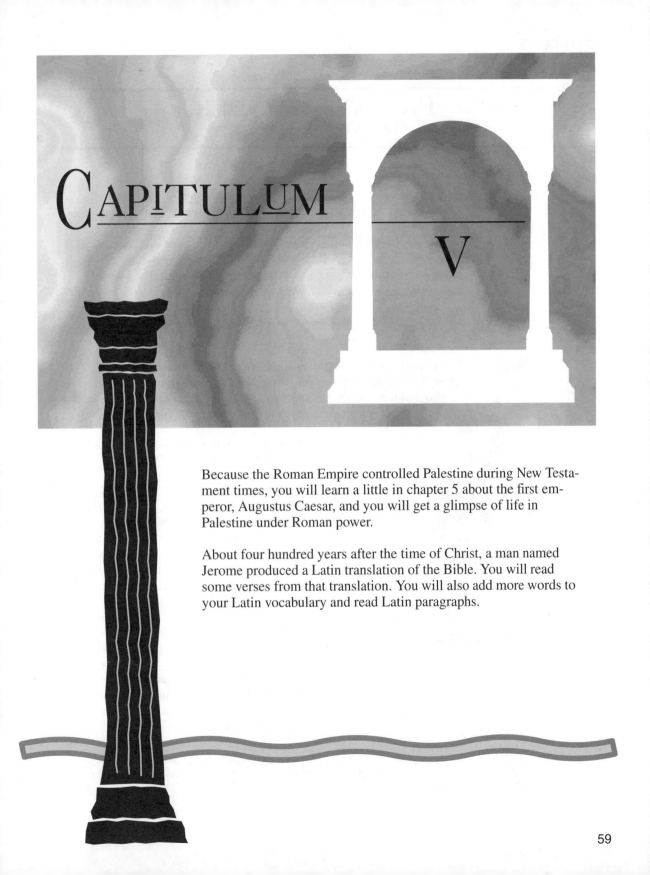

CAPITULUM V

Because the Roman Empire controlled Palestine during New Testament times, you will learn a little in chapter 5 about the first emperor, Augustus Caesar, and you will get a glimpse of life in Palestine under Roman power.

About four hundred years after the time of Christ, a man named Jerome produced a Latin translation of the Bible. You will read some verses from that translation. You will also add more words to your Latin vocabulary and read Latin paragraphs.

PALESTINE UNDER ROMAN RULE

Magister: Because the events recorded in the New Testament took place in the Roman Empire, learning about Rome at the time of Christ can help you understand those events. Rome controlled the whole Mediterranean world when Christ came to earth. You can see on the map (page 9) how much territory Rome had conquered by that time. Notice that **Judea** was a part of the empire. This period of history is called **Pāx Rōmāna,** which means "Roman peace."

Mark: How could it be Roman peace when Rome was conquering so many countries?

Magister: Pāx Rōmāna was enforced peace. Conquered peoples could not resist Roman military power. Throughout the conquered lands the people knew they were under the authority of **SPQR,** which stood for *Senātus Populusque Rōmānus,* "Roman Senate and People."

Lydia: I can see what the initials *S* and *P* and *R* stand for, but what does *Q* stand for?

Magister: Look for the letter *q.* Do you see *-que* at the end of *Populus? **Que** is an **enclitic** conjunction meaning "and." This enclitic is usually attached to the second of the two words it joins. It has the same meaning that the conjunction *et* would have if it were between *Senātus* and *Populus.*

The senate *and* the people shared the power, especially during the years of the republic. Rome began as a kingdom, then became a republic, and finally became an empire. **Augustus Caesar** was the first emperor. He ruled from **27 B.C.** to **A.D. 14.**

(1) Can you give the English meaning of (a) the phrase *Pāx Rōmāna* and (b) the abbreviation *SPQR?* (2) Can you give the meaning of the Latin enclitic *-que?*

Mark: So he reigned twenty-seven years before Christ was born and fourteen years afterwards. I know he was reigning when Christ was born because we read about him every Christmas. The first verse of Luke 2 states, "And it came to pass in those days, that there went out a decree from Caesar Augustus, that all the world should be taxed."

Magister: And it's because of that tax that Christ was born in Bethlehem. God worked through a Roman law to bring Mary and Joseph to Bethlehem. They had to go "every one into his own city" to be taxed. As you read the New Testament, you can learn much about Roman soldiers and rulers. Some were harsh or cruel to the people they ruled, but a few accepted Christ. Can you think of one who was saved?

Timothy: A man named **Cornelius.** I read about him in the book of Acts.

Magister: He was a **centurion;** that means he was an officer in the Roman army. His conversion shows that not all Romans were like Pilate. Acts 10:2 tells us that Cornelius "feared God." There were other Christian Romans. For example, in Philippians 4:22 the apostle Paul mentions **"saints . . . of Caesar's household."**

Knowing about Rome can clarify many events in the New Testament. And knowing the New Testament can show us some things about Roman law, the Roman army, and some individual Romans.

 Can you name (1) the Roman emperor who was ruling when Christ was born and (2) a Roman centurion who received Christ?

THE BIBLE IN LATIN

Working with Jerome's Translation

Magister: About four hundred years after Christ, a man named **Jerome** completed the first Latin translation of the entire Bible. The approximate date was **A.D. 405.** His complete Latin translation included revisions of earlier Latin translations of the New Testament and Psalms. This final translation made the Bible accessible to people who knew Latin but not Hebrew and Greek.

Activity A

Can you give the approximate date for Jerome's completion of the Latin translation of the whole Bible?

Metaphors in the Gospel of John

Magister: Remember from Chapter 3 how the word *pastor* can be used as a metaphor. In the Gospel of John are many metaphors (comparisons without such words as "like" or "as"). In the sentences of Activity B, the Lord Jesus reveals Himself with easily understood metaphors. To read the verses, you need some added information.

Grammar

- When a **verb inflection** is *-m,* the subject of that verb is "I." *Sum* means "I am." The pronoun *ego* means "I." The pronoun is not needed as the subject of a sentence because the verb inflection *-m* gives us the meaning of "I" as the subject. When the pronoun *ego* is in a sentence, the subject is being given special emphasis. Compare it with verbs ending in *-t,* which do not need a noun or pronoun subject because of the *-t* inflection. A sentence that has the *-t* inflection may have a subject—a noun or pronoun—for emphasis, or it may omit the subject.

  Verbum [The Word] Deī vēritātem docet. / Vēritātem docet. "The Word of God teaches truth. / It teaches truth."

  Ego sum Christiānus. / Sum Christiānus. "I am a Christian."

- *Verbum* is a subject form in the second declension. That form will be presented in a later chapter.

- The noun *ostium* ("door"), also a subject form, is in the second declension. Like *fīlius,* it has two possible genitive forms: *ostiī* or *ostī*

Pronunciation

- The consonants *gr* blend as in *a•gri•co•la;* therefore, they are in the same syllable.

- The letters *ti* do not blend to make an *sh* sound in Latin, as they often do in English. We pronounce *resurrection res•ur•rec′shən,* but in the Latin word *re•sur•rec′ti•o,* the letters *t* and *i* are pronounced separately. The subject form of the Latin word does not end with *n,* as the English derivative does.

Ego sum ostium

Can you (1) give the subject of any Latin verb having the *-m* inflection, (2) give two correct spellings of *ostium* in the genitive case, and (3) pronounce correctly the Latin word *resurrectiō?*

Magister: The metaphors in Activities B and C describe Christ vividly—His person and His ministry.

Activity D lists all the new words you have just worked with and asks you to use what you've learned in Activity B to answer the questions. To refresh your memory, here are the genitive inflections for the first three declensions: *-ae,* first; *-ī,* second; *-is,* third. (The list contains no fourth- or fifth-declension nouns.)

Activities B, C, D, E

More verses from the Gospel of John

Magister: In Activity B metaphors were expressed with common, everyday nouns. The noun *husbandman* means "farmer." You will find more verses from the Gospel of John in Activity F. Again, the Latin words are familiar. You have already worked with most of them and could no doubt figure out *Spiritus* and *prophēta* without help.

All the words in the list are nouns except those otherwise labeled. The **adverb** *vērē* looks much like the adjective *vēra.* To get the English meaning, we simply change the adjective to an adverb by using the *-ly* suffix: *true, truly.* In a similar manner, many Latin adjectives can be changed to adverbs by replacing the adjective inflection with the adverb inflection -*ē*: *vēra, vērē*. However, it is important to note that not every English word that ends in -*ly* is an adverb, nor is every Latin word that ends in -*ē* an adverb.

agricola, -ae, husbandman, farmer

bonus, *adj.,* good

Christiānus, -ī, Christian

ego, *pro.,* I

lux, lūcis, light

mundus, -ī, world

ostium, -iī/-ī, door

pānis, -is, bread

Pater, -tris, Father (God)

pater, -tris, father

populus, -ī, the people (refers to more than one but is used with a singular verb)

prophēta, -ae, prophet

-que, *enclitic conj., attached to the second of two words joined,* and

resurrectio, -ōnis, resurrection

Spīritus, -ūs, Spirit, the Holy Spirit

spiritus, -ūs, spirit

sum, *v.,* I am

vēra, *adj.,* true

verbum, -ī, word

vēritās, -tātis, truth

vērē, *adv.,* truly

vīvus, *adj.,* living

vītis, vītis, vine

Activities F, G, H, I

Reading Latin Paragraphs

Deus mundum dīligit. Deus peccātōrem dīligit. Christiānus vērus Patrem et Fīlium dīligit. Dominus est Salvātor meus. Estne Dominus Salvātor tuus?

Dominus viam vītae ostendit. Magna est glōria Dominī.

Derivatives

Magister: You have valuable clues to the meanings of many unfamiliar English words when you learn their Latin origins. Furthermore, knowing the Latin origin of a familiar English word can help you understand that word better. Activity J can clarify some English words for you.

Activity J

Essential Information

Grammar terms
- adverb, verb inflection
- enclitic

General terms
- Augustus Caesar, Pax Romana, SPQR
- Palestine (Israel); Cornelius, a centurion; saints of Caesar's household
- Jerome, Jerome's translation of the Bible
- metaphor

Dates
- 27 B.C., A.D. 14
- A.D. 405

Inflection
- The verb inflection *-m* means that the subject of the verb is the pronoun *I*. The subject pronoun is not needed in a Latin sentence, but for emphasis the pronoun *ego,* "I," can be used.

Loan phrase
- Pax Romana

Pronunciation
- The letters *ti* do not combine, as they do in English, to make the *sh* sound. The letters are pronounced separately, not as in the English word *resurrection.*
- The consonants *gr* form a blend, as in *agricola.*
- When the enclitic *-que,* like *-ne,* is added to a word, the enclitic becomes the new ultima. Accent the new penult unless it is short: the penult is long in *pu•e•rī′que* and *po•pu•lus′que;* the penult is short in *um′bra•ne.*

Vocabulary

Activity K

- For several of the new words, the meaning is obvious. The less familiar words should be easy to remember because you found them in easy-to-remember Bible verses. Most of them are common words that you will be using in future chapters, so you should learn their meanings now. Activity J can help you learn the meanings of some of the new words.

- From the genitive inflections you can tell what declension a noun is: *-ae,* first; *-iī/-ī,* second; *-is,* third; *-ūs,* fourth; *-ēī/-eī,* fifth.
- You are responsible for the words listed on page 64.

New Words in Legenda I

Nouns	Adjective
Claudia, -ae, a feminine name	**ūnus,** one
Terentia, -ae, a feminine name	**Adverb**
Tullia, -ae, a feminine name	**quoque,** also
fīlia, -ae, daughter	

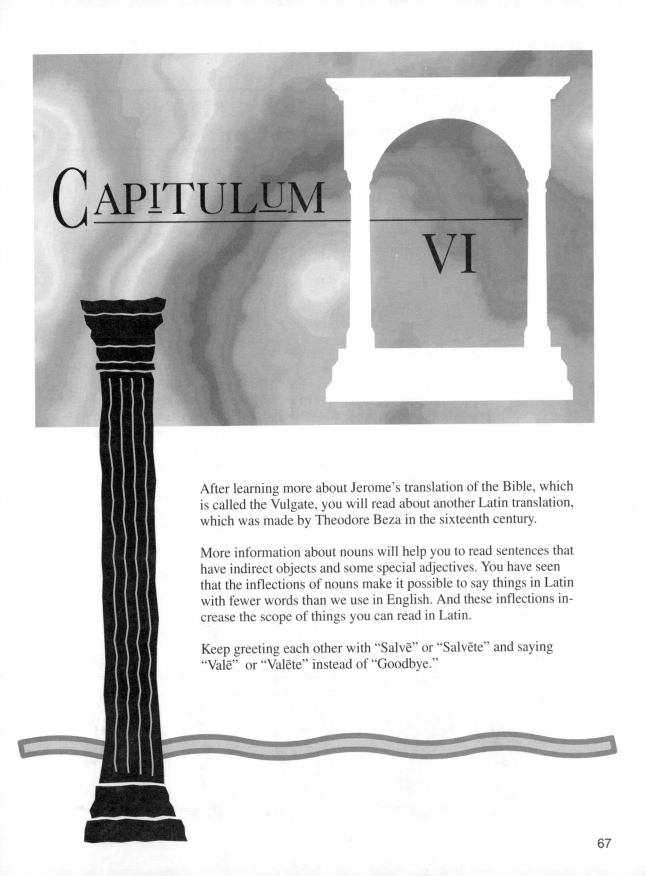

CAPITULUM VI

After learning more about Jerome's translation of the Bible, which is called the Vulgate, you will read about another Latin translation, which was made by Theodore Beza in the sixteenth century.

More information about nouns will help you to read sentences that have indirect objects and some special adjectives. You have seen that the inflections of nouns make it possible to say things in Latin with fewer words than we use in English. And these inflections increase the scope of things you can read in Latin.

Keep greeting each other with "Salvē" or "Salvēte" and saying "Valē" or "Valēte" instead of "Goodbye."

TWO LATIN TRANSLATIONS OF SCRIPTURE

Learning about the Vulgate

Magister: In Chapter 5 you read verses from Jerome's translation of the Bible. That translation is called the **Vulgate.**

Sylvia: Does that word mean *Bible* in Latin?

Magister: It has come to mean that. Let me explain why. Do you remember why Jerome translated the Bible?

Clara: So the people who didn't know Hebrew and Greek could read it.

Magister: Yes. By the time he lived, most of the people in western Europe were speaking Latin, not Greek or Hebrew. Jerome wanted the Bible to be in the language that the masses would understand. Some of the Bible had already been translated into Latin; Jerome improved the previous translations and translated the remaining portions into the kind of Latin that was spoken by the common people, not in the formal style used by orators and authors. The word *Vulgate* comes from the Latin word **vulgus,** which means "the people, the multitude, the masses." Ever since, the translation has been called the Vulgate (or **Vulgāta** in Latin). Surprisingly, another derivative of *vulgus* is *vulgar.*

Lydia: How could the name for the Bible and the word *vulgar* come from the same word?

Magister: Latin words, like English words, can have more than one meaning. Some derivatives develop from one meaning and other derivatives from a different meaning. For the Romans, the word *vulgus* sometimes meant simply "the multitude, the masses"; and sometimes it meant "the mob or rabble," suggesting disapproval of the behavior of the masses. The noun *Vulgate* comes from the first meaning and refers simply to the multitude; the adjective *vulgar* is related to the second meaning and refers to the lack of refinement or the violation of moral or social codes frequently found among the masses.

Timothy: I heard that the Vulgate is the Catholic Bible.

Magister: Jerome lived from A.D. 349 to 420. The Roman Catholic Church was just developing at that time. The Catholics have used his translation down through the centuries. In fact, it was the only translation in western Europe for centuries. It contains some books called the **Apocrypha,** which Jerome did not believe were inspired. He did not want to include them in the Bible, but the bishop of Rome required that he include these in the Vulgate. He did so with a statement that they are not canonical (authoritative).

 Can you (1) explain the reason for the name of Jerome's translation of Scripture and (2) tell why Jerome did not want to include the Apocrypha in his translation of the Bible?

Learning about Theodore Beza's Translation

Julia: The verses we translated from the Vulgate in the activities for Chapter 5 weren't very hard to read. Is all of it that easy?

Magister: No. I chose some rather easy verses. But as you gain more information about Latin grammar, you will be able to read some of the not-so-simple verses. You will also be reading some Bible selections from another translation of the New Testament and the Psalms—a translation made by **Theodore Beza.** He was a leader (with **John Calvin**) of the **Protestant Reformation** in Switzerland during the sixteenth century. He used the formal Latin style, which Cicero used, instead of the language of the common people, which Jerome used. Later on, you will notice the difference when you read from his translation.

Can you (1) tell in what period of time Theodore Beza translated the New Testament and (2) name a Roman whose writing style Beza used in his translation?

THE DATIVE CASE OF NOUNS

Working with Indirect Objects

Magister: So far you have learned about the following parts of speech and sentence functions:

> Parts of speech: nouns, adjectives, pronouns, verbs, (linking and transitive), adverbs, conjunctions
>
> Functions: *nouns*—subjects, direct objects, predicate nouns, genitive modifiers; *adjectives*—predicate adjectives

Here is a sentence that contains a new noun function: *Christ gives the sinner hope.* To discover what the new noun function is, first find the subject and the verb.

Clara: The subject is *Christ,* and the verb is *gives.*

Magister: Is the verb linking or transitive?

Julia: It's transitive because there's a direct object—*hope.* Then *sinner* is the word we don't have a name for.

Magister: Does anyone know the name for a noun or pronoun that's always right before the direct object?

Flora: I think it's the indirect object.

Magister: Can you give us a reason for calling it an **indirect object**?

Mark: Well, it doesn't really receive the action of the verb, but the action is done for that person.

Magister: That's a good answer, Mark. Usually the indirect object is a person or persons, but not always. We can test to find out whether an English or Latin word is an indirect object by using two English prepositions. Here is a sentence with an indirect object: "Magister read the class several Bible verses." Can you name two English prepositions that we can use to test for an indirect object, and can you restate that sentence with each of the test words?

Lydia: The **test words for indirect objects** are *to* and *for.* We could say, "Magister read *to* the pupils several Bible verses," or "Magister read *for* the pupils several Bible verses."

Magister: Very good. In English we can express the same idea with a prepositional phrase or with an indirect object. The phrase can come either before or after the direct object. "Magister read several Bible verses to the class." In Latin the only way to express this idea is with a noun in the dative case, not a prepositional phrase. "Magister read *the pupils* several Bible verses." So when you are translating from Latin to English, you may use either an indirect object or a **prepositional phrase.** However, if you are translating from English into Latin, you must use an indirect object. "Christ gives the sinner hope." The word for *sinner, peccātor,* is the indirect object and will have a dative-case inflection, *peccātōrī.* Latin has no word for *to* or *for* that would be used to express indirect objects.

Can you (1) state the location of an indirect object in an English sentence and (2) name two test words for an English indirect object?

Magister: A verb that is often used in sentences that have indirect objects is the verb for *"give."* Here it is in its present and past forms.

> **dat,** gives
>
> **dedit,** gave
>
> Christus peccātōrī spem dat.
>
> Although the indirect object in a Latin sentence is usually right before the direct object, Latin has **flexible word order.**

Flora: What does *flexible* mean?

Magister: It's an adjective that describes something that can be changed easily. Latin word order can be changed more easily than English word order because the Latin inflections tell us how the words are being used, regardless of the word order. For example, the inflection on a noun lets us know whether that noun is being used as a subject, a direct object, an indirect object, or a noun showing possession. In earlier chapters you've seen various possible ways words can be arranged in sentences. What is the usual location of an adjective or a possessive form in Latin?

Clara: Usually it comes after the noun it modifies.

Magister: The word *usually* indicates the flexibility of Latin word order, as compared to English word order. Remember, though, that Latin word order is not helter-skelter.

The dative inflection for some words is *-ī*. In the sentence *Christus peccatōrī spem dat*, the indirect object *peccatōrī* comes before the direct object *spem*. But if a writer wants to put the indirect object elsewhere, we can still recognize it as an indirect object by its dative-case inflection. We can say "Peccātōrī Christus spem dat."

By putting the word for "sinner" first in the sentence, the writer gives the indirect object special emphasis. Here are more sentences with indirect objects. Notice in each sentence which word is emphasized by being placed as the first word, and notice where the indirect object is.

> Salvātōrī grātiam° Christiānus ostendit.
> [°gratitude]
> Glōriam rēgī patria dat.
> Dux° rēgī glōriam dat.
> [°army general]

In the sentences you have just read, all the nouns in the dative case are in the third declension with *-ī* as the dative inflection. You need to know the dative inflections for nouns in all five declensions. Before you learn these new inflections, let's turn to page 45 and review the nominative, genitive, and accusative inflections.

In the list of Latin cases, the dative case follows the genitive case. Notice that in the first and the fifth declensions the dative inflection is identical with the genitive inflections.

Can you (1) state the usual location of an indirect object in a Latin sentence and (2) name the case of a Latin indirect object?

Dative case inflections

Singular Noun Inflections					
Case	**First**	**Second**	**Third**	**Fourth**	**Fifth**
Nominative	-a	-us/-er/-um	(varies)	-us	-ēs
Genitive	-ae	-ī	-is	-ūs	-ēī/-eī
Dative	*-ae*	*-ō*	*-ī*	*-uī*	*-ēī/-eī*
Accusative	-am	-um	-em	-um	-em

 Can you give the dative-case inflection for each of the five declensions?

Magister: As you saw in Chapter 4, the stem of a Latin noun is the genitive form with the inflection removed. Add the dative inflection to the stem of each of these nouns: *vīta, equus, rex, manus, diēs.* If you have forgotten the stems, you can find them on page 51.

Clara: The dative forms would be *vītae, equō, rēgī, manuī* and *diēī.*

Magister: Excellent! Which two of these forms are identical with the genitive forms?

Gloria: *Vītae* and *diēī.*

Magister: In Chapter 4 you saw that fifth-declension nouns in the genitive case have the inflection *-eī* following a consonant and *-ēī* following a vowel: *speī, diēī.*

Problem of identical forms

Magister: Which cases have identical inflections in two of the declensions?

Lydia: The genitive and dative.

Magister: In which declensions are the inflections for the genitive and dative cases identical?

Julia: The first and fifth declensions. Won't it be hard to tell whether a word with one of these inflections is an indirect object or a possessive?

Magister: Usually the problem is easy to solve. If the sentence has no direct object, is a word with the *-ae* or the *-eī* inflection in the dative case?

Rex: No, because there has to be a direct object if there is an indirect object. I learned that in English class.

Magister: That's a good test. To see whether the inflection is genitive, try making the noun modify another noun by using an apostrophe or the *of* phrase.

Victor: What about the long *-ī* inflection?

Magister: If you know the declension of the noun, this should be no problem. If the noun is second declension, what case is an *-ī* inflection?

Victor: Genitive.

Magister: And if it's a third-declension noun, what case is the *-ī* inflection?

Victor: Dative. I see now.

Magister: And the inflections *-uī* and *-ēī* are two-letter inflections, not to be confused with *-ī*.

Now you should be ready to work with dative forms. You will need some of these new nouns as you do Activities B, C, and D.

> **agnus, agnī,** lamb
>
> **dux, ducis,** leader, general, ruler
>
> **grātia, grātiae,** kindness, grace; gratitude
>
> **quercus, quercūs,** oak tree

Activities B, C, D

Can you (1) name the two cases that can have each of these inflections: *-ae* and *-ēī/-eī* and (2) give the four case inflections in order for each of the five declensions?

Context, an aid in translation

Magister: An important way to distinguish two identical inflections is to think about the **context** of the word. The context is the sentence (or sentences) in which the word occurs. First, get the main idea of the sentence from the subject and verb. If the verb is linking, can there be an indirect object? Of course not, because there is no direct object. If the sentence has a direct object and a word with an inflection that could be more than one case, you have a decision to make. Next, check the location of the noun. If it follows another noun, it may be genitive; if it precedes a direct object, it may be an indirect object. What if both things are true of the word in question? Only the general sense of the sentence can tell you the case of the noun. And remember that word order is flexible; so when words are in unusual positions, you again must decide the case of an ambiguous noun on the basis of its context.

Before you begin working with any group of sentences, it is good to read them all aloud in Latin. When you translate, put the words into normal English order.

Here are some reminders before you work with the Latin sentences in Activities E and F.

Translation of genitive and dative cases

A noun in the genitive case can be translated either with an apostrophe and an *s* or with an *of* phrase, whichever sounds more natural.

A noun in the dative case can be translated as an indirect object (right before the direct object) or in a prepositional phrase beginning with *to* or *for* (usually after the direct object).

Activity E calls for translations into English. Activity F reviews grammar. Try to complete it without translating the sentences.

Activities E, F

(1) Can you name the usual position of a noun (a) in the genitive case and (b) in the dative case? (2) Can you name a way other than position to determine the case of a noun if that noun has an inflection that can be either genitive or dative?

Magister: In Activity G, you are to apply what you know about case forms and the functions of each case. One noun is underlined in each sentence. For each underlined noun, you will need to decide (1) its declension, (2) its case, and (3) its function in the sentence.

In numbers 3 and 4, the underlined words are spelled the same but used differently. Sentences 7 and 8 are identical, but the underlined words (words to work with) are different.

Activity G

Magister: Test your skill at sight-reading by trying the Latin sentences below. Read the sentence aloud in Latin and then tell us what it means. Before you check word lists for the meaning of any new word or any word you have forgotten, try to figure out the meaning from the context.

• When a Latin word containing a diphthong comes into English, usually one of the letters in the diphthong is dropped. For example, the *ae* in *aeterna* becomes just *e* in *eternal.*

• *Praebet* is made by combining *prae,* "before, in front" with a shortened form of *habet,* "has, holds." So it means "holds before, offers."

Nouns

Christus, Christī, Christ

cor, cordis, heart

pāx, pācis, peace

Scriptūra, Scriptūrae, Scripture

scriptūra, scripturae, a writing

venia, veniae, grace, favor; pardon, forgiveness

Adjective

aeterna, eternal

Pronouns

cui, whom, to/for whom; what, to/for what

mihi, me, to/for me

tibi, you, to/for you

nōbīs, us, to/for us

Verb

praebet, offers

Verbum Deī est vēritās. Nōbīs viam ostendit.

Christus peccātōrī veniam praebet.

Dominus cordī Christiānī pācem dat.

Vītam aeternam dedit Christiānō Deus. (I John 5:11, Beza's translation)

 Can you (1) read all the sentences above, using correct pronunciation, (2) give their English meanings, and (3) give the case of each noun in those sentences?

Magister: In Activity H you are to write Latin answers to questions about the sentences you've just translated. In these sentences you will use the dative forms of some pronouns that are in the list of new words. In Activity I, you will give brief answers to Latin questions. Going directly from a Latin sentence to a Latin answer without stopping to translate into English is a good way to develop the skill of thinking in Latin.

In Activity J you will give the two possible translations of indirect objects.

Activities H, I, J

 Can you read the questions and your answers in Activity H, using correct pronunciation?

Using Dative-Case Nouns with Special Adjectives

Magister: The dative case has other uses besides showing that a word is the indirect object. In English we usually use the preposition *to* after certain adjectives: for example, *similar to, faithful to, friendly to*. In Latin these are called **special adjectives.** They are in the dative case without any word such as the English preposition *to*. Remember to use *to* when you translate these adjectives into English.

> LinguaLatīna est similis linguae Graecae.
>
> Quintus est fidēlis ducī.
>
> Ille puer est amīcus mihi.

Magister: You've worked with *amīcus* as a noun meaning "friend." It can also be an adjective. Clement, can you translate these three sentences?

Clement: I'll try. The first one says, "The Latin language is similar to the Greek language." The next one says, "Quintus is faithful to the general." And the last one says, "That boy is friendly to me."

Magister: Very good. The preposition *to* sounded normal each time, didn't it? Would someone please write these phrases in Latin on the chalkboard for us?

> similar to the king
>
> friendly to you
>
> faithful to God

Lydia: similis rēgī, amīcus tibi, and fidēlis Deō

Magister: Perfect translation. By now you should have a working knowledge of three new adjectives.

> **amīcus,** *adjective,* friendly
> **fidēlis,** faithful
> **similis,** similar

Using the Dative-Case Nouns to Show Purpose

Magister: In Chapter 1 you learned the English meaning of the Latin translation of the title of our textbook. What is the meaning?

Rex: "The Latin Language for Christian Schools." Why is the word *for* in the translation? The words for "Christian Schools" are dative case, but I don't see why.

Magister: The title of this section is your answer. The dative case sometimes is used to show purpose. In English we often use *for* in phrases like this: *a good place for a meeting* or *a name for the book.* Can you put these phrases into Latin?

Victor: The second one is easy. It's *nōmen librō.*

Flora: The first one is harder, but I'll try. *Locus bonus conventuī.*

Magister: Excellent! You even remembered that *conventus* is a fourth-declension noun. Now, back to the Latin title of our book. Tell us in Latin the purpose of this Latin book—without looking at the cover.

Clara: *Scholīs Christiānīs.*

Magister: Very good. Activities K and L give you practice in using the dative case with special adjectives. Since you will not be using the dative of purpose frequently, the activities do not have examples of it. I explained it here just so that you will understand the reason for the dative case in the Latin title of this textbook.

Activities K, L

Can you (1) name three Latin adjectives that can be used with the dative case and (2) name the English preposition that is used to translate these adjectives?

Reading Latin Paragraphs

Christus cordī Christiānī pācem dat. Pecūnia cordī Christiānī pācem nōn dat. Salvātor peccātōrī veniam praebet. Christus Christiānō vītam aeternam dat.

Christus est fidēlis mihi et tibi. Christiānus vērus est fidēlis Christō.

Derivatives

Magister: Latin, as you are beginning to see, can help you understand English words. For example, *vitality* is derived from *vīta,* so a person with vitality is "lively," or has lots of life. As you learn new Latin words, let them guide you to the basic meaning of English words that are fairly new or completely new to you.

Activities M and N show you how this can work.

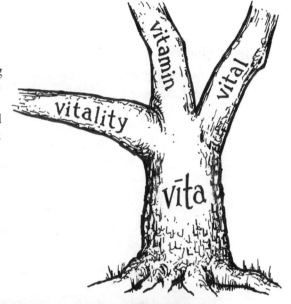

Activities M, N

Essential Information

Grammar terms

dative case, dative case inflections

indirect object (the test words *to* and *for* in prepositional phrases)

dative with special adjectives

dative of purpose

context, an aid to translation; flexible word order

General terms

Apocrypha, Vulgate, Vulgata, vulgus

Theodore Beza, John Calvin, Protestant Reformation

Inflections for the dative case

See page 73.

Translation

Indirect object

Translate a Latin indirect object (1) by placing it right before the direct object or (2) by putting it in a prepositional phrase beginning with *to* or *for*.

Special adjective

To translate such special adjectives as *similis, amīcus,* and *fidēlis,* use the preposition *to* after the adjective and before the dative-case noun.

Vocabulary

Activities O, P

From the genitive inflections you can tell what declension a noun is: *-ae,* first; *-iī/-ī,* second; *-is,* third; *-ūs,* fourth; *-ēī/-eī,* fifth.

You are responsible for all words in bold type listed on pages 74, 76, and 78, and for those in bold type listed below.

Nouns

Vulgata, -ae, translation of the Bible into Latin as used by the common people

aqua, -ae, water

historia, -ae, history

honos (*or honor*), honōris, honor

initium, -iī/-ī, beginning

ōrātiō, -iōnis, speech, oration

pecūnia, -ae, money

senātor, -tōris, senator

tempus, -poris, time

vulgus, -ī, multitude, masses; mob, rabble

Adjective

nostra, our

Adverb

nunc, now

Verbs

dat, gives

dedit, gave

legit, reads

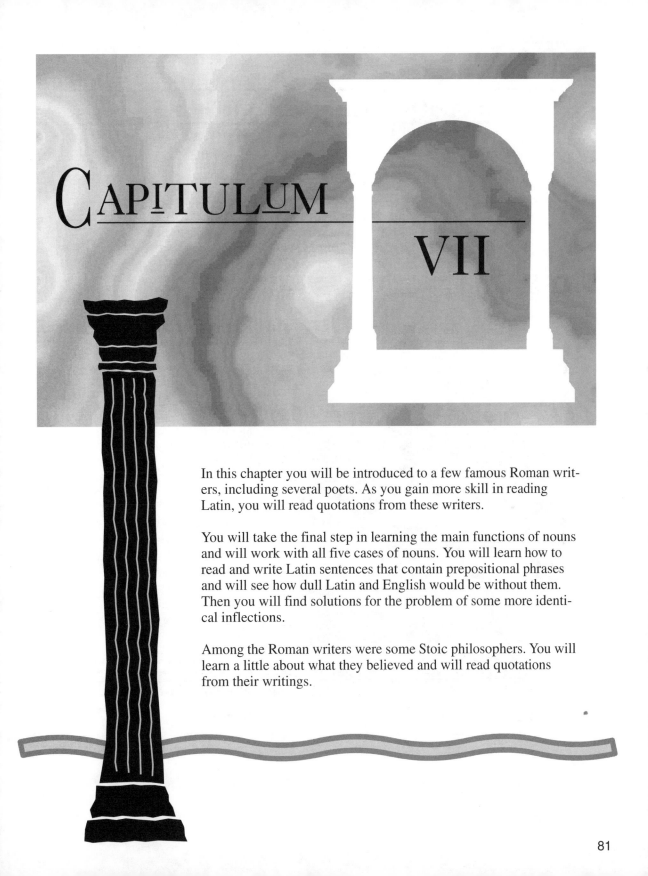

CAPITULUM VII

In this chapter you will be introduced to a few famous Roman writers, including several poets. As you gain more skill in reading Latin, you will read quotations from these writers.

You will take the final step in learning the main functions of nouns and will work with all five cases of nouns. You will learn how to read and write Latin sentences that contain prepositional phrases and will see how dull Latin and English would be without them. Then you will find solutions for the problem of some more identical inflections.

Among the Roman writers were some Stoic philosophers. You will learn a little about what they believed and will read quotations from their writings.

FAMOUS ROMAN WRITERS

Mark: Who are some famous Roman authors?

Magister: Two that you may have heard of are **Julius Caesar** and **Cicero**—both famous military and political leaders. To distinguish Julius Caesar from **Augustus Caesar,** we usually use their full names. Actually *Augustus* is a title rather than a name. (It means "inspiring awe; majestic.") Augustus Caesar's name was Octavius (or Octavian) Caesar.

Mark: Did Roman authors write poetry and novels?

Magister: Poetry, yes; novels, no. The novel didn't begin to develop as a literary form until the late Middle Ages (fourteenth century).

Timothy: Who were some Roman poets?

Magister: One of the best known is **Virgil.** He wrote an **epic poem** called the *Aeneid;* it is about the legendary history of early Rome. Like other epic poems, it is very long—as long as some novels.

Horace, Martial, and **Catullus** were also poets. You will be reading quotations from these and many more Roman writers. At first these quotations will be easy sentences, just as your first sentences from the Vulgate were easy ones.

Activity A

Can you name five important Roman writers?

ABLATIVE CASE OF NOUNS

Using the Ablative Case in Prepositional Phrases

Magister: Perhaps you haven't noticed, but so far you haven't read any Latin sentences that contained prepositional phrases, though you did sometimes use English prepositional phrases to translate the genitive and the dative cases. Roman writers used prepositional phrases as freely as we do, so the time has come to learn about them. This knowledge will greatly expand the amount of Latin you can read.

Objects of prepositions are in the **ablative case** or the accusative case. Here is good news: the ablative is the last of the cases that have separate inflections in all five declensions. There are two other cases, but they have only limited use, and you won't need to learn about them until later.

Below are some questions and answers that contain prepositional phrases—prepositions followed by nouns in the ablative case. After each preposition notice the noun inflection that you haven't seen before. Even a macron over a vowel makes the inflection different from a short-vowel inflection.

Three ways to translate present-tense verbs

- In Latin the present tense of a verb can be expressed in only one way, but English present tense can be expressed in three ways. The present form *discit*, for example, can be translated "learns," "is learning," or "does learn."

- In English questions, the subject is between the auxiliary and the main verb: "Does he learn?" or "Is he learning?"

Cover everything below the first question. Read aloud the question that I assign you and answer it in Latin. Then check what you said with the answer that follows. If you make a mistake, we'll need to solve the problem before moving to the next question.

Estne dux cum° rege?

[°with]

Est cum rege.

Dīcitne senātor in° senātū?

[°in]

In senātū dīcit.

Estne conventus° in Rōmā?

[°meeting]

Est in Rōmā.

Dīcitne senātor dē° pāce?

[°concerning]

Dīcit nōn dē pāce./Dīcit dē pāce.

Lydia: I think I've found four nouns with the ablative inflection. They are *rege, senātū, Rōmā,* and *pāce.* They come after prepositions, and they have inflections we haven't seen before. They must be objects of prepositions.

Magister: Very good. Notice the long ā in Rōmā—it is the only thing that distinguishes the ablative case from the nominative case. Pay close attention to macrons; they often make important distinctions in how words are used.

Here are all the **ablative singular inflections.** As you learn them, review the other four cases. The ablative inflection is a characteristic vowel of each declension; that is, you will find that vowel in other case inflections of that declension.

Singular Noun Inflections					
Case	**First**	**Second**	**Third**	**Fourth**	**Fifth**
Nominative	-a	-us/-er/-um	(varies)	-us	-ēs
Genitive	-ae	-ī	-is	-ūs	-ēī/-eī
Dative	-ae	-ō	-ī	-uī	-ēī/-eī
Accusative	-am	-um	-em	-um	-em
Ablative	*-ā*	*-ō*	*-e*	*-ū*	*-ē*

Activity B

Can you (1) recognize prepositional phrases in Latin questions and (2) answer those questions in Latin? Can you give the ablative inflection for each of the five declensions, using correct pronunciation?

Solving the Problem of Identical Forms

Rex: The dative and ablative cases are the same in the second declension. How can we know the case of a noun with an -ō inflection?

Magister: If the noun with this inflection comes before a direct object, what case is the word with the -ō inflection?

Rex: Dative case. And it's ablative if it comes after a preposition. But Latin word order is flexible, so what about sentences that have different word order?

Magister: The object of a preposition in a Latin sentence usually comes after the preposition, as it does in an English sentence. Later you will see exceptions with some pronoun objects, and you will find modifiers before some objects of prepositions.

If the sentence has no direct object and no special adjective that is logically followed by *to* in English, what case can you eliminate?

Rex: The dative. Then can we eliminate the ablative if there is no preposition?

Magister: Sorry. It's not that simple, because the ablative case is sometimes used without a preposition. You'll learn later about some uses of the ablative forms without prepositions. For now, your plan will work.

Can you name the usual position of indirect objects and of objects of prepositions in order to determine the case of a noun having the -ō inflection?

Using Ablative and Accusative Forms in Prepositional Phrases

Magister: Since some prepositions have objects in the accusative case, you must learn which case the preposition takes when you learn the meaning of a preposition. Here are some of the most commonly used prepositions.

Prepositions with the ablative

ā, ab, away from, from

cum, with

dē, down from, from; concerning, about

ē, ex, out from, out of, from

in, in, on, among

sine, without

Prepositions with the accusative

ad, to, toward, at, near

ante, before

in, into, upon, against

per, through, during

post, after, behind

trāns, across, over

Julia: I have two questions. First, why are some prepositions used with the ablative case and some with the accusative case? Also, why do the Latin words for "away from" and for "out from" have two different spellings?

Magister: I don't know why the Romans used some prepositions with the ablative and some with the accusative. Since they did, we have to learn which case each preposition takes.

To answer your second question, compare *ā/ab* and *ē/ex* with the English *a/an*. We use *an* before words that begin with vowels: *an apple.* But we say *a book.* The same principle applies for *ā/ab* and *ē/ex*. In Latin, however, *ab* is sometimes used before consonants, and nearly always before *h*.

> *ā lacū (away from the lake)*
> *ē lacū (out of the lake)*
> *ab aquā (away from the water)*
> *ex aquā (out of the water)*
> *ab hārēnā (from the sand)*
> *ex hārēnā (out of the sand)*

Notice that the word *in* is in both lists. When it is used with the ablative, it indicates location "in, on," or "among"; when it is used with the accusative, it usually implies motion "into, upon," or "against."

Can you tell when the spellings *ā* and *ē* are usually used instead of *ab* and *ex?* Can you name the case that is used with each preposition in the list?

Magister: Here are a noun and some action verbs you will find in the sentences.

Noun	Verbs
arbor, arboris, tree	**ambulat,** walks
	currit, runs
	iacet, lies
	natat, swims
	sedet, sits
	stat, stands

The verb *iacet*

The verb *iacet,* in Activity C, can also be spelled *jacet.* When *i* precedes a vowel at the beginning of a word, it is a consonant pronounced *y* and sometimes spelled *j.* Derivatives of these words are usually spelled with a *j. Adjacent* means "lying near."

Magister: When you translate the sentences in Activity C, you will notice how uninteresting they are without prepositional phrases. You are given the opportunity to make the dull sentences interesting by using the nouns that are listed below. The translations in Activity D should be very easy. In Activity E you can get some experience using these new nouns and some other nouns you already know as objects of prepositions. Be careful to use the right case with each preposition. Activities F and G give you still more practice with prepositional phrases.

In the new words below, notice that only the genitive inflections are given instead of the complete genitive forms. The shortened forms will be used from now on unless you need more of a noun to show any spelling change in the stem.

Nouns
aqua, -ae, water
hārēna, -ae, sand
īnsula, -ae, island

lacus, -ūs, lake
silva, -ae, forest, woods
terra, -ae, earth, ground, land

Activities C, D, E, F, G

Magister: As you practice writing Latin sentences that contain prepositional phrases, try to learn the meanings of the words you use.

Here are a set of sentences and a set of phrases that show which case follows each preposition in this chapter. Memorizing either set can speed your command of the cases used with each preposition and the meanings of the prepositions and the nouns.

Lucius ā lacū ad silvam ambulat.

Ē silvā et trāns hārēnam ambulat.

Dē monte° et per vulgum ambulat.
[°mountain]

In viā in Rōmam ambulat.

Cum amīcō et post carrum° ambulat.
[°wagon]

Sine Cornēliā et ante magistrum ambulat.

ante conventum° senātūs aut post conventum
[°meeting]
per lacum aut trāns lacum
ad urbem aut in urbem
in arbore aut dē arbore
cum aquā aut sine aquā
ab vulgō aut ex vulgō

Using the Five Cases

Magister: Now let's practice with the five cases of nouns. In Activity H you will review the functions of the five cases. In Activity I you will work with them in sentences. In Activity J you will practice putting

Latin words in the correct cases according to their functions in sentences.

Latin quotations containing figurative language

Magister: In Activity K you will begin reading sentences from Roman authors and later Latin writers. After each sentence is the writer's name (if it's known) and the period when he wrote.

Like modern writers, some Roman writers used figurative language. *Dominus est pastor meus* is figurative language—a metaphor, which makes a comparison without using a word such as *like* or *as*. Sentences 3 and 4 in Activity K are metaphors. A **simile** is a figure of speech that does have a word such as *like* or *as*. Sentence 1 is a simile. In Activity L you will review case functions.

Translation suggestions

- From the three ways that can express the present tense in English, always choose the one that best fits the context of the sentence.
- The verb *est* is usually translated "is"; it can occasionally be translated "is being."
- Often Latin writers omitted the linking verb. For sentences without a linking verb, supply the word *is* in your translation.

Flora: Most of the sentences in Activity K are by **Seneca.** Who was Seneca?

Magister: He was a Roman **Stoic philosopher** who was living at the time of Christ.

Stoic Philosophy

Timothy: What is a Stoic philosopher?

Magister: The word *philosopher* comes from two Greek words, and the literal meaning is "a lover of wisdom." The word *Stoic* comes from a Greek word meaning "porch," and it refers to the porch where a Greek philosopher named **Zeno** taught his followers in the fifth

Seneca

century B.C. The wisdom of the Stoics was man's wisdom, not the wisdom that God gives.

Seneca was one of the Roman philosophers who followed the teachings of Greek philosophers such as Zeno. The main teaching of Stoic philosophers was that people should accept both pleasure and pain without expressing emotion.

Julia: Did they believe in God?

Magister: The Greek religion had many gods instead of the God revealed in Scripture.

Clara: Did the Romans and the Greeks have the same religion?

Magister: Their religions were very similar. The Romans and Greeks were neighbors, and many of their gods were alike, though most of them had different names.

A few Romans believed in God and accepted Christ, as you saw in Chapter 5.

 Can you name two Stoic philosophers—one Roman and one Greek?

Reading Latin Paragraphs

Magister: You should be able to figure out the meaning of the unfamiliar word in the paragraph.

Sicilia est īnsula. Italia nōn est īnsula. Īnsula Siciliae est ad Italiam. In Siciliā est lacus magnus. Quintus in lacū natat. Marcus cum Quintō natat.

Pater Quintī in viā per silvam ambulat. Pater Quintī amīcō viam per silvam ostendit. Canis Quintī ē silvā ad lacum currit.

Derivatives and Loan Phrases

Magister: Have you thought of any English derivatives or loan words and phrases as you've worked with new words in this chapter? If you have thought of any words not included in Activities M and N, make a list of them and share them with the class.

Loan Words and Loan Phrases

- arbor (as in Arbor Day), arena (also spelled harena in Latin)
- aqua pura, terra firma, arbor vitae (*or* arborvitae)

Activities M, N

Essential Information

Grammar terms

- ablative case, ablative case inflections, identical forms
- prepositional phrase, object of a preposition (ablative or accusative case)
- singular noun inflections in the five declensions

General terms

- Virgil/Vergil, *Aeneid,* epic poem
- Augustus (Octavius/Octavian) Caesar, Julius Caesar, Cicero
- Catullus, Horace, Martial
- Zeno, Seneca, Stoic philosophy, Stoic philosopher
- simile

Inflections for the ablative case

- See inflections on page 84.
- All the ablative inflections are long vowels except for the third declension short *e.*

Variable prepositions

- Before words that begin with vowels or with the consonant *h* or sometimes other consonants, the forms *ab* and *ex* are used. Before words that begin with consonants other than the letter *h,* usually the forms *ā* and *ē* are used.

Spelling

- When the letter *i* precedes a vowel at the beginning of a word, that *i* is a consonant pronounced like the English letter *y.* It is sometimes spelled *j,* as in *jacet.* In this book the *i* spelling is used. The spelling variation is explained so that you will recognize derivatives from these words and will recognize words with the *j* spelling in other Latin books.

Translation

- Since English has three ways of expressing the present tense of verbs, you must choose the translation that best fits the context of each sentence: for example, *ambulat* can be translated "walks, is walking" or "does walk." Latin does not have the auxiliaries *is* and *does*.

- In English questions the word order is changed; therefore, "Ambulatne?" should be translated "Does he walk?" or "Is he walking?"

- The verb *est* is usually translated "is"; it can occasionally be translated "is being."

- Often Latin writers omitted the linking verb. For sentences without a linking verb, supply the word *is* in your translation.

Vocabulary

Activity O

- You are responsible for the words listed on pages 86, 87, and 88, and for the words in bold type below.

Nouns	Adjectives
bulla, -ae, bubble	**augustus,** inspiring awe, majestic
carrus, -ī, wagon	**nostra,** our
conventus, -ūs, meeting, assembly	
īra, -ae, anger, wrath, ire	**Adverbs**
mōns, montis, mountain	**tum,** then
mora, -ae, delay	**ubi,** where, when
nēmō, nobody, no one	**Verbs**
remedium, -iī/-ī, remedy	**insilit,** jumps into
sciūrus, -ī, squirrel	**mordet,** bites
umbra, -ae, shadow	**vīvit,** lives
virtus, -tūtis, courage, virtue	
vitium, -iī/-ī, fault	

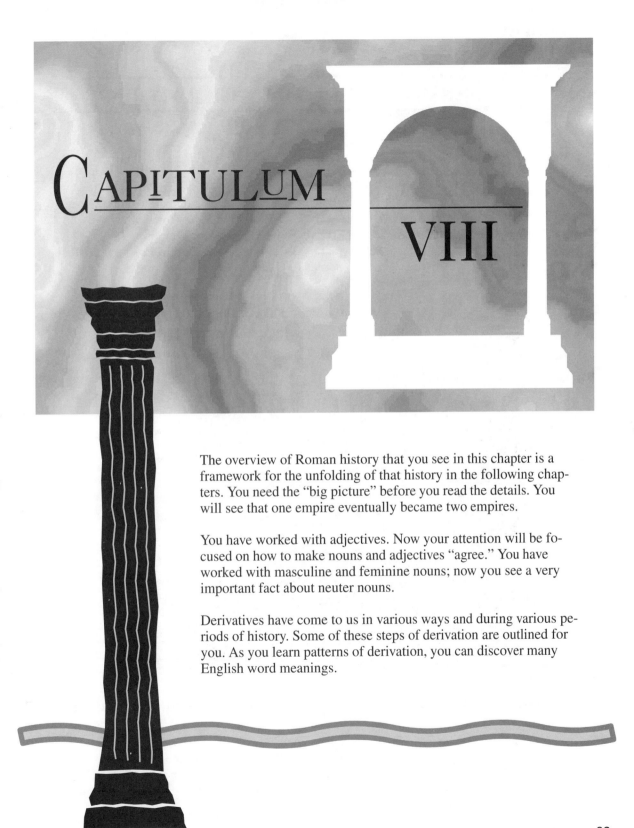

CAPITULUM VIII

The overview of Roman history that you see in this chapter is a framework for the unfolding of that history in the following chapters. You need the "big picture" before you read the details. You will see that one empire eventually became two empires.

You have worked with adjectives. Now your attention will be focused on how to make nouns and adjectives "agree." You have worked with masculine and feminine nouns; now you see a very important fact about neuter nouns.

Derivatives have come to us in various ways and during various periods of history. Some of these steps of derivation are outlined for you. As you learn patterns of derivation, you can discover many English word meanings.

OVERVIEW OF ROMAN HISTORY

Sylvia: Compared to the United States, how long was Rome a country?

Magister: Well, the time from the beginning of the earliest British colony in America (1607) until now is about 400 years. Compare that to the approximately 1,230 years from the beginning of Rome to the fall of the Western Roman Empire. Before Rome was an empire, it was a republic; and before that it was a kingdom. It grew from a very small district in the Italian peninsula (Latium) to a huge empire. Here is a brief summary.

Kingdom from **753 B.C.** to **509 B.C.**

Republic from **509 B.C.** to **27 B.C.**

Empire from **27 B.C.** to **A.D. 476**

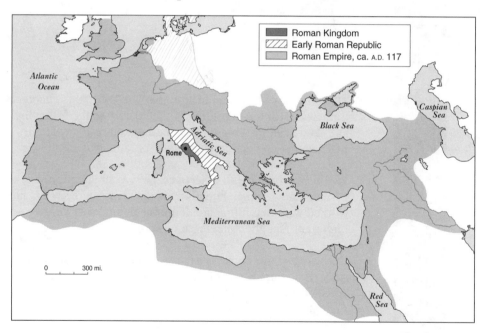

Distinguishing the Eastern from the Western Roman Empire

Magister: The date 753 B.C. is approximate because we have only legends, not accurate historical accounts, of the early years of the kingdom. While Rome was a republic (nearly 500 years), it increased greatly in size and strength. It grew still more during the years of the empire.

You've seen on the map how vast the western empire was. During the empire years the character of the people declined and Rome's military strength was weakened so that by A.D. 476 the **Western Roman Empire** had fallen to invaders.

Julia: Why do you call it the Western Roman Empire?

Magister: Because there was an eastern Roman empire. The Roman emperor **Constantine** established **Constantinople** in **A.D. 330,** intending to make this **"New Rome"** the capital of the Roman Empire. However, the people in western Europe still considered Rome the head of the empire. The eastern empire included Asia Minor, Palestine, much of eastern Europe, and parts of North Africa.

Paul: I've never heard of the eastern Roman empire. Did they speak Latin there?

Constantine the Great

Magister: Yes, when the Roman emperor first established Constantinople, the Romans brought their culture, including the Latin language, to New Rome. Gradually the Roman influence blended with the Greek culture, which already was predominant throughout the Mediterranean area, including Palestine. The fact that Greek influence had been strong in the eastern Mediterranean area explains why the New Testament was first written in Greek. Gradually Roman influence decreased in eastern Europe.

The name Constantinople means "city of Constantine." The word comes from the emperor's name and the Greek word *polis,* which means "city."

Germanic tribes plundered the city of Rome. Their continued attacks and a serious threat from the fierce **Huns** from northern Asia weakened the western empire until its final fall in A.D. 476 to Odovacar, the German commander. Meanwhile Constantinople was able to hold off the barbarians, and the eastern empire grew in size and strength. It was called the **Byzantine Empire** because its capital was built on the site of an ancient Greek city named Byzantium.

After about a thousand years, however, it too was weakened; and in **1453** Constantinople finally fell to the Turks.

References to the Roman Empire in this class will be mainly to the western empire. In the Western Roman Empire, Latin continued to be the dominant language, and the Romance languages developed from Latin. Although the Romans occupied Britain for nearly five hundred years, Latin had almost no influence on the English language during those years because the people of Britain did not mingle socially with their conquerors. The Latin influence on the English language came later, mainly through the Norman French invasion in A.D. 1066.

Roman Occupation of Britain

Julius Caesar led his army into Britain in **54 B.C.** His invasion was the first step toward the Roman occupation of Britain, which lasted until **A.D. 410,** near the end of the Western Roman Empire. The Romans built a wall, known as the Roman Wall, to prevent invasions of the warlike tribes in what is now Scotland. Much of that wall still stands. Many other evidences of the Roman occupation also remain. For example, there is a city called Bath, where public baths built in Roman times have been preserved. Roman coins are still being found and can be purchased in England. The photographs shown here were taken of four coins purchased there. From the inscriptions we can see who the Roman emperors were when these coins were in use. Claudius II Gothicus and Tetricus I ruled the Western Roman Empire; Constantine I and Constantine II ruled the Byzantine Empire. The western empire controlled Britain, but these coins indicate that there was trade between the people of Britain and those of the Byzantine Empire.

Claudius II Gothicus, A.D. 268-270
On one side: Claudius
On the reverse side: Victoria advancing

Tetricus I, A.D. 270-273
On one side: Tetricus
On the reverse side: Salus (safety) standing

Constantine I (the Great), A.D. 307-337

On one side: Constantine the Great

On the reverse side: "Glory of the Army" (two soldiers standing on each side of two standards)

Constantine II, A.D. 337-361

On one side: Constantine

On the reverse side: Soldier spearing a fallen horseman

Activity A

(1) Can you name the three major divisions of Roman history and give the dates for each? (2) Can you name the capitals of the Western Roman Empire and the Byzantine Empire? (3) Can you give the date when the capital of the Byzantine Empire was founded?

ADJECTIVES IN LATIN SENTENCES

Making Adjectives Agree with Nouns

Magister: If you were going to tell someone about Roman history, what are some English adjectives you could use? Try making up some very short, easy English sentences with an adjective in each one. In each sentence tell something about a stage of Roman history in the Western Roman Empire.

Victor: I'll try. "At first Rome was small. The republic had a long history. The empire was vast."

Magister: Good sentences. I'll put them into Latin for you.

> Prīmō Rōma erat parva.
>
> Rēs publica longam histōriam habēbat.
>
> Imperium erat vastum.

Clement: I can figure out the meanings of the verbs. ***Erat*** means "was" and ***habēbat*** means "had."

Timothy: I think I know what the adjectives are. ***Parva*** means "small," ***longa*** means "long," and ***vastum*** means "vast." ***Imperium*** means "empire," so it must be a noun. I don't know what part of speech ***publica*** is, but *public* and *republic* must be derivatives from it.

Magister: Very good. You're down to just three words. ***Prīmō*** is an adverb meaning "at first." ***Rēs*** is a noun that has many meanings, but the basic meaning is "thing." *Publica* is an adjective modifying *rēs*. ***Rēs publica*** literally means "public thing." The Romans applied the term to their form of government that replaced the kingdom. The two words were eventually combined. In French the *s* disappeared and the word became *république,* from which we get our word *republic.*

Let's think about the adjectives in the Latin version of Victor's sentences. Look at the first sentence. How is *parva* used? Your clue is the verb. What kind of verb is it?

Clement: It's linking, and *small* is a predicate adjective. There's another predicate adjective in the third sentence.

Magister: Excellent. Now tell us the case of the adjective in the first Latin sentence.

Clement: That's easy. It's nominative because it describes the subject.

Magister: Here's a challenge. Can you figure out the case of the words *rēs* and *publica?*

Flora: Well, *rēs* looks like *spēs* in the fifth declension. It must be nominative. And *publica* has the same inflection as nominative nouns like *lingua.*

Magister: You're right. *Publica* modifies *rēs*. Remember from *liber meus* that an adjective inflection doesn't have to be spelled like the inflection of the noun it modifies. English nouns and adjectives don't have inflections to show how they are used in sentences. But Latin adjectives, like Latin nouns, have case inflections. Noun-adjective agreement is essential. In other words, an adjective must be in the same case as the noun it modifies. *Publica* is nominative because *rēs* is nominative.

Clement: But *rēs* is in fifth declension, and *publica* is in the first declension.

Magister: An adjective doesn't have to be in the same declension as the noun it modifies. In Victor's second sentence, they happen to be in the same declension. Can you tell me the case and the function of *longam históriam?*

Mark: Both words are accusative. *Históriam* is the direct object. Why does this adjective come before the noun?

Magister: If an adjective precedes the noun it modifies, it receives emphasis. Perhaps the Romans considered **adjectives that express size and number** as emphatic, since Latin adjectives expressing those ideas *generally* precede the nouns they modify. Notice the location of the adjectives in Activity B.

Activity B

 Can you answer these two questions? (1) Must an adjective be in the same declension as the noun it modifies? (2) How are certain Latin adjectives given emphasis in sentences?

Working with Neuter Nouns and Adjectives

Magister: Let's look again at the sentence *Imperium erat vastum.* To decide whether *imperium* is the subject or the direct object, you need to look at the verb. What kind of verb is it?

Timothy: It's a linking verb. So it's connecting the subject with the predicate adjective.

Magister: You're right. Until now you've used the *-um* inflection only for direct objects when the nouns were masculine. And you've used the *-am* inflection for feminine nouns. *Imperium* is neuter. The word **neuter** is a loan word. It means "neither one nor the other; neither masculine nor feminine." *Imperium,* "an empire," is neither masculine nor feminine. Let's compare the inflections of a masculine noun and a neuter noun in the second declension.

Masculine	Neuter
mund*us*	verb*um*
mundī	verbī
mundō	verbō
mund*um*	verb*um*
mundō	verbō

Clement: I can see only one difference. It's in the nominative case. How can we tell whether a neuter noun that ends in *-um* is a subject or a direct object?

Neuter rule

Magister: Before I answer your question, let me give you a simple rule that has *no* exceptions. It's called the **neuter rule.** The nominative and the accusative cases of Latin neuter nouns, adjectives, and pronouns are *always* identical. For example, the noun for *heart* is *cor* for both the nominative and the accusative case.

Now, to answer your question, usually the word order and the kind of verb in the sentence tell you which case these nouns are. Although identical inflections can cause translation problems, there's nearly always an easy solution. Translate this sentence: "Quis vitium nōn habet?" The meaning of *vitium* is in the list below.

Timothy: "Who does not have a fault?"

Magister: Now translate this sentence: Vitium est meum.

Timothy: "The fault is mine." I see. That's like Imperium erat vastum. Because there's a linking verb, the words with a *-um* inflection have to be in the nominative case.

Magister: The problem isn't as great as it first appeared, is it? From the list of new neuter nouns below, translate these sentences.

Vitium magnum habet.
Remedium invenit.

Julia: "He has a great fault." "He finds a remedy."

Flora: Couldn't the subject of those sentences be *she?*

Magister: Yes. We would need a context to know which pronoun to use. Activity C illustrates the use of neuter nouns in the nominative and accusative cases.

Here is a list of neuter nouns, some review and some new. They are grouped according to declension.

> **imperium, -iī/-ī,** power or right to command; empire
> **initium, -iī/ī,** beginning
> **ostium, -iī/-ī,** door, mouth (of a river)
> **peccātum, -ī,** fault, sin
> **remedium, -ī,** remedy
> **vitium, -iī/ī,** fault, imperfection; crime, vice
>
> **genus, generis,** kind, class
> **iūs, iūris (jūs, jūris),** right, law
> **opus, operis,** work, labor
> **tempus, temporis,** time

Activity C

Can you (1) state the neuter rule and (2) state two ways to distinguish neuter subjects or predicate nouns from direct objects in Latin sentences?

Third-declension neuter nouns with *-us* inflections

Magister: You may be surprised when you find words such as *opus* and *tempus* used as direct objects, since you have previously seen *-us* only in second declension and only as a nominative form. In the third declension the nominative inflections are greatly varied. For neuter nouns the *-us* inflection is both nominative and accusative according to the neuter rule.

Let's compare the forms of two third-declension nouns: one masculine and one neuter.

Masculine	Neuter
pan*is*	op*us*
pan*is*	oper*is*
pan*ī*	oper*ī*
pan*em*	op*us*
pan*e*	oper*e*

Noun-adjective agreement

Magister: Here's some practice in translating neuter forms that have adjective modifiers. Read the sentences aloud before you translate them. Use context to decide the case of the nouns, especially neuter nominative and accusative forms.

Remember that the two words *rēs* and *publica* became a single English word.

Translation hints

- When a Latin sentence has the verb *est* or *erat* and doesn't have a predicate noun or predicate adjective, we can begin the English translation with "There is/was" to make the sentence sound like normal English. ("There is a book on the desk.") Apply this principle in the fourth sentence below. *There,* used in this way, is called an **expletive.** Latin doesn't have a parallel word.

- Often when a sentence contains *nōn,* the auxiliary *does* is needed in the English translation. Claudia linguam Germānam nōn dīcit. *Claudia* does *not speak the German language.*

Rōma erat magnum imperium.

Nōmen imperī est ā nōmine urbis.

Iūs in rēs publicā Rōmānā erat forte.°

[°strong]

Peccātum multum° erat in Imperiō Rōmānō.

[°much]

Remedium peccātī est in Verbō Deī.

Before doing Activity D, you should review all the case inflections. Use the table on page 86. Put the inflections for each declension on a familiar noun in that declension and say the nouns in each case. For second-declension nouns, decline three nouns, one for each nominative inflection. In Activity D you will use neuter nouns in phrases so that you can become more familiar with them in the various sentence functions. Can you identify the one phrase that does not contain a neuter noun?

Activity D

Can you determine whether a neuter noun with the inflection *-us* is the subject or direct object in a sentence?

Magister: Now you will be using adjectives you've already worked with to improve some Latin sentences. They are listed for your convenience.

aeternus, eternal	**magnus,** large
amīcus, friendly	**meus,** my
Anglicus, English	**noster,** our
bonus, good	**Rōmānus,** Roman
Christiānus, Christian	**similis,** similar
fidēlis, faithful	**tuus,** your
Germānus, German	**vērus,** true
Latīnus, Latin	**vīvus,** living, alive

Magister: In Activity E you'll supply appropriate adjectives to modify nouns in Latin sentences to get experience in making adjectives agree with the nouns they modify. In Activity F you will answer Latin questions in Latin for still more practice with neuter nouns. You may wish to use *yes* or *no* in your answers. To answer the questions, try to think in Latin instead of translating.

Yes and *no*

Latin has no words equal to our answer-words *yes* and *no*. Often the Latin answer is given in a complete sentence. Sometimes the answer is a phrase such as *ita vērē,* "thus truly, certainly." Later you will learn Latin words that convey the approximate meaning of *yes* and *no* when those words answer questions.

The word *Latin*

In the English Language the word *Latin* is both a noun and an adjective. In the Latin language *Latinus* is only an adjective.

Activities E, F

Magister: What case is the phrase *senātōris Rōmānī?*

Timothy: It's genitive case.

Magister: And the case of *urbe Rōmānā?*

Timothy: Ablative.

Reading Latin Paragraphs

Rōma est magna urbs. Urbs Rōmae historiam longam habet. Imperium Rōmānum erat vastum et forte. Peccātum in Imperiō Rōmānō erat magnum.

Opus illīus° senātoris Rōmānī erat bonum. Erat fortis et fidēlis. Ille° senātor grātiās magnās ab populō Rōmānō habēbat.

[°of that, °That]

Derivatives

Magister: Here's a group of derivatives that came to us directly or indirectly from the nouns in this chapter. Many of these came from Latin adjectives made from Latin nouns.

Abbreviations

These are the customary abbreviations that are used in dictionaries to identify the time period when the words with these labels were first used.

L — ancient Latin, until about A.D. 200

LL — Late Latin, between about A.D. 200 and 600

ML — Medieval Latin, during the Middle Ages (about A.D. 700 to about 1500)

NL — New Latin, since about 1500, especially for scientific terms

---

The Latin adjectives are given below the nouns from which they were derived.

Each italicized English word is borrowed directly from Latin.

cor, cordis
    ML — cordiālis: *cordial*
genus, generis
    ML — generālis: *general*
imperium, imperiī: empire
L — imperiōsus: *imperious*
    L — imperiālis: *imperial, imperialistic*

remedium, <u>remediī</u>: *remedy*

    L — remediālis: *remedial*

rēs, <u>reī</u> (as in rēs publica)

    ML — reālis: *real*

tempus, <u>tempor</u>is: *tempo* (through Italian)

    L — temporārius: *temporary*

    ML — temporālis *temporal*

verbum, <u>verbī</u>: *verb*

    LL — verbālis: *verbal*

vitium, <u>vitiī</u>: *vice*

    Old French: vitiōsus: *vicious*

Many Latin nouns are related to Latin verbs. An English derivative that seems to come from an English noun may actually come from the related Latin verb. Among such derivatives are *generate, generation, generator, operate, operation,* and *operator.* These come from verbs rather than from *genus, generis* and *opus, operis.* We'll discuss these when you've learned more about verbs.

You've probably figured out that *jury* and *juror* came from *iūs, <u>iūris</u>.*

From *nōmen* we get *nomenclature,* "a system of names, as in science." A *nomenclator* is a person who assigns names in classifications. Notice that these derivatives come from the nominative form.

Loan Words

Magister: Here are two nouns and an adjective that we borrowed letter for letter from Latin.

       genus, "a class or group, the members of which have common characteristics"

       opus, "a creative work, as a musical composition"

       neuter, "neither one nor the other; neither masculine nor feminine"

In Activity G you will see how the underlined derivatives can be used. This activity can improve your understanding of some English words.

Activity G

Essential Information

Grammar terms

- neuter, neuter rule; expletive
- noun-adjective agreement, adjectives that express size or number (their position in a sentence)

General terms

- Western Roman Empire; Germanic tribes, Huns
- Byzantine empire (eastern Roman empire), Constantine, Constantinople ("New Rome")

Major dates of Roman history

- Kingdom from 753 B.C. to 509 B.C.
- Republic from 509 B.C. to 27 B.C.
- Roman Empire from 27 B.C. to A.D. 476
- Byzantine Empire from A.D. 330 to A.D. 1453
- Roman occupation of Britain from 54 B.C. to A.D. 410

Inflections of neuter nouns

- See pages 99 and 101.

Translation

a. Latin has no words equivalent to our *yes* and *no.* Among the Latin ways of expressing the approximate meaning *yes* is the phrase *ita vērē,* "thus truly, certainly."

b. Latin has no expletive comparable to our word *there.* If a sentence with the verb *est* or *erat* has no predicate adjective or predicate noun, we can usually supply *there* to make a normal-sounding translation. Lacus est in silvā. *There is a lake in the forest.*

c. When a sentence contains *nōn,* often the auxiliary *does* is required to translate the sentence into English. Claudia linguam Germānam nōn dīcit. *Claudia does not speak the German language.*

Word order

- Adjectives that indicate size or number are usually placed before the nouns they modify.

Loan Words

- genus, neuter, opus

Vocabulary

Activity H

- For the genitive form, just the inflection is given unless a spelling change is involved. If the word is fairly long, enough of the word is given to show that change. Some words that you have already worked with are given in order to show the genitive forms.
- You are responsible for the words listed on pages 101 and 103 and for the words listed below in bold type.

Nouns

honos (or honor), -nōris, honor

investīgātio, -iōnis, examination, test

rēs, reī, thing, affair

rēs publica, reī -ae, republic

Adjectives

dūrus, hard

forte, strong, brave

longa, long

multus, much

neuter, neither one nor the other; neither masculine nor feminine

parva, small

publica, public

vastum, vast

Adverbs

interdum, sometimes

ita vērē, thus truly, certainly

prīmō, at first

Verbs

erat, was

habēbat, had

LEGENDA II

Colloquium

This Legenda is a **colloquium**—a conversation—between Horatius (we would call him Horace) and Licinius, two Roman boys, about their teachers, Magister Aurelius and Magister Silvanus. The time of the conversation is about A.D. 200. As you read it for the first time, cover the lines below and guess the meanings of the new words. Try to understand as much as you can directly in Latin. Then read it again and check the word meanings to see how well you did in guessing the meanings of new words.

Horatius: Quis est magister tuus?

Licinius: Magister Silvānus est magister meus. Linguam Latīnam et linguam Graecam° docet.
[°Greek (adj.)]

Horatius: Sum discipulus Magistrī Aurēliī.

Licinius: Nōmen magistrī tuī est quoque nōmen clārī° Rōmānī imperātōris.°
[°famous, °emperor]

Vīvitne° Magister Aurēlius in urbe?
[°lives]

Horatius: Ad Rōmam vīvit. Magnum equum et canem amīcum habet. Ubi° Magister Silvānus vīvit?
[°where]

Licinius: Ad lacum. Pacem silvae dīligit. Saepe° in silvā ambulat. Etiam° sub° arbore saepe cum librō sedet. Ē librō magnō dē Bellō Troiānō° legit.
[°often, °also, °under, °Trojan War]

Horatius: Puer est saepe cum magistrō tuō. Quis est?

Licinius: Est fīlius senātōris. Nōmen puerī est Octāvius. Puer quoque silvam
dīligit. Ē silvā ad lacum currit et in lacū natat.

Horatius: Magister Aurēlius librum dē historiā patriae nostrae scrībit.° In librō
senātuī magnam glōriam dat. Nōmen librī erit° *Cīvitās° Rōmāna.*
Liber in linguā Latīnā erit. Magister Aurēlius est scriptor° bonus.
[°writes, °will be, °state, °writer]

Dīcenda in Linguā Latīna

Answer each question in a complete Latin sentence, orally or in writing, as your
teacher directs. Use the correct case inflection for each noun and adjective. Try not to
think in English, but just react directly to the Latin question. You may look back at the
Colloquium if necessary.

1. Quis est magister Horātiī?
2. Quis est discipulus Magistrī Aurēliī?
3. Quis ad lacum vīvit, Magister Aurēlius aut Magister Silvānus?
4. Quis dē Bellō Troiānō legit?
5. Quis librum dē historiā scrībit?
6. Quis est puer cum Magistrō Silvānō?

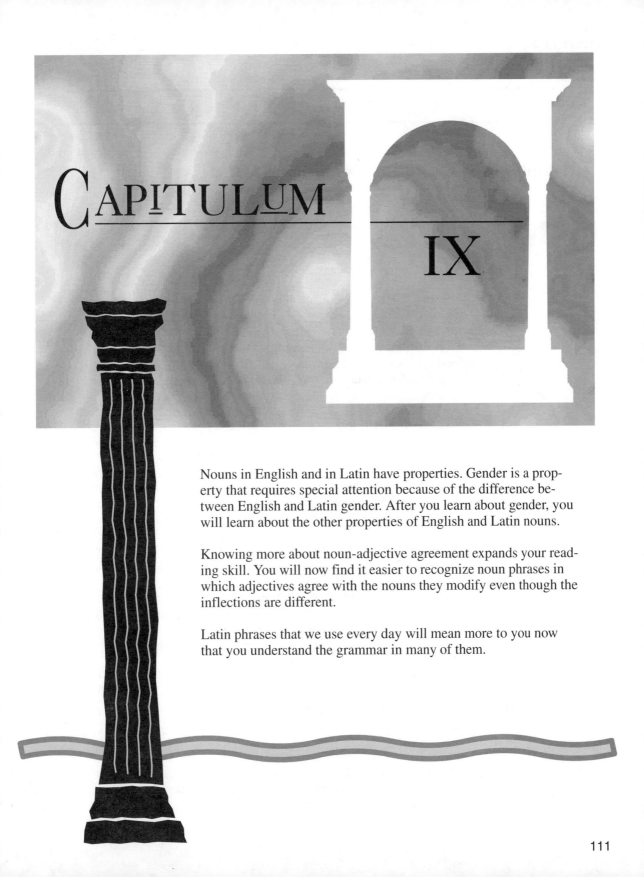

CAPITULUM IX

Nouns in English and in Latin have properties. Gender is a property that requires special attention because of the difference between English and Latin gender. After you learn about gender, you will learn about the other properties of English and Latin nouns.

Knowing more about noun-adjective agreement expands your reading skill. You will now find it easier to recognize noun phrases in which adjectives agree with the nouns they modify even though the inflections are different.

Latin phrases that we use every day will mean more to you now that you understand the grammar in many of them.

GENDER OF NOUNS

Comparing Gender in English and Latin

Magister: You've seen that adjectives must agree in case with the nouns they modify. There's another kind of agreement that is necessary. It's gender agreement.

Victor: You mean masculine and feminine and neuter?

Magister: Yes. In Chapter 3 we talked about English nouns like *waiter* and *waitress* that show a difference for males and females, but most English nouns don't have inflections that indicate gender. The few English gender forms of nouns don't affect the adjectives that modify them: *excellent waiter, excellent waitress.* In Latin, on the other hand, the gender of a noun determines the form of any modifying adjective(s): *discipulus bonus* and *discipula bona.*

Gloria: What about nouns that don't end in -*us* or -*a,* like *senātor?* How do we make the adjectives agree with them?

Magister: That's an important question. We would say *senātor bonus* because *senātor* is masculine. Roman senators were men, and nouns for men and boys are masculine gender. Nouns for women and girls are feminine gender.

In English, nouns that name neither males nor females are neuter, and we use the pronoun *it* to refer to these things. (Remember that the word *neuter* is a loan word meaning "neither.") However, in Latin the names of many of these things are masculine or feminine gender. For example, even though the words *world* and *earth* are names of things, in Latin the word for "world," *mundus,* is masculine; and the word for "earth, land," *terra,* is feminine.

Gloria: But that isn't logical.

Natural gender and grammatical gender

Magister: Here's the reason that it doesn't seem logical. In English, gender is **natural,** or as you would say, logical. In Latin, gender is **grammatical.** That is, many nouns that are logically neuter (from our point of view) have **assigned** masculine or feminine gender. *Mundus* and *terra* are examples.

Getting used to grammatical gender in Latin will help you if you study any of the Romance languages or German, which also have grammatical gender.

In English we need to consider the gender of nouns only when we make personal pronouns (*he, she, it*) agree with them in gender.

> I voted for *John,* and *he* was elected.
>
> *Susan* said *she* also voted for John.
>
> The *election* was on Tuesday. *It* is held each semester.

In Latin, adjectives must agree in gender with the nouns they modify.

> *longa via,* feminine
>
> *magnus lacus,* masculine
>
> *verbum vērum,* neuter

As you saw in Chapter 1, an adjective can agree with a noun even though the two inflections are not spelled the same: *liber meus.*

Clement: Calling *road* feminine and *lake* masculine still doesn't seem logical.

Gender in English poetic language

Magister: It will take a little time to get used to grammatical gender. But think for a moment about some things we say in English. What gender do poets often use when they speak of ships, boats, the moon, or the earth?

Julia: I guess they use feminine gender. Ships have names like the *Queen Mary,* and we talk about Mother Earth.

Magister: That's right. In English **poetic language,** we even use the pronoun *she* for these nouns. Are *Faith, Hope, Grace,* and *Joy* names of girls or of boys? The answer is obvious. What about *frost, winter,* and *time* in poetic language? Are they masculine or feminine nouns?

Timothy: I think they're masculine. We talk about Jack Frost and Old Man Winter and Father Time.

Magister: In English—other than in poetic language—what gender are *frost, winter,* and *time*?

Clara: They're neuter because they don't name males or females.

 Can you (1) name the kind of gender in English grammar and (2) name the kind of gender found in Latin grammar?

Learning the Gender of Nouns in the Five Declensions

Magister: You can see, then, that what we do in poetic language the Romans did in their basic grammar. Because adjectives must agree in gender with the nouns they modify, we must know the gender of every noun. Don't let that statement frighten you. It is only nouns with assigned gender that differ from the corresponding English nouns. Here is help for learning the genders of Latin nouns.

Genders in each declension

- First: nearly all feminine, few masculine, *no* neuter
- Second: *very* few feminine, many masculine, many neuter
- Third: many feminine, many masculine, many neuter
- Fourth: most masculine, few feminine, *very* few neuter
- Fifth: nearly all feminine, at least one masculine, *no* neuter

Here's another way of looking at noun genders. A few nouns are grouped according to gender, not for you to memorize but to show you what declensions the various genders are found in.

- *Masculine nouns:* masculine persons and other nouns with assigned masculine gender

  A *few* first-declension nouns (*agricola, prophēta, poēta [poet], nauta [sailor],* and so on.)

  Many second-declension nouns (*fīlius, puer, magister,* and so on.)

  Many third-declension nouns (*victor, rēx, pater, mors, panis,* and so on.)

  Most fourth-declension nouns (*conventus, senātus, spiritus, lacus,* and so on.)

  One fifth-declension noun (*diēs,* which is sometimes feminine)

- *Feminine nouns:* female persons and other nouns with assigned feminine gender

  Most first-declension nouns (*schola, Rōma, īra, lingua,* and so on.)

  Very few second-declension nouns (*Aegyptus, atomus,* and so on.)

  Many third-declension nouns (*pāx, vēritās, arbor, urbs,* etc.)

  Few fourth-declension nouns (*quercus, manus,* etc.)

  Most fifth-declension nouns (*spēs, rēs,* sometimes *diēs,* etc.)

- *Neuter nouns:* nouns naming things neither male nor female

  No first-declension nouns

  Many second-declension nouns (*verbum, ostium, peccatum,* etc.)

  Many third-declension nouns (*opus, nōmen, cor,* and so on.)

  Very few fourth-declension nouns (*cornū, genū,* and so on.)

  No fifth-declension nouns

Can you name and give the English meanings of several Latin nouns that have assigned gender?

Magister: If a noun can be either masculine or feminine, it is said to have **common gender.** Examples are *cīvis,* "citizen"; *mūs,* "mouse"; and *elephantus,* "elephant."

Regardless of the declension, most **abstract nouns** are feminine. An abstract noun is the name of any nonmaterial thing. Examples include *grātia* (first), *vēritās* (third), and *spēs* (fifth).

When you find a noun that doesn't fit the general rule of its class (the general rule is indicated by the term *most* in the lists you've just looked at), be sure to learn the gender of that noun. Learning the gender of the nouns that are the exceptions to the general rules will not be an impossible task.

Here is a bit of help for third-declension nouns with certain inflections:

> *-tās, -tūdo, -tiō* Feminine
>
> *-tor* Masculine

The more you work with the language, the more you will see spelling patterns that give you clues to the gender of nouns. However, I must be honest and tell you that you must memorize noun genders.

To bring you up to date, here are the nouns with assigned masculine, feminine, and common genders, as well as the neuter nouns that you have worked with. The list includes a few nouns that you have seen only once or twice in activities.

Part of a tiled floor uncovered in a house in Pompeii.

The sign reads, "Beware of the dog."

FIRST		SECOND	THIRD		FOURTH
Eurōpa, f.	īra, f.	liber, m.	cīvis, c.	conventus, m.	lacus, m.
Graecia, f.	lingua, f.	mundus, m.		pānis, m.	quercus, f.
Hispānia, f.	mora, f.	populus, m.	lūx, f.	senātus, m.	
Ītalia, f.	patria, f.	stilus, m.	pāx, f.	spiritus, m.	**FIFTH**
Rōma, f.	schola, f.	truncus, m.	resurrectiō, f.		diēs, f.
Scriptūra, f.	silva, f.		urbs, f.	cor, n.	spēs, f.
	terra, f.	imperium, n.	vēritās, f.	genus, n.	
aqua, f.	umbra, f.	initium, n.	virtus, f.	iūs, n.	
bulla, f.	venia, f.	ostium, n.	vītis, f.	nōmen, n.	
glōria, f.	via, f.	peccātum, n.		opus, n.	
grātia, f.	vīta, f.	remedium, n.		tempus, n.	
historia, f.		verbum, n.			
insula, f.	agricola, m	vitium, n.			

Rex: I know a little Spanish, and the genders are like they are in Latin. The words for *book* and *lake* are masculine. They are *libro* and *lago*. And the words *agua* and *lengua,* like *aqua* and *lingua* are feminine.

Magister: I'm glad you told us that. As I mentioned earlier, the Romance languages and German have grammatical gender. Some languages have *no* neuter nouns: all their nouns have assigned masculine or feminine gender. Gender in English differs because it is natural rather than grammatical.

Properties of nouns

Magister: Nouns have three **properties,** or characteristics: **gender, number, and case.** Each noun belongs to one of four genders. What are they?

Timothy: Masculine, feminine, neuter, and common.

Magister: Number means singular or plural. So far you are working only with singular forms. In later chapters you will work with plural forms.

Can you name the cases?

Gloria: Nominative, genitive, dative, accusative, and ablative.

Magister: Activity A reviews what you have learned about gender. Activity B asks you to identify two properties of some nouns: case and gender. Pay close attention to the gender agreement of adjectives and the nouns they modify. From the inflections decide what case each noun is. Before checking the list above for the gender of any noun, make a reasonable guess based on the information on page 115, where genders in the five declensions are listed ("Genders in each declension").

Activities A, B

Can you identify the case and gender of nouns and adjectives in noun phrases?

ADJECTIVE FORMS

Working with First-Second Declension Adjectives

Sylvia: In Activity B both *parva* and *urbs* are in the nominative case. But how do we know they agree in gender, since the inflections are different?

Magister: That's an important question. The answer requires an explanation of the adjective declensions. Good news. You don't have a whole new set of inflections to learn. The first- and second-declension noun inflections have been combined to make the **first-second declension adjective** inflections. Third-declension adjectives, which are in Chapters 10 and 13, have third-declension noun inflections with a slight variation. Fourth and fifth declensions have no adjectives.

Adjective stems

Magister: The adjective inflections are arranged in a three-column format, listing the genders in this order: masculine, feminine, neuter. First-declension (feminine) inflections come between the two sets of second-declension inflections (masculine and neuter). Unlike noun stems, adjective stems are in the nominative case. The stem is found by removing the inflection from either the feminine or the neuter form.

Masculine	Feminine	Neuter
bon*us*	bon*a*	<u>bon</u>*um*
bon*ī*	bon*ae*	bon*ī*
bon*ō*	bon*ae*	bon*ō*
bon*um*	bon*am*	bon*um*
bon*ō*	bon*ā*	bon*ō*

 Can you (1) say the inflections of *bonus* from memory, giving the three genders of each case before moving to the next case, and (2) write the forms in the order you said them?

Magister: Vocabulary lists give the spelling of all three genders in short form.

> bonus, -a, -um

There are **spelling variations** in adjectives that end in *-er.* Some adjectives that end in *-er* in the masculine singular keep the *e* before the final *r.* Other adjectives drop the *e*. Enough of the feminine and neuter forms is given to show whether the *e* is dropped.

> **līber, -era, -erum** ("free")
> noster, -tra, -trum ("our")

To review, then, the *e* in some adjectives occurs only in the masculine nominative form, and the stem is in the feminine and neuter nominative forms. Adjective stems differ from noun stems, which are in the genitive form.

The stems are underlined in the two examples below. You can easily give all the other case forms of these words. The inflections are the same as for *bonus.*

| lībe*r* | līber*a* | līber*um* |
| līber*ī* | līber*ae* | līber*ī* |

| noste*r* | nostr*a* | nostr*um* |
| nostr*ī* | nostr*ae* | nostr*ī* |

Magister: Don't confuse *līber* with *liber.* The macron makes the difference. Think of a derivative for each that can remind you of the meaning of each.

119

Paul: *Liberty* comes from *līber,* and *library* comes from *liber.* The *e* stays in *liberty,* and it's dropped in *library.*

Magister: When you are practicing the adjective inflections orally, read or say from memory the three genders of each case before moving to the next case. In this way you distinguish your review of adjectives from a review of nouns. The three-word rhythmic sound will distinguish adjective practice from noun practice.

 Can you give from memory the stem of each of these adjectives: *bonus, līber, noster?*

Achieving Noun-Adjective Agreement

Julia: I understand now why we have to learn the gender of nouns. If we don't know the gender, we can't make the adjectives agree with them.

Magister: Exactly right! When you read things in Latin, you can often discover the gender of nouns by noticing the inflections of adjectives that modify them. For example, in the phrase *parva urbs,* you can figure out the gender of *urbs* from the adjective that modifies it. What is the gender of *urbs,* and how do you know its gender?

Timothy: Well, the inflection of *parva* is in the feminine column. So *urbs* is feminine.

Magister: This technique will speed the process of learning the genders of the nouns you use.

Now is a good time to apply what you have learned.

In Activity C you will write the form of *bonus* that agrees with each of ten noun forms. Use the list on page 117 that shows whether a noun is masculine, feminine, or neuter to make the adjective agree with each noun form. In Activity D you will write noun phrases in the oblique cases, making adjectives agree with the nouns they modify in those cases. The **oblique cases** of nouns and adjectives are all the forms except the nominative forms. A first-second declension adjective can modify a noun in any of the five declensions.

Activity E gives you more practice with adjective-noun agreement.

Activities C, D, E

Here are noun phrases with a noun in each of the five declensions. Even if you don't know the gender of the nouns, you can figure out the gender from the adjective forms.

Let's read the phrases aloud. From the spelling of each adjective, decide the gender of each noun.

agricola bonus,
good farmer

initium bonum,
good beginning

lēx bona, good
law

senātus bonus,
good senate

rēs bona,
good thing

agricola bonus

Mark: *Agricola* is masculine, *initium* is neuter, *lēx* is feminine, *senātus* is masculine, and *rēs* is feminine.

Magister: Very good. Now let's think carefully through the steps needed to write the phrases correctly. To write *good farmer* in the nominative case, we begin with *agricola,* which is masculine. We select the masculine nominative inflection of *bonus* from the masculine column of the adjectives and complete the phrase: *agricola bonus.* The inflections of the noun and the adjective are not spelled the same, but they are the same gender and case. Can you write *a good senator* in the nominative case?

Flora: I'll try. *Senator* is spelled the same way in Latin, and it's masculine. So it would be *senātor bonus.*

Magister: Now try *large oak tree* in the accusative case.

Flora: *Quercus* is feminine. In the fourth declension the accusative case ends in *-um.* The feminine adjective for *large* in the accusative is *magnam.* I think this kind of adjective usually goes before the noun; so it would be *magnam quercum.*

Magister: If you will follow this method, you will always have correct noun-adjective agreement.

In Activities F and G you work with noun phrases in sentences. If you're unsure of the gender of any noun, check the Vocābulārium and make a point of learning the gender of that noun as you work with it. In Activity H you are to fit appropriate nouns and noun phrases into sentences. Be sure that the inflection of the noun is correct in both gender and case.

Activities F, G, H

Can you use noun phrases correctly in Latin sentences?

Reading a Latin Paragraph

Dux spem magnam victōriae habēbat. Opus ducis erat magnum. Patria nostra est lībera. Populus nōn timet et pacem dīligit. Ab victōriā patriae meae cor meum pācem invenit.

Latin Phrases in Our Daily Life

Magister: Latin didn't die when the Romans died. Latin expressions are common in everyday English. These expressions need not be puzzling to you. You may have already seen or heard some of the ones in Activity I. Even though you don't know the meanings of all the words, you can figure out what the expressions mean from Latin words you do know. As you learn more about Latin grammar, you'll be able to understand many more Latin expressions.

Activity I

Derivatives

Magister: Think of derivatives that can help you remember the meanings of the new Latin words that you worked with in this chapter.

Some of the Latin words in Activities J and K were first used in the activities for this chapter. If necessary, you may check the Vocābulārium for word meanings and genders. Take time to learn any words you must look for.

Activities J, K

Essential Information

Grammar terms

- gender

  English and Latin gender compared

  natural and grammatical (assigned) gender compared

  gender in English poetic language

  gender of nouns in the five declensions

  names of genders: masculine, feminine, neuter, common

  gender of abstract nouns

- properties of nouns: gender, number, case

- adjectives

  first-second declension adjectives

  adjective stems

  noun-adjective gender agreement

- oblique cases

Spelling

- Some adjectives that end in *-er* drop the *e* in the stem.

Inflections of first-second declension adjectives

- You are responsible for the forms of *bonus* on page 119.

Vocabulary

Activity L

Noun	Adjectives
Hispānia, -ae, *f.,* Spain	**breve,** short, brief
	līber, -bera, -berum, free
	prīmus, -a, -um, first

New Words in Legenda II

Nouns

Bellum Troiānum, -ī, ī, *n.,* Trojan War

cīvitās, -tātis, *f.,* state

imperātor, -tōris, *m.,* emperor

scriptor, -tōris, *m.,* writer

Adjectives

clārus, -a, -um, famous

Graecus, -a, -um, Greek

Adverbs

quoque, also

saepe, often

ubi, where (interrogative)

Verbs

erit, will be

scrībit, writes

vīvit, lives

Preposition

sub, under

Conjunction

etiam, also

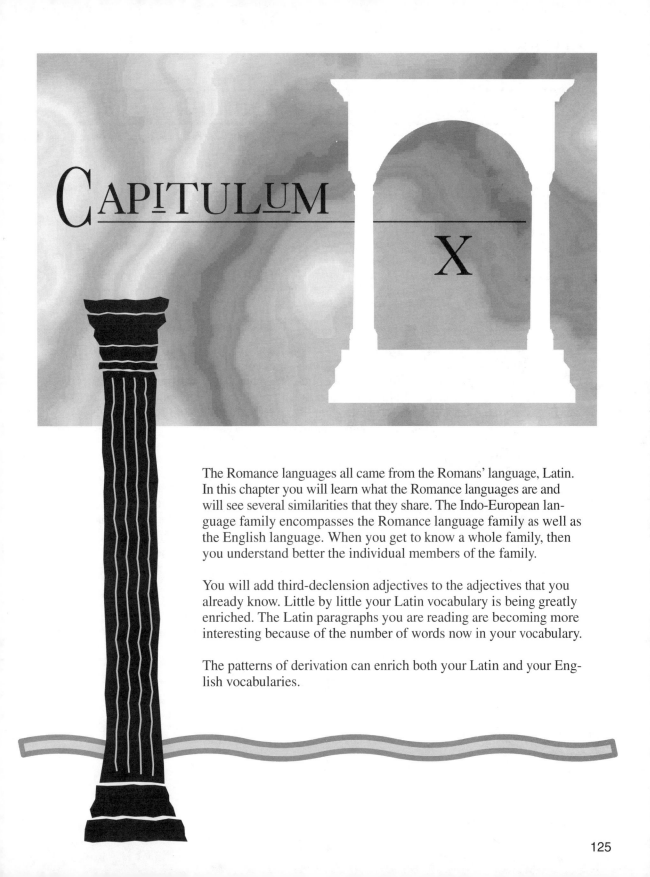

CAPITULUM X

The Romance languages all came from the Romans' language, Latin. In this chapter you will learn what the Romance languages are and will see several similarities that they share. The Indo-European language family encompasses the Romance language family as well as the English language. When you get to know a whole family, then you understand better the individual members of the family.

You will add third-declension adjectives to the adjectives that you already know. Little by little your Latin vocabulary is being greatly enriched. The Latin paragraphs you are reading are becoming more interesting because of the number of words now in your vocabulary.

The patterns of derivation can enrich both your Latin and your English vocabularies.

LANGUAGE FAMILIES

Seeing the Cognate Relationships in the Romance Language Family

Magister: You may remember from Chapter 3 that *amico, amigo,* and *ami* are words for "friend" in three of the Romance languages. Do you remember the Latin word they came from?

Victor: *Amīcus.* I've heard my Mexican friends use the Spanish word *amigo.*

Paul: I've heard the French word *ami.*

Magister: Sometime you may hear an Italian use *amico. Amīcus* is the **parent word** of those words. Similar words in different languages that come from the same parent word are cognates. The word *cognate* comes from two Latin words that mean "born together." Notice that all the *a*'s in those Romance language words are pronounced the same, as well as all the *i*'s and the two *o*'s.

Sylvia: The vowels *a* and *i* are pronounced just like the Latin vowels.

Magister: Pronunciation similarities among the Romance languages tell us how ancient Latin may have been pronounced. The rules in Latin textbooks are based largely on those similarities. Of course changes took place in ancient Latin just as they do in any other language. But because Latin is no longer a spoken language, pronunciation rules have been established and have changed very little in recent centuries. This makes possible the use of Latin by people of any language. Latin has been the language of the Roman Catholic Church ever since that church began; the pronunciation used by Catholics differs slightly from the classical pronunciation that you are using.

 Can you (1) give the meaning of *cognate,* based on its Latin origin and (2) name the parent language of the Romance languages?

Seeing the Cognate Relationships in the Indo-European Language Family

Clement: Did Latin words come from parent words in some other language?

Magister: Yes. Long before Rome became a nation, the **Indo-European language** family was used in India, in some other parts of Asia, and in Europe. Latin developed from the parent language of that family. Just as the Romance languages came from Latin, so many languages including Latin and Greek came from that parent of the Indo-European languages. The chart shows a few of the many languages in that family. These cognate languages were "born" from the same **parent language.** You may recall some similarities between Latin and ancient Greek that I mentioned earlier.

Indo-European Parent Language

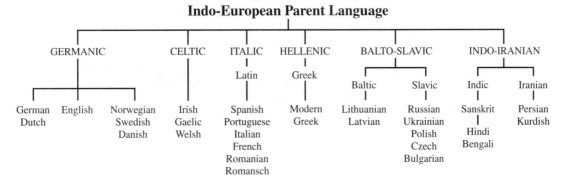

GERMANIC	CELTIC	ITALIC	HELLENIC	BALTO-SLAVIC	INDO-IRANIAN
		Latin	Greek	Baltic / Slavic	Indic / Iranian
German English Norwegian Dutch Swedish Danish	Irish Gaelic Welsh	Spanish Portuguese Italian French Romanian Romansch	Modern Greek	Lithuanian Russian Latvian Ukrainian Polish Czech Bulgarian	Sanskrit Persian Hindi Kurdish Bengali

Rex: Who spoke that first language?

Magister: We don't know the name of the people who spoke it or what the language was called when it was spoken. Nothing written in that language has been found.

Rex: Then how do we know it existed?

Magister: To answer your question, think about this. If we had no record of the Romans and nothing written in Latin, would we know there was a parent language of the Romance languages?

Rex: I guess so, because of words like *amigo, amico,* and *ami.*

Magister: Exactly right. There are hundreds of sets of cognate words in the Romance languages, and nothing can explain these words except a parent language. Then what would cause us to think that there was a parent language of all the Indo-European languages?

Clara: Well, Latin and Greek and those other languages probably have words that are similar to each other.

Magister: That's right. Similarities are found among all the Indo-European languages. The Indo-Europeans were the various peoples who lived in India and the countries of Europe.

Can you name four languages in the Indo-European language family?

Flora: Do you know any German words that are similar to Latin words?

Magister: Yes. Here are a few. The reason for the capital letters is that nouns are capitalized in the German language. The German word *Maus* is pronounced like our English word *mouse*. The nouns *Historiker* and *Historicus* mean "historian." You can make reasonable guesses about the meanings of the other cognates.

Latin	German
mūs	Maus
nōmen	Name
octō	acht (eight)
rēx, rēgis	Reich (kingdom, empire)

Latin, an aid in learning related languages

Victor: I hadn't thought about the similarity between *mūs* and *mouse* before. Maybe that's because we learned *mūrem* before we learned *mūs*. Now I can see the similarity of the German and English and Latin words.

Magister: English is a Germanic language; so we should expect many similarities between English and German.

Paul: Would Latin help us if we study German?

Magister: It certainly would, mainly because of some similar grammar structures. One example is the noun case forms in both German and Latin. Cognates and derivatives can also help, but in German there are not nearly as many derivatives from Latin as there are in English. English, as you may recall, was enriched by a great influx of Latin words and derivatives, largely through the French language, beginning at the time of the Norman Conquest in A.D.1066, when

England was ruled by the Norman French. Incidentally, the Normans were people from Scandinavia who had settled in northern France.

Timothy: What about Greek? Preachers study Greek. Latin would help them, wouldn't it?

Magister: It certainly would, both in vocabulary and in grammar. Also, knowing Latin can enable preachers to read what Christian leaders wrote as long ago as the first century of the Christian era.

Here's a comparison of cognate words in five of the Indo-European languages.

The Arch of Titus

English	German	Latin	Greek	Russian
I	ich	ego	ego	ia
me	mich	me	me	menya
mother	Mutter	mater	meter	mat'
yoke	Joch	iugum	zugon	igo
night	Nacht	noctis	nuktos	noch
is	ist	est	esti	jest'

Sylvia: The word *me* looks exactly the same in English and Latin and Greek.

Magister: And the words in all five languages are similar enough to suggest the same family origin.

Activity A

Can you state the main reason why a study of Latin can help in the study of German and Greek?

THIRD-DECLENSION ADJECTIVES

Learning and Working with the Adjective Forms

Magister: You've seen that adjectives in the first-second declension have the same inflections as the nouns in first and second declensions. Likewise adjectives in the third declension have the same inflections as nouns in the third declension, with one exception: the ablative singular inflection is -ī instead of -e. Here is an example of the difference: cum duce fortī ("with a brave general").

Three types of third-declension adjectives

Magister: Most third-declension adjectives are called **two-termination** because the inflections for masculine and feminine genders are the same. The neuter differs only in the nominative and accusative cases. The word *termination* means "ending, inflection." In the discussion of third-declension adjectives we use the word **termination** to avoid confusion with the usual use of the word *inflection* and to distinguish three groups: three-termination, two-termination, and one-termination.

We begin with the two-termination adjectives because most third-declension adjectives belong to this group. *Facilis, facile* is used below as an example of these. The group gets its name from the fact that the masculine and feminine inflections are the same in the singular nominative forms. Thus, instead of three forms (masculine, feminine, and neuter), there are only two forms to distinguish (masculine/feminine and neuter). The neuter forms differ only in the nominative and accusative cases. Once you learn the two-termination declension, you have to adjust only in the nominative case for the other two groups of third-declension adjectives. Notice that the stem is underlined in the neuter nominative form, but it is the same for all the genders.

For the masculine/feminine genders all the forms are given. Identical neuter forms are omitted. When you practice the forms to memorize them, you should *say aloud* the identical forms that are omitted in the list. The word *facilis, facile* means "easy."

Two-Termination Adjectives	
Masculine/Feminine	**Neuter**
facil*is*	facil*e*
facilis	
facilī	
facil*em*	facil*e*
facilī	

Adjectives must agree with the nouns they modify in gender, number, and case. They need not agree in declension. Any adjective can modify any noun, regardless of declension.

Activity B

Can you state the case and gender in which the stem is found for two-termination adjectives such as *facilis?*

Magister: The only difference between **three-termination adjectives** and two-termination adjectives is in the nominative singular forms, where the feminine termination differs from the masculine. The name of this group comes from the three nominative singular forms: masculine, feminine, and neuter. Here is an example: ***celer, celeris, celere,*** which means "swift, rapid, quick." Notice the **stem**, which is underlined in the feminine and neuter forms.

Good news. You don't have to memorize all the forms of all the kinds of third-declension adjectives. You need to learn only where an adjective differs from ***facilis, facile.*** Learn the three nominative forms of this adjective. Notice that the stem is underlined in the feminine and neuter forms and that the masculine and feminine are identical except in the nominative case. The neuter differs as it does in ***facilis, facile.***

Three-Termination Adjectives (celer type)		
Masculine	**Feminine**	**Neuter**
celer	cel*eris*	cel*ere*
	cel*eris*	
	celer*ī*	
celer*em*	celer*em*	celere
	celer*ī*	

Magister: Compare the nominative forms *celer, celeris, celere* with those of the first-second declension adjective *līber, lībera, līberum*. The *e* remains in the stem for both adjectives.

Here is a three-termination adjective—one that drops the *e* in the stem. Compare it with the first-second declension adjective *noster, nostra, nostrum*. **Acer, acris, acre** means "sharp, bitter, keen, painful, harsh."

Three-Termination Adjectives (acer type)		
Masculine	**Feminine**	**Neuter**
acer	ac*ris*	ac*re*
	ac*ris*	
	acr*ī*	
acr*em*	acr*em*	acre
	acr*ī*	

Clement: Are there derivatives that can help us remember whether to keep or drop the *e?*

Magister: From *celer, celeris, celere* think of a verb that means "to make something go faster" or a noun that names the part of a car that makes it go faster.

Rex: How about *accelerate* and *accelerator?*

Magister: Good. From *acer, acris, acre* we have *acrid.* Most people don't like the acrid odor of household ammonia. In Scripture we read about the children of Israel drinking bitter water. That *acrid* taste must have been very unpleasant.

Activity C

Magister: Now for the **one-termination adjectives.** As the name tells us, all three genders have the same form in the nominative singular. If it were not for the neuter rule, all the forms of one-termination adjectives could be written in a single column. An example is ***vetus*** (*gen.*, **veteris**), which means "old, ancient, experienced in."

To learn one-termination adjectives, you need to say aloud the nominative and genitive forms in all three genders. From there on the inflections are identical with all the other third-declension adjectives.

Paul: The genitive looks quite a bit different from the nominative.

Magister: That shouldn't surprise you. You've worked with third-declension nouns that have changed spellings, like *tempus, temporis* and *mūs, mūris.* Derivatives come from the **genitive stems.** Think of the noun *veteran* from the stem *veteris.*

One-Termination Adjectives
vetus
veter*is*
veterī
veter*em* (neuter: vetus)
veterī

Magister: In the Vocābulārium you will find the three kinds of third-declension adjectives listed like this:

- Two-termination: *facilis, -e*
- Three-termination: *celer, -eris, -ere; acer, acris, acre*
- One-termination, nominative and genitive forms: *vetus (gen., veteris)*

Some dictionaries list these adjectives without the label *gen.* (genitive). Instead, they are listed thus: *audāx, -ācis; vetus, -eris.*

Activities D, E

Can you state the form in which the stem is found in one-termination third-declension adjectives?

Using Third-Declension Adjectives

Magister: Here are more third-declension adjectives. Notice that they are all two-termination or one-termination adjectives.

audāx *(gen.,* **-dācis),** bold, daring, courageous; rash, foolhardy

brevis, -e, short, brief

gravis, -e, heavy, severe

iuvenis, -e (or **juvenis, -e**), young

omnis, -e, every

potēns *(gen.,* **-entis),** able, powerful, mighty

quālis, -e, what kind of

prūdēns *(gen.,* **-entis),** wise, prudent, judicious

tristis, -e, sad, dismal

vetus *(gen.,* **veteris),** old, ancient, experienced in

Magister: And here are the adjectives you have worked with in previous chapters, with all the nominative gender forms. Remember that in Chapter 7 you saw that *iustus* can also be spelled *justus.*

Anglicus, -a, -um	bonus, -a, -um	longus, -a, -um	publicus, -a, -um
Christiānus, -a, -um	brevis, -e	magnus, -a, -um	similis, -e
Germānus, -a, -um	clārus, -a, -um	meus, -a ,-um	tuus, -a, -um
Graecus, -a, -um	dūrus, -a, -um	multus, -a, -um	ūnus, -a, -um
Latīnus, -a, -um	fidēlis, -e	noster, -tra, -trum	vastus, -a, -um
Romānus, -a, -um	fortis, -e	novus, -a, -um	vērus, -a, -um
aeternus, -a, -um	iustus, -a, -um	parvus, -a, -um	vīvus, -a, -um
amīcus, -a, -um	līber, -era, -erum	prīmus, -a, -um	

Magister: To help you attain skill in writing and translating correct Latin noun phrases and sentences, I'm giving you several activities. Give special attention to the agreement of adjectives with the nouns they modify. They must agree in gender, number, and case. Remember that they need not agree in declension.

You may need to look up a few words in the Vocābulārium. If so, be sure to take time to learn those words right away.

Activities F, G, H, I, J

Activity K challenges you to translate some famous Latin quotations. They contain several words you've probably not seen before. Cover the meanings of the new words and read each sentence aloud. From the context, guess the meaning of the new words. Then check your guess by the meaning given. Since the Romans often omitted the *be* verb (*is,* etc.), you will need to supply this verb in some sentences.

Each sentence in Activity L contains a predicate adjective or a predicate noun. Notice the agreement of each with the subject of the sentence.

Activities K, L

The Arch of Constantine

Reading Latin Paragraphs

Puer est audāx. Pater puerī est audāx et fortis. Pater fīlium dē lēge docet. Fīlius dē lēge grāvī et acrī patriae discit. Patria puerī et patris nōn est America.

Historia Americae est brevis. Historia Rōmae erat longa. America est patria fortis. Rōma erat imperium potēns.

Derivatives

Magister: *Veteran* and *veterinarian* look like derivatives from *veteris,* the genitive form of *vetus.* Are both these English words derived from *veteris?*

Lydia: The spelling is similar, but the meaning of *veterinarian* doesn't have anything to do with *old.*

Magister: You're right. The dictionary tells us that *veterinarian* comes from a Latin word that means "a beast of burden." Perhaps that's the kind of animal that the first veterinarians took care of.

At first, you may think *patio* comes from *patiēns,* but it comes from another Latin word, *patēre,* which means "to be open." Can you think of any English words that come from *patiēns?*

Timothy: Probably *patience* and *patient.*

Magister: Right. Do you think *face* and *facial* come from *facilis?*

Julia: No, because there is no connection in the meaning.

Magister: You reasoned correctly. Now here are two derivatives of *facilis.* Such conveniences as electricity and running water are called *facilities* because they make our lives easier. To *facilitate* is to make something easier. Computers facilitate rapid calculations and record-keeping for businesses.

It's interesting to see how words develop. Within a language a noun may develop from an adjective and vice versa. Here is an example of two Latin nouns that came from Latin adjectives.

Latin nouns from Latin adjectives

facilis is to *facilitās* as *quālis* is to *quālitās*

We can state the comparison briefly in this manner:

facilis : facilitās :: quālis : quālitās

Latin adjectives from Latin nouns

Here is an example of the reverse development, forming an adjective from a noun:

rēgis : rēgālis :: lēgis : lēgālis

Now you have an opportunity to figure out some Latin words that came from other Latin words and some English words that came from Latin words. You will be asked to fill in the last word in each comparison. The symbol shows that the word before it is the source for the word after it. Here is an example.

Latin adjectives to Latin nouns
brevis : brevitās :: celer : <u>celeritās</u>
English adjectives to English nouns
brief : briefness :: swift : <u>swiftness</u>

Activities M, N, O

Essential Information

Grammar terms

- termination

    terminations of third-declension adjectives:

    of two-termination adjectives, of three-termination adjectives, of one-termination adjectives

- stems of third-declension adjectives

    in nominative forms (two- and three-termination adjectives)

    in genitive forms (one-termination adjectives)

General terms

- cognate, parent word
- parent languages: Indo-European language family, Romance language family
- Latin, an aid in learning related languages

Inflections of singular third-declension adjectives

- See pages 131, 132, and 133.

Vocabulary

Activity P

- You are responsible for the lists on page 134 and for the words listed below in bold type.

Nouns

ars, artis, *f.,* skill; art

bellum, -ī, *n.,* war

exercitus, -ūs, *m.,* army

fōns, fontis, *m.,* spring, fountain

inimīcus, -ī, *m.,* enemy

iūdex, -dicis, *m.,* judge

lēx, lēgis, *f.,* law

nēmo, *f.,* no one, nobody

Adjectives

acer, -cris, -cre, bitter, keen, painful

antīquus, -a, -um, ancient

celer, -eris, -ere, swift, quick, rapid

facilis, -e, easy

fēlix, -īcis, happy, favorable

fortis, -e, strong, brave

iustus, -a, -um, just, fair

patiēns (*gen.,* **-entis**), patient

pūrus, -a, -um, pure

Adverbs

iterum, again, a second time

nunc, now

Verbs

dēfluit, flows down

narrat, tells

praevalet, prevails, triumphs

CAPITULUM XI

In this chapter you will learn the plural noun forms for the nominative, genitive, and accusative cases in all five declensions.

The knowledge of plural noun forms will enable you to read and write about Romulus and Remus. It is with their story that the legend of early Rome and its seven kings begins. After the seven kings, Rome became a republic ruled by two consuls. Again, you need plural forms in order to read and write about Roman government.

One plural pronoun form that you will see here is *quorum,* which was to become an interesting loan word from Latin. Official business of an organization cannot be conducted without a quorum. You will learn what *quorum* means.

PLURAL VERB AND NOUN FORMS

⟡ Learning About a Legend

Clement: The Romulus and Remus story—is that true?

Magister: It's a legend. A **legend** is a story that may have originated with a historical event but has been retold down through the centuries and can't be verified by recorded history. In the legend of Romulus and Remus, the founder of Rome is said to have had a supernatural origin. Those who handed down the legend were using it to give glory to Rome.

Learning and Using Plural Verb Forms

Magister: You will be reading about Romulus and Remus later in this chapter. Since there were two of them, you need to learn some plural forms of nouns and verbs. We'll begin with verbs. The plural form of *est* is *sunt*. These are forms of the irregular verb that in English we call the *be* verb. Regular Latin verbs that end with *-at* or *-et* have plural inflections *-ant* or *-ent*. Regular verbs that end with *-it* have plural inflections *-unt* or *-iunt*. Later you will learn when to use *-unt* and when to use *-iunt*. The actual inflections are just *-t* and *-nt*. The difference in the vowels that precede the inflections will be explained in a later chapter.

In English, third person present-tense verbs have the singular inflection *-s* and no plural inflection. For example, we say *he walks, they walk.*

Here are the new verbs you will find in the story. *Capit* isn't new, but it is used with a new meaning. The list gives you both the singular and the plural Latin forms. Beginning with this chapter, the *-s* inflection is omitted from English meanings of Latin verbs because that English inflection is used only when the subject is a singular noun or pronoun.

A verb must **agree in number** with its subject. **Number** means singular or plural.

capit, capiunt, seize	intendit, intendunt, plan
condit, condunt, establish	necat, necant, kill
crescit, crescunt, grow	servat, servant, save
cūrat, cūrant, care for	est, sunt, is, are
ēvādit, ēvādunt, escape	

Magister: Since the story about Romulus and Remus happened in the past and you haven't learned how to make Latin verbs past tense, the events are told in the present tense. Telling about events of the past as if they were happening in the present is a technique that is sometimes used to make a story come alive. We call this the **historical present**. The use of historical present dates back to Roman writings.

 Can you (1) recognize and write plural verb forms and (2) explain why storytellers sometimes use the historical present?

Learning and Using Plural Noun Forms

Nominative and accusative cases

Magister: Now look at the plural nominative and accusative forms of nouns. The same inflections are also used for adjectives.

Plural Masculine and Feminine Nouns					
	First	**Second**	**Third**	**Fourth**	**Fifth**
Nom.	silv*ae*	puer*ī*	rēg*ēs*	senāt*ūs*	di*ēs*
Acc.	silv*ās*	puer*ōs*	rēg*ēs*	senāt*ūs*	di*ēs*
Plural Neuter Nouns					
		Second	**Third**	**Fourth**	
Nom.		peccā*ta*	nōmin*a*	corn*ua* (horns)	
Acc.		peccā*ta*	nōmin*a*	cornua	

When the inflection -*ī* follows a short *i* in a nominative plural ending, it does <u>not</u> form an elision by combining with the preceding *i* as it does in the **genitive singular**. The genitive singular of *fīlius* can be *fīliī* or *fīlī*. However, the nominative plural can be only *fīliī*.

Can you give (1) the plural nominative inflections for nouns in each of the five declensions and (2) the plural accusative inflections in each declension, including nouns in the neuter gender?

Some identical noun forms

Magister: You have no doubt noticed several identical forms in the list above. The neuter rule reminds you to expect identical neuter nominative and accusative forms. What other identical forms do you notice?

Victor: The third, fourth, and fifth declensions all have the same plural endings for both the nominative and the accusative cases. How can we tell the case of one of those nouns in a sentence? I guess I can answer my own question. We have to decide according to the context.

Magister: Yes. You faced that problem earlier. When you learned the neuter rule, you worked with some singular identical case forms. What other clue do you have besides the context?

Victor: Is it word order?

Magister: That's right. Occasionally in isolated sentences (sentences without a context) you may not be able to tell for certain which case a noun is, but in a paragraph you will nearly always have enough information to determine the case of these forms.

Besides the identical nominative and accusative plural forms, what other identical forms do you need to be aware of when you are reading Latin sentences?

Julia: For the first-declension nouns, the nominative plural form is just like the genitive and dative singular forms.

Paul: And the singular genitive of the second declension is just like the nominative plural.

Mars, god of war

Magister: Yes, if you're referring to the masculine gender. But the solution is the same: context and word order. Latin word order is more flexible than English word order, but it is often a clue to the case and number of a noun.

Can you find one more example of identical forms?

Clara: In the fifth declension, the plural nominative is like the singular nominative. That looks like a harder problem to solve.

Magister: Not usually. The verb will often solve the problem because it shows whether the subject is singular or plural.

Rex: The biggest problem I see is the short *a*. It can be singular feminine or plural neuter. I guess the answer is in whether the verb is singular or plural.

Magister: Yes, the number of the verb will solve the problem if the noun is the subject. Knowing the declension of the noun is the definite answer. If the noun is first declension, the *a* is definitely what case and number?

Rex: It's nominative singular. And if it's second declension, it's neuter plural, either nominative or accusative.

Magister: So we do have answers to most questions about identical forms.

Can you (1) give the possible cases and number(s) of nouns ending in *-ī, -ae, -ūs, -ēs,* or *-a* and (2) state the two clues that can help you decide which of the identical forms is being used in a particular Latin sentence?

Magister: Here are a few nouns and two adverbs you will need for the Romulus and Remus story. I am not listing proper nouns that name persons and places. You can figure those out from the context. In Latin the word *geminus, -a, -um* is an adjective meaning "twin-born; double." In this story the plural form is used as a noun, "twin-born boys" or just "twins." In Latin, as in English, adjectives can be used as nouns. The word *geminus* is listed here as a noun because in the Romulus and Remus story it is used as a noun.

fīlia, -ae, *f.,* daughter	**geminus, -ī,** *m.,* twin
flūmen, -minis, *n.,* river	**iuvenis, -is,** *c.,* a young man or woman
frāter, -tris, *m.,* brother	

> **māter, -tris,** *f.,* mother
> **mors, -rtis,** *f.,* death
> **mūrus, ī,** *m.,* wall
> **pīcus, -ī,** *m.,* woodpecker
> **regnum, -ī,** *n.,* kingdom
>
> **intendit,** to plan, entend
> **ēvādit,** to escape
> **autem,** *adv.,* however
> **mox,** *adv.,* soon

Magister: In Activity A you will work with plural noun and verb forms. In Activity B you are asked to write plural nouns in nominative and accusative forms. Activity C reviews prepositional phrases. In the Latin paragraphs that you will be reading, you will find several of these phrases. You may need to check the prepositions in the Essential Information section for Chapter 7 or the Vocābulārium if you're unsure of the case that a preposition takes.

Activities A, B, C

Reading the Legend of Romulus and Remus

Magister: I'll ask Flora to read this aloud. As she reads, try to think in Latin and follow what is happening.

Rōmulus et Remus

Pars I

Numitor est rēx **Albae Longae. Frāter Numitōris est Amūlius,** et fīlia Numitōris est **Rhea Silvia. Rōmulus** et **Remus** sunt geminī, fīliī Rheae Silviae. Amūlius est malus. Regnum ā Numitōre capit. Mortem Rōmulī et Remī in flūmine **Tibere** intendit.

Autem geminī in flūmine Tibere mortem ēvādunt. Lupus et pīcus vītās Rōmulī et Remī servant. In fābulā deus **Mars** est pater Rōmulī et Remī. Puerī crescunt,° et mox sunt iuvenēs.

[°grow]

Latin answers to Latin questions

Magister: You may look at the story as you answer my questions. Your answers need not be sentences. However, you should think of the complete sentence answer in order to use the right case and number for nouns and adjectives. The word *cuius,* you may remember, means "whose."

1. Quis est rēx Albae Longae?
2. Cuius frāter est Numitor?
3. Cuius fīlia est Rhea Silvia?
4. Cuius māter est Rhea Silvia?
5. Quis est rēx novus?
6. Quis mortem Rōmulī et Remī intendit?
7. Ēvāduntne mortem geminī in flūmine Tibere?
8. Quis est pater Rōmulī et Remī?

Mythological terms

- The Latin word *geminī* has been borrowed as a proper noun (a loan word) in English. It is the name of a constellation containing the stars Castor and Pollux. The term is also used in astrology, which is the false belief that the stars and planets influence human lives.

- The names of the Roman gods are used by astronomers for the planets in our solar system. Mars is named for the god of war because of its red color, the color of blood.

Origin of pagan gods

- Romans 1:21-23 tells how pagan gods came to be. Men "became vain in their imaginations, and . . . changed the glory of the uncorruptible God into an image made like to corruptible man."

Plural nouns: genitive case

Magister: There are some questions that I couldn't ask you about the story of Romulus and Remus because you didn't know the genitive plural forms. Here are those endings.

First declension	Second declension	Third declension	Fourth declension	Fifth declension
fīli*ārum*	fīli*ōrum*	patrum	senāt*uum*	di*ērum*

Plural form of *cuius*

Magister: The plural of *cuius* is *quōrum/quārum*. The plural endings may suggest to you that these words are in the first and second declensions. They do happen to have the same endings as first-second declension adjectives. However, pronouns do not belong to declensions, as nouns and adjectives do.

Which form would you use to ask a question if you expected the answer to be a plural feminine noun?

Lydia: Quārum.

Magister: You're right. And *quōrum* is used for masculine and neuter nouns. It means "whose" or "of what." Some of the questions in Activity E are asked with these interrogative pronouns.

Reading about the Founding of Rome

Paul: I heard that Romulus founded Rome. What happened to Remus?

Magister: That is the subject of Part II of our story. First, Paul will read the story aloud for us. Try to think in Latin as he reads, because you will be asked some Latin questions that you are to answer in Latin in Activity E.

Rōmulus et Remus

Pars II

Pastor parvōs puerōs invenit et cūrat°. Post paucōs° annōs° dē Amūliō malō discunt. Amūlium necant. Oppidum° Rōmae condunt. Rōmulus mūrum circum° oppidum construit.° Remus ridet° et mūrum trānsilit.° Rōmulus Remum necat. Rōmulus est rēx prīmus Rōmae.

[°care for, °few, °years, °town, °around, °build, °laugh, °jump over]

Magister: Read the Latin paragraphs in English now. You may check the word lists if necessary; but for the words marked with circles, make educated guesses from the context before looking for the meaning at the end of the paragraph.

Latin answers to Latin questions

Magister: Activity D reviews information about Romulus and Remus. In Activities E, F, and G are examples of plural genitive forms. One of the plural pronouns, *quōrum,* is a commonly used English word.

Quōrum

We have borrowed and made a noun of the genitive form *quōrum,* which means "whose" or "of whom." In English it refers to the number of members of a committee or an organization required at a meeting in order to conduct official business (the number "of whom" the meeting must consist).

Activities D, E, F, G

Can you (1) give the genitive plural ending for words in each of the five declensions and for the pronoun *cuius* and (2) use the noun *quorum* correctly in an English sentence?

ROMAN KINGS AND THE EARLY ROMAN REPUBLIC

Magister: Now that you know about the legendary first king, let me tell you a little about the first period of Roman history when there were kings. Several peoples lived in the area now known as the **seven hills of Rome.** Two of these peoples were the **Latins** and the **Sabines.** They had **Etruscan** neighbors to the north and **Greek neighbors** to the south—all in the **Italian peninsula.**

Tradition, not recorded history, gives us the names of the **kings: Romulus, Numa Pompilius, Tullus Hostilius, Ancus Marcius, Tarquinius Priscus, Servius Tullius,** and **Lucius Tarquinius Superbus.**

I don't expect you to memorize their names, but it's good to be familiar with them so that you will recognize them when you see or hear them mentioned. Why were there only seven? Why did Rome become a republic? The answers to these questions are important.

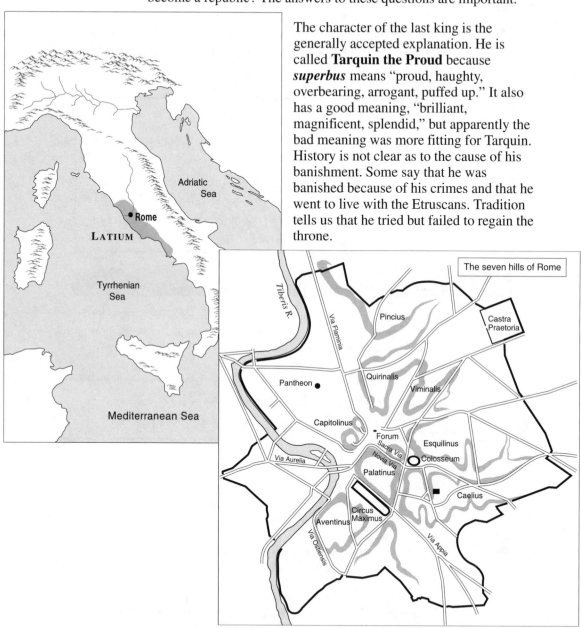

The character of the last king is the generally accepted explanation. He is called **Tarquin the Proud** because *superbus* means "proud, haughty, overbearing, arrogant, puffed up." It also has a good meaning, "brilliant, magnificent, splendid," but apparently the bad meaning was more fitting for Tarquin. History is not clear as to the cause of his banishment. Some say that he was banished because of his crimes and that he went to live with the Etruscans. Tradition tells us that he tried but failed to regain the throne.

The kingdom probably lasted less than 250 years. What were the dates of the kingdom, and what form of government did Rome have next?

Victor: The kingdom existed from 753 to 509 B.C. Then it became a republic.

Magister: The government of the United States is patterned to some extent after the **Roman republic.** One major difference, though, is that Rome had two **consuls** of equal power instead of a president and vice president. The Romans changed the government from a kingdom to a republic so that the head of the government would no longer have "all power." You will learn more about the republic in later chapters.

Magister: Use Activities H and I to check your memory of case functions and the information about the end of the kingdom and the beginning of the republic of Rome.

Activities H, I

Can you (1) identify each person named in the discussion of the Roman kingdom and Roman republic and (2) state the probable reason for the end of the kingdom in Rome and the establishment of the republic?

- Roman kings are a part of the past. As we look to the future through prophecy in the book of the Revelation (19:16), we read about Christ, who will reign for a thousand years as KING OF KINGS AND LORD OF LORDS. The Vulgate and Beza's translation use these words: "RĒX RĒGUM ET DOMINUS DOMINAN-TIUM." Note the genitive plural forms. The word *dominantium* means "of lords, of the ones ruling or holding sway."

- Even for the reigns of the very best kings in history, there has always been an end. But Christ has said, "I am alive for ever-more" (Rev. 1:18). The Vulgate reads, "Sum vivēns in saecula saeculōrum" (translated literally, "I am living into the ages of the ages").

Learning Latin Words: Help from English Words

Magister: Often you can see a relationship in meaning between an English word and a Latin word even though the English word may not be borrowed directly from that particular Latin word. The relationships you will see in Activity J should help you remember the meanings of the Latin words.

Activity J

Derivatives

Magister: English has many adjectives made from Latin adjectives that came from Latin nouns. Most of these nouns date back to the **classical period** (500 B.C. to A.D. 200). Most of the adjectives were developed during the **Middle Ages** (about A.D. 476-1453).

Here are three English adjectives that entered our language in the Middle Ages. Beginning with the Latin noun(s), we move to the Latin adjective and finally to the English adjective.

fīlius/fīlia > fīliālis > filial

frāter > frāternālis > fraternal

pater > paternālis > paternal

Clara: The English adjectives are just the Latin adjectives with the *-is* inflections gone. Why isn't *maternal* in the list?

Magister: *Maternal* came to us through the French *maternel.* The paths of derivation aren't always exactly the same.

The basic definition of these adjectives is "pertaining to a son or daughter / to a brother / to a father / to a mother." Try going from other Latin nouns to English adjectives.

Activities K, L, M

Essential Information

Grammar terms

- number: plural
- noun: nom., gen., and acc. forms
- verb: two forms
- tense: historical present

General terms

- legend: founding of Rome
- Numitor, Amulius, Rhea Silvia, Romulus, Remus, Tarquin the Proud
- Latins, Sabines, Etruscans, Greeks
- Mars
- Alba Longa, Seven Hills of Rome, Italian Peninsula, Tiber River
- Roman kings, Roman Republic, consuls; classical period, Middle Ages

Verb inflections

- Singular: -a*t* -e*t* -i*t*
- Plural: -a*nt* -e*nt* -u*nt*

Plural noun inflections

- For nominative- and accusative-case inflections, see page 141. For genitive-case inflections see page 146.

Spelling

- The nominative plural, masculine gender, of *i*-stem nouns is always -*iī*. The *i* in the stem never elides with the -*ī* inflection, as it sometimes does in the genitive singular. For example, the nominative plural of *fīlius* is always *fīliī*.

Loan words

- Gemini, quorum

Vocabulary

- Use the clues to English meanings in Activities H, I, J, K, L, and M to review the vocabulary words.
- You are responsible for the words on page 141, 143, and 144 and for the words in bold type listed below.

Noun	**Verbs**
cūra, -ae, *f.,* care	**construit, construunt,** construct, build
Pronouns	**ridet, rident,** laugh
quī, *interrogative, nom. pl.,* who?	**trānsilit, trānsiliunt,** leap across, jump over
quōrum, *interrogative, gen. pl.,* whose? of whom?	**Preposition**
Adjective	**circum,** *with acc.,* around
superbus, -a, -um, haughty, proud	
Adverb	
quoque, also	

CAPITULUM XII

There were two classes of people in the Roman Republic, and they were represented in two different ways in the government. As you learn about the two classes, you will understand the abbreviation for the Roman Empire, SPQR. A similar abbreviation for the United States of America is USA.

Plural forms for the dative case are given for nouns in all the declensions.

You will read paragraphs about Coriolanus and Cincinnatus, two important Romans in the early republic. In the first of these, you will learn Coriolanus's real name. In the second historical account, you will learn the meaning of the name of an American city: Cincinnati, Ohio.

PATRICIANS AND PLEBEIANS

Victor: If Romulus and Remus are just part of a legend, when did the real history of Rome begin?

Magister: There is no simple answer to your question. The accounts of events in the kingdom and the early republic are based largely on legends. A Roman named **Livy** (Titus Livius) is the best-known ancient writer of Roman history. He lived from 59 B.C. to A.D. 17. His books include legendary stories as well as historical events. One historical fact that is clear from his writings is that there was strife between the patricians and the plebeians even in the very early years of Rome.

Flora: Who were the patricians and plebeians?

Magister: The **patricians** were the wealthy upper class, which consisted of about ten percent of the population. The **senators** were patricians, and the Roman senate had great power, especially throughout the period of the Roman Republic. The **plebeians** were the other ninety percent of the Roman citizens. Their demand for a voice in the government was granted in the early days of the republic. They were allowed to have tribunes to represent them. The abbreviation SPQR shows the two parts of Roman government. Do you recall what SPQR means?

Julia: "The Roman Senate and People." Were the tribunes senators?

Magister: No, but they held positions of power. The influence of the tribunes of the plebs was great because they represented such a large part of the population. Later in this chapter you will read about some of the friction between patricians and plebeians. Frequently, though, patrician leaders worked with tribunes of the plebs for the good of Rome. Activity A reviews what we have just discussed.

Activity A

Can you give the name of (1) the small, rich upper class of Romans, (2) the powerful officials who belonged to the upper class, (3) the class consisting of about ninety percent of the Romans, and (4) the officials who represented the majority?

DATIVE CASE: PLURAL FORMS

Magister: To learn about the events of early Roman history as told in Latin, you need plural nouns in the dative case. These inflections are emphasized for you in this list of sample nouns chosen from each of the five declensions. And let me remind you from Chapter 11 that neuter nouns always have a short *a* inflection for the nominative and accusative plural forms: for example, *verba, iura,* "words, laws."

	First	Second	Third	Fourth	Fifth
Nominative	silv*ae*	puer*ī*	rēg*ēs*	senāt*ūs*	di*ēs*
Genitive	silv*ārum*	puer*ōrum*	rēg*um*	senāt*uum*	di*ērum*
Dative	silv*īs*	puer*īs*	rēg*ibus*	senāt*ibus*	di*ēbus*
Accusative	silv*ās*	puer*ōs*	rēg*ēs*	senāt*ūs*	di*ēs*

Magister: What similarities do you find that will make learning these easy?

Sylvia: The first and second declensions are alike, and the third and fourth are alike. The fifth is almost the same as the third and fourth. These inflections are simple to learn!

Magister: Do you see any potential problem?

Julia: Yes, I see a problem. We learned the *-is* inflection for the genitive singular in the third declension.

Magister: Do you see a solution?

Timothy: The *-i* in the genitive singular is short, and the *-ī* in these plural inflections is long.

Magister: Problem solved. Remember the solution when you see these forms in context.

Activity B asks you to recognize the translations of singular and plural inflections of the four cases you have studied. In Activity C you will answer questions in Latin. Try to think only in Latin.

Activities B, C

Can you (1) give the dative plural inflections for nouns in each of the five declensions and (2) state the case and number of nouns with the *-is* inflection and nouns with the *-īs* inflection?

Reading about Coriolanus, a Patrician

Magister: Here are new words you will need in order to read the paragraph about Coriolanus. As you read, remember the difference between the inflections *-is* and *-īs*. The words *exercitus* and *plebs,* like *populus,* are **collective nouns:** they refer to more than one person, but they are singular in form.

ager, agrī, *m.,* field, farm

contrā, *prep. with acc.,* against

dēnique, *adv.,* finally

exercitus, -ūs, *m., collective noun,* army

inimīcus, -a, -um, unfriendly, hostile

inimīcus, -ī, *m.,* enemy

oppidum, -ī, *n.,* town

patricius, -a, -um, pertaining to the patrician class or to a member of that class

patricius, -iī/-ī, *m.,* a patrician, nobleman

plēbēius, -a, -um, pertaining to the plebeian class or to a member of that class

plebs, plēbis, (*sometimes a fifth-declension noun,* **plēbēs, -eī**) *f., collective noun,* the plebeians, the common people

pugnat, pugnant, fight

trībūnus, -ī, *m.,* a tribune, or magistrate, who protected the plebeians and performed important government functions

ubī, *adv.,* where

Special adjective

- Compare the adjective *inimīcus* with the adjective *amīcus*. When *in-* was placed at the beginning of the word, the letter *a* changed to *i*. Frequently a prefix placed at the beginning of a word causes the first vowel in the original word to be replaced with a vowel that takes less time to pronounce.

- The prefix *in-* in the word *inimīcus* means "not" and makes the adjective *friendly* mean "not friendly, unfriendly, or hostile." Like *amīcus, -a, -um,* the adjective *inimīcus* is a **special adjective** used with the dative case.

- Inimīcus, like *amīcus,* is both an adjective and a noun. Notice the separate listings for these parts of speech.

Genitive case for renaming

- Just as we speak of "the city *of Rome*," so the Romans sometimes used the genitive case for a noun that renames another noun: for example, "oppidum *Coriolōrum*" means "the town of *Coriolī.*" (**Coriolī** was the name of a town.)

Magister: Read the paragraphs about Coriolanus two or three times. A few new words are so close in meaning to familiar English derivatives that definitions are not given. The word *inimīcus* in its various forms in these paragraphs is an adjective. Verb meanings in the margin are in their simple form instead of the *-s* translation form.

Coriolānus

Gnaeus Marcius est patricius in rē publicā Rōmānā. Est dux exercitūs in bellō contrā oppidum **Coriolōrum.** Vincit oppidum in victōriā magnā. Patriciī in Rōmā ducī nōmen Coriolānī in honōre victōriae dant.

Plebs Coriolānō honōrem nōn dat. **Coriolānus** est inimīcus tribūnīs plēbis. Dēnique Coriolānus ab Rōmā ad oppidum Volscōrum° abit° et est inimīcus Rōmae.

[°**Volscī,** (*sc = sk*), a tribe of people in Latium; °goes away]

Latin answers to Latin questions

Magister: Now answer some questions about Coriolanus in Activities D and E.

Activities D, E

Reading about Cincinnatus, Another Patrician

Magister: Cincinnati, Ohio, was named for an American organization that honored another patrician who fought for Rome in the early republic. His name was Cincinnatus, and he had a small farm.

Below is a Latin paragraph about Cincinnatus. It contains several new words. Their context and their similarity to English words will suggest the meaning of most of these. Where the meaning of a word is obvious, no translation is given. Read the paragraph twice without looking at the meanings below. Then check the meanings to see how close you were in your guessing. Remember, only simple verb translation forms are given.

In the Coriolanus and Cincinnatus stories, past events are still being told in the historical present. Soon you will learn how to express ideas in past time.

Read Cincinnatus's story in Latin. Definitions are not given for words almost identical to their English spellings.

Cincinnātus

Historia et fābula° dē Cincinnātō narrant.° Exercitus Rōmānus contrā **Aequōs** pugnat. Aequī superant.° Rōmānī Cincinnātum inveniunt. Cincinnātus est agricola. In agrō labōrat. Ducēs Rōmānī Cincinnātō titulum° dictātōris dant.

In unō° diē Cincinnātus et exercitus Rōmānus Aequīs magnam clādem° dant. Rōmānī victōriam celebrant. Tum° Cincinnātus ad agrum redit°.

[°legend, °tell, °win, °title, °one, °defeat, °then, °goes back]

Latin answers to Latin questions

Lydia: Then Cincinnati, Ohio, was named for Cincinnatus. But why is it spelled with a plural Latin ending?

Magister: After the American War of Independence in 1783, officers of the American army formed the **Society of Cincinnati.** The first president of the society was **George Washington.** Membership was for officers and their oldest descendants. The plural form of *Cincinnatus* stands for the members of the society. They called themselves Cincinnati because they imitated Cincinnatus. After serving their country in war, they returned to their previous occupations. Like Cincinnatus, George Washington returned to his farm after serving his country. His service, though, was several years as general and president, whereas Cincinnatus's service to Rome as dictator lasted only sixteen days.

Before Ohio became a state, the governor of the Northwest Territory renamed a town in what is now Ohio. He called it Cincinnati in honor of the men in the original Society of Cincinnati.

You are now ready to answer the questions about Cincinnatus in Activity F and review the plural case forms in Activity G.

Activities F, G

Can you (1) state a comparison between George Washington and the Roman dictator Cincinnatus and (2) explain how Cincinnati, Ohio, got its name?

Ancient Latin sentences

Magister: Activity H contains quotations from a famous Roman poet named Horace. It gives you more practice with plural dative forms.

> **Activity H**

Derivatives

Magister: Use Activity I as a two-way help: improving your English vocabulary and helping you remember the meanings of Latin words.

> **Activity I**

Essential Information

Grammar terms
- collective noun, special adjective

General terms
- patricians, plebeians, senators, tribunes
- Livy, Cincinnatus, Coriolanus, Gnaeus Marcius
- George Washington, Society of Cincinnati
- Aequians, Volsci
- Corioli

Inflections for plural dative forms
- See plural noun forms on page 156.

Grammar
- The genitive case is sometimes used for nouns that rename other nouns: *city of Rome, office of dictator.*

Pronunciation
- *g—not silent: Gnaeus*

Loan words
- Cincinnati; dictator, plebs

Vocabulary

Activities J, K

- You are responsible for the words listed on page 157 and for the words in bold type listed below.

Nouns

Aequī, -ōrum, *m.,* Aequians, a tribe of people in central Italy

Cincinnātus, -ī, *m.,* a Roman farmer, dictator, and farmer again

Coriolānus, -ī, *m.,* a patrician army general

Coriolī, -ōrum, *m.,* a town of the Volscians in Latium

Martius, Gnaeus, -iī (-ī), *m.,* a patrician, later called Coriolanus

Volscī, -ōrum, *m.,* a tribe of people in Latium to whom Coriolanus went when he left Rome

carmen, -inis, *n.,* song

cibus, -ī, *m.,* food

clādēs, -is, *f.,* defeat, disaster

crūstulum, -ī, *n.,* little cake, cookie

dictātor, -ōris, *m.,* dictator, chief magistrate

fābula, -ae, *f.,* tale, legend, fable

fīnis, -is, *m. (sometimes f.),* end

nihil, *n.,* nothing

puella, -ae, *f.,* girl

titulus, -ī, *m.,* inscription, label, title

victōria, -ae, *f.,* victory

vir, virī, *m.,* man

LEGENDA III

Legenda

Livy (59 B.C.-A.D. 17) wrote a series of books about the history of Rome. He records a great variety of legends concerning the founding of Rome. In the paragraphs below you will read about the one which, according to him, is most believed. (Virgil's epic poem, the *Aeneid,* contains another version of how the city of Rome began.)

Read these paragraphs aloud and then silently in Latin. When you finish, you should be able to complete the Legenda that follows.

Initium Rōmae

Livius in historiā Rōmae dē Bellō Trōiānō° narrat°. Graecī antīquī Trōiānōs vincunt° et urbem Trōiae incendunt°. Post Bellum Trōiānum dux Aenēas cum fīliō eius° Ascaniō venit° ad Ītaliam ab Troiā. Aeneas oppidum° Lāvīnī condit, et posteā° Ascanius oppidum Albae Longae condit.
[°Trojan War, °tell, °conquer, °burn, °his, °come, °town, °afterwards]

Post multōs° annōs° Numitor est rēx Albae Longae. Amūlius, frāter suus°, eum° necat. Fīlia Numitōris est Rhea Silvia. Est māter geminōrum, Rōmulī et Remī. Rōmulus est prīmus rēx Rōmae. Omnēs rēgēs Rōmae erant septem° in numerō.°
[°many, °years, °his own, °him, °seven, °number]

Dīcenda in Linguā Latīnā

Fill in the blanks with the needed Latin words. Use the correct inflection. Try to think in Latin instead of translating the sentences. Then, according to your teacher's instructions, read aloud or write the sentences.

1. Līvius dē Bellō _____ narrat.
2. Graecī _____ vincunt.
3. Quoque Graecī urbem Trōiae_____.
4. Ascanius et pater eius ad _____ veniunt.
5. Lāvinium est _____.
6. _____ quoque est oppidum.
7. _____ et _____ Lāvinium et Albam Longam condunt.
8. Amulius _____ necat.
9. Numitor est pater _____.
10. Rōma septem _____ habet.

Answer these questions in English. You may use complete sentences or short answers.

1. Who wins the Trojan War? _____

2. What happens to ancient Troy?_____

3. Where do Aeneas and his son go after the Trojan War? _____

4. Is Aeneas on the winning side or the losing side of the Trojan War? _____

5. Who travels with Aeneas? _____

6. According to the legend, what does each of these men accomplish? _____

7. Which king of Alba Longa is murdered? _____

8. Who is the grandfather of Romulus and Remus? _____

9. Romulus is the first of how many kings? _____

CAPITULUM XIII

Father, mother, sister, brother—nearly all the terms for family members are given in this chapter. Many derivatives will become clear to you once you know their Latin origins.

You conclude the study of plural noun forms by learning the ablative plurals. The next step is to put all the singular and plural forms together in each separate declension.

Then you will combine singular and plural adjective forms—adjectives in the first-second declension and in the third declension.

You will use new vocabulary words and the noun and adjective inflections as you translate passages from the Vulgate.

FAMILY NAMES

Clara: We know the Latin words for *mother* and *father*. What are the words for *grandmother* and *grandfather?*

Magister: Good question. Let's meet the whole Roman family. You already know several nouns in this list. You will practice using these names in Activity A.

---

familia, -ae, *f.,* the entire household including family members and servants or slaves

avus, -ī, *m.,* grandfather

avia, -ae, *f.,* grandmother

paterfamiliās, patrisfamiliās or -ae, *m., (sometimes written as two words),* father of the family, head of the household

māterfamiliās, mātrisfamiliās or -ae, *f., (sometimes written as two words),* mother of the family, mistress of the household

vir, virī, *m.,* man, husband

fēmina, -ae, *f.,* woman

mulier, -eris, *f.,* woman, wife, matron

uxor, -ōris, *f.,* wife

parēns, -ntis, *c.,* parent, father, mother; grandfather, ancestor pater, -tris, *m.*, father

māter, -tris, *f.*, mother

līberī, -ōrum, *m. pl.*, children

fīlius, -iī, -ī, *m.*, son

fīlia, -ae, *f.*, daughter

frāter, -tris, *m.*, brother

soror, -ōris, *f.*, sister

puella, -ae, *f.*, girl; young woman; sweetheart

puer, -erī, *m.*, boy; child of either sex

infāns, -antis, *c.*, a little child

nepos, -ōtis, *m., f.*, grandson or granddaughter; nephew; any descendant

fīlia sorōris or fīlia frātris, *f.*, niece

- *Vir* is irregular because it ends in *-ir;* except for the *i* instead of *e,* it has the same forms as *puer.*

- The noun *līberī* is always plural in form and meaning. Its form is identical with the masculine plural forms of the adjective *līber, -era, -erum,* meaning "free." The context of any form of *līberī* will tell you whether the word means "free" or "children."

- The genitive plural of *parēns* is *parentium,* not *parentum.* Nouns that end in *-ns* have the genitive plural inflection *-ium* instead of *-um.*

- The noun *pater* in its plural form sometimes means "parents, ancestors, forefathers; heroes, senators." Compare the American title for George Washington: "father of the country."

Activity A

Derivatives

Magister: Instead of ending the chapter with derivatives, we'll begin with them this time. Let's begin with the noun *familia* and an adjective made from it—*familiāris.* What English adjective came from that Latin adjective?

Sylvia: *Familiar.* It's just the Latin word without the inflection.

Magister: A *familiar* friend is like a *family* member. Just as a person knows his family very well, so another person or a thing that he knows very well is *familiar.*

Another derivative from *familia* is *familial,* which means "pertaining to a family." Familial characteristics are the ones that are handed down from one generation to another.

Another family word gives us the derivative *filial.* What word is its origin?

Gloria: *Fīlia.* It must mean "pertaining to a daughter."

Magister: You could also have said *filius* because it also means "pertaining to a son." It comes from the Late Latin adjective *filiālis. Filial* love is the love of a son or daughter for the parents.

Another adjective derived from a family word refers to the love of a father or mother for a child. What kind of love is that?

Clara: That's *parental* love.

Magister: Good. Now can you define these words: *paternal, maternal, fraternal, sororal?*

Clement: "Pertaining to a father, a mother, a brother, a sister."

Magister: Then whose parents are your maternal grandparents?

Sylvia: They must be my mother's parents. I always wondered what that meant. Then my father's parents are my paternal grandparents.

Magister: That's right. Now for another derivative. There are organizations such as the Lions Club and the Elks Club in which the members treat each other like brothers. What is an appropriate adjective to describe organizations like that?

Rex: *Fraternal.*

Victor: *Fraternity* must be another derivative.

Magister: Yes. You may recall from Chapter 10 that many Latin words ending in *-tās* become English words ending in *-ty. Fraternity* from *frāternitās* is an example.

The English suffix *-ity* means "state, quality." So *fraternity* means "state of being a brother or like a brother." It has come to mean "an organization of people with similar backgrounds and interests."

Words continued to enter the Latin language for many centuries. Many of the words that entered in later periods developed from earlier Latin words, such as nouns from other nouns and adjectives from nouns. On page 104 you can find the dates of the periods when most of those additions were made—Latin, Late Latin, and Medieval Latin. Here are a few nouns that developed from other nouns.

> frāternitās, -tātis—L
> paternitās, -tātis—LL
> sororitās, -tātis—ML
> māternitās, -tātis—ML

In Chapter 4 you saw the word *puerile.* Do you remember what it means?

Victor: I think it means "childish."

Magister: Yes. Remember that *puer* means both "boy" and "child," so *puerile* can describe childish behavior of any child—boy or girl.

You may have heard of someone in public office being accused of *nepotism* because of some government appointments he made. What person or persons is he accused of appointing?

Flora: He must have appointed relatives.

Magister: Yes. And the term *nepotism,* which now means "favoritism in making official appointments," has been expanded to include close friends.

The Latin noun *cāritas* is the origin of the English noun *charity.* The *h* in *charity* dates back to the Old French word from which the English word was later derived.

Magister: Activity B provides more experience with English nouns ending in *-ty* that come from Latin nouns that end in *-tās.* Activity C contains various derivation patterns. Activity D includes derivatives coming from Latin words with *-us* and *-a* inflections. These activities can enrich both your English and your Latin vocabulary if you note other sets of parallel words and conclude from Latin origins what the English parallel words mean or vice versa.

Activities B, C, D

 Can you give the Latin nouns for the various members of a family?

ABLATIVE CASE: PLURAL FORMS

Learning Plural Ablative Inflections

Magister: Now let's resume the study of plural noun forms. We conclude the list of plural forms with the ablative plurals.

In Chapter 7 you learned how to write prepositional phrases, putting singular objects of prepositions into the ablative case. Now look at the plural ablative forms of sample words.

	First	**Second**	**Third**	**Fourth**	**Fifth**
	Masculine and Feminine				
Nom.	fīli*ae*	fīli*ī*	frātr*ēs*	exercit*ūs*	di*ēs*
Gen.	fīli*ārum*	fīli*ōrum*	frātr*um*	exercit*uum*	di*ērum*
Dat.	fīli*īs*	fīli*īs*	frātr*ibus*	exercit*ibus*	di*ēbus*
Acc.	fīli*ās*	fīli*ōs*	frātr*ēs*	exercit*ūs*	di*ēs*
Abl.	fīli*īs*	fīli*īs*	frātr*ibus*	exercit*ibus*	di*ēbus*
	Neuter				
Nom.		regn*a*	nōmin*a*	cornu*a*	
Gen.		regn*ōrum*	nōmin*um*	cornu*um*	
Dat.		regn*īs*	nōmin*ibus*	corn*ibus*	
Acc.		regn*a*	nōmin*a*	cornu*a*	
Abl.		regn*īs*	nōmin*ibus*	corn*ibus*	

Victor: There's nothing new to learn! These new endings are exactly like the dative endings.

Magister: Only context can reveal whether these plural forms are dative or ablative.

Working with Nouns in Plural Ablative Forms

Magister: In Activity E, ablative forms are used in prepositional phrases. You may need to look again at the list of prepositions in Chapter 7 for the various meanings of the prepositions.

Activity E

 Can you give the plural ablative inflection for a noun in each of the five declensions?

DECLENSION: SECOND MEANING

Learning to Decline Latin Nouns

Magister: The word **declension** has two meanings in Latin grammar. You've been using it as a term to classify Latin nouns into five categories. Here is the **second meaning:** "a declension is a list of all the singular and plural case forms of any noun, pronoun, or adjective." The **cases** of these three parts of speech are shown by their inflections, which tell us how the word is being used in the sentence: for example, subject, possessive, indirect object, direct object, or object of a preposition. You will learn the declensions of pronouns in future chapters.

Ponder the two meanings of *declension* in the next sentence. The Appendix contains sample *declensions* of nouns in all five *declensions*. The meaning of the grammatical term **decline** is "to say or write the declension of a noun, pronoun, or adjective; that is, to give all the forms in order." Until now you have been learning inflections according to their cases. You have seen many inflection similarities for the various cases. Now it is time to practice declining a noun in each of the five declensions. Turn to Appendix A and read at least one noun declension in each of the five declensions. Say aloud the singular forms and then the plural forms. Repeating this practice for a few days should give you a command of all five declensions. Omit *ars* and *mare*.

 Can you (1) give the two meanings of the term *declension* and (2) explain how to decline a noun?

Working with Nouns in Five Cases, Singular and Plural

Magister: The sentences in Activity F contain both singular and plural forms in the five cases. Activities G and H emphasize the functions and inflections of the five cases, both singular and plural.

Activities F, G, H

Can you decline a noun in each of the five declensions, adjusting for neuter differences?

Third-declension i-stem nouns

Magister: Some third-declension nouns are i-stems. There are three groups of these. The first two groups include nouns that are masculine or feminine. Here are examples of these in the nominative and genitive forms. Look carefully at the two cases of all these nouns. How are the cases alike?

> • *Masculine and feminine:* auris, auris; fēles, fēlis; cīvis, cīvis; senex, senis; classis, classis; finis, finis; panis, panis

Sylvia: All I can see is that they are the same length.

Magister: Yes, they have the same number of syllables. Nearly all nouns having the same number of syllables in the nominative and genitive cases are i-stems.

In the next group the similarity is harder to see. The last letter in the nominative form is either an *s* or an *x*. Now look at the genitive forms. How many consonants precede the inflection *-is* in each genitive form?

> • *Masculine and feminine:* ars, artis; arx, arcis; fōns, fontis; gēns, gentis; infāns, infantis; mors, mortis; parēns, parentis; pars, partis; pōns, pontis; urbs, urbis

Clement: It's always two consonants.

Magister: Good observation. These two groups of i-stem nouns differ from other third-declension nouns only in the two inflections shown in bold type in the word *finis*, declined below. What are the two differences?

Clara: The ablative singular is a long *-ī* or short *e.* The genitive plural is *-ium.*

Neuter i-stem nouns

The third group of these i-stem nouns are neuter gender. Only a very few neuter nouns are i-stem. Here are two that you will work with.

animal, -is; mare, -is

You need to keep the differences in mind as you do the activities for this chapter and later chapters. In what four forms does the letter *i* occur in these nouns but not in other third-declension nouns?

Julia: In the singular it's in the ablative and in the plural it's in the nominative, genitive, and accusative.

Masculine/Feminine		Neuter	
Singular	**Plural**	**Singular**	**Plural**
fīnis	fīnēs	mare	mar*ia*
fīnis	fīn*ium*	maris	mar*ium*
fīnī	fīnibus	marī	maribus
fīnem	fīnēs	mare	mar*ia*
fīnī/e	fīnibus	marī	maribus

Can you (1) describe two kinds of masculine and feminine i-stem nouns and name two neuter i-stem nouns and (2) name the forms in which the *-i* occurs before the inflection?

PLURAL ADJECTIVE DECLENSIONS

Magister: You need the plural forms of adjectives so that you can write adjectives to agree with plural nouns. Latin has only two adjective declensions: first-second declension and third declension. (The singular forms of these were presented in Chapters 9 and 10.) Fourth and fifth declensions have no adjectives.

Learning Plural Adjective Forms

First-second declension adjectives

	Masculine	**Feminine**	**Neuter**
Nom.	long*ī*	long*ae*	long*a*
Gen.	long*ōrum*	long*ārum*	long*ōrum*
Dat.		long*īs*	
Acc.	long*ōs*	long*ās*	long*a*
Abl.		long*īs*	

Magister: Practice making adjectives agree with nouns in Activity I. Remember that the adjective must agree with the noun in gender, number, and case. It does not always agree in declension.

Activity I

Can you decline orally and in writing any first-second declension adjective?

Third-declension adjectives

Magister: Most third-declension adjectives are i-stems. That means they have an *i* before the inflection in these plural forms:

> all genders—genitive
>
> neuter—also nominative and accusative

In the singular, only one form differs:

> all genders—ablative has a long -*ī* or short -*e* inflection.

Vetus, veteris, as you saw in Chapter 10, belongs to a small group that are not i-stems. In the plural declension below, the underlining shows the three plural forms that lack the letter *i* before the inflections, making *vetus* different from *gravis* and *celer.* In Chapter 21 you will work with one-termination adjectives that are i-stems.

We will work first with the two-termination declension because most third-declension adjectives are in this group. Three-termination adjectives are the second most common, and one-termination adjectives are the least common.

	Two-Termination		Three-Termination			One-Termination
	M/F	**N**	**M**	**F**	**N**	**M/F/N**
Nom.	gravēs	gravia	celerēs	celerēs	celeria	veterēs (n. vetera)
Gen.	gravium			celerium		veterum
Dat.	gravibus			celeribus		veteribus
Acc.	gravēs	gravia	celerēs	celerēs	celeria	veterēs (n. vetera)
Abl.	gravibus			celeribus		veteribus

Magister: Activity J contains adjectives in both the first-second declension and the third declension, singular and plural. Three kinds of agreement are necessary: gender, number, and case.

Substantive Use of Adjectives

In both Latin and English, a noun is often omitted if the context makes clear what noun is understood. In English we can say, "Many will come." The listener or reader knows that we mean "Many men" or "Many people." In Latin the adjective form indicates the gender, number, and case of the understood noun. For example *bonī* means "many men" or "many people," not "many things." *Mortalia omnia* means "all mortal *things*," not "all mortal *men*." Adjectives used as nouns are called **substantives.**

Activity J

Can you (1) give the plural forms for adjectives in first-second declension and third declension and (2) use singular and plural forms correctly to modify nouns?

Translating Ancient Latin Sentences

Magister: In Activity K you are to translate sentences quoted from several Roman writers. Note the agreement of the adjectives with the nouns they modify. In number 3 the words are rearranged to make the translation easier for you. In parentheses you see the sentence just as Horace wrote it. Romans, especially poets, often used varied word order for emphasis. With more experience you will be able to understand sentences just as the Romans wrote them.

Activity K

Reading about Horatius, a Legendary Hero

Magister: When Tarquin the Proud, Rome's last king, was banished, he went to **Etruria,** just north of Rome. The Tarquins had originally come from Etruria, so he went back to his own people.

The **Etruscans** wanted to regain power over Rome, and they made several attacks against Rome. **Lars Porsena,** king of the Etruscan town Clusium, came with his army to the river Tiber. **Lucius Junius Brutus,** one of the first two consuls in the newly established republic of Rome, withstood Lars Porsena. However, the Romans were at a great disadvantage against the huge well-trained, well-equipped Etruscan army. Now read about **Horatius,** Rome's hero. Try to understand what happens without translating. Here are a few new words you will find in the story. You will also need them for the activities that follow. Read through the list before reading the paragraphs.

Brūtus, Lucius Junius, -ī, -ī (-ī), -ī (-ī), *m.,* one of the first two consuls in the Roman republic

Etrūria, -ae, *f.,* a district in northwest Italy

Etruscus, -a, -um, pertaining to or belonging to Etruria

Etruscus, -ī, an Etruscan man

Horātius, -ī (-ī), hero in the early Roman republic

Porsena, Lars (*or* Porsenna), **-ae,** *m.,* a king in Etruria

cadit, fall

duo, duae, duo, two

magnopere, *adv.,* greatly

nullus, -a, -um, no, not any

pons, -ntis, *m.,* bridge

secūrus, -a, -um, secure, safe

sōlus, -a, -um alone

super, *prep. with abl.,* over; *prep. with acc.,* upon

Horātius ad Pontem

Ad° pontem super flūmine Tibere Rōmānī stant. Omnēs—virī, fēminae, puerī, puellae—exercitum Etruscōrum magnopere timent. Exercitus fortis Etruscus est trāns flūmen.

[°at]

In ponte Horātius stat. Duo amīcī cum eō° stant. Horātius sōlus Etruscōs pugnat. Eōdem tempore° amīcī suī° pontem post Horātium succīdunt°.

[°him, °at the same time, °his, his own, °cut down]

Dēnique duo amīcī ad terram natant. Rōmānī ad Horātium vocant, "Revenī°, revenī!" Tōtus pons in flūmen cadit. Horātius ad terram natat.

[°come back]

Sine ponte nullam viam ad Rōmam Etruscī habent. Rōma est secūra!

Latin answers to Latin questions

Magister: Activities L, M, and N are based on the events at the end of the kingdom of Rome. Legend and history are intermingled in the story of Horatius. In some accounts Horatius fights back the Etruscans until the bridge is cut down, and he drowns when the bridge finally falls. In any case, he is one of Rome's heroes. To him the protection of Rome was more important than his own life.

In answering the questions in Activities M and N, try to think in Latin instead of translating into English.

Activities L, M, N

Can you (1) identify all the important people and places in the story of Horatius and (2) translate sentences into Latin with accurate noun-adjective agreement?

VERSES FROM THE VULGATE

Translating Latin Scripture Verses

Magister: We go now to the Scriptures, and in Activity O you will read some verses about fathers, mothers, and other members of the family. Because you are not ready to read the entire verses that are quoted, part of each verse is given in English. Translate the Latin portions. (The English portions of the sentences are taken from the King James Version. A few sentences are shortened, and one phrase is replaced with more familiar words.)

Activity O

Borrowed Plural Forms

Magister: In some English classes you may be asked to learn a group of unusual plural forms of nouns. Both the singular and the plural Latin forms are now English forms. Having learned them in Latin will make them easy to remember. Here are a few. Give the singular form of each.

alumnae, antennae, formulae; alumni, stimuli, nuclei; addenda, bacteria, data, errata, memoranda; criteria, phenomena; appendices, indices, analyses, crises, parentheses

A few of these have both English and Latin plural forms. The word *data* is now both a singular and a plural form. For details about any of these words, check a standard dictionary.

Latin Sayings in English

Magister: Your friends will turn to you for help when they find out that you have studied Latin. They will ask you the meanings of phrases and mottoes. Do them a favor by translating and explaining the phrases whenever you can. In the next two activities are phrases that you should be able to figure out. For now, you are not asked to translate—only to recognize the meanings.

The English phrases in Activities P and Q have no macrons because the Romans did not use macrons.

The italicized words are supplied to make the translations clear. What follows the slash is a paraphrase (another way of expressing the same idea).

Activities P, Q

Can you translate at least ten of the nineteen Latin words and phrases in Activities P and Q without looking at the second column?

Essential Information

Grammar terms

- ablative case, substantive use of adjectives
- declension (second meaning), decline

History and geography terms

- Etruscans, Horatius, Lars Porsena, Lucius Junius Brutus
- Etruria

Declensions of nouns and adjectives, singular and plural

Plural ablative noun forms in the five declensions

- See the lists of plural noun forms on page 170.

Third-declension i-stem noun forms

- See declensions of masculine-feminine nouns and neuter nouns on page 173.

First-Second declension plural adjective forms

- See plural adjective declensions on page 174.

Third-declension plural adjective forms

- See plural adjective declensions on page 175.

Patterns of derivation

- Latin noun, -tās (lībertās) > English noun, -ty (liberty)
- Latin noun (fīlia) > LL adjective (fīliālis) > English adjective (filial)
- Latin noun (frāter) > LL adjective (frāternālis) > English adjective (fraternal)

Vocabulary

Activity R

- You are responsible for the words in bold type listed on pages 166, 167, and 176. You are also responsible for the words listed below.

Nouns

cāritās, -tātis, *f.*, affection, love, esteem

perīculum, -ī, *n.*, danger

mūtātiō, -ōnis, *f.*, a change

Pronoun

qui, who

Adjective

suus, -a, -um, his, her, its own; their own (their)

Adverb

cur, *inter.*, why

Verbs

aedificiō, to build

facit, do

revenī, (command form) come back

succidit, cut down

New Words in Legenda III

Nouns

annus, -ī, *m.*, year

numerus, -ī, *m.*, number

mūtātiō, -ōnis, *f.* a change

Pronouns

eius, his

eum, him

Adjectives

mortālis, -e, mortal, pertaining to human beings; subject to death

multus, -a, -um, much (*sing.*), many (*pl.*)

septem, seven

Adverb

posteā, afterwards

Verbs

incendunt, burn

narrat, tells

veniunt, come

vincunt, conquer

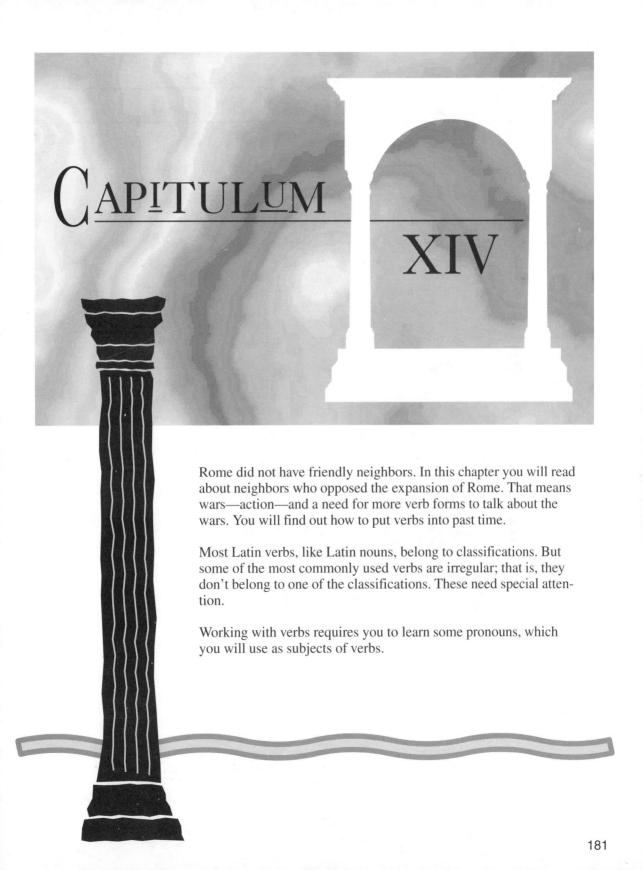

CAPITULUM XIV

Rome did not have friendly neighbors. In this chapter you will read about neighbors who opposed the expansion of Rome. That means wars—action—and a need for more verb forms to talk about the wars. You will find out how to put verbs into past time.

Most Latin verbs, like Latin nouns, belong to classifications. But some of the most commonly used verbs are irregular; that is, they don't belong to one of the classifications. These need special attention.

Working with verbs requires you to learn some pronouns, which you will use as subjects of verbs.

THE EARLY ROMAN REPUBLIC

Magister: You've read about a few heroes of Rome during the early republic: for instance, Horatius and Cincinnatus. In the first two hundred years of the Roman republic, Rome was becoming the dominant power in central Italy, but it still occupied only a small part of the Italian peninsula.

Mark: What other powers were there?

Magister: Rome's strongest early rivals were the **Samnites.** The Romans and the Samnites fought three wars before making a treaty. In the second war, the Samnites defeated the Romans. They made the Roman soldiers give up their weapons and march under a yoke.

Clement: What is a yoke?

Magister: It's a crossbar used to join a team of oxen so they can pull something, such as a plow or a wagon. You can understand the humiliation of a conquered army when the men had to walk under the yoke as a symbol of their defeat. In the third Samnite war, the Romans defeated the Samnites and made the Samnites walk under the yoke. Instead of holding up heavy yokes, the conquerors usually held up spears under which the conquered had to walk.

Then the two sides made a treaty, but the Samnites soon broke the treaty. For about twelve years, Rome fought them, and at the same time they were fighting three other neighboring peoples: the Etruscans, the **Umbrians,** and the **Gauls.**

Victor: Did the Romans finally win?

Magister: Yes, gradually they gained the upper hand over all these neighbors.

See if you can answer some questions about the early Roman Republic. Give short Latin answers.

> Eratne rēs publica magna aut parva prīmō?
>
> Erantne victōriae Rōmānōrum facilēs aut dūrae?
>
> Ambulantne Rōmānī sub iugō°?
>
> [°yoke]
>
> Ambulantne Samnītēs sub iugō?

 Can you name four peoples against whom Rome fought during the early years of the republic? Can you (1) explain the meaning of walking under the yoke and (2) name two armies that were forced to walk under the yoke?

VERB FORMS

Learning about Verb Tenses

Magister: The historical present tense forms have served us well during the lessons about nouns and adjectives. But when we write and speak, we generally use more than one tense. As you read the Latin paragraph below, you can discover the tense of a verb from its context.

The **tense** of a verb is the time that it refers to. In this chapter you will learn about two Latin tenses. The first of these is the present tense. Definitions of verbs in word lists, such as the **Vocābulārium,** are always given in the **present tense.** Likewise, definitions following Latin portions in this text are in the present tense, even though the verb form being used may be a different tense.

In the paragraph below, verbs in three Latin tenses are used. In English we would identify these three as present, past, and future. You will be asked to identify the tenses of these verbs, using English tense names. The context will make the tenses perfectly clear. A few of the new words are not defined for you because the context and familiar English derivatives make the meanings obvious. **Bella** is a neuter plural noun that means "wars." To translate the last sentence, you may use the expletive *there,* which was explained in Chapter 8.

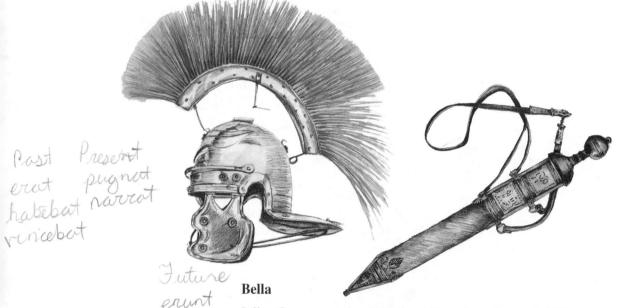

[Handwritten notes:]
Past Present
erat pugnat
habebat narrat
vincebat

Future
erunt

Bella

Iulius Caesar erat dux Rōmānus. Exercitum fortem habēbat. Exercitus Caesaris magnam partem° Eurōpae vincēbat.° Hodiē° patriae in Eurōpā adhūc° bella pugnant. Librī histōriae nunc° dē bellīs antīquīs° et bellīs recentibus narrant.° Bella erunt quoque° in futūrō (Matt. 24:6).

[°part, °conquer, °today, °still, °now, °ancient, °tell, °also]

Magister: Now write headings for three columns on a piece of paper. Label them past, present, and future. Under each heading, list all the verbs in that tense that you find in the paragraph you just read. I'll wait for your answers.

Paul: The context does make the tenses easy to figure out. I think I have them all in the right columns.

Magister: Tell us which verbs you put in each list and why.

Paul: For the past I have *erat, habēbat,* and *vincēbat* because Julius Caesar lived in the past. For the present I have *pugnant* and *narrant* because of the word for "today." I have *erunt* for the future because of the word for "future."

Magister: Excellent work. You had more context help in this paragraph than you will ordinarily find. However, even without context clues, you will soon be able to identify the tense of a Latin verb. In Activity A the context clues are essential for right answers.

Activity A

Regular and irregular verbs

Magister: Verbs in both Latin and English are classified as **regular** or **irregular.** *Walk* is regular because its past form ends in *-ed; run* is irregular because its past form does not end in *-ed.* Also irregular is the *be* verb with such forms as *am, is, are, was,* and *were.*

You will learn about Latin irregular verbs one at a time. The one you've worked with so far is *sum,* which is the Latin word for our English *be* verb. *Est* is a form of *sum.* In the paragraph you just read about wars, *erat* and *erunt* are other tenses of *est.* Using context help, tell me the English meanings of *erat* and *erunt* as you reread the Latin paragraph called "Bella."

Flora: *Erat* must mean "was" because it is in a sentence about Julius Caesar. *Erunt* is in a sentence about the future, so it means "will be."

Magister: Excellent use of context to solve problems. You will learn about the future tense in Chapter 15.

The imperfect tense of regular verbs

Magister: The Latin imperfect tense is not exactly equivalent to the English past tense. It's called the **imperfect tense** because it shows incomplete action, or action that continued in the past. The English past tense can show either complete or incomplete action. The grammatical term *perfect* means "complete" and *imperfect* means "not complete." To express the idea of incomplete action in English, we can say "he was walking," "he used to walk," "he would walk," "he did walk," or "he walked." The English verb form that expresses past continuous action is called the *past progressive.*

In the paragraph about wars, find two words that indicate continued action in the past—verbs other than *erat*. What are the last three letters of those two verbs?

Victor: Well, in the sentences about Julius Caesar's army I see *habēbat* and *vincēbat*. The last three letters are *bat*.

Tense sign for the imperfect tense

Magister: Yes. The *-t* is the inflection you have been using to show that the subject is a singular noun or pronoun. When we translate, the subjects are *he* and *army*. Right before the inflection *-t* are two letters that we call a **tense sign.** This tense sign tells us that the verb is in the imperfect tense of a regular verb. How is the tense sign spelled?

Clara: It's spelled *ba.*

Magister: Actually the tense sign is **-bā-,** but the vowel has been shortened in those verbs because of the following consonant. Vowels are never long before the inflections *-t* and *-nt*.

Translation of verbs in the imperfect tense

Magister: This tense sign for the imperfect tense is used in regular verbs. Let's review the possible translations for the imperfect tense. What are the possible translations of *ambulābat?*

Clara: "He was walking," "he used to walk," "he would walk," "he did walk," or "he walked."

Magister: Very good. "He walked" does not show continued action, but this is an acceptable translation if the context makes it clear that the action is continued. For example, we could show continued action by saying, "Last year he walked to school every day." If we say "This morning he walked to school," the context shows completed action. Latin has another tense to show completed action. You will learn about it later.

In Activity B you will practice with present and imperfect verb forms. In Activity C you will translate sentences into English, being careful to use the correct tense forms. Activity D contains parts of verses from Jerome's translation of the Gospel of Mark. Since some of the vocabulary is unfamiliar to you, you are not asked to translate the words in brackets. Meanings of some new verbs are so obvious from the context and from English derivatives that the meanings are not given.

Activities B, C, D

Can you name an irregular Latin verb? Can you give (1) the tense sign for regular Latin verbs in the imperfect tense and (2) three ways of translating *pugnābat* into English?

Learning the Four Conjugations of Regular Verbs

Magister: You've seen that nouns and adjectives belong to declensions. Verbs, likewise, are grouped. Each regular verb belongs to one of **four conjugations.**

First, look at the two forms of the sample verb of each conjugation. Notice the letters in bold type. The translation shows that the inflection *-ō* means the same thing as the pronoun subject *I*. Notice that in the present tense of the second and fourth conjugations the stem vowel is shortened and remains in the verb forms, whereas in the present tense of the first and third conjugations, the stem vowel is dropped.

Next, look at the translation of the second form of each word. Can you figure out the meaning of the *-re?*

Sylvia: It must mean "to."

Magister: Yes. Because of inflections, Latin verbs are often briefer than their English translations. *Narrō* is a verb with the subject *I* included. It's the first person singular in the present tense. *Narrāre* is an **infinitive** with the *to* included. It's translated "to tell." The *-re* inflection tells us that a verb form is an infinitive. These are the first two principal parts. Let's read together the two forms of each verb.

First conjugation	Second conjugation	Third conjugation	Fourth conjugation
narr**ō**, narrā**re**	doce**ō**, docē**re**	dīc**ō**, dīce**re**	audi**ō**, audī**re**
I narrate, to narrate	I teach, to teach	I speak, to speak	I hear, to hear

Principal parts and stem vowels of regular verbs

Magister: The verb forms listed above are the first two principal parts. Latin verbs have four principal parts, whereas English verbs have only three. The first two principal parts of a Latin verb are equivalent to the first principal part of an English verb. Since English infinitives have the word *to* before the verb, one English principal part serves for the two Latin principal parts.

Principal parts are the simple forms used to make verbs in the six tenses. You'll learn about the other principal parts and tenses in later chapters.

The second Latin principal part, the infinitive, tells us the conjugation (classification) of a verb. I mentioned the **stem vowel** earlier. In regular Latin verbs, the stem vowel is immediately before the inflection *-re*; it tells us what conjugation the verb is. It is different in each conjugation. The difference between second and third conjugations is shown by a macron over the stem vowel in second conjugation.

Would someone name the stem vowel in each of the four conjugations, stating whether it is long or short?

Rex: In first conjugation it is a long *ā*, in second it is a long *ē*, in third it is a short *e*, and in fourth it is a long *ī*.

Magister: In Activity E you will translate the first two principal parts of some verbs in each of the four conjugations and will use the Latin infinitive to identify the conjugation of each verb.

Activity E

Can you (1) write the infinitive form for a verb in each of the four conjugations and (2) name the stem vowel for each conjugation?

Learning to Conjugate and Translate Verbs

> The verb *conjugate* comes from the Latin prefix *com-* from *cum,* "together with," and the verb *jugāre,* "to join." To conjugate a verb is "to join the forms of a verb together."

Sylvia: What if I want to say "you tell" or "we tell"?

Magister: To know singular and plural forms for *I, we, you, he* (or *she* or *it*), or *they,* you need to know how to **conjugate** verbs. That means "to list the verb forms in order." An organized list of verb forms is a **conjugation,** just as an organized list of noun or adjective forms is a *declension.* Here is an English conjugation of a present-tense verb:

	Singular	**Plural**
First person	I tell	we tell
Second person	you tell	you tell
Third person	he/she/it tells	they tell

Notice the pronouns used in the English conjugation. They are the subjects that show the **person** and number of the verbs. If the subject is *I* or *we,* the verb is first person. If the subject is *you,* the verb is second person. If the subject is *he, she, it, they,* another pronoun, or any noun, the verb is third person.

Latin verb inflections show the person and number of a verb: *-ō, -s, -t; -mus, -tis, -nt* (I, you, he/she/it; we, you, they). Here is the present-tense conjugation of a first-conjugation verb.

	Singular	**Plural**
First person	narr*ō*	narrā***mus***
Second person	narrā*s*	narrā***tis***
Third person	narra*t*	narra***nt***

- Before the inflection *ō,* the stem vowel *ā* disappears.
- A vowel is never long before an inflection *-m, -t,* or *-nt.*

Pronoun subjects

Clara: Didn't the Romans have pronouns?

Magister: Yes, but they didn't need them to show the person of a verb. Here are the nominative-case forms of the **personal pronouns,** which they seldom used. The syllables are divided to help you pronounce the words correctly.

	Singular	**Plural**
First person	e•go (I)	nōs (we)
Second person	tū (you, *sing.*)	vōs (you, *pl.*)
Third person	is, e•a, id (he, she, it)	e•ī, e•ae, e•a (they)

In Activity F you will review the infinitive forms (second principal parts) of verbs and practice using pronoun subjects for verbs. For Activity G you need to know the English pronoun subject for each of the verb inflections and to distinguish the imperfect tense from the present tense. In Activity H you will translate English to Latin, working with some pronoun subjects.

Pronoun subjects for first and second person are used in Latin sentences only when the writer wants to give special emphasis to the subject. Third-person pronouns are frequently used. When they are not, you must determine from the context what pronoun to use in translation. You will learn all the case forms of these pronouns in Chapters 15 and 16. For now you need only the nominative forms.

Activities F, G, H

 Can you (1) give the Latin pronoun subject for first, second, and third persons, singular and plural, and (2) use these pronouns correctly in sentences?

Learning the Forms of Narrō in Two Tenses

Magister: To pronounce Latin verb forms correctly, read the pronunciation reminders carefully.

> ***Pronunciation reminders***
> - Latin has no silent letters. Pronounce all the *r*'s in *narrāre*.
> - Accent the penult when it is long.
> - Never accent the ultima, even when you are conjugating a verb and thinking carefully about the inflections.
>
> ***Inflection variation***
> - In the imperfect tense, the first-person inflection is *-m* instead of *-ō*.

Present Tense		
Singular		
First person	I tell, I am telling, I do tell	narr**ō**
Second person	you tell, you are telling, you do tell	narr**ās**
Third person	he tells, he is telling, he does tell	narra**t**
Plural		
First person	we tell, we are telling, we do tell	narrā**mus**
Second person	you tell, you are telling, you do tell	narrā**tis**
Third person	they tell, they are telling, they do tell	narr**ant**
Past Tense/ Imperfect Tense		
Singular		
First person	I told, I was telling, I did tell	narrā**bam**
Second person	you told, you were telling, you did tell	narrā**bās**
Third person	he told, he was telling, he did tell	narrā**bat**
Plural		
First person	we told, we were telling, we did tell	narrā**bāmus**
Second person	you told, you were telling, you did tell	narrā**bātis**
Third person	they told, they were telling, they did tell	narrā**bant**

(handwritten margin notes:) pugnō, pugnā, pugnā, pugnamus, pugnatis, pugnant, pugnaba, pugnabas, pugnabit, pugnabamus, pugnabatis, pugnabant

Magister: Practice saying all the present and imperfect forms of *narrō* until you know them and can give their meanings.

Clara: Why do those Latin words have so many English translations?

Magister: Because we have many auxiliaries in English. Auxiliaries make it possible for us to express more ideas for some tenses than are possible in Latin, especially in the present and imperfect tenses. When you're translating from Latin, use the English verb or verb phrase (verb with auxiliaries) that best fits the context.

Now let's review the stem vowels for the four conjugations. Can you name them?

Julia: Long *ā,* long *ē,* short *e,* and long *ī.*

Magister: Do you recall the explanation of the word **stem** from Chapter 4? You may recall that the word *stem* can be a metaphor, comparing a word to part of a plant. You were learning then about the stems of nouns.

Paul: You mean we're comparing what's left of a plant when the flowers and leaves are gone?

Magister: Yes. The metaphor applies to verbs in the same way that it applies to nouns and adjectives. From verbs we simply remove the infinitive inflection *-re* to get the stem. In the metaphorical term *stem vowel,* what do the leaves or the flower represent?

Julia: The inflection that is removed. Now I see why it's called the stem vowel.

Victor: Why isn't there a stem vowel in *narrō?*

Magister: The *ā* disappeared before the *ō* inflection probably because the sounds of the *ā* and the *ō* are similar enough that the Romans, over a period of time, made them into a single sound.

You need to know the verb inflections as well as you know the spelling of your own name. Take time to learn them now: *-ō, -s, -t; -mus, -tis, -nt.*

Now write *ambulō* in the present and the imperfect tenses. Compare your work with *narrō* in the chart, checking for (1) the omission of macrons before *-t* and *-nt,* (2) the change from *-o* to *-m* in the first person singular, imperfect tense. Read aloud what you have written.

Here are the first-conjugation verbs you have worked with in the chapters so far:

ambulō, ambulāre, to walk	pugnō, pugnāre, to fight
cūrō, cūrāre, to care for	servō, servāre, to save, keep, watch over
dō, dare, to give	stō, stāre, to stand
natō, natāre, to swim	
necō, necāre, to kill	

Victor: The stem vowel for *dō* is short. Is that right?

Magister: Yes, *dō* is a rare first-conjugation verb with short *a* for a stem vowel. However, the conjugation forms are sometimes written with macrons.

 Can you (1) conjugate a first-conjugation verb in the present and the imperfect tenses and (2) translate that verb correctly in a sentence?

Learning the Forms of the Irregular Verb Sum, Esse *in Two Tenses*

Magister: The first two principal parts of the irregular verb that you know as *est* are *sum, esse.* When you compare *esse* with the infinitives of regular verbs, you can see how irregular this verb is. You have already worked with the forms *sum, est,* and *sunt.* Here are all the present and imperfect forms with their translations. Notice that the imperfect tense sign *bā* is not used with this irregular verb.

Beginning with this chart, we will simplify the translation of third person by using just *he* for the singular. This will save time when we discuss verb forms. Of course in sentences where the context shows that the subject is *she* or *it,* those pronouns should be used.

Present Tense		
Singular		
First person	I am	su*m*
Second person	you are	e*s*
Third person	he is	es*t*
Plural		
First person	we are	su*mus*
Second person	you are	es*tis*
Third person	they are	su*nt*

Past Tense/Imperfect Tense		
Singular		
First person	I was	era*m*
Second person	you were	erā*s*
Third person	he was	era*t*
Plural		
First person	we were	erā*mus*
Second person	you were	erā*tis*
Third person	they were	era*nt*

Magister: In Activity I are some verses from the Vulgate that contain these new pronoun and verb forms. Activities J and K review verbs, nouns, pronouns, and adjectives.

Activities I, J, K

Can you conjugate the verb *sum* in the present and imperfect tenses? Can you translate sentences with verbs in first, second, or third person, singular or plural?

Derivatives

Magister: Activity L can help you remember the meanings of verbs you have worked with, and it can introduce new English words that will be valuable in your vocabulary.

Activity L

Essential Information

Grammar terms

- regular verbs, irregular verbs
- principal parts (first two), infinitive (See the principal parts of eight first-conjugation verbs on p. 192.)
- conjugations (four verb classifications)
- conjugation (listing of six verb forms), conjugate
- verb stems, stem vowels
- verb tense: present tense, imperfect tense
- verb translations
- tenses, tense sign *bā*
- person of verbs
- personal pronouns

History terms

- Gauls, Samnites, Umbrians

Infinitive forms

First conjugation	Second conjugation	Third conjugation	Fourth conjugation
narrō, narrā*re*	doceō, docē*re*	dīcō, dīce*re*	audiō, audī*re*
I narrate, to narrate	I teach, to teach	I speak, to speak	I hear, to hear

Present and imperfect inflections

Regular verbs

- See the conjugations of the present and imperfect tenses of *narrō* on page 191.

An irregular verb

- See the conjugations of the present and imperfect tenses of *sum* on pages 193 and 194.

Macron rules

- A vowel is never long before a final *-t.*
- A vowel is never long before the consonants *-nt* whether those letters are final or not.

Vocabulary

Activity M

You are responsible for the words listed below.

Nouns

bellum, -ī, *n.,* war

consilium, -iī/-ī, *n.,* plan, advice

pars, partis, *f.,* part

Pronouns

ego, I

is, ea, id (pl., eī, eae, ea), he, she, it

nōs, we

tū, you (sing.)

vōs, you (pl.)

Adjective

antīquus, -a, -um, old, ancient

Adverbs

adhūc, thus far, hitherto; still, even now

hodiē, today

nunc, now

Verbs

audiō, -īre, to hear

clāmō, -āre, to call, shout, cry aloud

cōnveniō, -īre, to come together

inrīdeō, -ēre, to laugh at, ridicule

interrogō, -āre, to ask

narrō, -āre, to tell, narrate

veniō, -īre, to come

vincō, -ere, to conquer

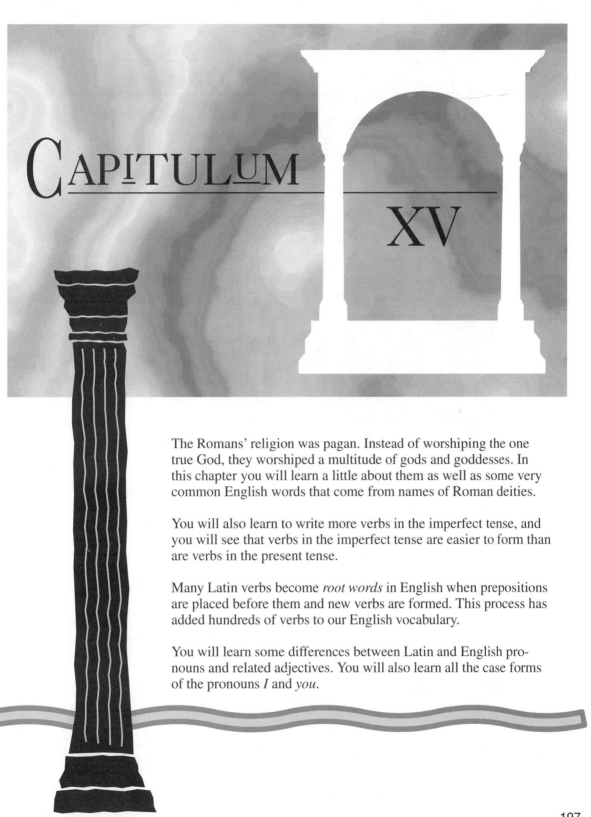

CAPITULUM XV

The Romans' religion was pagan. Instead of worshiping the one true God, they worshiped a multitude of gods and goddesses. In this chapter you will learn a little about them as well as some very common English words that come from names of Roman deities.

You will also learn to write more verbs in the imperfect tense, and you will see that verbs in the imperfect tense are easier to form than are verbs in the present tense.

Many Latin verbs become *root words* in English when prepositions are placed before them and new verbs are formed. This process has added hundreds of verbs to our English vocabulary.

You will learn some differences between Latin and English pronouns and related adjectives. You will also learn all the case forms of the pronouns *I* and *you*.

RELIGION OF THE ROMANS

Religiō Rōmānōrum erat similis religiōnī Graecōrum. Rōmānī et Graecī multōs deōs et deās habēbant. Rōmānī et Graecī deōs et deās timēbant.

Deōs et deās māiōrēs habēbant; deōs et deās minōrēs quoque habēbant. Iuppiter, Neptūnus, et Plūto erant deī māiōrēs Rōmānī. Iūno, Vesta, et Cerēs erant deae māiōrēs Rōmānae.

Christiānī ūnum Deum vērum adōrant.

Magister: In the second paragraph are the words *māiōrēs* and *minōrēs*. Do you recognize two English words? One of them will be obvious if you recall the spelling adjustment by which an *i* before another vowel was changed to the consonant *j* in later Latin.

Clement: *Major* and *minor.*

Magister: Yes. Can you tell us the difference between *deōs* and *deās?*

Clement: *Deōs* must be masculine and *deās* must be feminine—something like *discipulus* and *discipula.* I think they mean "gods" and "goddesses."

Magister: Good thinking. Now, can someone tell us three things about the Roman religion that you read in the first paragraph?

Victor: They had many gods and goddesses, their religion was similar to the Greek religion, and they feared the gods and goddesses.

Magister: Very good. From the second paragraph, tell us more about their religion.

Lydia: The Romans had major gods and goddesses and minor gods and goddesses. Jupiter, Neptune, and Pluto were major gods; and Juno, Vesta, and Ceres were major goddesses. I have two questions. Is *Jupiter* spelled with one or two *p*s? And who were the minor gods and goddesses?

Magister: In Latin, *Jupiter* has two *p*s; in English it has only one. Gods and goddesses can be called **deities.** The plural masculine form, *deī,* is often used to refer to both gods and goddesses. There were many, many minor deities, and there were more major deities than the six that I've named.

What does the third paragraph tell us about Christians?

Mark: We worship only one God. He is the true God.

Magister: That's right. From the spelling of *adōrant* and from its derivatives, you figured out the meaning. Can you change the verb so that the sentence says, "*We* worship the one true God"?

Mark: Adōrāmus.

Magister: That's right. From our discussion of Roman religion, you should know the meanings of these words.

adōrō (1), to worship

dea, -ae, *f.,* goddess

deus, -ī, *m.,* a god, a deity

deī, -ōrum, *m.,* gods and goddesses, deities

māior, -ius, *gen.,* **māiōris,** greater, larger

minor, -us, *gen.,* **minōris,** smaller, less, lesser

Magister: In Activity A you will review four noun cases, singular and plural; you will also review verbs in the present and imperfect tenses. In Activity B you will answer questions in Latin, giving careful attention to noun and verb inflections.

Activities A, B

Can you name three major Roman gods and three major Roman goddesses?

VERB FORMS

Learning More about Verb Tenses

The present tense

Magister: So far you've been working mainly with the present tense, but you haven't learned how present-tense verbs differ from one another in the four conjugations. In Chapter 14 you saw the stem vowel in each of the four conjugations, and you worked with the stem vowel *ā* in the first conjugation. Let's quickly review the conjugation of *narrō*.

What are the stem vowels of the other three conjugations?

Sylvia: Long *e*, short *e*, and long *i*.

Magister: Sample verbs from the other conjugations are conjugated here in the present tense: *doceō,* teach; *discō,* learn; *capiō,* take; *audiō,* hear.

Present Tense			
Singular			
Second	**Third**	**Third -iō**	**Fourth**
doce*ō*	disc*ō*	cap*iō*	aud*iō*
doc*ēs*	disc*is*	cap*is*	aud*īs*
doce*t*	disc*it*	cap*it*	aud*it*
Plural			
doc*ēmus*	disc*imus*	cap*imus*	aud*īmus*
doc*ētis*	disc*itis*	cap*itis*	aud*ītis*
doc*ent*	disc*unt*	cap*iunt*	aud*iunt*

Look carefully at the stem vowel in the two third-conjugation verbs. What unexpected vowel change do you see?

Julia: The stem vowel is *i* instead of *e*.

Magister: Right. The reason for two third-conjugation verbs is that some in that conjugation are **i-stem verbs.** That means that the stem ends with *i;* so we have *capiō,* as compared with a regular third-declension verb such as *discō.*

What other difference do you see between the two kinds of third-conjugation verbs?

Clara: The third-person plural form of *capiō* ends with *-iunt,* but *discō* just ends with *-unt.*

Magister: So the only differences between i-stem verbs and other third-conjugation verbs in the present tense are in the first person singular and third person plural. Now compare the i-stem third conjugation verb with the fourth conjugation. What differences do you see?

Flora: The only difference is the long *i* in some fourth-conjugation forms.

Magister: The *i* in those forms is long because the stem vowel is long. Notice carefully the three forms that have the long *i.* You should practice saying the conjugations on your own until you're sure you know them. The sounds can help you remember the spelling. Then write them from memory until you get them right.

Gloria: How can we tell a third-conjugation i-stem from a fourth conjugation verb? They both end in *-iō.*

Magister: You can tell only by the infinitive: *-ere* for third i-stem and *-īre* for fourth. Be sure to practice the principal parts aloud so that you hear the accent in the infinitives of all the conjugations: *narrā're, docē're, dis'cere, ca'pere,* and *audī're.* The accent is on the penult of each infinitive except those in the third conjugation, including the third i-stem. Because the stem vowel in these is short, the accent is on the antepenult.

Stem-vowel spelling adjustments in present tense

All stem vowels are short before the inflections -*ō*, -*t*, and -*nt*. Very rarely in Latin does one long vowel precede another. Therefore in second and fourth conjugations, the long stem vowels become short in the first-person singular forms: -*eō*, -*iō*.

First conjugation The stem vowel *ā* disappears before inflection -*ō*.

Second conjugation The stem vowel remains but becomes short before the final -*t* and -*nt*.

Third conjugation The stem vowel changes to *i* and disappears before the inflection -*ō*. The stem vowel changes to *u* before the inflection -*nt*.

Third conjugation, i-stem The letter *i* precedes the inflection -*ō*, and in third-person plural it remains before the *u* so that the verb ends with -*iunt*.

Fourth conjugation The spelling is exactly like that of third-conjugation i-stem verbs except that the stem vowel is long where inflections do not prevent a long vowel: *audīs, audīmus,* and *audītis*.

Magister: Activity C provides practice with the stem vowels in present-tense verbs of all four conjugations. Activity D asks you to use verb forms correctly in Latin sentences.

Activities C, D

 Can you (1) conjugate any regular verb in the present tense and (2) translate all the forms into English?

The imperfect tense

Magister: For the imperfect forms, I am giving you only the first-person singular. Starting with that form, you can easily give the other forms for each conjugation because the tense sign and inflections are the same as for *narrō* in Chapter 14. Remember that the first-person singular inflection is -*m*, not -*ō*, and that there is no macron before a final -*m*, -*t*, or -*nt*.

As you conjugate these verbs orally, notice what precedes the tense sign in each verb.

First	Second	Third	Third *-iō*	Fourth
narrā**ba***m*	docē**ba***m*	discē**ba***m*	capiē**ba***m*	audiē**ba***m*

Stem vowels and tense sign in the imperfect tense

First conjugation Stem vowel *ā* precedes the tense sign *bā*.

All other conjugations An *ē* precedes the tense sign.

Third-conjugation The *i* found in the present tense changes to *ē*.

Third i-stem and fourth conjugations The letters *iē* precede the tense sign.

All conjugations In the tense sign, the *ā* becomes a short *a* before the inflections *-m, -t,* and *-nt.*

Magister: The imperfect tense is easy to learn. Remember these spelling variations as you do your own practicing. Writing the forms from memory will tell you whether you need more review.

In Activity E you will write and translate imperfect-tense verbs in all four conjugations. In Activities F and G you will use verbs in sentences. In these activities be sure (1) to use the right letters before the tense sign and (2) to use macrons correctly.

Activities E, F, G

(1) Can you write a Latin verb in each conjugation in the present and imperfect tenses? (2) In those two tenses can you correctly translate verbs from Latin to English and from English to Latin?

Reviewing Verbs in the Four Conjugations

Magister: Here are the verbs you've worked with. Those in bold type are verbs you've been asked to learn; you may already know most of the others because you've seen them often. The list is here to help you review until you are sure of the conjugation and meaning of each verb.

First Conjugation

ambulō, -āre, to walk

necō, -āre, to kill

cantō, āre, to sing

celebrō, -āre, to celebrate

cūrō, -āre, to care for

dō, dare, to give

narrō, -āre, to tell

natō, -āre, to swim

pugnō, -āre, to fight

servō, -āre, to save

stō, stāre, to stand

vocō, -āre, to call

at

Second Conjugation

doceō, ēre, to teach

habeō, -ēre, to have

iaceō, -ēre, to lie (rest)

mordeō, -ēre, to bite

praebeō, -ēre, to offer

praevaleō, -ēre, to prevail

rīdeō, -ēre, to laugh

sedeō, -ēre, to sit

timeō, -ēre, to fear

et

Third Conjugation

cadō, -ere, to fall

condō, -ere, to build

construō, -ere, to construct

crescō, -ere, to increase

currō, -ere, to run

dēfendō, -ere, to defend

dēfluō, -ere, to flow down

dīcō, -ere, to speak

dīligō, -ere, to love

discō, -ere, to learn

dūcō, -ere, to lead

incendō, -ere, to burn

intendō, -ere, to plan

legō, -ere, to read

ostendō, -ere, to show

pascō, -ere, to feed

scrībō, -ere, to write

succidō, -ere, to fall under

vincō, -ere, to conquer

vīvō, -ere, to live

it

Third *i*-stem Conjugation

capiō, -ere, to take

faciō, -ere, to make

it

Fourth Conjugation

audiō, -īre, to hear

insiliō, īre, to jump into

inveniō, -īre, to find

redeō, -īre, to return (irregular)

trānsiliō, (*or* trānssiliō), -īre, to jump across

veniō, -īre, to come

Can you (1) identify the conjugation of each verb in the list above by writing its infinitive and (2) give the meaning of each of those verbs?

Using Verbs in Two Tenses

Magister: From now on, when you find a word in bold type followed by the definition and sometimes other information, that word will be included in Essential Information as a vocabulary word to be learned. As usual, if the meaning of a Latin word is obvious from an English derivative, the meaning is not given.

Opus manuum virorum

Fābulae Graecōrum et Rōmānōrum

Graecī et Rōmānī multās° fābulās° dē deīs narrābant. In fābulīs deī erant similēs mortālibus. Deī Graecōrum et Rōmānōrum nōn mortālēs audiēbant ubi° supplicābant.° In Scriptūrā Deus noster vērus nōbīs vēritātem ostendit dē mortālibus quī° deōs pāgānōs° adōrant. Adōrant "opus manuum suārum" ["the work of their own hands"]. (Jer. 1:16)

[°many; °tales, stories, or myths; °when; °they prayed; °who; °pagan]

Lydia: The definition for *fābula* is "myth." Isn't *fābula* the word for *legend* in the story about Romulus and Remus? I remembered it because I wondered whether a legend was a fable.

Magister: The Latin word is the same for *fable, legend,* and *myth.* In English we distinguish them. A **fable** is a story, usually with animals as characters, that teaches a lesson. A **legend** is a popular story that is not based on historical record; it is handed down from earlier times. A **myth** is a story with supernatural beings and sometimes human heroes as characters; it also is usually handed down from earlier times.

To answer the questions in Activity H, use the information in the paragraph entitled "Fābulae Graecōrum et Rōmānōrum."

Activity H

Can you tell how myths, fables, and legends differ from each other in the English language?

Learning Verbs Made from Root Words and Prefixes

Magister: The list of verbs in this chapter is long. But here is help. Several of the verbs were formed by combining a preposition with a verb. A preposition at the beginning of a verb is called a **prefix.** You learned several of these prepositions in Chapter 7.

> The *a* in *salīre* becomes an *i* when a **prefix** is added. A vowel is frequently replaced by one that takes less time to say in the longer new word. The **root word** is the main part of the word to which the prefix is attached.
>
> The spelling of the preposition *cum* is changed to *com, con,* or *co* when it is a prefix. The *m* may also change to the first letter of the root word. Often, as in *construere,* it does not add the meaning "with" to the word; instead it intensifies (makes stronger) the meaning of the root word.
>
> In an English definition of a Latin word, the prefix and verb meanings are in reverse order: *dēfluere* means "to flow down."
>
> invenīre—in + venīre—to come <u>upon</u>, to find
>
> insilīre—in + salīre—to jump, leap <u>into</u>
>
> trānsilīre—trāns + salīre—to jump, leap <u>across</u>
>
> construere—cum + struere—to put in order, to build

Magister: Activity I contains words made from prepositions and root words. In numbers 2 through 5, you need to decide whether *con-* (from cum) means "with, together" or is making the root word stronger. In English, unless we use a modifier such as *very* we can't show that the verb is stronger. After you complete the activity, you may want to look up the words in a dictionary to see how close your meaning is to the dictionary meaning.

 Can you state the usual order of the parts of words made from Latin prefixes and roots when the words are defined in English?

PRONOUNS

Learning to Decline First-Person and Second-Person Pronouns

Magister: You've used pronouns occasionally in the previous chapters. **Pronouns** are words that take the place of nouns. The cases are the same as for nouns and adjectives. However, the forms of pronouns are far less regular. We'll begin with the first-person and second-person pronouns. A first-person pronoun refers to the person speaking; a second-person pronoun refers to the person spoken to.

In the declensions below, the functions of the pronouns are given in the first column.

	First Person, Singular		First Person, Plural	
S/PN	ego	I	nōs	we
Mod	meī	of me (*not* my/mine)	nostrum/ nostrī	of us (*not* our/ours)
IO	mihi	me (*or* to/for me)	nōbīs	us (*or* to/for us)
DO/OP	mē	me	nōs	us
OP	mē	me	nōbīs	us

	Second Person, Singular		Second Person, Plural	
S/PN	tū	you	vōs	you
Mod	tuī	of you (*not* your/yours)	vestrum/ vestrī	of you (*not* your/yours)
IO	tibi	you (*or* to/for you)	vōbīs	you (*or* to/for you)
DO/OP	tē	you	vōs	you
OP	tē	you	vōbīs	you

Using First-Person and Second-Person Pronouns

Magister: The genitive forms of these two pronouns do not show possession. Instead, possession is shown by adjectives. Here are the adjectives for *my, our,* or *your.* These **possessive adjectives** are declined like any other first-second declension adjectives.

Singular adjectives	Plural adjectives
meus, -a, -um; my, mine	noster, -stra, -strum; our, ours
tuus, -a, -um; your, yours	vester, -tra, -trum; your, yours

Timothy: If the genitives of the pronouns don't show possession, then what are they for?

Magister: They have two main functions. First, they can express part of a whole. For example, I could say "All *of us (Omnēs nostrum)* use Latin derivatives every day." Or you may say "A part of me *(Pars meī)* looks forward to winter because I like to ski." The examples I've given you are **genitives of the whole.**

The other use of these genitive forms is the **objective genitive.** If a noun suggests some kind of action, its genitive-case modifier may be the receiver of the suggested action. For example, "The boy's fear of us *(timor nostrī)* was easy to see." If the noun *fear* were a verb, the thought would be, "The boy fears us." The object of his fear would be *us (nostrī).*

Genitive of the whole: meī, nostrum; tuī, vestrum (all of me/us/you)

Objective genitive: meī, nostrī; tuī, vestrī (fear of me/us/you)

The fact that these pronoun forms are identical with some of the adjective forms creates a problem. The only solution is to pay close attention to the context. Compare these sentences.

1. Librī meī sunt novī.°

    [°new]

2. Opus vestrum est dūrum.

3. "Repulsus° meī et exercitūs meī nōn est facilis."

    [°Defeat]

4. Dominātiō nostrum et imperiī nostrī est dūra.

Magister: Translate number 1 and then tell us whether *meī* is an adjective or a pronoun.

Sylvia: It means "My books are new." *Meī* has to be an adjective because it modifies *librī*.

Magister: Now translate number 2 and explain *vestrum*.

Julia: "Your work is hard." That's like the first sentence. *Vestrum* is an adjective.

Magister: Number 3 presents a greater challenge. *Meī* has two functions. See whether you can distinguish them.

Flora: *Repulsus* and *meī* are in different cases. *Defeat* can be a verb. So I think *meī* is objective genitive: "the defeat of me." *Exercitūs* is genitive; *meī* comes right after it and agrees with it. *Meī* must be an adjective. "The defeat of me and of my army is not easy."

Magister: After that excellent explanation, number 4 should be easy. *Dominātiō* isn't a verb. It's a noun related to the verb meaning "to dominate." Therefore, it can function like *defeat* in number 3. In this sentence, *imperium* means "empire," and *dūra* means "harsh." Are you ready to try?

Clara: I'll try. *Nostrum* is objective genitive, and *nostrī* is an adjective describing *imperiī*. "The domination of us and of our empire is harsh."

Magister: Good work. Practice using these pronoun forms in Activity J. Then go on to Activity K, where you will translate parts of sentences from the Gospel of John in the Vulgate. Since you are not ready to translate each entire verse, you are to translate only what is not in brackets. The bracketed portions are translations or other information that gives you the context of the Latin portions. The capital letters and punctuation do not correspond exactly with the rules you learn in English class.

Activities J, K

Can you (1) write and say the case forms for first-person and second-person pronouns, (2) state two functions of the genitive case of these pronouns, and (3) name the four Latin adjectives that show possession?

Derivatives

June, the goddess Juno

July, Julius Caesar

August, Augustus Caesar

cereal, Ceres, the goddess of grain

deity, *deus, dea,* a god or goddess [the state of being a god]

majority, *māior,* larger [larger number or part]

minority, *minor,* smaller [smaller number or part]

adoration, *adōrāre,* to worship [worship; great love or regard]

docile, *docēre,* to teach [easily taught]

disciplinarian, *discere,* to learn [one who enforces rules in order to teach proper conduct]

audible, *audīre,* to hear [able to be heard]

Word Order in Prepositional Phrases

In an English prepositional phrase, the first word is always the preposition. In a Latin prepositional phrase of three words, the preposition is often between the adjective and the noun it modifies: *magna cum laude,* "with great praise."

The Romans often attached the preposition *cum* to a pronoun object: *mēcum, vōbīscum,* and so on.

Loan Phrases

alter ego, another I, another self, a close friend

Alter ego est amicus. A friend is another self.

Dominus tecum. The Lord *be* with you (plural).

Dominus vobiscum. The Lord *be* with you (singular).

Pax tecum. Peace *be* with you (plural).

Pax vobiscum. Peace *be* with you (plural).

cum laude, with praise

magna cum laude, with great praise

summa cum laude, with highest praise

Magister: Here are helps to understand the loan phrases. (1) No macrons are used in the loan words and phrases because they are now a part of our language. (2) The phrases beginning with *Dominus* and *Pax* are used in the Roman Catholic Church. You may see them in stories that you read. (3) The last three are used to honor college graduates who have high grade-point averages.

Essential Information

Grammar terms

- i-stem verbs
- prefix, root word
- possessive adjectives, genitive of the whole, objective genitive

General terms

- deities: Jupiter, Neptune, Pluto, Juno, Vesta, Ceres
- fable, legend, myth

Pronouns

- See first-person pronoun declension on page 207.
- See second-person pronoun declension on page 208.

Spelling

- An *i* before another vowel can be changed to a *j*.
- For stem-vowel adjustments, see page 202.

Verbs

Stem vowels of the four conjugations

- First, *ā;* second, *ē;* third, *e;* fourth, *ī*

Tense sign

- Imperfect tense: *bā*

Present and imperfect tenses

- See stem-vowel variations for present-tense verbs on page 202.
- See stem-vowel variations for imperfect-tense verbs on page 203.

Word order

- Latin prepositions sometimes occur within a prepositional phrase: *magnā cum laude.*
- The preposition *cum* is often attached to a pronoun object: *tēcum, vōbīscum.*

Vocabulary

Activity L

- You are responsible for the words listed in the section called "Religion of the Romans" on page 199.
- You should know the verbs listed in bold type under "Reviewing Verbs in the Four Conjugations" on pages 205 and 205. A review of the words in that list that are not in bold type will help you in later chapters.
- You are responsible for the words listed below.

Nouns	Adjective
cibus, -ī, *m.,* food	**novus, -a, -um,** new
fābula, -ae, *f.,* tale, story, myth	**Verbs**
Pronoun	**sciō, -īre,** to know
vester, -tra, -trum, your (pl.)	**supplicō (1),** to pray

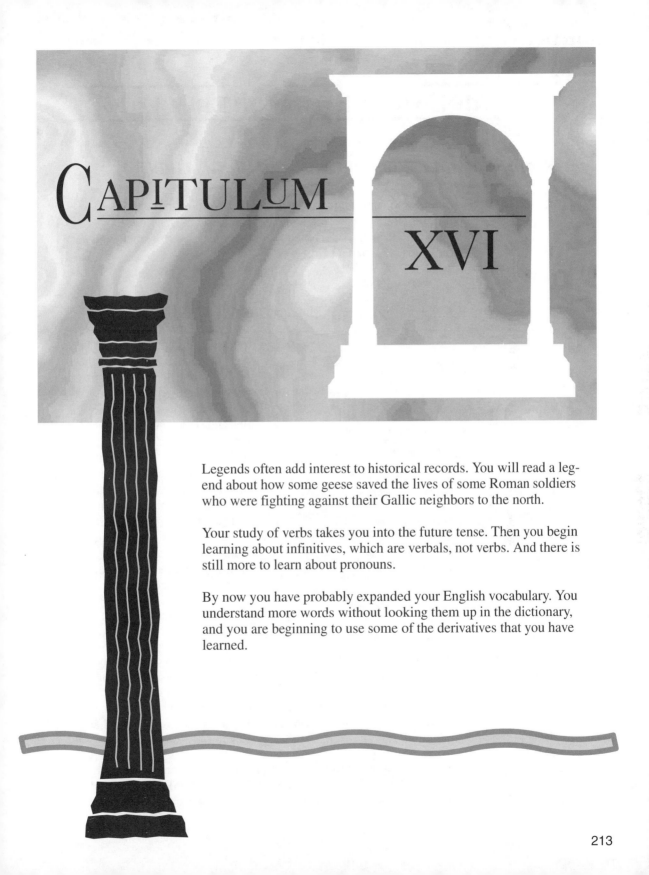

CAPITULUM XVI

Legends often add interest to historical records. You will read a legend about how some geese saved the lives of some Roman soldiers who were fighting against their Gallic neighbors to the north.

Your study of verbs takes you into the future tense. Then you begin learning about infinitives, which are verbals, not verbs. And there is still more to learn about pronouns.

By now you have probably expanded your English vocabulary. You understand more words without looking them up in the dictionary, and you are beginning to use some of the derivatives that you have learned.

THE EARLY ROMAN REPUBLIC

Reading about a Roman Conflict with the Gauls

Magister: While Rome was conquering neighboring peoples in the Italian peninsula, the Gauls seized some of the Etruscans' land north of Rome. The Romans intervened in the argument over the land, and a Roman leader killed a Gallic leader.

Victor: Who were the **Gauls**?

Magister: They were people who lived mainly in the area called by the Romans Transalpine Gaul ("across the Alps"). That was the area in Europe that is now France and the countries near France. Some Gallic tribes crossed the Alps and settled in Cisalpine Gaul ("this side of the Alps" from the Romans' point of view); it is the area south and east of the Alps. The Alps, as you probably know, are a mountain range in south central Europe. Because of the Gauls who had moved into what is now northern Italy, Rome's neighbors were looking to Rome for protection.

Victor: Let me see if I understand. Close to Rome were Gauls and other warlike tribes, right?

Magister: Yes, you're right. In one of these struggles, the Gauls defeated the Roman army and besieged the city of Rome. Many Roman soldiers were killed. The remaining Roman soldiers fled up a steep hill to a fortress. Legend tells us that their lives were saved by some geese. In the Roman religion, geese were sacred to the goddess Juno. In the paragraph called "Anserēs," this legend is retold.

Before reading in Latin the paragraph about this event, I want you to pronounce the Latin words in the list. For each word give the whole genitive form of each noun and the infinitive of each verb. Then give the meaning. The words are listed in the order that they occur in the paragraph.

> The letters *oe* are a diphthong that is pronounced like the letters *oi* in the English word *oil*.

anser, -eris, *m.,* goose

Gallus, -ī, *m.,* a Gaul, member of a Gallic tribe in Europe

propter, *prep. with acc.,* on account of, because of

proelium, -iī/-ī, *n.,* battle

exsultō, -āre, to rejoice, triumph

mīles, -litis, *m.,* soldier

locus, -ī, *m., sing.; n., pl.,* place

tutus, -a, -um, safe

fugiō, -ere, to flee

arx, arcis, *f.,* fortress, citadel

ascendō, -ere, to climb up, ascend

noctu, *adv.,* at night (from **nox, noctis,** *f.,* night)

ubi, *conj.,* when, where

strīdor, -dōris, *m.,* a loud noise

Magister: Paul, please read aloud this Latin paragraph.

Anserēs

Gallī propter victōriam in proeliō contrā Rōmānōs exsultābant. Mīlitēs Rōmānī ex proeliō currēbant. Familiae Rōmānae ex urbe Rōmae ad locum tutum fugiēbant. Militēs Rōmānī in arcem ascendēbant. Noctū Gallī veniēbant ad arcem ubi mīlitēs Rōmānī erant. Anserēs strīdōrem faciēbant. Rōmānī anserēs audiēbant et Gallōs repellēbant.

Magister: Now translate "Anserēs." If you don't recall the meanings of some of these words, first use the context to guess the meanings. Then check the vocabulary list. For verbs in the imperfect tense, choose the translation that best fits the context. Remember, there are three possible translations for any verb in the imperfect tense.

Keep thinking in Latin as you answer the questions in Activity A. Be sure you understand the reason for any errors that you make.

Continue thinking in Latin as you answer the questions in Activity B.

Activities A, B

 Can you (1) name two areas in southeastern Europe where the Gauls lived, (2) tell why the Romans fought against the Gauls, and (3) tell how the conflict ended?

VERB FORMS

Learning and Using the Future Tense Forms

Magister: Let's move today to the Latin forms of the future tense. Here are the future forms of a sample word in each of the four conjugations and the future forms of the *be* verb, which is an **irregular verb.** As we read through them together, you will notice a shift in the tense sign. The first and second conjugations are alike; then the third and fourth conjugations have a different tense sign. The irregular *be* verb doesn't have a tense sign.

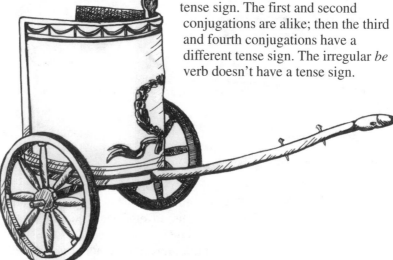

Future Tense					
First	**Second**	**Third**	**Third iō**	**Fourth**	**Irregular**
narrō, -āre	doceō, -ēre	discō, -ere	capiō, -ere	audiō, -īre	sum, esse
Singular					
narrā**bō**	docē**bō**	disc**am**	capi**am**	audi**am**	er**ō**
narrā**bis**	docē**bis**	disc**ēs**	capi**ēs**	audi**ēs**	er**is**
narrā**bit**	docē**bit**	disc**et**	capi**et**	audi**et**	er**it**
Plural					
narrā**bimus**	docē**bimus**	disc**ēmus**	capi**ēmus**	audi**ēmus**	er**imus**
narrā**bitis**	docē**bitis**	disc**ētis**	capi**ētis**	audi**ētis**	er**itis**
narrā**bunt**	docē**bunt**	disc**ent**	capi**ent**	audi**ent**	er**unt**

Julia: What do these mean in English? Is the future "I will tell, you will tell" and so on?

Magister: Yes, but the auxiliary for first person singular and plural is either *shall* or *will*. When you practice, use *shall*. It takes three English words to translate any future form. Here is an example of a first-conjugation verb.

> *I* (subject)
> *shall* (future auxiliary)
> *tell* (verb meaning).

In a Latin verb these three parts are in reverse order from the parts of the English translation. *Narrābō* illustrates the difference.

> *narrā* (verb meaning) *tell*
> *b(i)* (tense sign) *shall*
> *ō* (subject inflection) *I*

Read from the end to the beginning to give the English meaning for this word. Notice that the *i* disappears before the inflection -*ō*. Let's read it together.

Now let's do the same with a third-conjugation verb, *discam*.

> *disc* (verb meaning) *learn*
> *a* (tense sign) *shall*
> *m* (subject inflection) *I*

Read the meaning in reverse order.

Flora: "I shall learn." I expected the future to be easy, like the imperfect tense. But it isn't.

Magister: I agree that the imperfect forms are easier to learn. The major difference is that in the future tense we have the **tense sign** *bi* for the first and second conjugations and *ē* for the third and fourth conjugations, with *a* for first person. Here are some questions to help you discover the two different tense signs for the future tense. Let's begin with some questions about the verbs in the first and second conjugations.

1. What two letters occur in nearly all the forms? Those two letters are the tense sign.
2. Which forms don't have *bi?*
3. What happened to the *i* in first person singular?
4. What happened to the *i* in the third-person plural form?
5. What is the stem vowel that precedes the tense sign in the first conjugation?
6. What is the stem vowel that precedes the tense sign in the second conjugation?
7. Which principal part tells you the stem vowel of any regular verb?

Let's read together the complete conjugation of the verbs *narrābō* and *docēbō*. Pay close attention to the tense sign in these **first- and second-conjugation** verbs. Notice the *bi* and the **two variations** of it.

Paul: For third and fourth conjugations, the first-person inflection is different.

Magister: Yes, it's an *-m.* Here are questions about the third and fourth conjugations. Look carefully at the forms as you answer the questions.

1. After the singular first-person form, what letter occurs before all the inflections?
2. In which forms is the *e* long?
3. Why are the others short vowels?
4. What is the inflection for the first person singular?
5. Where else have you seen that inflection?

6. Except for the *a* in the first person singular, what is the future tense sign for the third and fourth declensions?

7. Is it a long or a short *e?*

8. What letter precedes the tense sign in verbs that are in the third i-stem and the fourth conjugations?

9. Are there any differences between a third i-stem verb and a fourth conjugation verb in the future tense, besides, of course, the meaning of the verbs?

Remember that the third i-stem verbs are like fourth-conjugation verbs in the imperfect tense also.

Let's practice saying the future tense of the verbs of the third, the third i-stem, and the fourth conjugations. Note the one form that has the tense sign **a** and note where the ē becomes short. Saying, hearing, and seeing the words will help you to write them correctly in Activity C.

Lydia: The future of *sum* looks easy.

In later wars, the Romans faced the Greeks and the Carthaginians, who fought with elephants.

Magister: Oral practice of that verb will help too. You should practice saying and writing each of the verb conjugations until you know that you know them. Practice now will save you much time in the future. Activity C calls for future tense forms of verbs in all four conjugations and of the irregular *be* verb. Then in Activity D you will translate future forms.

Can you (1) give the future tense sign for each conjugation and (2) state the variations for the first-person singular and third-person plural forms? Can you conjugate in the future tense (1) a sample verb in each of the conjugations and (2) the verb *sum?*

Distinguishing Present and Future Forms in Second and Third Conjugations

Sylvia: When we are reading, how do we know whether words like *discēmus* and *docēmus* are present or future?

Magister: That's a very important question. We must know the stem vowel that we find in the infinitive form. For second-conjugation verbs like *doceō,* what is the stem vowel?

Sylvia: It's a long *e.*

Magister: And what is the stem vowel in third-conjugation verbs such as *discō?*

Timothy: It's a short *e.*

Magister: Compare the present-tense forms of *doceō* with those of *discō.* An oral practice of both verbs will help.

Singular	Plural	Singular	Plural
doce*ō*	doc*ē*mus	disc*ō*	disc*i*mus
doc*ēs*	doc*ē*tis	disc*is*	disc*i*tis
doce*t*	doce*nt*	disc*it*	disc*u*nt

Sylvia: I remember now. Third-conjugation verbs, like *discō,* have an *i* instead of an *ē* in the present tense.

Magister: In *docēmus,* is the *ē* the stem vowel or the tense sign?

Sylvia: It's the stem vowel.

Magister: Now go back to page 217 in this chapter and compare the future of *doceō* with the future of *discō.* Is the *ē* in *discēmus* the stem vowel or the tense sign?

Sylvia: It's the tense sign. I see now. Present-tense verbs don't have a tense sign, so the *ē* in *docēs* is the stem vowel. But in the third conjugation the *ē* is the tense sign for the future. In other words, if we don't know what conjugation a verb is, we won't know what tense a verb is when it has that long *e*.

Magister: That's true for verbs in the second and third conjugations. It isn't a problem for verbs in the third i-stem and fourth conjugations because they always have an *i* before the *ē* tense sign, and verbs in the second conjugation do not. Some practice with verbs in the present, imperfect, and future tenses will help you feel more secure when you begin to meet all three tenses in sentences.

Magister: Activity E will help you distinguish the present, imperfect, and future tenses. The distinction between present and future tenses requires that you know which conjugation the verb is and what the tense sign is for that conjugation. In Activity F, which contains sentences from famous Roman writers, you will work with verbs in two of the three tenses.

Activities E, F

Can you (1) name the tense of the two verbs *dēfendent* and *timent* and (2) state how you determined the tense?

INFINITIVES

Recognizing Two Uses of Infinitives

Noun uses

Magister: You use infinitives every day in English and may not be aware of how often you use them. You need to recognize infinitives and to understand their uses. Look back at the preceding sentence and find the two infinitives.

Mark: *To recognize* and *to understand.*

Magister: Treat the two words of an infinitive as if they were, like a Latin infinitive, just one word. Tell me the function of the two infinitives in the sample sentence I just gave you. Are they used as the subject, direct object, or object of a preposition?

Mark: *You* is subject. The infinitives are the direct object of *need.*

Magister: Right. The complete direct object is *to recognize infinitives and to understand their uses.* The word *infinitives* is the object of the infinitive *to understand,* and the phrase *their uses* is the object of the infinitive *to understand.* You can see, then, that infinitives can have objects just as verbs can.

Julia: How can a noun have an object?

Magister: They can't unless they are nouns made from verbs. An infinitive is a **verbal.** A verbal acts like a verb in every way except that it cannot be the predicate of a sentence.

Mark: How would we say this in Latin: "We are learning to read Latin"?

Magister: Try it yourself. I suggest that you emphasize the subject by using the pronoun for "we." To write "Latin," as you saw in the Latin title of this book, you'll have to use the phrase *lingua Latīna* because *Latīnus, -a, -um* is an adjective. There isn't a Latin noun meaning "the Latin language," as we have in English.

Mark: How's this? Nōs discimus legere linguam Latīnam. But I guess I should have put the verb last.

Magister: Generally it would come last. However, as you begin to read more and more from Roman authors, you will find that Latin word order can vary much more than English word order can. The verb is not always at the end of a sentence. Changes from the normal word order show emphasis. By putting "Latin language" at the end, you gave it emphasis. And *nōs* at the beginning emphasizes the subject both by its position and by the fact that Latin verbs don't need pronoun subjects.

Infinitives can also be subjects: *To recognize infinitives is important.* And they can be predicate nouns: *My responsibility is to recognize infinitives.*

Subjects, direct objects, and predicate nouns—what parts of speech are they?

Clement: Nouns or pronouns.

Magister: Pronouns and nouns have the same functions, so I'll just use the word *noun* and say that infinitives can function as nouns. Here is a sentence that contains two examples of the **noun function of infinitives:** "To study is to grow mentally." Notice that the adverb *mentally* modifies the verbal *to grow.*

Clement: The subject is an infinitive and so is the predicate noun.

Magister: Right. Infinitives can have other noun functions as well.

The sentences in Activity G are translated for your convenience. You are to decide how infinitives are used in the sentences.

Activity G

Complementary infinitives

Magister: One of the most common uses of the infinitive is called the complementary infinitive. Some verbs require an infinitive to complete the idea. For example, *I ought* is an incomplete idea without an infinitive. The Latin word for "I ought" is **dēbeō, debēre.** Here is a complete sentence: *Dēbeō legere.* It means "I ought to read."

Another verb that requires a complementary infinitive is the irregular verb **possum, posse.** It means "I am able." Notice that both of the principal parts are irregular. The sentence *Possum legere* means "I am able to read" or "I can read." The first of these translations shows clearly the use of the infinitive in the Latin sentence.

You've probably guessed that *possum* is made from *sum.* Put the letters *pos* before word forms that begin with *s* and *pot* before word forms that begin with *e.*

Present		Imperfect		Future	
possu*m*	possu*mus*	potera*m*	poterā*mus*	poter*ō*	poteri*mus*
pote*s*	potes*tis*	poterā*s*	poterā*tis*	poter*is*	poter*itis*
pote*st*	possu*nt*	potera*t*	potera*nt*	poter*it*	poteru*nt*

The word *complementary* is related to *complete.* Complementary infinitives complete the meaning of the main verb.

In Activity H are sentences with forms of *possum* and *debeō,* used with complementary infinitives. Activity I includes both noun uses and complementary uses of infinitives. Try to determine the function of the infinitive in each sentence before you translate the sentence.

You will learn about other verbals later.

Can you name two ways that Latin infinitives are used in sentences?
Can you name two Latin verbs that require a complementary infinitive?

PRONOUNS

Learning and Using Third-Person Pronouns

Magister: Let's review the **person of pronouns.** The **first person** is *ego* (the person speaking) and the **second person** is *tū* (the person spoken to). Now let's look at the **third-person** pronouns (the persons or things spoken about).

A third-person pronoun usually renames a previously mentioned noun, which is called its **antecedent.** It must agree with its antecedent in gender and number. The forms of these pronouns are similar to those of first-second declension adjectives in the accusative and ablative singular forms and in all the plural forms.

These words have several translations and functions. Notice the possible translations.

- **Personal pronoun** Caesar erat dux clārus. <u>Is</u> [He] exercitum fortem habēbat.
- **Demonstrative pronoun** Id [This/That] erat exercitus quod° plūrimum° Eurōpae vincēbat.
  [°which, °most]

These same words can be used as demonstrative modifiers: "this book" or "that book." Like any other adjective, a **demonstrative adjective** must agree with the noun it modifies in gender, number, and case.

- Demonstrative adjective: Caesar <u>eum exercitum</u> [that army] in Eurōpā et Britānniā dūcēbat°.
  [°led]

As you use the table below, remember that each pronoun can also mean "this" or "that" in the singular and "these" or "those" in the plural.

Third-Person Pronouns					
Singular					
Masc.	**Fem.**	**Neut.**	**Masc.**	**Fem.**	**Neut.**
is	ea	id	he	she	it
	eius/ejus		his, of him	her/hers, of her	its, of it
	eī		to/for him	to/for her	to/for it
eum	eam	id	him	her	it
eō	eā	eō	him	her	it
Plural					
Masc.	**Fem.**	**Neut.**	**All**		
eī/iī	eae	ea	they		
eōrum	eārum	eōrum	their/theirs, of them		
	eīs		to/for them		
eōs	eās	ea	them		
	eīs		them		

Magister: Activity J asks you to translate sentences into Latin, using the various cases of pronouns. Activity K contains sentences from Beza's translation of Scripture. Give special attention to the pronouns as you translate the required portions of these sentences.

Activities J, K

  Can you (1) decline the third-person pronoun in both singular and plural and (2) give the possible translations of each form?

Derivatives

Magister: I hope that you are finding out how much Latin helps English and how English derivatives can help you remember the meanings of Latin words. In Activity L the derivatives are your clues to the meanings of new Latin words as well as a few review words.

Activity L

Essential Information

Grammar terms

- verbs: future tense, tense signs *bi* and *ē* (*ā*), variations of future tense sign in four conjugations, future tense of the irregular verb *sum*
- verbal, infinitive, noun functions of the infinitive, complementary infinitive
- personal pronouns: first-, second-, and third-person
- demonstrative pronoun, demonstrative adjective
- antecedent
- irregular verb *possum, posse*

General terms

- Alps, Cisalpine Gaul, Transalpine Gaul
- Gauls

Third-person pronoun forms

- See page 225.

Pronunciation

- The diphthong *oe* = *oi* as in *oil*

Tense signs and inflections for future tense

- Tense signs

    First and second conjugations: **bi**

    Third and fourth conjugations: **ē**

    First person singular only: **a**

- Inflections

    First and second conjugations: *-ō, -s, -t, -mus, -tis, -nt*

    Third and fourth conjugations: *-m, -s, -t, -mus, -tis, -nt*

Verb conjugations

- For the future tense of the four conjugations and the irregular verb *sum,* see page 217.
- For the irregular verb *possum, posse* in the present, imperfect, and future tenses, see page 223.

Vocabulary

Activity M

- You are responsible for the words listed on pages 215 and for the words in bold type listed below.

Nouns

crustulum, -ī, *n.,* a little cake, cookie

cūra, -ae, *f.,* care, concern, attention

horreum, -ī, *n.,* barn

paenīnsula, -ae, *f.,* peninsula

principium, -iī/-ī, *n.,* beginning

voluntās, -tātis, *f.,* will, wish

Pronouns

is, ea, id, *personal and demonstrative,* he, she, it; this, that

quod, which, that

Adjectives

Ītalius, -a, -um, Italian

perpetuus, -a, -um, continuous, uninterrupted

sacer, sacra, sacrum, sacred

ūnus, -a, -um, one

Adverbs

rapidē, rapidly, fast

semper, always

tum, then

Verbs

agō, -ere, to do

crēdō, -ere, to believe

dēbeō, -ēre, to owe, to be obligated (ought)

incipiō, -ere, to begin

maneō, -ēre, to remain

possum, posse, to be able

sum, esse, to be

LEGENDA IV

Legenda

You will probably have little difficulty reading these verses from the Vulgate translation of the Gospel of John. Try to think in Latin as you read. Cover the meanings below each line until you have decided the probable meaning of each word with the mark °.

If you have not learned to read Roman numerals, here are some pointers.

I = 1, V = 5, X = 10, L = 50, C = 100, D = 500, M = 1,000. Placing a letter to the left of a larger numeral subtracts that amount from the larger numeral; placing a letter to the right of another adds it. IV subtracts I from V, making 4. VI adds I to V, making 6. The first verse in Arabic numbers is Chapter 1, verse 9 (1:9)

Evangelium Secundum Johannem

[Iēsus] erat lūx vēra quae° inlūminat° omnem hominem° venientem° in mundum. (I:ix)
[°which; °illuminates; °man, person; °coming]

Hic est [he] qui baptīzat in Spiritū Sanctō. (I:xxxiii)

Ecce° agnus Deī. (I:xxxvi)
[°behold (an exclamation, not a command)]

Tū es Simon, fīlius Iohanna.° (I:xlii)
[°Jona]

Ego sum via et vēritās et vīta. Nēmō venit ad Patrem nisi° per mē. (XIV:vi)
[°except, unless]

Quia° vīvō et° vōs vīvētis. (XIV:xix)
[°because, °also]

[He] qui° manet in mē et ego in eō, hic fert° frūctum° multum quia° sine mē nihil
potestis facere. (XV:v)
[°who, °bears, °fruit, °for, because]

Ego nōn sōlus sum quia Pater mēcum est. (XVI:xxxii)

Dīcenda in Linguā Latīnā

According to your teacher's directions, read or write each sentence. More than one correct word could be used to complete some of the sentences, but you are requested to use
the words found in these quotations from the Vulgate version of the Gospel of John.

Many names in the Bible do not have Latin inflections. Use the spellings given in
the verses. The inflection -*ū* is used for the genitive and ablative forms of the name
Iēsus.

I:ix   Iēsus erat lūx _____.

I:ix   Iēsus omnem _____ venientem in mundum inlūminat.

I:xxxiii   Iēsus _____ in Spiritū Sanctō.

I:xxxvi   Iēsus est _____ Deī.

I:xlii   Pater Simōnis, discipulus Iēsū, erat _____.

XIV:vi   _____ est sōla via ad Deum Patrem.

XIV:vi   _____ ad Patrem sine Iēsū venit.

XIV:xix   Quia Iēsus _____, vīvere possumus.

XV:v   Sine Iēsū, _____ facere possumus.

XVI:xxxii   Iēsus erat nōn sōlus quia _____ erat cum eō.

Answer these questions in complete Latin sentences.

1. Quis omnī hominī venientī in mundum lūcem dat?
2. Quis in Spiritū Sanctō baptīzat?
3. Quis est agnus Deī?
4. Iohanna fīlium habēbat. Quid erat nōmen fīlī eius?
5. Potesne venīre ad Patrem sine Iēsū?
6. Cur vīvere possumus?
7. Quis multum frūctum fert?
8. Iēsus nōn sōlus erat. Quis cum eō erat?

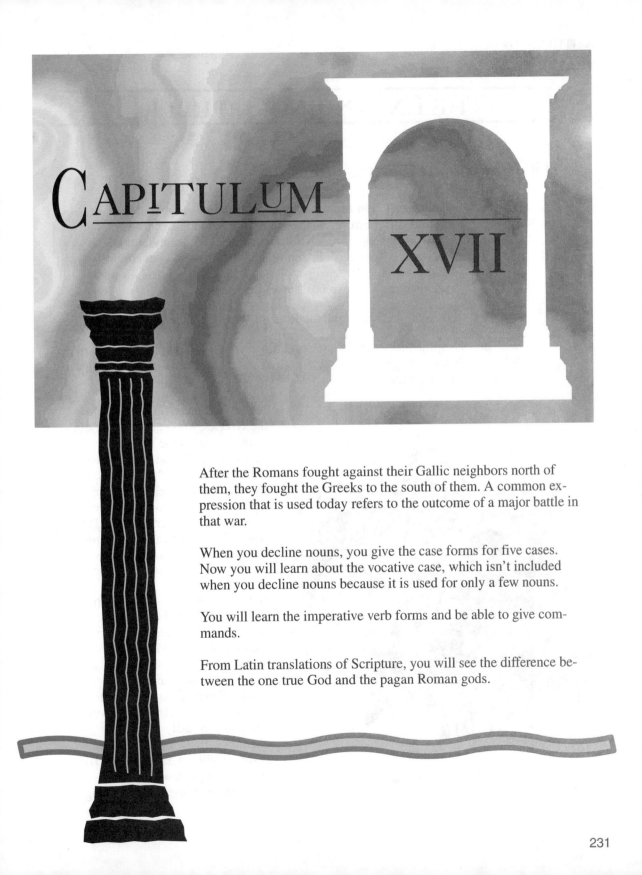

CAPITULUM XVII

After the Romans fought against their Gallic neighbors north of them, they fought the Greeks to the south of them. A common expression that is used today refers to the outcome of a major battle in that war.

When you decline nouns, you give the case forms for five cases. Now you will learn about the vocative case, which isn't included when you decline nouns because it is used for only a few nouns.

You will learn the imperative verb forms and be able to give commands.

From Latin translations of Scripture, you will see the difference between the one true God and the pagan Roman gods.

THE EXPANDING REPUBLIC

Learning about Pyrrhus of Epirus

Magister: The Romans didn't find it easy to gain control of the Italian peninsula. The Etruscans, the Latins, the Samnites, and several other neighboring peoples resisted Roman power. After subduing these peoples, the Romans didn't continue treating them as enemies. By dealing with the defeated peoples on a friendly basis, the Romans strengthened their own position as leaders in the area.

Rex: I thought the Latins and the Romans were the same people.

Magister: It's true that Rome began as a little town in Latium; but as the town grew stronger, it controlled Latium and the neighboring peoples that it conquered.

Elephantī in proeliō

As the Roman territory expanded, the **Greeks,** who held much of the southern part of the Italian peninsula, called on **Pyrrhus** to help them against the Romans. Pyrrhus was a Greek general in **Epirus,** which is now in northern Greece and southern Albania. He was a distant relative of **Alexander the Great,** the famous Greek general.

Here are new words listed in the order you will find them in the account of Pyrrhus's conflict with the Romans. You will probably recognize many of these words because you have used them before. Some of the new words are so much like English derivatives that you can easily guess their meanings. Read through the list before reading the paragraph. The contexts of the new words will help you learn the word meanings.

multus, -a, -um, many

colonia, -ae, *f.,* colony

paenīnsula, -ae, *f.,* peninsula

Ītalicus, -a, -um, Italian

clārus, -a, -um, famous

adiuvō, -āre, to help

quod, *conj.,* because

ars, artis, *f.,* art

bellum, ī, *n.,* war

terreō, terrēre, to frighten, terrify

vincō, -ere, to defeat

sed, *conj.,* but

revertō, -ere, to return

austrālis, -e, southern

- The **English expletive** *there* can introduce a sentence, making it possible to put the verb before the subject. *There* as an expletive does not indicate place. Latin does not have an equivalent word.

- A noun that follows another noun and renames that noun is called an **appositive.** In the paragraph below, *Pyrrhum* is an appositive that renames the direct object *ducem clārum.*

- The adjective *duobus* is the ablative form of the irregular adjective *duo,* which means "two."

Pyrrhus et Rōmānī

Multae colōniae Graecōrum erant in paenīnsulā Ītālicā. Graecī Rōmānōs timēbant, et ducem clārum Pyrrhum ab Epirō suōs° adiuvāre vōcābant. Pyrrhus artem bellī bene° sciēbat. Elephantī eius Rōmānōs terrēbant. In duōbus proeliīs Rōmānōs vincēbat, sed Rōmānī multōs virōs in exercitū Pyrrhī necābant. Pyrrhus nōn in Italiā remanēbat. Ad Graeciam revertēbat. Tum Rōmānī tōtam partem austrālem paenīnsulae Italiae habēbant.

[°them °well]

Clement: I can translate the first sentence. "Many colonies of Greeks were on the Italian peninsula."

Magister: Good. Now I would like all of you to read silently the whole paragraph, thinking in Latin, not English, if you can.

We're going to talk about what you've read. When I ask a question, look for the answer in the Latin paragraph and give the answer in Latin. Use a piece of paper or a card as a mask to cover all the material below the question. Move the mask down only after the correct answer is given. Not all answers will be words, phrases, or sentences lifted from the paragraph. You may need to make your own sentences by changing word forms or word order. Your answers may be brief statements or complete sentences. Here is my first question: Quī erant in parte austrālī paenīnsulae Italicae prīmō?

Clement: Multae colōniae Graecōrum.

Magister: Timēbantne Rōmānī Graecōs aut timēbantne Graecī Rōmānōs prīmō?

Clara: Graecī Rōmānōs timēbant.

Magister: Quī Pyrrhum ad Italiam vocābant?

Victor: Graecī

Magister: Ubi [Where] erat Pyrrhus quandō [when] eum vocābant?

Flora: In Epirō

Magister: Cūr [Why] Graecī Pyrrhum vocābant?

Lydia: Artem bellī bene sciēbat.

Magister: Quī elephantōs timēbant, Graecī aut Rōmānī?

Timothy: Rōmānī

Magister: Quī inimīcōs eōrum in duōbus proeliīs vincēbant?

Paul: Graecī

Magister: Cūr erat victōria nōn magna?

Gloria: Rōmānī multōs virōs Graecōs necābant.

Magister: Post bellum quī [who] tōtam austrālem partem paenīnsulae Italicae habēbant?

Julia: Rōmānī

Pyrrhic victory

Magister: A common term in our language is **Pyrrhic victory.** Perhaps you've already heard or seen the term. Its modern use is an **allusion** to Pyrrhus's victory over the Romans. An allusion is a reference to history, literature, the Bible, or some other source of knowledge. It suggests a comparison between two events or situations.

Pyrrhus's victory was in the long run a defeat. In what sense can it be called a defeat?

Flora: He went back to Greece, and the Romans took control of the southern part of Italy.

Magister: In what other way was it a defeat for Pyrrhus?

Flora: He lost so many men.

Magister: Here are two dictionary definitions of a Pyrrhic victory: "a victory that is offset by staggering losses"; "a victory won at excessive cost." People make allusions to Pyrrhus's victory when they speak of victories that turn out as Pyrrhus's did. For example, if a candidate wins his party's nomination for an office but his leadership divides the party and they lose the final election, his nomination would be a Pyrrhic victory for him and his followers. Activity A asks you questions about Pyrrhus.

Activity A

Can you (1) explain why Pyrrhus went from Epirus to Italy with his army, (2) tell who won the two important battles that he fought, (3) tell why he left Italy, and (4) explain the term *Pyrrhic victory*?

THE VOCATIVE CASE

Magister: Students, have you heard of the **noun of address?** If you've not heard the term before, I just now gave you an example. I used the noun *students* to address you. To address a person is to call his attention to what you are saying. A noun of address in Latin is in the **vocative case.**

Because words used to call someone's attention are usually nouns, the term is *noun* of address. Pronouns can also be used, but this usage is not common. A parent or teacher might emphasize a command by saying, "You, pick up that paper"; however, in English this use of the pronoun is rare. The Latin pronouns *tū* and *vōs* are occasionally used as "nouns" of address, but they do not show the same extreme emphasis as the English pronoun *you.*

Here's some good news. You don't have a whole new set of inflections to learn for the vocative case. All vocative-case inflections—nouns, pronouns, and adjectives—are identical with nominative case inflections with one exception: second-declension masculine nouns and adjectives that end in *-us*.

- The vocative case inflection of second-declension masculine nouns ending in *-us* is *-e.*

  Nominative: amīcus

  Vocative: amīce

- The vocative inflection if the noun is an i-stem is *-ī.*

  Nominative: fīlius

  Vocative: fīlī

- The vocative inflection of first-second declension masculine adjectives ending in *-us* is *-e.*

  Nominative: bonus

  Vocative: bone

- The singular vocative of *meus* is irregular: *mī.*

- The vocative inflection of i-stem adjectives, which are rare, is *-ie.* (*Eximius* means "exceptional, distinguished.")

  Nominative: eximius

  Vocative: eximie

Magister: Activity B has nouns and adjectives in the vocative case. The sentences are quotations from the writings of famous Roman authors. Activity C requires that you translate a few sentences into Latin, using the vocative case.

Activities B, C

Can you (1) explain the use of the noun of address and (2) give the vocative case form of second-declension nouns and adjectives that have the nominative singular inflection *-us?*

THE IMPERATIVE MOOD OF VERBS

Magister: All the verbs you have worked with so far have been in the **indicative mood.** The word *indicative* means that we *indicate* or state something as a fact. It may not be a fact, but it is stated as a fact. For example, on Tuesday I may mistakenly say, "This is

Wednesday." The statement is in the indicative mood because I have stated it as a fact. A corresponding question, asking about a fact, is also in the indicative mood: "Is this Wednesday?"

You may recall from Chapter 8 that the noun *imperium,* means "a command or order." The **imperative mood** is used when we give commands. Here are the imperative forms of sample verbs in each conjugation and the irregular *be* verb. These forms are very simple.

	First	Second	Third	Third i-stem	Fourth	Irregular
Imperative Verb Forms by Conjugation						
Singular	narr*ā*	man*ē*	crēd*e*	cap*e*	aud*ī*	e*s*
Plural	narr*āte*	man*ēte*	crēd*ite*	cap*ite*	aud*īte*	es*te*

Magister: Here are two sentences that contain commands. Think *about command forms in English.* Tell *me the subject of* think *and* tell in these two English sentences.

Clara: They don't need subjects because we know you are speaking to us.

Magister: You're exactly right. But when the verb is in the imperative mood the noun of address is often used. Go back to Activity B and look at the first word in numbers 2, 3, and 5. There you will see the imperative forms of these verbs:

> **salveō, -ēre,** to be well; Good day! Good morning! Hail!
>
> **valeō, -ēre,** to be strong, to be in good health; Farewell! Good-bye!

The Roman greeting *Salvē* or *Salvēte* means "Be well!" or "Be in good health!" The farewell *Valē* or *Valēte* also means "Be well!" or "Be in good health!" Compare those greetings and farewells with ours. We often greet a person with a question, "How are you?" Our farewell is usually "Good-bye," which is a shortened form of "God be with you."

The Romans used another imperative form, *avē* or *avēte,* as either a greeting or a farewell. These are forms of the verb

> **aveō,** *or* **haveō, -ēre,** to be well.

In Luke 1:28 the Beza translation reads: Ave, gratis dilecta: Dominus tēcum *est*: benedicta [es] tū inter mulierēs. ("Hail/Greeting, [thou] chosen of grace: The Lord be with you: you are blessed among women.") This begins the angel Gabriel's message to the virgin Mary. These translations should help you to understand better the greetings and farewells in Scripture.

The next two activities provide practice with verbs in the imperative mood. Activity D asks you to translate into English, and Activity E asks you to translate into Latin.

Activities D, E

Can you (1) state the function of the imperative mood and of the indicative mood, (2) write verbs of all five conjugations in the imperative mood, singular and plural, and (3) translate sentences containing imperative forms?

ROMAN DEITIES

Comparing Roman and Greek Deities

Magister: The culture of Rome included much that was borrowed from neighboring peoples. Roman myths show the influence especially of Greek mythology. Many Greek and Roman deities are parallel. Here are a few examples.

Roman	Greek	Mythical realm
Jupiter	Zeus	Heaven and earth
Neptune	Poseidon	Seas
Pluto	Hades	Underworld
Juno	Hera	Heavens
Vesta	Hestia	Hearth (home)
Ceres	Demeter	Grain (crops)

Seeing the One True God in Scripture

Magister: The only true God, who has revealed Himself in the Scriptures, describes for us the gods that men make for themselves. One description of men's deities is in Psalm 115. This passage makes a person wonder why anyone would believe in such gods. Romans 1:20-23 answers the question.

Many Roman myths are attempts to explain things in nature. People who don't acknowledge the Creator must seek explanations for natural phenomena through their imaginations. The Romans and the Greeks had one god for the heavens, another for the earth, and still another for the underworld. They had a god of the universe, a god of the sun, a goddess of the moon, a goddess of the earth, a goddess of grain, a god of the harvest, and so on.

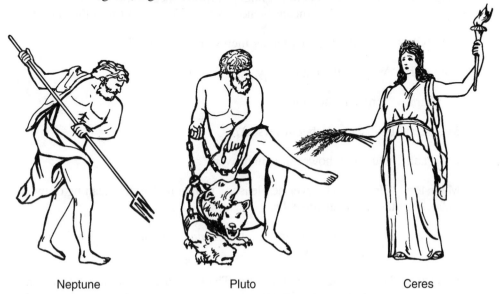

| Neptune | Pluto | Ceres |

Here are passages from Latin versions of Psalm 115:1-9*a*. The verses are mainly from the Vulgate, but parts of some verses are taken from the Beza translation because those parts are easier for you to understand.

Let's read the verses in unison twice. You will probably discover the meaning of several words from their context and be able to translate much of the passage. I want you to translate the italicized portions. I'll translate or will help you translate what is not in italics.

Psalm 115:1-8

1. *Nōn nōbīs, Domine, nōn nōbīs sed nōminī tuō dā glōriam* propter misericordiam tuam *et vēritātem tuam.*

2. Quārē dīcerent gentēs, *Ubi est Deus eōrum?*

3. *Deus autem noster in coelīs;* quicquid placet, facit.

4. Idola gentium sunt argentum et aurum, opus manuum hominum.

5. Ōs habent sed nōn loquuntur; *oculōs habent et nōn vident.*

6. *Aurēs habent et nōn audiunt;* nāsum habent et nōn odōrantur.

7. Manūs habent et nōn palpant; *pedēs habent et nōn ambulābunt,* nec sonābunt in gutture suō.

8. Similēs illīs fiant quī faciunt ea.

Victor: I can translate the first part of the first sentence. "Not to us, Lord, not to us but to your name give glory."

Magister: That's an excellent beginning. *Propter* means "on account of" and *misericordiam* means "tender mercy." Who can finish the verse?

Sylvia: "on account of thy tender mercy and thy truth."

Magister: "Why do the nations say. . .?" Finish the verse.

Clara: "Where is their God?"

Magister: Paul, can you begin verse 3?

Paul: "Our God, however, is in heaven."

Magister: "He does whatever he pleases." Can you give the meaning of two of the words in verse 4?

Rex: *Idola* probably means "idol" and *manuum* means "of hands" because it is genitive plural.

Magister: *Idola* is a neuter plural form. The verse means "Idols are gold and silver, the work of the hands of men." The next verses are parallel to each other in form. Verse 5 begins, "A mouth they have but they do not talk." Can someone make reasonable guesses and complete the verse?

Flora: "They have eyes and they do not see."

Magister: How did you figure out the meaning of *oculōs?*

Flora: I guessed that *vident* means "see" because I know that videos are something you see; so *oculōs* must be "eyes." I can translate the first part of verse 6. "They have ears and they do not hear."

Magister: You're making good use of context clues. Let the derivative clue in this sentence help you with the word *nāsum.* Nasal congestion is a common problem when we have a cold. So what does *nāsum* mean?

Mark: It must mean "nose."

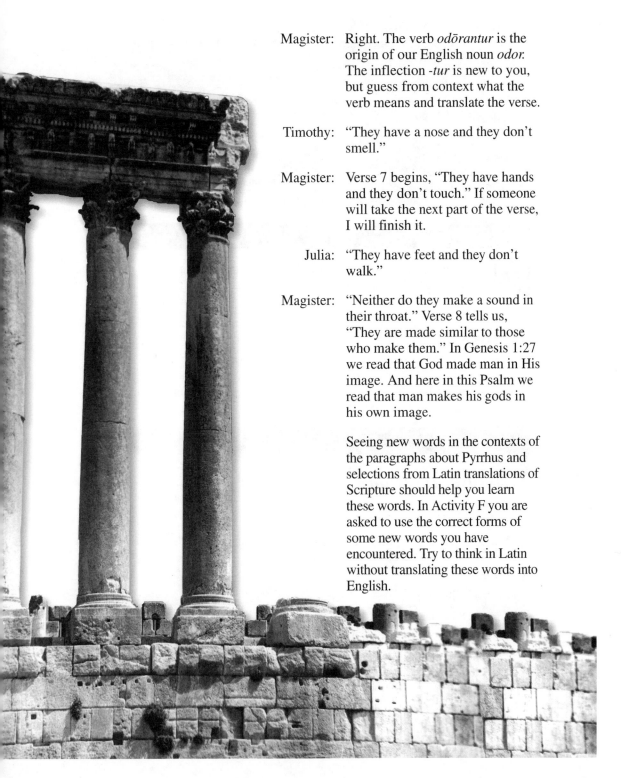

Magister: Right. The verb *odōrantur* is the origin of our English noun *odor.* The inflection *-tur* is new to you, but guess from context what the verb means and translate the verse.

Timothy: "They have a nose and they don't smell."

Magister: Verse 7 begins, "They have hands and they don't touch." If someone will take the next part of the verse, I will finish it.

Julia: "They have feet and they don't walk."

Magister: "Neither do they make a sound in their throat." Verse 8 tells us, "They are made similar to those who make them." In Genesis 1:27 we read that God made man in His image. And here in this Psalm we read that man makes his gods in his own image.

Seeing new words in the contexts of the paragraphs about Pyrrhus and selections from Latin translations of Scripture should help you learn these words. In Activity F you are asked to use the correct forms of some new words you have encountered. Try to think in Latin without translating these words into English.

argentum, -ī, *n.,* silver

auris, -is, *f.,* ear

aurum, -ī, *n.,* gold

caelum, -ī or coelum, -ī, *n.,* the heaven, the sky

gēns, gentis, f., a people, a nation

homo, -minis, *m.,* a human be-ing, a man

manus, -ūs, *f.,* hand; a band of men

nāsus, -ī, *m.,* nose

oculus, -ī, *m.,* eye

ōs, ōris, *n.,* mouth

pēs, pedis, *m.,* foot

videō, -ēre, to see

Activity F

Can you (1) name six major Roman deities, (2) name five parts of nature for which the Romans had deities, and (3) name at least five abilities that people have but man-made gods do not have?

Derivatives

Magister: Activity G gives you contexts for derivatives of words presented in this chapter. Let these derivatives help you to remember the meanings of the vocabulary words.

Activity G

Essential Information

Grammar terms

- appositive, English expletive *there,* noun of address, vocative case, imperative mood, indicative mood

General terms

- allusion
- Greeks, Pyrrhus, Pyrrhic victory, Epirus, Alexander the Great
- Roman deities: Jupiter, Neptune, Pluto, Juno, Vesta, Ceres
- Greek deities: Zeus, Poseidon, Hades, Hera, Hestia, Demeter

Imperative forms of verbs

- See page 237.

Vocative case of nouns

- nearly all forms, same as nominative forms
- Second declension singular forms
  that end in *-us: -e,* Marc*e*
  that end in *-ius: -e*
  (i-stems): *-ī*, Luc*ī*
  the adjective *meus:* m*ī*

Vocabulary

Activity H

- You are responsible for the words listed on on pages 233 and 242 and for the words listed below in bold type.

Verbs	**valeō, -ēre,** to be strong; Farewell! Good-bye!
aveō, -ēre, to be well; Good day! or Farewell!	**Conjunction**
cogitō, -āre, to think	**sī,** if
salveō, -ēre, to be well; Good day! Good morning!	

New words from Legenda IV

Noun	**Verb**
fructus, -ūs, *m.,* fruit	inluminat, illuminate
Pronoun	**Conjunctions**
quae, which	nisi, if not, unless
Adverbs	quia, because
bene, well	
ecce, behold	

CAPITULUM XVIII

Rome, now in control of most of the Italian peninsula, engaged in wars against Carthage. The first of these was a struggle to control the island of Sicily. Find out who won.

The three perfect tenses will be fairly easy to learn because Latin and English have similarities in those tenses. With oral practice you will soon learn the principal parts of the verbs you have worked with.

You can already ask questions with the enclitic *-ne.* Now you will learn how to ask more questions by using interrogative pronouns.

The names of Roman numerals will explain four "incorrect" names of months on our calendars.

THE FIRST PUNIC WAR

Magister: Pyrrhus's departure left the Romans in control of the entire Italian peninsula. New gains for the Romans brought new problems. All the peoples in the peninsula were allied under the leadership of Rome by 265 B.C. However, Rome now had to protect the borders of the entire peninsula. **Sicily,** an island at the "toe of the boot" of Italy, was partly under the control of Carthage, which had a strong navy to protect her merchant ships.

Lydia: What do you mean by the "toe of the boot"?

Magister: Look at the map. Notice that the Italian peninsula looks like a boot, and the island of Sicily is positioned like a ball about to be kicked by the boot. Now look beyond Sicily to the north coast of Africa and find the city of **Carthage.** That was a strong city that had been settled by **Phoenicians** about 800 B.C. Carthage fought the Greeks in a long-term struggle for supremacy in the Mediterranean area. At the time of Pyrrhus, the Greeks had a treaty with Carthage.

Bellum Prīmum Pūnicum

Victor: Was Carthage likely to attack Rome?

Magister: Rome had to consider the possibility. Until about 265 B.C., there had been no cause for concern. The navy of Carthage had been no threat to Rome because Rome had very little sea trade and no navy. History indicates a possible agreement between Rome and Carthage that Rome would not hinder Carthage's sea trade if Carthage would not establish colonies in Italy.

Julia: Did Carthage try to build colonies in Italy?

Magister: No, but a conflict between Rome and Carthage began in Sicily. Carthage controlled about half of the island, and strife arose over a town in the other part of the island. Rome and Carthage were soon at war. Carthage had the advantage of having a strong mercenary navy.

Victor: What is a mercenary navy?

Magister: **Mercenaries** are professional soldiers or sailors, usually from other countries, who are hired to fight. The word *mercenary* comes from *mercēs,* which means "wages, pay."

Rex: Do you mean like the Hessians, who were hired by the British to fight in the Revolutionary War?

Magister: Yes, except that England had her own army and hired the mercenaries for added strength. Carthage depended entirely on mercenaries. Such military forces are well trained, but they aren't motivated by loyalty and love for the country they are fighting for.

The First Punic War (264-241 B.C.) resulted from Rome's decision to keep Carthage from gaining possession of the part of Sicily nearest Italy. If Carthage should control that part of Sicily, Rome would be in danger.

Lydia: Why would a war between Rome and Carthage be called a **Punic War?**

Magister: Because the people who had settled at Carthage in **North Africa** were the Phoenicians, whom the Romans called **Poenī.** The word *Punic* comes from *Poenī.* Three Latin adjectives—**Poenicī, Punicī,** and **Carthāginiēnsēs**—can describe these people. The Poenī had come from the city of **Tyre** to North Africa and to Sicily.

You will need a few new words to read about this war. They are listed in the order you will find them in the paragraph.

After you read the paragraph aloud, I'll ask you questions about it. Please answer in Latin. Your answers may be brief. Be careful to use the correct inflections in your answers.

Adjectives can modify understood nouns, as explained in Chapter 13. When the modified noun is understood, the adjective is called a *substantive.* The three adjectives—*Pūnicus, Poenīcus,* and *Carthāginiēnsis*—can be translated "a Carthaginian." Don't mistake these adjectives for nouns.

Pūnicus, -a, -um, or **Poenicus, -a, -um,** Phoenician, Carthaginian	**dominātiō, -ōnis,** *f.,* mastery, irresponsible power, despotism
Poenī, -ōrum, *m.,* the Carthaginians	**mare, maris,** *n.,* sea
Carthāginiēnsis, -e, pertaining to Carthage; Carthaginian, Punic	**igitur,** *adv.,* therefore
Carthāgō, -inis, *f.,* the city of Carthage in North Africa	**classis, -is,** *f.,* fleet
	iactūra, -ae, *f.,* loss

Bellum Prīmum Pūnicum

Initium Prīmī Pūnīcī Bellī erat in insulā Siciliae. Voluntās Rōmae et Carthāginis erat potestātem habēre super Siciliam. Multae urbēs in insulā erant amīcae Rōmae quod dominātiō Carthāginis super eās erat dūra.

In proeliīs contrā Rōmānōs, Poenī elephantōs habēbant. Rōmānī in proeliīs Poenōs vincēbant, sed potestātem super mare ad paeninsulam nōn habēbant. Igitur Rōmānī classem construēbant et in marī pugnābant. Bellum erat longum, et iactūra vītārum erat magna in exercitū Rōmānōrum et in exercitū Poenōrum. Rōma erat victor. Rōma nunc Siciliam habēbat. Rōma et Carthāgō erant "amīcae."

Magister: Quae [what] urbēs Prīmum Pūnicum Bellum pugnābant?

Flora: Rōma et Carthāgō.

Magister: Ubi erat initium bellī?

Timothy: In insulā Siciliae.

Magister: Erantne elephantī pars exercitūs Rōmānī aut exercitūs Carthāginiēnsis?

Mark: Erant pars exercitūs Carthāginiēnsis.

Magister: Quī [who] prīmō potestātem in marī nōn habēbant?

Lydia: Rōmānī.

Magister: Erantne Rōmānī aut Poenī victōrēs in fīnī [the end] bellī?

Paul: Rōmānī erant victōrēs.

Magister: Activity A reviews what we have just talked about.

Activity A

Can you (1) give the dates when the First Punic War began and ended, (2) give the cause of the war, and (3) tell how the war ended?

VERBS IN THE PERFECT TENSES

Magister: Latin has a **present verb system** and a **perfect verb system.**

> *Present system: present, imperfect,* and *future tenses*
> They are built on the present infinitive stem (second principal part).
>
> *Perfect system: present perfect, past perfect,* and *future perfect* They are built on the stem that is found in the third principal part. The present perfect is often called just the **perfect tense.**

Clement: Why are they called perfect tenses?

Magister: The word *perfect* in grammar means "complete." The first word in the name of each of the three perfect tenses indicates the time when the action of the verb is complete.

The action of a *present perfect verb* was done in the past and is now complete. Here is an example: *I have completed my assignment.* The action of a *past perfect verb* was done before a stated time in the past. *I had completed my assignment before I came to class.* The tense of the auxiliary in those sentences provides the name for the tense. What is the tense of each of those auxiliaries?

Rex: *Have* is present, and *had* is past. So that's why we say ***present** perfect* and ***past** perfect* tense. That makes sense.

Julia: What about the future perfect tense?

Magister: *I will have completed my lesson before I will come to class.*

Julia: Would anybody ever say that?

Magister: Probably not. More likely you would say, "I will have completed my lesson by nine o'clock," or "I will complete my lesson by nine o'clock." Future time is suggested by the words *nine o'clock.* In English conversation we don't express the ideas of the future and future perfect tenses very logically. We use the future for the future perfect and the present for the future in sentences like this: "I will complete my lesson before I come to class."

In English, context words and phrases usually indicate the time of the verb: for example, "I have a meeting [now], [tomorrow], [after this class]."

Can you (1) name the two tense systems and (2) name the three tenses in each system?

Identifying the Stem for the Perfect Tenses

Magister: The perfect tenses are built on the stem found in the **third principal part.**

Lydia: What are principal parts, anyway?

Magister: They are simple verb forms that are used as a basis of other verb forms. In Latin they provide the stems to which the inflections are added.

The first two principal parts, which you have been using in the present-system verbs, are equivalent to the first principal part of an English verb, the infinitive. In English the infinitive is the same as the first-person singular present tense in all verbs except *be.* In Latin, the two forms differ and are distinguished as the first two principal parts. Compare the first two English principal parts with the first three in Latin.

> do, did
>
> agō, agere, ēgī

The third principal part of a Latin verb is equivalent to the second one of an English verb. It is a verb, not an infinitive. The inflection -*ī* shows that the verb is first person singular, *I,* just as the -*ō* or -*m* does on the first principal part. Here are three principal parts of a verb in each conjugation and an irregular verb. The stems are underlined.

> vocō, voc<u>ā</u>re, <u>vocāvī</u>
>
> timeō, <u>timē</u>re, <u>timuī</u>
>
> agō, <u>age</u>re, <u>ēgī</u>
>
> veniō, <u>venī</u>re, <u>vēnī</u>
>
> sum, esse, <u>fuī</u>

Paul: Is the third principal part of *agō* misspelled?

Magister: No. This is an example of the verbs that have an important spelling change between the second and third principal parts. Compare this with the difference between the first two principal parts of our verb *eat* and *ate*. You can see the importance of learning the spelling of all the principal parts. Only the first principal part of each verb is listed in many Latin dictionaries or word lists. If you look in the *e* section for *ēgī*, the third principal part of *agō*, you won't find it because the dictionary makers assume that you know all the principal parts of all the verbs. A dictionary that lists irregular spellings such as *ēgī* is the *Collins Gem Latin Dictionary, Second Edition.*

 Can you name (1) which principal part provides the stem for verbs in the perfect system and (2) the verb inflection that is removed in order to form the stem for perfect-system verbs?

Learning the Present Perfect Inflections

Magister: The present perfect has its own set of inflections, which are used only in the present perfect tense. Let's practice saying and writing the three persons in the singular and plural until you know them well.

Singular: ***-ī, -istī, -it***

Plural: ***-imus, -istis, -ērunt***

Identifying the Tense Sign for Two Tenses

Rex: Are there tense signs in the perfect tenses?

Magister: The present perfect tense doesn't have a tense sign, just as the present tense doesn't. Here are the tense signs for the other two tenses:

Past perfect: **erā**

Future perfect: **eri**

I'll give you two mnemonic aids to help you remember which vowels are long.

(1) The imperfect, *bā,* and the past perfect, *erā,* have long vowels. The English auxiliary *was* also contains the letter *a.*

(2) The future, *-bi-* (for first and second declensions only), and the future perfect, *-eri-*, have short vowels. The English auxiliary *will* also contains the short vowel *i*.

Conjugating in the Three Perfect Tenses

Magister: Here are the conjugations of a sample verb in all three perfect tenses. Remember that the diphthong *au* is pronounced like the English diphthong *ou* (as in cloud).

Present Perfect

laudāv*ī*, I have praised, I praised

laudāv*istī*, you have praised, you praised

laudāv*it*, he/she/it has praised, he praised

laudāv*imus*, we have praised, we praised

laudāv*istis*, you have praised, you praised

laudāv*ērunt*, they have praised, they praised

Past Perfect

laudāv**eram**, I had praised

laudāv**erās**, you had praised

laudāv**erat**, he had praised

laudāv**erā***mus*, we had praised

laudāv**erā***tis*, you had praised

laudāv**erant**, they had praised

Future Perfect

laudāv**erō**, I will/shall have praised

laudāv**eris**, you will have praised

laudāv**erit**, he will have praised

laudāv**eri***mus*, we will/shall have praised

laudāv**eri***tis*, you will have praised

laudāv**eri***nt*, they will have praised

Magister: For all four conjugations and for irregular verbs, the method of forming the perfect tenses is easy because it is *always* the same. These verbs have no stem vowels. Just follow these simple directions:

> ***Present perfect tense*** Add the inflections (*-ī, -istī, -it; -imus, -istis,* or *-ērunt*) to the stem (found in the third principal part).

Past perfect tense Add the tense sign *erā* to the perfect stem; then add the correct inflection (*-m, -s, -t; -mus, -tis,* or *-nt*).

Future perfect tense Add the tense sign *eri* to the perfect stem; then add the correct inflection (*-ō, -s, -t; -mus, -tis,* or *-nt*). Remember to make long vowels short before the inflections *-t* and *-nt.*

Can you conjugate each of these verbs in the three perfect tenses: *vocō, timeō, agō, veniō,* and *sum?*

Learning the Four Principal Parts

Clara: Is there an easy way to learn all the principal parts?

Magister: For first-conjugation verbs, yes. They are nearly all alike. Verbs in the other conjugations will require memorization of the principal parts of each verb. Most Latin verbs have four principal parts. Since you will soon be working with the fourth one, you may as well learn it now. It is an adjective form, having masculine, feminine, and neuter first-second declension forms. The reason for these adjective forms will soon be clear. In the list below, the feminine and neuter adjective endings are omitted.

When you work with a verb whose meaning you already know, learn its principal parts. If first-conjugation verbs have the same forms as *laudō,* they have *(1)* after them in most vocabulary lists and dictionaries; otherwise all the principal parts are given.

In the list below, verbs with the same pattern of principal parts are grouped together. The principal parts are given only for the first verb in each group. Some verbs have only three principal parts, marked (3), and some have only two, marked (2).

> The verb *ostendō occurs twice in the list because its fourth principal part can end with *-sus* or *-tus.*
>
> The two verbs *vincō* and *vīvō* have identical fourth principal parts: **victus.*
>
> The macron is very important over the *e* in the third principal part of some verbs, such as *veniō* and *legō,* and compounds made from them. For some forms, that is the only way the present tense (*venit, venimus; legit, legimus*) can be distinguished from the present perfect tense (*vēnit, vēnimus; lēgit, lēgimus*).

First Conjugation

laudō, laudāre, laudāvī, laudātus

adiuvō, adiuvāre, adiūvī, adiūtus

dō, dare, dedī, datus

stō, stāre, stetī, status

Second Conjugation

doceō, docēre, docuī, doctus

habeō, iaceō (3)

praebeō, praevaleō (3)

timeō (3), aveō (2)

salveō (2), valeō (2)

maneō, manēre, mansī, mansus

mordeō, mordēre, momordī, morsus

sedeō, sedēre, sēdī, sessus

terreō, terrēre, terruī, territus

videō, vidēre, vīdī, vīsus

rīdeō, rīdēre, rīsī, rīsus

irrideō (3)

Third Conjugation

agō, agere, ēgī, actus,

ascendō, ascendere, ascendī, ascensus; dēfendō; incendō; *ostendō

intendō, intendere, intendī, intentus; *ostendō; revertō (3)

capiō, capere, cēpī, captus; faciō

cadō, cadere, cecidī, casus

condō, condere, condidī, conditus; crēdō

crescō, crescere, crēvī, crētus

currō, currere, cucurrī, cursus

dīligō, dīligere, dīlēxī, dīlectus

discō, discere, didicī

dūcō, dūcere, dūxī, ductus; dīcō; dēfluō; construō

fugiō, fugere, fūgī, fūgitus

incipiō, incipere, incēpī, inceptus

legō, legere, lēgī, lectus

pascō, pascere, pāvī, pastus

repellō, repellere, reppulī, repulsus

resurgō, resurgere, resurrexī, resurrectus

scrībō, scrībere, scrīpsī, scriptus

succidō, succidere, succidī

vincō, vincere, vīcī, **victus

Fourth Conjugation

audiō, audīre, audīvī, audītus
insiliō, insilīre, insiluī
transiliō (3)

sciō, scīre, scīvī (sciī), scītus
veniō, venīre, vēnī, ventus;
  reveniō; conveniō; inveniō

Irregular

sum, esse, fuī, futūrus
possum, posse, potuī

abeō, abīre, abiī, abitus;
  redeō

Magister: For practice with the new tenses, translate these sentences.

> Rōma Pyrrhum vīcerat ante Prīmum Pūnicum Bellum pugnāvit.
>
> Post bellum contrā Rōmam Pyrrhus ad Graeciam revēnit.°
>
> [°return]
>
> Dē Secundō Pūnicō Bellō lēgerimus antequam° dē Tertiō Pūnicō Bellō legēmus.
>
> [°before]

Gloria: That doesn't sound right. Wouldn't we say, "We will read about the Second Punic War before we read about the Third Punic War"?

Magister: You're right. As I mentioned earlier in this chapter, when we speak and write in English, we seldom use the future perfect tense. When you do Activity E, you may think that number 4 sounds strange. However, it can be easily translated into Latin because of the accurate use in Latin of the future and future perfect tenses.

To become skilled in the use of these three new tenses, you have four activities. They include translations from Latin to English and from English to Latin. Activities B and C focus on the verb forms of the three perfect tenses. In Activities D and E, the perfect tenses are used in sentences. In all four activities, be careful to use the right auxiliaries in your English translations and the right tense signs and inflections in your Latin translations.

Can you translate verbs in the three perfect tenses, using the correct English auxiliary for each?

THE INTERROGATIVE PRONOUN

Magister: One way to ask questions in Latin is to use the enclitic *-ne.* We don't have the enclitic in English. But our languages are alike in another kind of question. The interrogative pronoun is used in both languages. In English, how would you ask a new acquaintance what her name is?

Clara: What is your name?

Magister: In Latin you would say, "Quid est nōmen tuum?" You've already worked with several forms of the interrogative pronoun. As you look at the declension of it, you will see that some forms resemble first-second declension adjectives, some resemble third-declension adjectives, and some don't resemble any adjectives. Where the genders are all alike, the form is given only once. Notice that in the singular, the masculine and feminine forms are the same, but in the plural they are different in three cases.

Timothy: The neuter rule will make some forms easy to learn.

Magister: Yes. Keep it in mind as we practice saying the forms. Where a form is used for all the genders, say it for each of the genders. For oral practice, follow the same pattern we did for adjectives, saying all the gender forms for each case before going to the next case.

Interrogative Pronoun		
Singular		
M/F	**N**	
quis	quid	who/what
cuius		whose, of whom/what
cui		to/for whom/what
quem	quid	whom/what
quō		by (etc.) whom/what

Plural			
M	**F**	**N**	
quī	quae	quae	who/what
quōrum	quārum	quōrum	whose, of whom/what
	quibus		to/for whom/what
quōs	quās	quae	whom/what
	quibus		by (etc.) whom/what

Magister: Activity F gives you practice with the forms and uses of the interrogative pronoun. Activities G and H use interrogative pronouns in sentences. In Activity H the questions are about Roman history, including what you have studied in earlier chapters. You may refer to the declension of *quis, quid* and the translations of the forms.

Activities F, G, H

Can you (1) give the case(s), number, and gender(s) of each interrogative pronoun form and (2) translate these pronoun forms in sentences?

LATIN NUMBERS

Using Ordinal and Cardinal Numbers

Magister: Rōma et Carthāgo Prīmum Pūnicum Bellum, Secundum Pūnicum Bellum, et Tertium Pūnicum Bellum pugnāvērunt. What have I just said?

Clara: "Rome and Carthage fought the First Punic War, the Second Punic War, and the Third Punic War."

Magister: Nōn unum bellum, nōn duo bella, sed trēs bella pugnāvērunt. Can you translate this sentence?

Sylvia: "They fought not one war, not two wars, but three wars."

Magister: The two Latin sentences you just read contain two kinds of numbers. One kind puts things in order. The other counts things. Which sentence puts things in order?

Victor: The first sentence: first, second, third. The other sentence counts the wars: one, two, three.

Magister: You have just defined two kinds of numbers. We use **cardinal numbers** for counting: for example, *ūnus, duo, trēs*. We use **ordinal numbers** to put things in order: for example, *prīmus, secundus, tertius.*

Listed below are the numbers up to ten. In Appendix B you can find the numbers up to a thousand, counting only by tens and then by hundreds.

The Romans used letters instead of numerals.

I = 1, V = 5, X = 10, L = 50,

C = 100, D = 500, M = 1,000

Roman numerals are read from left to right. If a lesser number comes before a greater number, subtract the lesser from the greater. Otherwise add the numbers.

IV = 4, but VI = 6

XC = 90, but CX = 110

XIV = 14, but XVI = 16

To represent subtraction, the letters *I, X, C,* and *M* can be placed only before the next larger of these letters. The letters *V, L,* and *D* can never be placed before any larger letter.

XCIX = 99

CMX = 910

MDXCIX = 1,599

A few numbers can be written in either of two ways.

4 = IV or IIII; 9 = IX or VIIII; 14 = XIV or XIIII, 19 = XIX or XVIIII, and so on.

The year 1998 in Roman numerals is MCMXCVIII.

Cardinal numbers are counting numbers.

ūnus = one or 1, duo = two or 2, and so on.

They are indeclinable except for *ūnus, duo, trēs,* and *mīlle.* (You will find these declensions in Chapter 19.)

Ordinal numbers are declined like any other first-second declension adjectives.

prīmus, -a, -um, and so on.

Numbers		
Numerals (Roman)	**Cardinal**	**Ordinal**
I, i	**ūnus, -a, -um**	**prīmus, -a, -um**
II, ii	**duo, duae, duo**	secundus
III, iii	**trēs, tria**	tertius
IV, iv *or* IIII	**quattuor**	**quārtus**
V, v	**quinque**	**quīntus**
VI, vi	**sex**	sextus
VII, vii	**septem**	septimus
VIII, viii	**octō**	**octāvus**
IX, ix *or* VIIII	**novem**	**nōnus**
X, x	**decem**	decimus

Magister: The only cardinal numbers that have case forms are *ūnus, duo, trēs,* and *mīlle. Mīlle* means "a thousand." The declensions of these four numbers are irregular. The forms are given in Chapter 19. (You can find a more complete listing of the numbers in Appendix B.)

All the ordinal numbers are regular first-second declension adjectives. In this list the three gender forms are shown only for *prīmus* (to save space). Notice that when *decem* is part of another word, the spelling changes to *decim.* Watch for other spelling adjustments in combined forms.

Flora: *September, October, November,* and *December* must be made from the numbers seven through ten. But that doesn't make sense! December isn't the tenth month, and September isn't the seventh month.

Magister: The earliest Roman calendar was lunar; that is, it was ten months long and based on the changes of the moon. It is called the *lunar* calendar, named for the word *luna, -ae, f.,* meaning "moon." March was the first month. January and February were added to make the calendar fit the seasons. After centuries of confusion, Julius Caesar, with the help of an Egyptian astronomer, changed the Roman calendar from lunar to solar. The *solar* calendar is named for *sol, solis, m.,* meaning "sun." He made January the first month. This seemed appropriate because **Janus** was the god of beginnings, a god that had two faces—one looking back and one looking forward into the new year.

To honor Caesar for these changes, the senate changed the fifth month, Quintilis, to July. Later Augustus Caesar made some minor improvements in the calendar; and at his request, the sixth month, Sextilis, was named August.

Now to answer your question, the names of the seventh through the tenth months were kept in spite of their erroneous meanings.

Julia: Where did the names for the other months come from?

Magister: As I mentioned, *January* was named for Janus. Statues of him were at the gates of cities, looking into and out of the cities.

February is from a religious festival which was first celebrated by the Sabines.

March is from **Mars,** the Roman god of war. You may recall that in Roman mythology he was the father of Romulus, who was the founder of Rome.

April may come from the verb *aperiō, -īre,* which means "to open." It is the month when buds and blossoms begin to open. Not all authorities agree about the origin of the word.

May was named for **Maia,** one of Jupiter's many wives.

June was named in honor of the goddess **Juno,** queen of the gods, wife of Jupiter, and goddess of weddings. Hence, June is considered the month of weddings.

July, again, honors Julius Caesar.

August honors Augustus Caesar.

Mark: What about the days of the week? Do they come from Latin?

Magister: Only *Saturday,* which was named for the god **Saturn,** one of the earliest gods worshiped in Italy. Beginning on December 17, the Romans held **Saturnalia,** which was a seven-day festival. Customs of that festival influenced early Christians in their celebration of Christmas. One of the Saturnalia customs was gift giving.

Sunday is named for the sun, *Monday* for the moon; the rest of the days are named for Norse (Germanic) gods.

Roman Calendar

The Roman lunar calendar began during the kingdom years. It had ten months of 30 or 31 days. This calendar caused many problems. The change to a solar calendar that was made by Julius Caesar in about 46 B.C. set the length of the calendar year at 365.25 days and established a leap year by adding one day to February every fourth year. This calendar lost 11 minutes a year, or 187 hours every 1,000 years.

In A.D. 1582, the Gregorian calendar corrected the Julian calendar so that it loses only 8 hours every 1,000 years. Most of the world has now adopted the Gregorian calendar.

Magister: Activity I gives you practice with a few of the ordinal and cardinal numbers. Use the number chart as you make your choices. This will help you remember the distinction between the two kinds of numbers.

Activity I

Derivatives

Magister: Activities J and K can increase both your Latin and your English vocabulary as you learn some new English words related to Latin words you are working with.

Activities J, K

Essential Information

Grammar terms

tenses in present verb system: present, imperfect, future

tenses in perfect verb system: present perfect (perfect), past perfect, future perfect

verb stems: second principal part (present system), third principal part (perfect system)

inflections for present perfect tense

four principal parts

interrogative pronoun

History and geography terms

Phoenicians (Poenī)

Sicily, Carthage, Tyre, North Africa

Punic wars, First Punic War, mercenaries

Roman deities: Janus, Mars, Maia, Juno, Saturn

Roman festival: Saturnalia

Dates

First Punic War, 264-241 B.C.

Inflections

Present perfect tense: *-ī, -istī, -it; -imus, -istis, -ērunt*

Past perfect tense: *-m, -s, -t; -mus, -tis, -nt*

Future perfect tense: *-ō, -s, -t; -mus, -tis, -nt*

Tense signs

Present perfect tense: none

Past perfect tense: **erā**

Future perfect tense: **eri**

Pronoun forms

Interrogative pronoun. See pages 256 and 257 for forms and translations.

Numbers

Roman numerals, cardinal numbers, ordinal numbers. See page 259.

Calendar names

Names of the months

Saturday from Saturn

Vocabulary

(1) Review the meanings of the verbs listed on pages 254 and 255. Use the Vocābulārium when necessary. (2) Begin a systematic plan for learning the principal parts of these verbs: practice saying the principal parts of a group each day. Be sure that you know the principal parts of each verb when you use it.

You are responsible for the words in the list on page 248 and for the ordinal and cardinal numbers *1-10* on page 259.

Learn the new words listed below. Some of them are used in Activity D.

Nouns	**Adverb**
luna, -ae, *f.,* moon	**prius,** before
mensis, -is, *m.,* month	**Verb**
Poenī, -ōrum, *m., pl.,* the Carthaginians	**abeō, -īre, -iī, -itus, -a, -um,** to go away, leave
sol, solis, *m.,* sun	**Preposition**
Adjective	**inter,** between, among
malus, -a, -um, bad, evil	

CAPITULUM XIX

The Second Punic War was long and hard. In this chapter you will meet Hannibal, Hamilcar, two Scipios (father and son), and other generals.

We will discuss the passive voice of verbs, which should not be difficult since you have learned the whole verb structure in the active voice.

Only four Latin names for numbers can be declined. Learning these declensions will lead you to the meanings of many derivatives that come from them.

You will learn the relative pronoun forms. This pronoun opens the door to more interesting sentences—complex sentences with adjective clauses.

THE SECOND PUNIC WAR

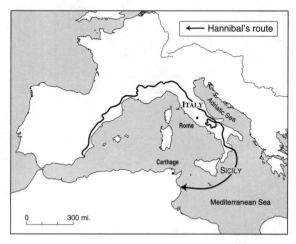

← Hannibal's route

Bellum Secundum Pūnicum

Magister: The First Punic War lasted twenty-three years. Interestingly, it was twenty-three years between the end of that first war and the beginning of the **Second Punic War,** which lasted seventeen years (**218-201** B.C.).

The military leaders on both sides of that war are fascinating character studies. Here are brief introductions to a few of those leaders. First read the sentences aloud. Think in Latin about the meaning of each sentence and then answer the question in Latin.

Hannibal in Siciliā prīmō vīvēbat. Pater Hannibalis erat **Hamilcar,** dux clārus Carthāginiēnsis.

Quis erat fīlius Hamilcaris?

Paul: Hannibal erat fīlius Hamilcaris.

Magister: Eratne Hannibal Rōmānus aut Poenus?

Lydia: Hannibal erat Poenus.

Magister: **Hasdrubal** erat frāter Hannibalis. Quoque erat dux in Secundō Punicō Bellō.

Quī erant trēs ducēs Poenī in Secundō Punicō Bellō?

Victor: Hamilcar, Hannibal, et Hasdrubal erant trēs ducēs in Secundō Punicō Bellō.

Magister: **Scīpio** fīlium habēbat. Nōmen fīlī quoque erat Scīpio. Pater et fīlius erant ducēs clārī Rōmānī.

Quis erat fīlius Scīpiōnis?

Flora: Scīpio erat fīlius Scīpiōnis.

Magister: **Quintus Fabius** erat dux Romānus et tum dictātor. Contrā mīlitēs Carthāginiēnsēs in Ītaliā pugnābat. Ubi° Quintus Fabius contrā Poenōs pugnābat?

[°where]

Rex: In Ītaliā contrā eōs pugnābat.

Two Scipios

Scipio the father is known as Scipio Maior (Scipio the Elder). Scipio the son is called Scipio Minor (Scipio the Younger). Scipio Maior was called Scipio Africanus after he defeated the Carthaginians in Africa.

Four Hasdrubals

There were four famous Carthaginian generals with the name Hasdrubal in the Punic Wars. One was Hannibal's brother, and another was his brother-in-law. One was the cavalry commander in the battle at Cannae. The fourth was forced to surrender the city of Carthage at the end of the Third Punic War.

Magister: Hannibal was born in Sicily toward the end of the First Punic War. His father instilled in him a hatred for the Romans. When the lad was nine years old, Hamilcar took him to a statue of the god Baal and had him take an oath of eternal hatred for the Romans. Throughout Hannibal's life he lived according to that oath.

Both Rome and Carthage were claiming power over the island of Sardinia and over a Greek colony in Spain. Both nations now had a strong army and navy.

Timothy: Who won the war?

Magister: I'll help you answer your question by asking you a question about Bible prophecy. Four world empires are prophesied in the book of Daniel, chapters 2 and 7. It is clear in Scripture that the first three empires described are Babylon, the Medes and Persians, and the Greeks. Do you know what the fourth one is?

Timothy: I think it's Rome.

Magister: That's right. If Rome had lost to Carthage, what nation would have been the dominant power that replaced the power of Greece in the Mediterranean region?

Timothy: Carthage.

Magister: Throughout the war, Carthage seemed to have the upper hand. But finally Rome won. We haven't time in class to talk about all that happened in the seventeen years that the two great powers fought each other. If you'd like to know more about it, look for articles in encyclopedias about Hannibal, Scipio, and Quintus Fabius. Books about ancient history also give interesting details about the war.

Here is a brief narration of the highlights of the war. First, I'll ask you to read the narration aloud in Latin. Try to think in Latin as you read. Then I'll ask you to translate the paragraphs into English.

Here are the new vocabulary words used in the paragraphs.

Compound verbs with *eō*

Nearly all verbs that end in *eō* are in the second conjugation. However, there is an unrelated irregular verb which means "to go". It is spelled *eō, īre, īvī/iī, itūrus, -a, -um*. Several other verbs are made by combining it with prefixes: *abeō, transeō, pereō, redeō*. The principal parts of these compound forms are the same as for *eō*. See Appendix A for the forms of *eō*.

Hannibal, -balis, *m.,* Carthaginian general in the Second Punic War

consilium, -iī/-ī, *n.,* plan, advice

invādō, -ere, -vāsī, -vāsus, -a, -um, to go in, enter; to attack; to seize

Scipiō Maior, -iōnis -ōris, *m.,* Scipio the Elder, Roman general in the Second Punic War

discō, -ere, didicī, to learn, know

contendō, -ere, -tendī, -tentus, -a, -um, to hasten

maior, maius, larger, greater; **Maior,** the Elder

transeō, -īre, -iī, -itus, -a, -um, to go over, cross, pass over

parātus, -a, -um, prepared

suus, -a, -um, his own, her own, its own, their own

fulmen, -minis, *n.,* a stroke of lightning, a thunderbolt

feriō, -īre, -īvī, -ītus, -a, -um, to strike, hit, smite

Scīpio Minor, -iōnis -ōris, *m.,* Scipio the Younger, Roman general in the Second Punic War

minor, minus, smaller, less; the younger

vulnus, -neris, *n.,* a wound

pereō, -īre, -iī/īvī, -itus, -a, -um, to go through, be lost, die, perish

tribus, -ūs, *f.,* a tribe

Cannae, -ārum, *f.,* an ancient city in southern Italy

auxilium, -iī/-ī, *n.,* help, aid

grandis, -e, great, grand, important

Capua, -ae, *f.,* a town in central Italy

revertō, -ere, -vertī, to turn back, return

Zama, -ae, *f.,* ancient town in northern Africa

dūcō, -ere, dūxī, ductus, -a, -um, to lead

fīnis, -is, *m., sometimes f.,* end; boundary

The Carthaginian and Roman generals, Hannibal and Scipio, meet before battle.

Locative Case

The locative case is used only for names of cities and for a very few common nouns such as *locī* for *locus,* "home." From the word *locative* we get the word *location*. The **locative case** is used to indicate where something is or where an event occurred. Since this case is used for a very small number of words, it is not included in declension listings.

The locative inflection for first-declension place names is *-ae* (*Rōmae,* "at Rome") for singular and *-īs* for plural forms (*Cannīs,* "at Cannae" because *Cannae* has only plural forms).

Distinguishing Possessive Forms

The pronoun genitive forms *eius, eōrum, eārum* are used to refer to someone other than the subject. To indicate in Latin that the owner of something is the same person as the subject, the adjective forms of *suus, -a, -um* are used. The adjective *suus, -a, -um* agrees in gender, number, and case with the noun it modifies, but it refers to the subject. To avoid misunderstanding, use "his own, her own," or "its own" to translate *suus, -a, -um. Hannibal fought his (eius [Scipio's]) exercitum. Hannibal took his (suum [his own]) exercitum to Carthage.*

Bellum Secundum Pūnicum

Hannibal magnum et fortem exercitum in Hispāniā habēbat. Consilium eius erat invadere Ītaliam. Ubi Scīpio Maior didicerat dē consiliō Hannibalis, cum exercitū Rōmānō ab Hispāniā ad Ītaliam contendit. Poteratne Hannibal transīre Alpēs cum magnō exercitū et trīgintā septem° elephantīs? Poterat transīre, sed iactūra virōrum et elephantōrum erat magna.

[°thirty-seven]

Rōmānī erant nōn parātī. Hannibal et mīlitēs suī et elephantī suī fuērunt similēs fulminī ubi eī ferivērunt. Scīpio Minor vītam patris suī servāvit, sed vulnus Scīpiōnis Maiōris erat grave. Tum Scīpio Minor contrā Hannibālem pugnābat. In proeliīs multī Rōmānī et multī Poenī periērunt.

Cannīs° duo exercitūs pugnāvērunt et Hannibal in grandī victōriā superāvit.

[°at Cannae]

Rōmānī Poenōs et trīgintā trēs° elephantōs eōrum (novōs ex Carthāgine) in proeliō Capuae° vīcērunt. Tum Hannibal ad Carthāginem cum exercitū suō revertit. Scīpiō Maior quoque ad Carthāginem exercitum suum dūxit. Zamae° in parte aquilōniā° Africae exercitus Scīpiōnis exercitum Hannabālis vīcit. Victōria Rōmāna Zamae fuit finis Secundī Punicī Bellī.

[°thirty-three, °at Capua, °at Zama, °northern]

Magister: You may look back at "Bellum Secundum Pūnicum" when necessary to answer the questions in Activity A. Before beginning Activity B, read very carefully the information (1) about the locative case and (2) about distinguishing possessive forms.

Activities A, B

Can you (1) name three military leaders on each side of the Second Punic War; (2) name the victor in the battle of **Cannae,** of **Capua,** and of **Zama**; and (3) tell how the war ended?

THE PASSIVE VOICE OF VERBS

Learning and Using Passive Verb Forms

Magister: You have worked with many transitive verbs, such as *adiuvāre,* "to help," and *condere,* "to build." You have also worked with some intransitive verbs, such as *exsultāre,* "to rejoice," and *resurgere,* "to rise again." How are the transitive verbs different from the intransitive verbs?

Julia: The transitive verbs have direct objects, but the intransitive verbs don't.

Magister: Verbs, like nouns, have **properties.** The verb properties that you have already worked with are person (first, second, and third), number (singular and plural), and tense (the six tenses). Another property is called **voice.** A transitive verb is in either the **active voice** or the **passive voice.** If the verb has a direct object, it is active. If the subject receives the action, the verb is passive. Compare the function of *many battles* in these two sentences.

The Romans fought many battles.

Many battles were fought by the Romans.

What is the voice of the verb in the first sentence?

Clara: It has a direct object, so it's active.

Magister: And what is the voice of the verb in the second sentence?

Clara: It must be passive because the subject receives the action.

Magister: Very good. When the subject is the *actor,* the verb is active. When the subject is the *receiver* of the action, the verb is passive. Now name the verb in each of those two sentences.

Mark: *Fought* and *were fought.*

Magister: English passive verbs always have an auxiliary—a form of the *be* verb. Compare the active and passive forms of the English verb *warn* in the three tenses.

Present Tense	
Active	**Passive**
I warn	I **am** warned.
You warn	You **are** warned.
He warns	He **is** warned.
We warn	We **are** warned.
You (pl.) warn	You (pl.) **are** warned.
They warn	They **are** warned.

Past Tense	
Active	**Passive**
I warned	I **was** warned.
You warned	You **were** warned.
He warned	He **was** warned.
We warned	We **were** warned.
You (pl.) warned	You (pl.) **were** warned.
They warned	They **were** warned.

Future Tense	
Active	**Passive**
I shall/will warn	I shall/will **be** warned.
You will warn	You will **be** warned.
He will warn	He will **be** warned.
We shall/will warn	We shall/will **be** warned.
You (pl.) will warn	You will **be** warned.
They will warn	They will **be** warned.

Julia: Why are there periods for all the passive forms but not for the active forms?

Magister: Read the active forms again. What do they lack?

Julia: Oh, I see. They don't have receivers of the action.

Magister: Unless the context makes clear who the receiver of action is, those in the active columns would not make good sentences.

Victor: What about this sentence: *I am warning him.* It has the auxiliary *am,* but it has a direct object.

Magister: To make the verb passive in English, we must use the third principal part. It is *warned,* not *warning.*

Here are both the active and the passive inflections for verbs in the present system. For the imperfect and future tenses, these inflections follow the tense signs.

Singular		Plural	
Active	**Passive**	**Active**	**Passive**
-ō/-m	-r	-mus	-mur
-s	-ris	-tis	-minī
-t	-tur	-nt	-ntur

Take time right now to memorize these inflections by spelling them. Then practice saying the passive verbs in the three present-system tenses. The forms marked with an asterisk illustrate these general rules.

- A macron is omitted before any final *r: laudor,* etc.
- The stem vowel in first-conjugation verbs and third-conjugation verbs that are not *i*-stems is omitted before *-or: laudor, dūcor.*
- A short *i* changes to a short *e* before the inflection *-ris: dūceris, caperis.*

Give special attention to the underlined vowels in the passive conjugations below, and notice where the corresponding vowels are missing or different in the other verb forms.

Stem Vowel or Tense Sign?

Remember that the long *e* (short before final *r* or *t,* or *nt,* whether it is final or not) is the stem vowel in second-conjugation verbs, but it is also the tense sign for the future tense in third-conjugation verbs.

monet, monētur; monent, monentur (present)

dūcet, dūcētur; dūcent, dūcentur (future)

Present Tense				
Singular				
First	**Second**	**Third**	**Third i-stem**	**Fourth**
laudor*	moneor*	dūcor*	capior*	audior*
laudāris	monēris	dūceris*	caperis*	audīris
laudātur	monētur	dūcitur	capitur	audītur
Plural				
laudāmur	monēmur	dūcimur	capimur	audīmur
laudāminī	monēminī	dūciminī	capiminī	audīminī
laudantur	monentur	dūcuntur	capiuntur	audiuntur

Imperfect Tense				
Singular				
First	**Second**	**Third**	**Third i-stem**	**Fourth**
laudā**bar**	monē**bar**	dūcē**bar**	capiē**bar**	audiē**bar**
laudā**bā***ris*	monē**bā***ris*	dūcē**bā***ris*	capiebā*ris*	audiebā*ris*
laudā**bā***tur*	monē**bā***tur*	dūcē**bā***tur*	capiē**bā***tur*	audiē**bā***tur*
Plural				
laudā**bā***mur*	monē**bā***mur*	dūcē**bā***mur*	capiē**bā***mur*	audiē**bā***mur*
laudā**bā***minī*	monē**bā***minī*	dūcē**bā***minī*	capiē**bā***minī*	audiē**bā***minī*
laudā**ba***ntur*	monē**ba***ntur*	dūcē**ba***ntur*	capiē**ba***ntur*	audiē**ba***ntur*

Future Tense				
Singular				
First	**Second**	**Third**	**Third i-stem**	**Fourth**
laudā**bor**	monē**bor**	dūc**ar**	capi**ar**	audi**ar**
laudā**beris***	monē**beris***	dūc**ēris**	capi**ēris**	audi**ēris**
laudā**bi***tur*	monē**bi***tur*	dūc**ē***tur*	capi**ē***tur*	audi**ē***tur*
Plural				
laudā**bi***mur*	monē**bi***mur*	dūc**ē***mur*	capi**ē***mur*	audi**ē***mur*
laudā**bi***minī*	monē**bi***minī*	duc**ē***minī*	capi**ē***minī*	audi**ē***minī*
laudā**bu***ntur*	monē**bu***ntur*	dūc**e***ntur*	capi**e***ntur*	audi**e***ntur*

Timothy: Are all those forms right? The present and the future of *dūcō* are the same in the second person singular.

Magister: They are correct. Look carefully and you will see a difference.

Timothy: Now I see. There's a macron in the future tense because the tense sign is a long *e*, and that *e* in the present is one of the rules you just gave us. But the Romans didn't use macrons; so how would they know the tense of a verb like this?

Magister: Only from the context.

Timothy: Now I see the answer to another problem. That rule of *i* changing to *e* before *-ris* explains why the future forms of *laudō* and *moneō* are *laudāberis* and *monēberis*.

Magister: Notice that every passive inflection ends with an *r* except the second-person plural. You will need to practice each verb in the three tenses. Say them aloud and write them. Remember, you learn Latin by hearing it, saying it, reading it, and writing it. In Activity C, you are asked to determine the tense of verbs that are in the passive voice. The translations of imperfect tense forms contain the word *being* because that is generally the preferable translation, although that auxiliary can be omitted in some contexts. Correct answers for Activity C require the recognition of stem vowels and tense signs in each tense of the four conjugations.

In Activity D you will write verbs in the present, imperfect, and future tenses. Remember that a macron, used or omitted, determines the tense of some verbs. Activity E calls for translations of sentences into English and into Latin. If you use the English-Latin Vocābulārium to find Latin words to use, take time to learn those words in order to save time later.

Activities C, D, E

Can you (1) say and write the passive inflections for the present, imperfect, and future tenses and (2) conjugate verbs in the passive voice of those three tenses?

MORE ABOUT NUMBERS

Magister: In Chapter 18 I told you that most of the cardinal numbers are indeclinable. Here are the declensions of the numbers that are declinable: *ūnus, duo, trēs* and *mīlle. Mīlle* means "one thousand." Obviously, *ūnus* has no plural forms, and *duō* and *trēs* have no singular forms. *Mīlle* has both singular and plural forms ("one thousand", "thousands").

The forms of *ūnus* are like any other first-second declension adjective except in the genitive and dative cases. The forms of *duo* and *trēs* are very irregular. The word **mīlle** changes its case forms only in the plural.

Declensions of Numbers					
M	F	N	M	F	N
ūnus	ūna	ūnum	duo	duae	duo
	ūnius		duōrum	duārum	duōbus
	ūnī		duōbus	duābus	duōrum
ūnum	ūnam	ūnum	duōs	duās	duo
ūnō	ūnā	ūnō	duōbus	duābus	duōbus

M/F	N	Singular	Plural
trēs	tria	mīlle	mīlia
trium		mīlle	mīlium
tribus		mīlle	mīlibus
trēs	tria	mīlle	mīlia
tribus		mīlle	mīlibus

Magister: Activity F calls for Latin translations of sentences containing the various forms of the four cardinal numbers that have case forms.

Appendix B contains a listing of many Roman numbers above the number ten: Roman numerals, cardinal numbers, and ordinal numbers.

Activity F

Can you give the case forms for *ūnus, duo, trēs,* and *mīlle?*

Ablative of Time When

In Latin, the time when something occurs is expressed in the ablative case without a preposition. It can be translated with or without a preposition. *In templō diē tertiā erat.* "He was in the temple on the third day. / He was in the temple the third day."

Magister: In Activity G you will practice with cardinal and ordinal numbers and the ablative of "time when." Activity H contains verses from the Vulgate. Each sentence contains either a cardinal or an ordinal number. After completing the activity, you may wish to read Acts 10-12 in your Bible to see the context of the passages in Acts that you translated.

Activities G, H

RELATIVE PRONOUN

Magister: In Chapter 18 you worked with the interrogative pronoun. Those forms are similar to the forms of the **relative pronoun.** It's called *relative* because it *relates* the clause it is in to a noun that the clause modifies. The modifying clause is called a **relative (adjective) clause.** Perhaps you're wondering what a **clause** is. It's a group of words having a subject and a predicate.

Independent and Dependent Clauses

Every sentence must have at least one independent clause, which contains a complete thought. A sentence may contain one or more dependent clauses. A dependent clause can modify some word in the independent clause. It cannot stand alone as a sentence. A relative clause is a dependent clause.

Hannibal, who was a Carthaginian general, was the son of Hamilcar.

Hannibal, quī erat dux Carthāginiēnsis, erat fīlius Hamilcaris.

The sentence you just read has two clauses. What is the independent clause?

Victor: "Hannibal was the son of Hamilcar."

Magister: Right. The remaining clause is dependent because it is not a sentence by itself. Since it describes the noun Hannibal, it's an adjective, or relative, clause.

Here are the forms of the relative pronoun.

Relative Pronoun			
Singular			
M	**F**	**N**	
quī	quae	quod	who/which/that
	cuius		whose/of whom/of which
	cui		to/for whom/which
quem	quam	quod	whom/which/that
quō	quā	quō	by, *etc.* whom/which
Plural			
M	**F**	**N**	
quī	quae	quae	who/which/that
quōrum	quārum	quōrum	whose/of whom/which
	quibus		to/for whom/which
quōs	quās	quae	whom/which/that
	quibus		by, *etc.*/whom/which

Victor: Would you explain how these forms are used in sentences?

Magister: The plural of this pronoun is just like the plural of the interrogative pronoun. You have to make two decisions. First, how is the pronoun used in its own clause? Is it the subject, the direct object, the indirect object, object of a preposition, or a possessive? No matter what function it has, it will nearly always be the first or second word in its clause. Use the right case to show its function.

Second, what is the gender and the number of its antecedent? Make it agree with its antecedent in gender and number.

Activities I and J provide practice with the relative pronouns. In Activity J you will review the events of the Second Punic War.

Activities I, J

Can you (1) write and say all the forms of the relative pronoun and (2) explain how relative pronouns are used in sentences?

Derivatives

Magister: To complete Activity K, you may refer to the verb list on pages 254 and 255 in Chapter 18. As you've seen in earlier chapters, words generally come from Latin into English according to patterns such as these:

> L verb L noun E noun.
> L verb LL adjective E adjective.

This activity does not show all the steps; instead, it shows just the Latin origin and the final English derivative.

Activity L asks you for the Latin origins of English derivatives. This will help you trace many familiar as well as unfamiliar English words back to their origins and help you understand their basic meanings.

Activities K, L

Common Latin Sayings

Magister: You will frequently find Latin phrases in your reading. In Activity M are some that are commonly used. Although you do not know all the words in these sayings, you can probably figure out their meanings from the choices in column 2.

Activity M

Essential Information

Grammar terms
- properties of verbs: voice
  active voice, passive voice
- stem vowel distinguished from tense sign
- locative case
- possessive forms *eius, suus*
- relative pronoun
- clauses: independent, dependent
  relative (adjective) clause
- ablative of time when
- irregular verb *eō*

History and geography terms

- Second Punic War
- Hannibal, Hamilcar, Hasdrubal
- Scipio Maior (Scipio Africanus), Scipio Minor, Quintus Fabius
- Cannae, Capua, Zama

Dates

- Second Punic War 218-201 B.C.

Inflections

- Passive voice inflections for verbs in the present-system tenses: *-r, -ris, -tur; -mur, -minī, -ntur*

Passive verb forms

- See pages 274 and 275 for verbs in the passive voice of the present, imperfect, and future tenses in the four conjugations.

Pronoun forms

- See page 279 for the forms of the relative pronoun.

Declensions of cardinal numbers

- See page 277 for the forms of *ūnus, duo,* trēs, and *mīlle.*

Vocabulary

Activity N

- You are responsible for the words in the list on pages 268 and 269, and for those in bold type in the list below.

Nouns

aquilo, -ōnis, *m.,* the north wind; the north

catēna, -ae, *f.,* chain, fetter; restraint

diēs, -diēī, *m.,* day, as opposed to night; *f.,* a particular day

domus, -ūs, *f.,* a house, a home

hōra, -ae, *f.,* hour

odium, -iī/-ī, *n.,* hatred

trīginta septem, thirty-seven

trīginta trēs, thirty-three

Verbs

eō, īre, īvī/iī, itūrus, -a, -um, to go

laudō (1), to praise

ministrō (1), to serve, to wait upon

quaerō, -ere, quaesīvī/iī, -sītus, -a, -um, to seek

suscitō (1), to make to rise

Adverbs

ecce, behold! look!

quasi, approximately, about

sicut, even as, as

Prepositions

circa, *with acc.,* about, around

apud, *with acc.,* at, near, with, before, in the presence of

CAPITULUM XX

The third and final Punic War ends with Rome in control of the Mediterranean area. Find out what happened to her enemy, Carthage.

In this chapter you will learn the passive voice in the perfect system. This is one of the easiest things to learn in Latin, and it is similar to the same tenses in English.

You will also learn two special uses of the ablative case and the interrogative adjective as distinguished from the relative pronoun and the interrogative pronoun.

THE THIRD PUNIC WAR

Magister: We are covering only the highlights of Roman history. Concerning the Punic Wars, the chapters include

- the countries that fought
- when, where, and why they fought
- some important generals
- the outcome of the wars.

The historical accounts of the three Punic Wars show us something about the character of some Roman military leaders. One remarkable general in the First Punic War was **Regulus.** About a century after the end of the First Punic War, the Roman orator Cicero and the poet Horace wrote of a difficult decision that Regulus made. He was captured by the Carthaginians and was allowed to return to Rome. Some historians state that he was allowed to return on condition that he persuade the senate to release the captured Carthaginian generals. According to other historians, he was to persuade the Roman senate to stop the war. In any case, he agreed that if he did not persuade the senate, he would return to Carthage and accept a cruel death. He did return to Rome, but he persuaded the senate *not* to release the captured generals or, according to some historians, *not* to stop the war. Then, true to his agreement, he returned to Carthage and accepted a very cruel death.

Regulus leaving Rome for Carthage during the First Punic War

Paul: Why would anyone do that?

Magister: If this narrative is true, we see that even among pagan Romans there was a man with a sense of honor that led him not only to die for his country but also to keep his word even to the enemy.

Paul: Did Carthage or Rome start the Third Punic War? I can't see why Carthage would start another war after Rome had defeated them twice.

Magister: Before answering your question, I need to mention that after the Second Punic War, Rome had gained dominance in the eastern Mediterranean area. She had conquered a vast territory including **Macedonia,** formerly conquered by the Macedonian general **Philip V** and the Greek general **Alexander the Great.**

The short, decisive Third Punic War was fought because some Romans, especially a senator named **Cato,** convinced the Roman senate that Carthage remained a serious threat to Rome's safety. Rome's victory in the final Punic War gave her dominance throughout the Mediterranean area.

Paul: How did the Third Punic War get started?

Magister: Let's read about it in Latin. This narrative contains more than the usual number of new words. However, the context and familiar derivatives should enable you to figure out the meanings of several of them without referring to the list. The context and derivatives will make it easier for you to remember the meanings. As usual, the words are listed in the order in which they occur in the paragraphs.

dum, *conj.,* while

crescō, -ere, crēvī, crētus, -a, -um, to increase

vīs, *f., irregular noun,* strength, force, power

iterum, *adv.,* again

mercātus, -ūs, *m.,* trade, business

validus, -a, -um, strong, powerful

clam, *adv.,* secretly

armō (1), to arm, equip for war

nāvis, -is, *f.,* a ship

ad, *prep. with acc.,* (to express purpose), for

pactiō, -iōnis, *f.,* a treaty, agreement

prōmissiō, -iōnis, *f.,* a promise

lēgātus, -ī, *m.,* a delegate, deputy

mittō, -ere, mīsī, missus, -a, -um, to send

ratiō, -iōnis, *f.,* reason

insolēns, -entis, rude, ill-mannered

adversus or **adversum,** *prep. with acc.,* towards, against

dēnuntiō (1), to declare [war]

statim, at once, immediately

dedō, -ere, dedidī, deditus, -a, -um, to give up, surrender

arma, -ōrum, *n. pl.,* weapons, arms

postulō (1), to demand, require

circumclūdō, -ere, -clūsī, -clūsus, -a, -um, to surround, shut in

flamma, -ae, *f.,* flame

superbus, -a, -um, proud, haughty

The Irregular Noun *vīs*

This very irregular noun will cause translation problems unless you distinguish it from *vir, virī,* meaning "man." This word means "strength, force, power." We have borrowed the accusative singular form. The phrase "vim, vigor, and vitality" should help you remember its meaning. The plural form is easily confused with *vir* unless you remember that *vir* is second declension and *virēs* is the plural of an irregular third-declension noun.

vīs	virēs		vir	virī
—	virium		virī	virōrum
—	viribus		virō	virīs
vim	virēs		virum	virōs
vī	viribus		virō	virīs

Vīs, virēs lacks genitive and dative singular forms.

Magister: Let's read the paragraphs aloud. Try to follow the narrative as you read.

Bellum Tertium Punicum

Dum Rōma contrā Macedoniam pugnābat, Carthāgō in vī crescēbat. Iterum Carthāgō mercātum validum in marī habēbat. Clam Carthāgō navēs armābat. Post Secundum Punicum Bellum, Carthāgō pactiōnem cum Rōmā fēcerat. In pactiōne Carthāgō promissiōnem nōn navēs armāre iterum fēcerat.

Cato, senātor Rōmānus, in ōrātiōne omnī dīcēbat, "Carthāgō delenda est."° Rōma lēgātōs ad Carthāginem mīsit. Rātiō erat loquī° dē pactione et dē navibus Carthāginiensibus. Poenī erant insolentēs adversus legātōs Rōmānōs.

[°"Carthage must be destroyed." °to talk]

Igitur senātus Rōmānus bellum contrā Carthāginem dēnuntiāvit. Statim Poenī Rōmānīs sē° dedidērunt. Rōmānī omnia arma Poenōrum postulāvērunt. Poenī multa arma dedidērunt, sed urbem nōn excēssērunt° ubi Rōmāni eīs mandātum dedērunt. Tum mīlitēs Rōmānī circumclūsērunt Carthāginem. Hasdrubal urbem dēfendēbat sed mox urbs erat in flammīs. Uxor et līberī° Hasdrubalis in flammīs periērunt. Urbs superba dēstructa est.° Post ignem° Rōmānī urbem sale° contexērunt.°

[°themselves, °leave, °children, °was destroyed, °fire, °with salt, °covered]

Magister: For these questions, some answers can be brief: for example, *Ita vērē* or *Nōn* plus the verb. Other answers require complete sentences. Let's begin.

Ubi Rōma post Secundum Punicum Bellum pugnābat?

Clara: In Macedoniā.

Magister: Habēbātne Carthāgō iterum mercātum validum in marī?

Gloria: Ita vērē.

Magister: Poenīne clam condēbant navēs ad bellum?

Mark: Ita vērē.

Magister: Fēcerantne Poenī promissiōnem nōn navēs armāre ad bellum iterum?

Timothy: Ita vērē.

Magister: Quis dīcēbat iterum et iterum "Carthāgō delenda est"?

Sylvia: Cato, senātor Rōmānus.

Magister: Erantne Poenī amīcī legātīs Rōmānīs?

Clement: Nōn amīcī erant. / Poenī erant nōn amīcī legātīs Rōmānīs.

Magister: Pugnābantne Poenī contrā Rōmānōs?

Paul: Nōn pugnābant. / Poenī sē Rōmānīs dedidērunt.

Magister: Quī Carthāginem circumclusērunt, Poenī aut Rōmānī?

Lydia: Rōmānī.

Magister: Quis Carthāginem dēfendit?

Julia: Hasdrubal/Poenī.

Roman soldiers storm the citadel of Carthage, the Byrsa.

Magister: Quae Carthāginem dēstruxērunt°? [°destroyed]

Flora: Flammae.

Magister: Now let's translate the three paragraphs that you've just read.

Based on our discussion of the Third Punic War and on what you have just translated, you should be ready to complete the sentences in Activity A. Then translate the sentences in Activity B.

Activities A, B

Can you tell (1) why Regulus died a cruel death in the First Punic War, (2) what people Rome fought between the Second and Third Punic Wars, and (3) the means by which Rome destroyed Carthage in the Third Punic War?

THE PASSIVE VOICE: PERFECT VERB SYSTEM

Learning the Perfect Passive Forms

Magister: In Chapter 18 you saw that most Latin verbs have four principal parts. When used with an auxiliary, the fourth principal part forms the passive voice in the perfect tenses. In English the third principal part functions in the same way.

Carthage *has been conquered* by Rome. (*Has been conquered* is the present perfect tense, passive voice.)

The fourth principal part of a Latin verb and the third principal part of an English verb can also be used as an adjective.

The *conquered* city of Carthage was destroyed by fire. (*Conquered* is an adjective describing *city*. Compare its use with *was destroyed,* a passive verb.)

We will begin working with passive verb forms made with the fourth principal part of Latin verbs. In both Latin and English, the passive forms require a form of the auxiliary *be*. Here are the Latin conjugations in the passive voice of the three perfect tenses.

Passive Forms	
Present Perfect	
Singular	**Plural**
duc*tus, -a, -um sum*	duc*tī, -ae, -a sumus*
duc*tus, -a, -um es*	duc*tī, -ae, -a estis*
duc*tus, -a, -um est*	duc*tī, -ae, -a sunt*
Past Perfect	
duc*tus, -a, -um eram*	duc*tī, -ae, -a erāmus*
duc*tus, -a, -um erās*	duc*tī, -ae, -a erātis*
duc*tus, -a, -um erat*	duc*tī, -ae, -a erant*
Future Perfect	
duc*tus, -a, -um erō*	duc*tī, -ae, -a erimus*
duc*tus, -a, -um eris*	duc*tī, -ae, -a eritis*
duc*tus, -a, -um erit*	duc*tī, -ae, -a erunt*

Victor: Would you please explain why there are different adjective inflections?

Magister: Yes. Since the fourth principal part is an adjective, it has to agree with the subject in gender and number. Since the subject is always in the nominative case, this adjective will always be nominative singular or plural. If Clara is speaking, she says, "Ducta sum." If she is speaking for herself and Lydia, she says, "Ductae sumus." Mark, what inflections would you use to speak for yourself, and how would you change it to include another boy?

Mark: "Ductus sum." For the plural I'd say, "Ductī sumus."

Magister: Good. You made the right gender and number choices.

Learning to Translate Verbs in the Perfect System

Julia: How do we translate these verbs?

Magister: Let's begin with a review of the translations of the verb forms you've worked with so far. To save time, we'll take just the third person singular in all the tenses and compare the active and passive translations. This shortened list of only third person singular is called a **synopsis.** To make a synopsis, any person and number can be used.

Bold type is used for the auxiliaries in the passive forms. Notice that the only Latin auxiliaries are forms of the *be* word, but the English translations have other auxiliaries as well. From the synopsis you can probably figure out the Latin forms for the other persons and numbers. If not, check the verb section in Appendix A.

Present System		
	Active	**Passive**
Present	dūcit, *he leads, he is leading, he does lead*	dūcitur, *he **is** led, he **is** **being** led*
Imperfect	dūcēbat, *he led, he was leading, he did lead*	dūcēbātur, *he **was** led, he **was being** led*
Future	dūcet, *he will lead, he will be leading*	dūcētur, *he will **be** led, he will **be being** led*

Perfect System		
	Active	**Passive**
Pres. Perf.	dūxit, *he has led, he led, he did lead*	ductus **est**, *he has **been** led, he **was** led*
Past Perf.	dūxerat, *he had led*	ductus **erat**, *he had **been** led*
Fut. Perf.	dūxerit, *he will have led*	ductus **erit**, *he will have **been** led*

Magister: Look at the passives in the perfect system. Where are the auxiliaries in the Latin verbs—before or after the principal part?

Sylvia: After it. But in the English verbs the auxiliaries come before the principal part. The English verbs have more auxiliaries than Latin verbs have.

Magister: Good observations. In English we can express more shades of verb meanings by using auxiliaries: for example, "is leading" shows progressive action and "does lead" makes the verb emphatic. And notice that forms of *have* are frequently used in English but never in Latin.

English is more limited in word order. We would never put an auxiliary after the main verb. In Latin the auxiliary usually follows the main verb, but it can precede it.

Rex: Would you please explain more about the voice of verbs?

Magister: Yes, but first, let's review the other properties. Can you name what's included under the headings of number, tense, and person?

Clement: Number is singular and plural. The six tenses are listed in the synopsis of *dūcō* forms. Person is first, second, or third—what we use when we conjugate.

Magister: Very good. Who is the subject for each person?

Clement: For first person the speaker is *I* or *we*. For second person the subject is *you*. For third person the subject is *he, she, it, they,* or any noun.

Magister: Now concerning voice, it is a property of transitive verbs. A transitive verb is active if it has a direct object. It is passive if the action of the verb is received by the subject.

In Activity C you will translate short sentences into English. Most of the verbs have third-person subjects, so note carefully the few with first- and second-person verbs. Activity D has eight pairs of sentences in which the first is active and the second is passive. You are to determine the receiver of action in each sentence. In Activity E you are to identify each verb and to give its four properties; then you will translate each sentence. These sentences are quoted from famous Roman writers; some are simplified to make them easier for you to read. Activity F asks you to translate some verses from the Vulgate version of the Gospels. In number 5 commas have been added in order to make some word functions clear.

Activities C, D, E, F

Paul: In these activities I noticed that whenever the verb is passive the sentence usually doesn't tell who did the action.

Magister: I selected sentences that do not state who the actors are. In some of the sentences, the identity of the actor is clear from the context; in others the actor is unknown or unimportant. In such sentences the passive voice is appropriate. Good writers, both Latin and English, avoid excessive use of the passive voice.

Julia: How do we show who the actor is with a passive verb, since the subject is the receiver of the action?

Magister: In English, we use a prepositional phrase: "The victory was won *by the Romans*." In Latin we use the ablative case, sometimes with a preposition and sometimes without, as you will see in the next section.

Can you (1) conjugate verbs in the passive voice in any tense, (2) use the correct adjective inflections in sentences for passive verbs in the perfect tenses, (3) translate verbs in both the active and passive voice of any tense, and (4) state the function of the receiver of action when the verb is passive?

~~~ OF AGENT AND ~~VE OF MEANS

Two Functions of the Ablative

Magister: If the actor is a person, a group of persons (such as a country or an army), or something acting as a person, we use the **ablative of agent.** The ablative of agent is a prepositional phrase containing *ā/ab* and the name of the actor in the ablative case. In these phrases the preposition *ā/ab* means "by." In other prepositional phrases beginning with *ā/ab,* this preposition means "from, away from," as you have already seen.

Here is the second part of the first four sentences in Activity D with the name of the actor(s) added in ablative of means phrases.

1b Nāvēs ā Carthāgine armātae sunt.
2b Prōmissiō ā Carthāgine facta erat.
3b Lēgātī ā Rōmā mīsī sunt.
4b Bellum ā senātū Rōmānō dēnuntiātum est.

In number 3b the phrase *ā Rōmā* could be translated "from Rome." However, the context in the second paragraph makes clear that Rome is the actor. Because the active voice has been changed to passive, *Rōmā* has become the ablative of agent (a city acting as a person). Activity G is based on the last four sentence pairs in Activity D. You are asked to supply the ablative of agent phrases in sentences 5b-8b. Sentences 5a-8a provide the name(s) of the actor(s).

Activity G

Magister: One important fact about the Third Punic War was omitted from Activities D and E. How was Carthage destroyed?

Flora: By flames.

Magister: How did the wife and children of Hasdrubal die?

Clara: By flames.

Magister: That fact leads me to explain the **ablative of means.** When the actor is a thing, not a person, the ablative case is used with *no* preposition. Incidentally, in very old Latin books the ablative of means is called the instrumental case. Here is an example.

I write with a pencil. Stilō scrībō.

From the final paragraph about the Third Punic War, can you find another example? It is the means by which "Urbs superba dēstructa est."

Paul: Flammīs.

Magister: You've had eight examples of ablative of agent and only two of ablative of means. Even one example can be as good as eight. Try to remember this vivid example.

In Activity H you are asked to translate English sentences into Latin. You must decide whether to use the ablative of means or the ablative of agent for each prepositional phrase.

Activity H

Can you use correctly the ablative of agent and the ablative of means in Latin sentences?

INTERROGATIVE ADJECTIVE

Distinguishing Interrogative Adjectives, Interrogative Pronouns, and Relative Pronouns

Magister: Remember the relative pronoun from Chapter 19? The very same forms can be used as **interrogative adjectives.** Those forms are identical in the plural with the interrogative pronouns.

Interrogative pronouns act alone in asking a question.

Translate these two sentences and tell how the interrogative pronoun is used in each.

<u>Quis</u> erat Scīpio? <u>Quem</u> Scīpio pugnābat?

Julia: "Who was Scipio? Whom did Scipio fight?" *Quis* is the subject, and *quem* is the direct object.

Magister: Right. A relative pronoun is used in a clause that describes a noun.

- *Scīpio, <u>quī</u> erat dux Rōmānus, contrā Hannibalem pugnābat.*
- *Hannibal, pater <u>cuius</u> erat Hamilcar, contrā Scīpiōnem pugnābat.*

Each of the sentences I just said has two clauses: one independent clause and one dependent clause. In the first sentence the independent clause is *Scīpio contrā Hannibalem pugnābat.* That's the main idea of the sentence. The clause *quī erat dux Rōmānus* describes *Scīpio.* It's a dependent clause. To distinguish it from other kinds of dependent clauses, we can call it by its more specific name, **relative (or adjective) clause,** which you read about in Chapter 19.

The interrogative adjective has the same form as the relative pronoun. When it modifies a noun, it asks a question. Try translating this question.

In <u>quō</u> bellō mīlitēs Rōmānī Carthāginem dēstruxērunt?

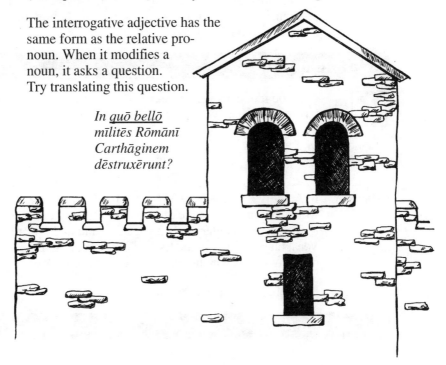

Arx Rōmāna

Rex: "In what war did the Roman soldiers destroy Carthage?" If the forms of interrogative adjectives and relative pronouns are the same, how can we tell these apart in sentences?

Magister: I think you can answer your own question. In the sentence you translated, does *quō* modify a noun?

Rex: Yes. Then it must be an adjective.

Magister: Does it help to ask a question?

Rex: Yes. Oh, I see. If it's forming a question and it's an adjective, it must be an interrogative adjective.

Magister: Activity I gives you practice with interrogative adjectives.

Activity I

Magister: Let's practice again the forms on page 279, remembering that those forms can be either relative pronouns or interrogative adjectives. The sentences in Activity J, quoted from Roman writers, contain interrogative pronouns, interrogative adjectives, and relative pronouns. Remember that all adjectives, including interrogative adjectives, modify nouns.

Activity J

Can you identify in Latin sentences the interrogative pronoun, the interrogative adjective, and the relative pronoun?

Derivatives

Magister: In Activity K you are asked to give the English meaning of Latin words that are the source of some derivatives. If necessary, you may look at the vocabulary list on page 286 and at the words in the Vocabulary section in the Essential Information. Be sure to learn now any words which you find necessary to look up.

In number 1, the prefix *in-*, *im-* means "not."

Activity K

Borrowed Phrases

Magister: You will frequently meet Latin phrases, some of which are more common as abbreviations. From what you have learned this year, you should be able to understand many of these. Activity L contains a few of them.

Activity L

Essential Information

Grammar terms

- passive voice, perfect verb system
- synopsis of a verb
- ablative of agent, ablative of means
- interrogative pronoun, interrogative adjective, relative pronoun
- independent clause, dependent clause, relative/adjective clause

History terms

- Regulus, Hasdrubal
- Philip V, Alexander the Great
- Macedonia

Dates

- Third Punic War, 149-146 B.C.

Passive verb forms in the perfect verb system

- See page 290.

Translations of active and passive verbs in the perfect system

- See page 291.

Relative adjective

- The forms are identical with the forms of the relative pronoun. See page 279 for those forms.

Vocabulary

Activity M

- You are responsible for the words listed on page 286 and for those in bold type listed below.

Nouns

carmen, -minis, *n.,* a song, poem

cīvis, -is, *c.,* a citizen

cīvitās, -tātis, *f.,* city; citizenship, state

evangelium, -iī/-ī, *n.,* gospel

faciēs, -ēī, *f.,* face

ignis, -is, *m.,* fire

passer, -eris, *m.,* sparrow, small bird

probitās, -tātis, *f.,* honesty, up-rightness

sāl, salis, *m.,* salt

senex, senis, *c.,* an old man or woman

Adjective

altissimus, -a, -um, highest

Adverbs

ante, before

sīcut, even as

statim, at once, immediately

Verbs

contegō, -ere, -texī, -tectus, -a, -um, to cover

dēstruō, -ere, -struxī, -struc-tus, -a, -um, to destroy

līberō (1), to set free

maneō, -ēre, mansī, mansus, -a, -um, to remain

mūtō (1), to change

nāvigō (1), to sail

vīvō, -ere, vīxī, vīctus, -a, -um, to live, be alive

LEGENDA V

Legenda

    Some pagan myths attempt to explain natural events. The following narrative is one such myth. Read the paragraphs in Latin without referring to the word list. Make reasonable guesses of the meanings of words you don't know. Then read the myth a second time and check the accuracy of your guesses by looking at the word list.

    New words are not included in the list if the context and the similarity to a common English derivative make the meaning obvious.

Cerēs, -eris, *f.,* goddess of grain, of growing things

Iuppiter, Iovis, *m.,* Jupiter, god of the heavens, highest of the Roman gods

frūmentum, -ī, *n.,* grain, growing things

Plūtō, -ōnis, *m.,* god of the lower regions

inferī, inferōrum, *m.,* the lower regions, the lower world

Proserpina, -ae, *f.,* daughter of Ceres and Jupiter, wife of Pluto, goddess of the underworld

mortuus, -a, -um, dead (here, pl., dead people)

aliquandō, *adv.,* once

alius, -a, -um, other, another

flōs, flōris, *m.,* flower

carpō, -ere, carpsī, carptus, -a, -um, to pick, pluck

carrus, -ī, *m.,* chariot, wagon

capiō, -ere, cēpī, captus, -a, -um, to take, snatch

dolor, -ōris, *m.,* sorrow, pain, anguish

quaerō, -ere, quaesīvī, quaesītus, -a, -um, to seek, search for

mandātum, -ī, *n.,* command, order, decree

remittō, -ere, -mīsī, -missus, -a, -um, to send back

nunc, *adv.,* now

rēgīna, -ae, *f.,* queen

annus, -ī, *m.,* year

Cerēs et Proserpina

Cerēs erat dea frūmentī. Fīlia Cereris erat **Proserpina.** **Plūto** erat frāter Iovis et **Neptūnī.** Plūto erat deus **inferōrum,** locus sub terrā ubi mortuī erant.

Aliquandō Proserpina, puella iuvenis, erat cum aliīs puellīs iuvenibus in Siciliā. Flōrēs carpēbat ubi Plūto vēnit ex inferīs in carrō. Proserpinam in carrum cēpit. Proserpina vocābat "Adiuvāte, adiuvāte!" Sed nēmo eam adiuvāvit. Plutō eam ad inferōs cēpit.

Cerēs, in dolōre, nōn agrōs et frūmentum cūrābat quod fīliam suam quaerēbat. Juppiter Plūtōnī mandātum dedit. Mandātum erat remittere Proserpinam, nunc rēgīna inferōrum, ad mātrem suam per partem annī cuiusque. Cerēs erat fēlix ubi Proserpina cum eā erat. Frūgēs iterum crēvērunt. Erat aestās. Sed posteā ubi Proserpina erat cum Plūtōne, per partem annī cuiusque, Ceres erat tristis. Frūgēs nōn crēvērunt. Erat hiems.

Dīcenda in Linguā Latīna

Your answers may be complete sentences or brief statements. If you answer briefly, the inflections should be the same as they would be in complete sentences. Give your answers orally or in writing, according to your teacher's directions.

1. Quis erat fīlia deae frūmentī?

2. Da nomina trium frātrōrum quī erant deī.

3. Ubi Proserpina habitābat?

4. Quis ex inferīs vēnit et Proserpinam ad inferōs cēpit?

5. Tum quis erat in dolōre?

6. In hāc fabulā, quae dea aestātem et hiemem fēcit?

7. Eratne aestās aut hiems ubi Proserpina erat in inferīs?

8. Erat Cerēs tristis aut fēlix in aestāte?

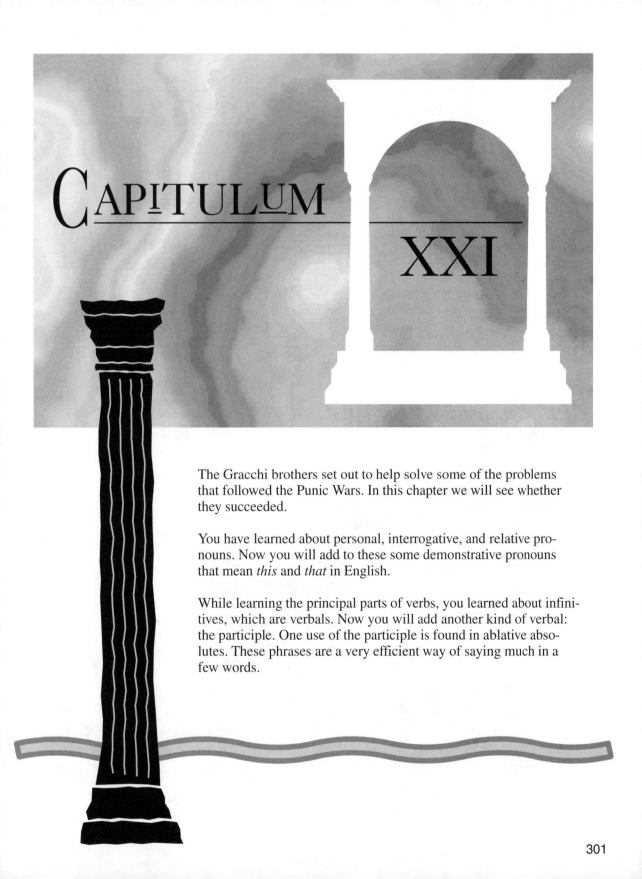

CAPITULUM XXI

The Gracchi brothers set out to help solve some of the problems that followed the Punic Wars. In this chapter we will see whether they succeeded.

You have learned about personal, interrogative, and relative pronouns. Now you will add to these some demonstrative pronouns that mean *this* and *that* in English.

While learning the principal parts of verbs, you learned about infinitives, which are verbals. Now you will add another kind of verbal: the participle. One use of the participle is found in ablative absolutes. These phrases are a very efficient way of saying much in a few words.

THE GRACCHI BROTHERS

Magister: After the Third Punic War and Rome's wars of expansion that followed, many veterans were discontent. They had suffered great losses, even losing their farms. Business men and public officials were buying the small farms and becoming rich as a result of Rome's expansion.

Mark: Where was Rome expanding?

Magister: In addition to Macedonia, Rome conquered most of the territory around the Mediterranean Sea, including **Syria** and **Egypt.** Much of this territory became Roman provinces.

Flora: What happened to the veterans who lost their farms?

A scene along the Appian Way

Magister: Many went to the city of Rome, hoping to make a living there. Two remarkable young men of a patrician family became greatly concerned about them and about other Romans who had no means of making a living. The two young men were the Gracchi brothers: **Tiberius** and **Gaius Gracchus.** Their mother was **Cornelia Gracchus,** the daughter of Scipio Africanus. What do you remember about the grandfather of these young men?

Clement: He defeated Hannibal in the Second Punic War.

Magister: Right! The father of the Gracchi brothers also belonged to a famous Roman family. One of his ancestors in the fourth century before Christ was **Appius Claudius.** He is famous because under his leadership a road 132 miles long was built from Rome to the seaport city of Capua. It is called *Via Appia,* the **Appian Way.** Parts of it are still used today.

Let's read more about these brothers. But first, read through the new words that you will find in the paragraphs. Afterwards, I will ask you to read the paragraphs aloud twice and to try to get the main idea by thinking in Latin. Then, translating the paragraphs should not be difficult.

appellō (1), to name, call

ēdūcō (1), to bring up, rear

praeclārus, -a, -um, remarkable, admirable, excellent

obeō, -īre, -īvī, -itus, -a, -um, to go away, to die

sum, esse, fuī, futūrus, -a, -um, to be

optō (1), to wish, desire

dīvēs, -itis, rich, wealthy

alius, -a, -um, other

pauper, -eris, poor, not wealthy

moveō, -ēre, mōvī, mōtus, -a, -um, to move

corrigō, -rigere, -rexī, -rectus, -a, -um, to correct, set right

iniustitia, -ae, *f.,* injustice

mūtātiō, -ionis, *f.,* a change

sectātor, -tōris, *m.,* follower

pugna, -ae, *f.,* fight, battle

iacio, -ere, iēcī, iactus, -a, -um, to throw, hurl

trecentī, three hundred

suffōcō (1), to choke, drown, suffocate

gūbernātiō, -iōnis, *f.,* government

et . . . et, *correlative conjunctions,* both . . . and

avārus, -a, -um, greedy

labor, -ōris, *m.,* labor, work

The consonant *i*

The letter *i* when used as a consonant gradually changed to the letter *j,* as you have seen in earlier chapters. This change took place during the Middle Ages. In ancient Roman times the *i* was a consonant when it came between two vowels or before a vowel at the beginning of a word. It was probably pronounced like *y.* A prefix does not affect the consonant pronunciation at the beginning of a word. *Iniustitia* is pronounced *inyustitia*

Correlative conjunctions

Correlative conjunctions act in pairs. In English the correlative pairs are *both . . . and, either . . . or, neither . . . nor,* and *not only . . . but also.* In each pair of Latin correlatives, the words are the same. The first pair is in the last paragraph below. Translate the first *et* "both" and the second *et* "and."

Gracchī Frātrēs

Tiberius et Gaius Gracchus appellābantur "gemmae° Cornēliae" quod mater sua eōs bene ēdūcāvit et eī erant virī iuvenēs praeclārī. Pater Gracchōrum frātrum obīverat ubi frātrēs erant puerī.

[°gems]

Familia Gracchōrum erat patricia. Pater Gracchōrum frātrum fuerat consul. Frātrēs adiuvāre omnēs virōs quī in bellīs pugnāverant optāvērunt. Dīvitēs familiae agrōs mīlitum et agrōs familiārum aliārum pauperum cēperant. Igitur multae familiae pauperēs ad urbem Rōmae mōverant. Gracchī frātrēs corrigere omnēs hās iniustitiās optāvērunt. Senātōrēs mūtātiōnēs nōn optāvērunt.

Tiberius Gracchus erat tribūnus patricius, nōn tribūnus plēbis. Sectātōrēs et inimīcōs habēbat. Dēnique erat pugna inter sectātōrēs suōs et inimīcōs suōs. Inimīcī suī eum in flūmen Tiberim iēcit et eum suffōcāvērunt. Quoque trecentōs (CCC) sectātōrum eius necāvērunt.

Similis frātrī suō, Gaius Gracchus erat dux praeclārus. Similis frātrī suō, Gaius erat tribūnus patricius quī facere mūtātiōnēs in gubernātiōne reī publicae Rōmānae optāvit. Ubi inimīcī contrā Gaium vēnērunt, "amīcī" suī fūgērunt. Gaius necātus est.

Quod et dīvitēs Rōmānī et pauperēs Rōmānī erant avārī, labōrēs Gracchōrum frātrum Rōmam nōn adiūvērunt.

Magister: Now translate the paragraphs into English. You may look at the list
of new words when necessary. When you finish translating, I will
ask you to memorize the new vocabulary.

Answering Questions about the Gracchi Brothers

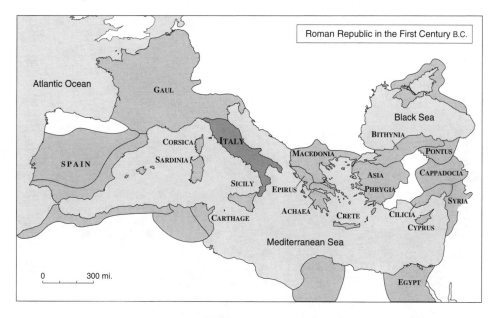

Magister: Take time to learn the new vocabulary words before you begin
Activity A.

You will find verbs in the imperfect, present perfect, and past perfect
tenses. If necessary, look back to Chapters 15 and 18-20 for the
forms and translations of those tenses in the active voice and the
passive voice.

Activity B reviews the information in *"Gracchī Frātrēs."* Try to
think in Latin to answer the questions.

The word *quod* has several different meanings. These include "because" when the word is a conjunction and
"which" or "that" when it is a neuter relative pronoun or a
neuter interrogative pronoun. You can tell from the context
how to translate this word.

Activities A, B

Can you (1) identify the members of the Gracchi family, (2) state the reason for the changes that the Gracchi brothers wanted to make, and (3) state the outcome and the reason for the outcome of their efforts?

An intersection of two Roman aqueducts

DEMONSTRATIVE PRONOUNS

Learning the Forms and Translations of Hic, Ille, *and* Iste

Magister: As you have probably noticed, pronouns do not belong to declensions. Each pronoun must be learned separately. However, there are similarities in the forms that make learning them easier.

In Chapter 1 you learned two demonstrative pronoun forms. *Hic est liber. Ille est liber.* What do *hic* and *ille* mean?

Lydia: "This" and "that."

Magister: *Hic* and *ille* are masculine nominative forms. Soon you will see other gender forms of these. But some cases will have the same form for all three genders. Think back to the declension of *quī, quae, quod.* Are the singular forms the same or different for the three genders in the genitive case and in the dative case?

Julia: They're the same.

Magister: Right. And that is true for *hic* and *ille.* What cases do you think will have identical forms in the plural?

Julia: The dative and the ablative.

Magister: That's true. Now think about the name of these two new pronouns. The word *demonstrative* is related to what English verb?

Paul: *Demonstrate.*

Magister: When we demonstrate, we point out something. Does *hic* point out something near or something far?

Lydia: Something near.

Magister: And *ille?*

Timothy: Something farther away.

Magister: Right. And *iste* means "that of yours" or "that near you." Often it suggests disapproval or contempt toward the person or thing being pointed out: "That thief [iste fūr] should be punished."

These three pronouns, like *is, ea, id* (introduced in Chapter 16), can be used as adjectives; so they are also called **demonstrative adjectives.** *Hic, ille,* and *iste* are strong, emphatic demonstratives. When the forms of *is, ea, id* are used as demonstrative pronouns, they are unemphatic. They may be translated either "this" or "that." If a demonstrative pronoun clearly modifies an understood noun, you may supply that noun when you translate, as illustrated beside the declensions of these pronouns.

The forms of *iste, ista, istud* are identical with those of *ille.*

Demonstrative Pronouns			
Singular			
hic	haec	hoc	this man, woman, thing; he, she, it
	huius		of this man, woman, thing; of him, her, it
	huic		to, for this man, woman, thing; to, for him, her, it
hunc	hanc	hoc	this man, woman, thing; him, her, it
hōc	hāc	hōc	by this man, woman, thing; by him, her, it
Plural			
hī	hae	haec	these men, women, things; these, they
hōrum	hārum	hōrum	of these men, women, things; of these, them
	hīs		to, for these men, women, things; to, for these, them
hōs	hās	haec	these men, women, things; them
	hīs		by these men, women, things; by them

Singular (Translate like *hic, haec, hoc,* but replace *this* with *that*.)			**Plural** (Translate like *hī, hae, haec,* but replace *these* with *those*.)		
ille	illa	illud	illī	illae	illa
	illius		illōrum	illārum	illōrum
	illī			illīs	
illum	illam	illud	illōs	illās	illa
illō	illā	illō		illīs	

Magister: Activity C provides practice with the demonstrative pronouns. Activities D and E contain various pronouns in verses from the Bible.

Activities C, D, E

Can you (1) give all the forms of *hic, ille, iste,* (2) translate the case forms of those pronouns into English, and (3) write the correct forms in Latin sentences?

Magister: We have worked with several kinds of pronouns. A review of some of these can help you to distinguish the different kinds. Activity F reviews demonstrative, interrogative, and relative pronouns.

Activity F

PARTICIPLES

Learning the Forms and Functions of Participles

Magister: **Participles** are verbals. In Chapter 16 you worked with another kind of verbal: the infinitive. You saw that **verbals** are verb forms but are not used as the main verbs in a sentence. The **main verbs** are called **predicate verbs.**

Verbals are verb forms used as another part of speech. Infinitives, as you saw, can function as nouns. They can *be* objects of verbs, and as verb forms they can *have* objects.

I want *to read.*
To read that book is easy.

Participles are adjectives; they often follow the noun they modify. They can *have* objects, but they cannot *be* objects.

A person *reading* the Bible finds truth there.

In Chapter 20 you saw **perfect passive participles** used with auxiliaries to form predicate verbs in the passive voice. Now you will work with them without auxiliaries, used as adjectives. This should not be difficult because we use them in the same way in English. Compare the participle in this English sentence with its Latin translation.

> The Gracchi brothers, *killed* by their enemies, were not able to help the Roman poor people.
>
> Gracchi frātrēs, *necātī* ab inimīcīs, adiuvāre Rōmānōs pauperēs nōn poterant.

What is the main verb in the sentence?

Gloria: *Poterant.*

Magister: What word means "killed"?

Gloria: Is it *necātī?*

Magister: Yes. Since *poterant* is the main verb, *necātī* can't be the main verb. It is a participle without an auxiliary. Then what part of speech is it?

Clara: It must be an adjective.

Magister: What noun does it modify?

Clara: *Frātrēs.*

Magister: Correct. The translation can be just "killed" or "having been killed." Think about these auxiliaries.

> (1) *Having* indicates the time of the main verb. The **time indicated by a perfect passive participle** is previous to the time of the main verb. The *-ing* ending shows that *having* is a participle.
>
> (2) *Been* indicates passive voice, showing that the word modified by the participle is the receiver of the action, not the actor.

Since the participle is a first-second declension adjective, it is declined like *longus, -a, -um*. It agrees with the noun it modifies (*frātrēs)* in gender, number, and case.

Another kind of participle is called the **present active participle.** Here is a sentence containing one.

> The Gracchi brothers, *seeing* the Roman poor people, wished to help them.
>
> Gracchī frātrēs, *videntēs* Rōmānōs pauperēs, eōs adiuvāre optāvērunt.

Like the perfect passive participle, it has no auxiliary in Latin.

(1) Every form contains the letters *ns* or *nt*. The English translation always ends in *-ing.*

(2) The main verb in the sentence about the Gracchi brothers is in the present perfect tense (past time); the participle is also speaking of past time, even though it is called a present participle. The **time indicated by present active participles** is the same as the time of the main verb.

What is the verb in the predicate of the sentence?

Clement: *Optāvērunt.*

Magister: Correct. Now find the participle that modifies *frātrēs* and tell us how you recognize it.

Clement: *Videntēs.* It's right next to *frātrēs,* and it looks something like the verb that means "see."

Magister: Very good. The participle in English is *"seeing."* Since the predicate verb shows past time, what time does *videntēs* show?

Mark: Past time.

Magister: Does *videntēs* show that the *frātrēs* are acting or receiving the action?

Rex: The brothers are seeing. That means *frātrēs* are acting, not receiving the action.

Magister: Right. To form a present active participle, we add *ns* to the present stem. The vowel before *ns* is long. Notice the slight variations in spelling in these examples from each conjugation.

> First: laudāre laudāns
> Second: vidēre vidēns
> Third: dīcere dīcēns
> Third: i-stem capere capiēns
> Fourth: audīre audiēns

After the nominative singular form, *ns* changes to *nt* for all the other forms, and a vowel before *nt* is always short. Present participles are easy to recognize if you remember that the word *present* contains *nt.*

The English translations of present participles always end in *-ing* or have auxiliaries that end in *-ing.*

You've seen that perfect passive participles are first-second declension adjectives: *scriptus, -a, -um,* "having been written."

Present active participles, on the other hand, are third-declension adjectives of the one-termination type: *scrībēns, -entis,* "writing." They are declined like *vetus,* gen., *veteris,* with a slight difference: they are i-stems. In the declension below, the *i*'s that distinguish i-stem adjectives are underlined.

Potēns is the present participle of the commonly used irregular verb *possum, posse, potuī.* It means "being powerful", or " powerful." The present stem has two spellings: *pos-* when the next letter is *s* (po**ss**um, po**ss**umus, po**ss**unt) and *pot-* when the next letter is *e* (po**t**es, po**t**est, po**t**estis). The present participle stem is *pot-.*

Present Participle					
Singular			Plural		
M	**F**	**N**	**M**	**F**	**N**
potēns	potēns	potēns	potentēs	potentēs	potent<u>i</u>a
	potentis			potent<u>i</u>um	
	potentī			potentibus	
potentem	potentem	potēns	potentēs	potentēs	potent<u>i</u>a
	potentī			potentibus	

Magister: Here is a simple comparison of the two kinds of participles you have seen so far.

Present Active	Perfect Passive
Form: (1) present stem plus *ns* or *nt* followed by the appropriate inflection after *nt* (2) no auxiliary Translation example: "leading"	Form: (1) fourth principle part of any transitive verb Translation example: "having been led"

Magister: In Activities G and H you will be working with both kinds of participles. The complete names are often shortened to *present participle* and *perfect participle.*

Activities G, H

Can you (1) recognize perfect passive and present active participles in Latin sentences, (2) decline those participles, and (3) translate Latin sentences containing those participles?

Our God is *omniscient, omnipotent,* and *omnipresent.* The Latin origins make clear the meanings of these words. *Omnis,* which means "all, every," combines with present participles to form adjectives that mean "all-knowing, all-powerful" and "every[where] present." *Present* comes from *prae+esse,* which means "to be before, to preside over." The English word *present* refers to something "existing or happening now."

Understanding and Using the Ablative Absolute

Magister: One of the most common uses of participles in Latin is in **ablative absolute phrases.** In English we have a parallel structure called the subjective (or nominative) absolute. Here is an example.

> The chapter having been completed, the students were ready for the test.

What is the main idea—that is, the independent clause—in this sample sentence?

Flora: "The students were ready for the test." And I see a participle. It's "having been completed."

Magister: Very good. What does the participle modify?

Flora: It modifies *chapter.* But what is *chapter* in the sentence?

Magister: A noun modified by the participle. The two words form a nominative absolute, sometimes called a subjective absolute. *The chapter having been completed* acts as a unit to modify the entire main clause. It's not related to any one word in the clause. In Latin the noun *chapter* and the participle *completed* would be in the ablative case. In both languages such phrases are *absolutely* independent grammatically from the rest of the sentence; therefore, they are called subjective or ablative *absolutes.* They add to the meaning of the whole sentence.

In Latin, the ablative absolute occurs very frequently; the English nominative absolute is less common. We often express the same ideas in adverb clauses or prepositional phrases. Therefore, to make English translations sound normal, you may choose to translate these phrases as if they were adverb clauses or prepositional phrases.

Compare the translations of this Latin sentence. The participle, as you can see, is perfect passive.

> Patriā victā, populus rēgem novum habēbat.
>
> The country having been conquered, the people had a new king.
>
> Because the country was conquered, the people had a new king.
>
> When the country was conquered, the people had a new king.
>
> After the conquering of the country, the people had a new king.

Notice that the translations show time *before* the time of the main verb.

Here is an example of the present active participle.

> Patriā rēgem novum habentī, populus nōn timēbant.
>
> The country having a new king, the people did not fear.
>
> Because the country had a new king, the people did not fear.
>
> When the country had a new king, the people did not fear.

The time of the present participles in the translations of ablative absolutes is the *same* as the time of the main verb.

If you had a context for these sample sentences, you would know what idea the ablative absolute is expressing: reason, time, or some other adverbial idea.

Ordinarily we should not change grammar structure when we translate. The ablative absolute is an exception. However, it is important that you know the literal meaning of an ablative absolute phrase before you translate it freely, as you will see in Activities I and J. Moreover, using English subjective absolutes is often a simple and effective way of speaking or writing. For example, "That done, we are ready to move to the next project."

> The participle for the *be* verb is omitted in ablative absolute phrases. The phrase *Augustō Caesāre prīmō imperātōre* is translated "Augustus Caesar *being* the first emperor."

Activities I, J

Can you (1) recognize ablative absolutes in Latin sentences and (2) translate them literally and then freely to express the idea suggested by the context?

Derivatives

Magister: Nearly all English derivatives from Latin verbs come from the second or the fourth principal part. In Activity K you will work with derivatives from the present participle, which is formed from the present infinitive (second principal part). Although spelling changes have occurred, you can identify participles from the second principal part because they contain the letter *n* from the *ns* or *nt* in the prese<u>nt</u> participle.

If necessary you may refer to the Vocābulārium. This would be a good time to review the principal parts and meanings of all these verbs. One of the words has a meaning very different from the meaning of the original Latin verb.

Activity K

Magister: In three Romance languages the demonstrative pronouns *illa* and *ille* were shortened and became articles. What gender do you think *la* is in Spanish, Italian, and French?

Clara: It's probably feminine.

Magister: You're right. The masculine form differs in those languages. In Spanish it is *el,* in Italian it is *il,* and in French it is *le.*

Loan Words

Magister: Have you noticed some loan words in this chapter?

Flora: Yes. *Extra* and *medium.*

Sylvia: Two more are *labor* and *pauper.*

Magister: Another one is an antonym for *pauper.* It's *Dives* (pronounced *dī'vēz*), which means "a very rich man."

Essential Information

Grammar terms

correlative conjunctions

demonstrative pronouns: *hic, ille, iste*

demonstrative adjectives: *hic, ille, iste*

predicate verb

verbals, participles, present active participle, perfect passive participle

verbals distinguished from predicate verbs

time indicated by present active and perfect passive participles

ablative absolute phrase

Spelling

consonant *i (j)*

History terms

Egypt, Syria

Gracchi: Tiberius Gracchus, Gaius Gracchus

Cornelia Gracchus

Appius Claudius

Appian Way

Pronoun declensions

See page 308.

Participle declension

See page 312.

Vocabulary

Activities L, M

You are responsible for the words listed on page 303. You are also responsible for the following words that are in bold type.

Nouns

dextra (*or* dextera), *f.*, the right hand

dolus, -ī, *m.*, deceit, guile

medium, -ī, *n.*, the middle, midst

mōns, montis, *m.*, mountain

vōx, vōcis, *f.*, voice

Adjective

maximus, -a, -um, very great

Adverbs

ergo, therefore

semper, always

Demonstrative Pronouns

hic, haec, hoc, this (man, woman, thing); he, she, it

ille, illa, illud, that (man, woman, thing); he, she, it

iste, ista, istud, that (man, woman, thing) near you, often expressing disapproval of the one indicated

Other Pronouns

quī, *interrog.*, who

quaecumque, *indef.*, whatsoever

Preposition

extrā, *with acc.*, outside

Verbs

adstō, -āre, -stitī, to stand, stand by

aperiō, -īre, -uī, -pertus, -a, -um, to open

conspiciō, -ere, -spexī, -spectus, -a, -um, to behold, perceive

ēiciō, -ere, iēcī, iectus, -a, -um, to throw out, cast out

exsiliō, -īre, -uī, to leap, leap up

exsurgō, -ere, -surrexī, to rise up

intrō (1), to enter

levō (1), to lift up

repleō, -ēre, -ēvī, -ētus, -a, -um, to fill, make full

Mythology terms in Legenda V

Ceres, Jupiter, Proserpina, Pluto, Neptune

New words in Legenda V

See the list there.

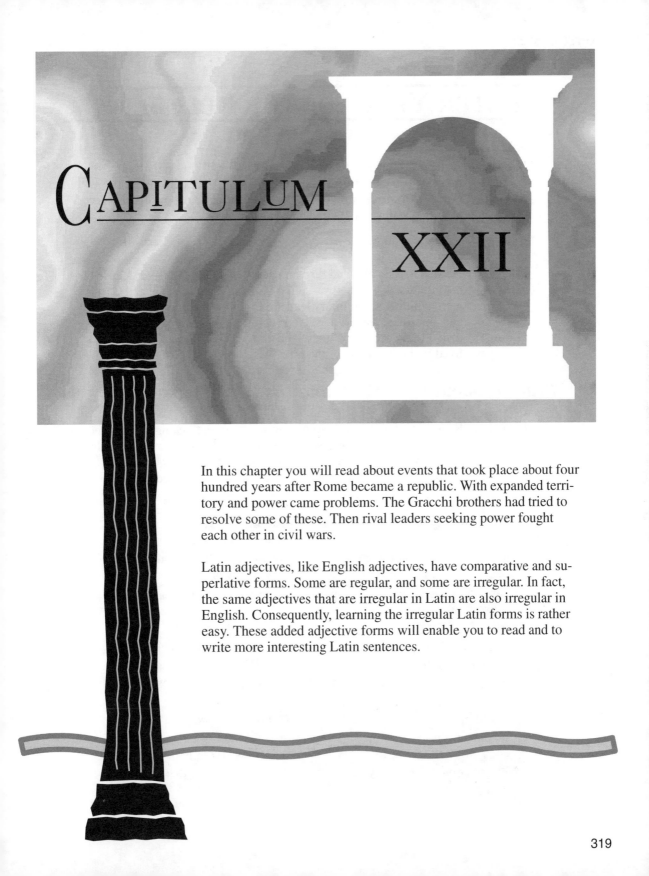

CAPITULUM XXII

In this chapter you will read about events that took place about four hundred years after Rome became a republic. With expanded territory and power came problems. The Gracchi brothers had tried to resolve some of these. Then rival leaders seeking power fought each other in civil wars.

Latin adjectives, like English adjectives, have comparative and superlative forms. Some are regular, and some are irregular. In fact, the same adjectives that are irregular in Latin are also irregular in English. Consequently, learning the irregular Latin forms is rather easy. These added adjective forms will enable you to read and to write more interesting Latin sentences.

LATER YEARS OF THE REPUBLIC

Magister: At the beginning of the first century before Christ, in the years 100 B.C. and 106 B.C., **Julius Caesar, Marcus Tullius Cicero,** and **Gnaeus Pompey** were born. This was about a quarter of a century after the deaths of the Gracchi brothers.

Timothy: I've heard of Caesar and Cicero, but who was Pompey?

Magister: He was first an ally and then an enemy of Julius Caesar. Because of his military power, he was called Pompey the Great. He and Caesar were political and military leaders. Cicero was famous as an orator and a political leader; he served for a time in Pompey's army. Let's read a Latin account of these and some other famous Romans who lived in the last years of the republic.

Reading about Civil Wars and the First Triumvirate

Magister: Read this brief historical account through twice, thinking in Latin and using the context to suggest the meanings of the new words. Read the paragraphs silently and learn the meanings of the new words. Loan words for which the meanings are obvious are not included in the list.

dēminūtiō, -ōnis, *f.,* decline, lessening

Marius, -iī/ī, *m.,* a military leader who was a rival of Sulla

conscrībō, -ere, -scrīpsī, -scrīptus, -a, -um, to enroll

stipendium, -iī/ī, *n.,* a soldier's pay

pro, *prep. with abl.,* as a reward for; in behalf of, for

Sulla, -ae, *m.,* a Roman general and dictator who fought against Marius

sē, *reflexive pronoun,* himself, herself, itself, themselves

cīvilis, -e, civil, relating to the state

terminō (1), to close, end

coniungō, -ere, -iunxī, -iunctus, -a, -um, to join together

triumvirātus, -ūs, *m.,* the office or power of three men

Gallia, -ae, *f.,* Gaul, area now called France and including neighboring territory

invideō, -ēre, -vīdī, invīsus, -a, -um, to envy

rogātiō, -ōnis, *f.,* request, entreaty

Rubicō, -ōnis, *m.,* small river in northern Italy

Aegyptus, -ī, *f.,* Egypt

illīc, *adv.,* there, at that place

Pompēius and Pompēii

Pompēius was the Roman general. **Pompēii** was the city that was destroyed by the volcanic eruption of **Mount Vesuvius** in A.D. 79. Notice the difference in the pronunciation of these words in their English forms: Pompey, Pom'pē (the man); Pompēii, Pom•pā' (the city).

Dēminūtiō Reī Publicae Rōmānae

Post mortem Gracchōrum frātrum, dux appellātus **Marius** multōs Rōmānōs pauperes in exercitum suum conscripsit. Stipendium militum erat agrī et pecūnia. Exercitus Mariī erat initium exercituum Rōmānōrum habentium mīlitēs quī erant fidēlēs ūnō ducī. Ante Marium, cīvēs in exercitibus Rōmānīs pugnābant prō Rōmā, nōn prō ducibus suīs. Exercitus Mariī contrā exercitum **Sullae** pugnābat in prīmō bellō cīvīlī. Illud bellum erat longum et acre.

The First Triumvirate

Julius Caesar

Pompey the Great

Crassus Dives

Bellō terminātō, Rōma trēs magnōs ducēs habebat: Pompeius Magnus, Iulius Caesar, et **Crassus Dīvēs.** (Nōmen *Dīvēs* significat virum habentem multam pecūniam.) Illī autem° sē coniunxērunt et Prīmum Triumvirātum fēcērunt. Triumvirātus erat regnum virōrum trium.

[°moreover]

The Rubicon River

0   200 miles

Atlantic Ocean

CISALPINE GAUL

Rubicon River
ITALY
Adriatic Sea

Mediterranean Sea

Caesar et exercitus suus **Galliam** vīcērunt. Populus Caesarem propter victoriās eius dīligēbat. Pompēius Caesarem invidit; et senātus, propter rogātiōnēs ab Pompeiō, Caesarem redīre ad Rōmam sine exercitū suō iussit. Caesar autem cum exercitū suō **Rubicōnem** flūmen transit et ad Rōmam redit.

Pompeius et senātōrēs ad Graeciam fūgērunt, et exercitum contrā Caesarem conscriptērunt. Exercitus Pompeiī contrā exercitum Caesaris in Secundō Civīlī Bellō pugnāvit et Caesar erat victor. Pompeius Magnus ad Aegyptum fūgit, et illic necātus est. Caesar dictātor °reliquum suae vītae factus est.

[°for the remainder]

Latin answers to Latin questions

Magister: Now that you are familiar with two civil wars fought by strong military leaders of the Roman republic, you should be able to answer the questions in Activities A and B about the generals and the wars.

Activities A, B

Now let's translate the paragraphs about the lessening of the unity in the Roman republic. Read through each sentence to get the whole idea in mind. Check the meanings of any new words. As you translate, put the words in normal English order.

When we finish the translation, you may correct any errors you made in Activities A and B. Draw a line through your first answer and write the correction above or after it.

Can you (1) tell how the Roman armies before Marius differed from those after Marius, (2) name the members of the First Triumvirate, and (3) tell how the second civil war ended?

COMPARISON OF ADJECTIVES

Learning the Three Degree Forms of Regular Adjectives

Magister: In both English and Latin, most adjectives have three **degrees: positive, comparative,** and **superlative.** For example, in English we have *tall* (positive degree), *taller* (comparative degree), and *tallest* (superlative degree). Here are some Latin adjectives you have worked with, showing the forms in the three degrees. Positive-degree adjectives are in either the first-second or the third declension. Comparative-degree adjectives are always in the third declension. Superlative-degree adjectives are always in the first-second declension.

audāx, -dācis	audācior, -ius	audācissimus, -a, -um
brevis, -e	brevior, -ius	brevissimus, -a, -um
fortis, -e	fortior, -ius	fortissimus, -a, -um
longus, -a, -um	longior, -ius	longissimus, -a, -um
novus, -a, -um	novior, -ius	novissimus, -a, -um
parātus, -a, -um	parātior, -ius	parātissimus, -a, -um
tristis, -e	tristior, -ius	

Sylvia: Would we translate the first one *bold, bolder, boldest* in English?

Magister: Yes, if you are clearly comparing two people (comparative form) or more than two (superlative form). You have several things to consider when you translate comparative and superlative forms into English.

- If two people or things are being compared, use a comparative form such as "long*er*" or a phrase like "more prepared" and translate the word *quam* with the word *than.*
- If the comparative form is not comparing two but is just strengthening the meaning of the adjective, you should translate it, for example, "rather bold" or "too bold."
- If the superlative form is not comparing three or more but giving emphasis to the adjective, translate it, for example, "very bold."
- If the word *quam* precedes the superlative adjective, translate the phrase, for example, "as bold as possible."

There are four differences between the forms of comparative-degree adjectives and other third-declension adjectives. In the adjective declension below, three of the inflections in bold type are not preceded by the letter *i.* The fourth difference is in the ablative singular, where the inflection is *-e* instead of *-ī.*

Refer to this declension of *fortior* while you do Activities C through J. In Activity C you will translate into Latin some phrases containing adjectives in the comparative and superlative degrees. In Activity D you will translate into English some sentences with the same kind of adjectives.

Comparative-Degree Adjectives			
Singular		**Plural**	
M/F	**N**	**M/F**	**N**
fortior	fortius	fortiōrēs	fortiō*ra*
fortiōris		fortiō*rum*	
fortiōrī		fortiSribus	
fortiōrem	fortius	fortiōrēs	fortiō*ra*
fortiō*re*		fortiōribus	

Activities C, D

Can you (1) give the correct case forms for adjectives in each of the three degrees and (2) translate these forms correctly according to their use in context?

Learning about Adjectives That End with Liquid Consonants

Magister: What is the final letter of the stem in each of these adjectives?

facilis, fidēlis, similis

Clement: It's *l* when you drop the inflection *-is*.

Magister: That's right. We call *l* a **liquid consonant.** The other liquid consonant is *r*. In words that end in *r*, you need to note whether the *e* before the final *r* disappears in the stem. Compare *acer, acris; celer, celeris;* and *pauper, pauperis.*

What's the last letter of each of those stems?

Victor: It's *r*. Why are *l* and *r* called liquid consonants?

Magister: Liquids blend easily with the consonants that precede them: for example, *tr, gr, cr, pl, gl, cl.* In the superlative forms the Romans usually "doubled the liquid" before the *imus* ending instead of using the *iss* sign of superlative forms. See if you can form the superlative degree of these adjectives that have stems ending with *r: acer, celer,* and *pauper.* Use *acer,* not *acr* for the stem of the superlative.

Flora: *Acerrimus, celerrimus,* and *pauperrimus.*

Magister: Now, give the superlative forms of *facilis, fidēlis,* and *similis.*

Clara: *Facillimus, fidellimus,* and *simillimus.*

Magister: Very good. Occasionally you will find the superlative forms of these words spelled with the letters *iss,* like other adjectives. The comparative forms are made the same way as the other adjectives you've worked with. Activities E and F include superlative-degree adjectives having roots that end with liquid consonants.

When the word *quam* means "than," the case of a noun that follows *quam* is the same as the case of the first word in the comparison.

See Chapter 6 for the case of nouns that follow such adjectives as *fidēlis* and *similis.*

Activities E, F

Can you (1) recognize superlative adjective forms in any of their possible spellings and (2) translate adjectives correctly in each of the three degrees?

Learning about Irregular Adjective Comparisons

Magister: In English we say *long, longer, longest,* but we don't say *bad, badder, baddest.* The word *bad* is a positive adjective form. What are the comparative and superlative forms of *bad?*

Clara: *Bad, worse, worst.* And for *good* we say *good, better, best.*

Magister: Fortunately, the list of irregular adjectives is about the same in Latin as in English. Here are the most commonly used ones. Notice that *plūs* has no masculine-feminine form and *prior* has no positive form.

bonus, -a, -um (good)	**melior, -ius** (better)	**optimus, -a, -um** (best)
malus, -a, -um (bad)	**peior, -ius** (worse)	**pessimus, -a, -um** (worst)
magnus, -a, -um (large)	**maior, -ius** (larger)	**maximus, -a, -um** (largest)
parvus, -a, -um (small)	**minor, -us** (smaller, less)	**minimus, -a, -um** (smallest, least)
multus, -a, -um (many)	——, **plūs,** (*gen.* **plūris**) (more)	**plūrimus, -a, -um** (most)
	prior, -is (former)	**prīmus, -a, -um** (first)
superus, -a, -um (above)	**superior, -ius** (higher)	**summus, -a, -um** (highest) *or* **suprēmus, -a, -um** (last)

Magister: Derivatives and loan words will be a great help to you in memorizing these. See how many unaltered loan words you can find in the list.

Lydia: *bonus, minor, minus, prior, plus, superior*

Magister: Very good. Now you can add another if I remind you that in later years an *i* between two vowels was written as a *j.*

Lydia: Then *maior* becomes *major.*

Magister: You can add two or three more by simply using the neuter inflection instead of the masculine.

Lydia: *Maximum* and *minimum* are the only ones I see.

Magister: You may not be familiar with the word *optimum*. It is a noun and an adjective. It refers to the best amount or degree of something or the most favorable condition.

Derivatives will help you to remember what these words mean. How many can you think of?

Sylvia: *magnify, malicious, multiply, super, majority, minority, minimize, priority, optimist, pessimist, plural, minimal, prime, summit, supreme*

Magister: I can say only "super" to such a good list. Even though these are irregular, they should not be hard to remember. In Activity G the sentences by Latin writers contain some of the irregular forms. In Activity H you will translate portions of Scripture verses containing irregular adjectives.

Activities G, H

 Can you (1) give the comparative and superlative forms of irregular Latin adjectives and (2) translate these forms correctly?

Seeing Four Differences in Comparative-Degree Adjective Forms

Magister: Go back to page 326 and look at the declension of comparative-degree forms. Notice that

- the singular ablative form is *e*, not *ī*.
- in the plural genitive forms there is no letter *i* before the inflection.
- in the neuter nominative and accusative forms there is no *i* before the inflections.

Therefore, these adjectives are not i-stems, as other third-declension adjectives are. Activity I contains adjectives that illustrate the fact that comparative-degree adjectives are not i-stems. Activity J gives practice with the varied possible translations of comparative and superlative-degree adjectives.

Activities I, J

Can you use correctly the comparative and superlative forms of regular and irregular Latin adjectives?

Derivatives

Magister: Activity K can help you build your English vocabulary. As you see patterns or methods by which many Latin words become English words, you can begin to solve many word-meaning problems from Latin words you are learning.

Activity K

Some of the words you used to fill in the blanks in Activity K may be new to you. From this activity you probably have a good idea of the meanings of these new words. Watch for them in things you read and listen for them. Then try using them.

We have borrowed into English several comparative and superlative forms of irregular adjectives. Some of these are words you probably use frequently. In Activity L you are to match the meanings with commonly used loan words and phrases.

In Activity M are derivatives from the comparative and superlative forms of the irregular adjectives. This activity should increase your working vocabulary.

Activities L, M

Essential Information

Grammar terms

- Comparison of regular and of irregular adjectives: positive, comparative, and superlative degrees
- Adjectives ending in liquid consonants: *l* and *r*

History terms

- Julius Caesar, Marcus Tullius Cicero, Gnaeus Pompeius Magnus (Pompey the Great), Marius, Sulla, Crassus Dives (Crassus the Rich)
- First Triumvirate
- Civil Wars

Geography terms

- Pompeii, Mount Vesuvius
- Gallia, Rubicon River

Comparative degree adjective inflections

- See declensions on page 324.

Vocabulary

Activity N

- You are responsible for the vocabulary words listed on page 320 and for the comparative and superlative forms listed on pages 323 and 326.
- You worked with the following new words in the activities.

certus, -a, -um, certain

dīvitiae, -ārum, *f.,* riches

exsistō (*or* **existō), -ere, -stitī, -sistus, -a, -um,** to arise

CAPITULUM XXIII

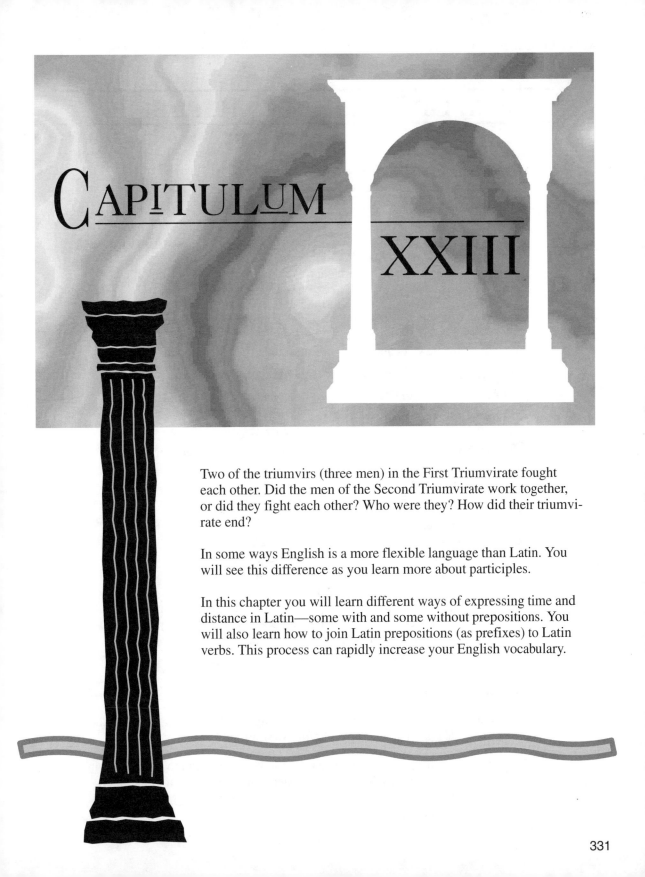

Two of the triumvirs (three men) in the First Triumvirate fought each other. Did the men of the Second Triumvirate work together, or did they fight each other? Who were they? How did their triumvirate end?

In some ways English is a more flexible language than Latin. You will see this difference as you learn more about participles.

In this chapter you will learn different ways of expressing time and distance in Latin—some with and some without prepositions. You will also learn how to join Latin prepositions (as prefixes) to Latin verbs. This process can rapidly increase your English vocabulary.

END OF THE ROMAN REPUBLIC

Learning about the Second Triumvirate

Magister: In Chapter 22 you saw how the First Triumvirate dissolved and two of its members, Julius Caesar and Gnaeus Pompey, fought each other in a civil war. Not long afterwards **Octavius Caesar, Mark Antony, and Marcus Lepidus** formed the **Second Triumvirate**. This triumvirate, unlike the first one, was made official.

Just as two members of the First Triumvirate had fought each other, so two members of the Second Triumvirate fought each other in another civil war. Let's read about it in Latin. But first, read through the new vocabulary words and three translation helps.

ōrātor, -ōris, *m.* orator

inimīcitia, -ae, *f.,* hatred, hostility

consentiō, -īre, -sensī, -sensus, -a, -um, to agree

constituō, -ere, -tuī, -tutus, -a, -um, to found, establish

ultimus, -a, -um, last

perficiō, -ere, -fēcī, -fectus, -a, -um, to accomplish, complete

- A noun in the genitive case can modify another noun in the genitive case: for example, *partem <u>exercitūs Caesaris</u>* (part <u>of the army of Caesar</u> or part <u>of Caesar's army</u>).

- A word that follows a direct object and renames or describes it is called an **objective complement.** It shows the effect of the action of the verb on the direct object. In the English translation, the words *to be* are understood between the direct object and the objective complement: for example, *sē dictātor fēcit,* "He made himself (to be) dictator."

- A Latin sentence can begin with a verb for emphasis.

Clement: When we read the paragraphs through twice, it helps me to get the idea of what's going on before we translate.

Magister: Yes. It helps you get used to Latin word order and to think in Latin. The meanings of words are easier to figure out and to remember when you see them in context. Let's read the paragraphs, first orally and then silently.

Secundus Triumvirātus

Dum Iūlius Caesar contrā Pompēium in Hispāniā pugnābat, Marcus Antōnius partem exercitūs Caesaris in Italiā dūcēbat. Marcus Antōnius erat dux bonus, sed vitia multa habēbat. Cicero, senātor et ōrātor, ōrātiōnēs dē vitiīs Marcī Antōnī faciēbat. Marcus Antōnius igitur inimīcitiam magnam ad Cicerōnem habēbat.

Iūlius Caesar dictātōr reliquum° suae vītāe factus erat. Tum senātōrēs quī fuerant inimīcī Caesaris eum necāvērunt. Duo virī Prīmī Triumvirātūs, Pompeius et Caesar, erant nunc mortuī.

[°for the remainder]

Trēs virī tum sē coniunxērunt et Secundus Triumvirātus constitutus est. Illī virī erant Marcus Antōnius, Octāvius Caesar, et Marcus Lepidus. Sed illī virī erant nōn amīcī. Consensērunt necāre omnēs inimīcōs cuiusque.° Quisque igitur tabulam inimīcōrum suōrum° fēcit. Cicerō erat in tabulā Marcī Antōnī. Is necātus est. Mox posteā Marcus Antōnius contrā Octāvium Caesarem in ultimō bellō cīvilī reī publicae Rōmānae pugnāvit. Octāvius Caesar Marcum Antōnium superāvit. Marcus Antōnius igitur sē necāvit. Victōriā perfectā, Octāvius Caesar imperium Rōmānum constituit.

[°of each one, °his own]

The Second Triumvirate

Octavian Caesar

Marc Antony

Marcus Lepidus

Magister: Now you should be ready to translate. Let's begin.

As you answer the questions in Activity A, think in Latin instead of translating. Activity B reviews some Latin grammar from earlier chapters.

Activities A, B

 Can you (1) name the members of the First and Second Triumvirates, and (2) state the main events of the third civil war?

PARTICIPLES

Learning About All Four Latin Participles

Magister: We can express things with English participles that are not possible in Latin. We can say, "The language being taught is the Latin language." *Being taught* is in the passive voice. Latin doesn't have a present passive participle. Also in English we can say, "*Having taught* the English language, Magister now teaches the language of the Romans." Latin doesn't have a perfect active participle. Here are the participles for the verb *doceō*. Most verbs follow this pattern.

	Active	**Passive**
Present	docēns, -ntis *teaching*	NONE
Present Perfect	NONE	doctus, -a, -um *having been taught, taught*
Future	doctūrus, -a, -um *going to teach, about to teach*	docendus, -a, -um *necessary to be taught, to be taught*

Timothy: What about words like *sum* that are never passive?

Magister: *Sum* has only one participle, the future active. For *sum* the future participle is *futūrus, -a, -um*. Regular intransitive verbs have only present active and future active participles: for example *ambulāns, -ntis* and *ambulātūrus, -a, -um*.

Lydia: The word *future* must come from *futūrus*.

Magister: Yes, and the letters *ūr* before the inflection are a very helpful clue to help you recognize all other **future active participles.** Notice those letters in *doctūrus, -a, -um.* The letters *nd* are a clue for remembering the translation of **future passive participles.** You may have heard of an *agenda.* It is a list of things that are "necessary to be done." Even though the Latin origin of *memorandum* is unfamiliar to you, still you can see its connection with the word *remember.* Can you make up a definition?

Sylvia: It must be something "necessary to be remembered."

Magister: Good. Now look carefully at the **stems of the four participles** of *doceō,* which are underlined in the table above. Notice that the stem vowels are not long. Before an *nt* and an *nd,* a vowel is never long. Which two participles are built on the present infinitive stem?

Paul: The present active and the future passive.

Magister: Which principal part provides the stem for the other two participles?

Flora: The fourth principal part.

Magister: Which participle is in the third declension? And what declension are the other three?

Clara: The present active is in third declension. The rest are in the first-second declension.

Magister: Two of the four participles should look very familiar to you. Which ones have you already worked with?

Sylvia: *Docēns* and *doctus.* We used *doctus* when we conjugated the three perfect tenses in the passive.

Magister: Exactly right! You may recall from working with these in Chapter 21 that they are the present active and the perfect passive participles. And you should recall that participles are adjectives. By using a verb, not verbal, form of the *be* verb as an auxiliary with the perfect active participle, we make a verb; for example, *Liber lectus est.* The future active and passive participles are often used with verbs. Here are two examples. *Hic liber est legendus. Hunc librum sumus lectūrī.* Can you translate them?

Rex: "This book is necessary to be read. We are going to read this book."

Magister: Very good. As you do Activities C and D, refer to the table and to this discussion when necessary. Try to learn all this information about participles as you work with them.

Activities C, D

 Can you (1) name the four kinds of Latin participles and (2) write them correctly in English and in Latin?

PREPOSITIONS: USES AND OMISSIONS

Reviewing Some Ablative Case Uses, With and Without Prepositions

Magister: While you are learning more about the uses of the ablative case, you will also be finding out more in the activities about the Roman pagan gods.

Here is a review of the meanings of three prepositions and of the information in Chapter 20 about ablative of means and ablative of agent.

- *Ā, ab* means "from" or, more specifically, "away from" when it refers to location or direction. When its object is the actor of a passive-voice verb, the phrase is called ablative of agent and the preposition means "by."
- Ablative of means is expressed without a preposition.
- *Dē* means "from" or "down from" when it refers to location. Otherwise it means "concerning, about."
- *Ē, ex* means "from" or "out from."

In Activity E are sentences that review uses of the ablative case, with and without prepositions. It includes the use of ablative of agent and ablative of means.

Meanings of Some Words in Activity E

- *Oriēns, -entis* is a present participle that means "rising." When it is used with the noun *sōl, sōlis,* the phrase *oriēns sōlis* means "the rising of the sun." Our English word *orient,* then, means "the east." Countries in Asia are in the Eastern Hemisphere and are called oriental.

- *Occidēns, -entis* is a present participle that means "falling." When it is used with *sōl, sōlis,* it means "the falling, or setting, of the sun." Our English word *occident* refers to the Western Hemisphere, which includes Europe and North and South America. Countries on these continents are called occidental.

Activity E

Can you (1) correctly translate sentences containing the prepositions *ā, ab; ē, ex;* and *dē,* and (2) distinguish ablative of means from ablative of agent?

The Roman Forum today . . .

and as it probably appeared at its height

Learning About Latin Forms Expressing Place

Magister: By comparing these English and Latin sentences, you will see some similarities and some differences.

- We live in the city. *In urbe* vivimus.
- We live in Rome. *Rōmā* vivimus.
- We moved from the city. *Ab urbe* mōvimus.
- We moved from Rome. *Rōmā* mōvimus.
- We moved to the city. *Ad urbem* mōvimus.
- We moved to Rome. *Rōmam* mōvimus.

Let's take the sentences in three pairs. Compare the Latin with the English in each pair. What difference do you find?

Victor: The preposition is missing in every Latin sentence that has the word *Rome* in it.

Magister: Right. We need grammar terms for the word *Rome* in each Latin sentence. The first use can be called **ablative of place where,** or **locative case,** which you read about in Chapter 19. It is used only for names of cities, such as *Rōma* and *Cannae.* The word *locative* comes from the Latin word *locus,* which means "place." We don't list the locative with the other five cases because it is used only for names of cities and for the common noun *domus,* which means "home." It is not used for other place names: we do use prepositions for phrases like *in Italiā* and *in patriā.* Most locative forms are the same as dative forms, but the locative of *domus* is *domī.*

The names of the Latin forms of *Rome* in the other two sentences are **ablative of place from which** and **accusative of place to which.** These forms without the Latin prepositions are also used only for names of cities and for *domus (domō).* They don't have case names, such as the locative case.

Learning About Latin Forms Expressing Time and Distance

Magister: Again we will compare English and Latin.

- We were at home on that day.
  We were at home that day.
  Domī illō diē erāmus.

- We finished the work in/within a few hours.
  Opus hōrīs paucīs confēcimus.
- We worked for four hours.
  We worked four hours.
  Hōrās quattuor laborābāmus.
- We saw a tree twenty feet tall.
  Arborem vīgintī pedēs altam vīdimus.

The first English set of sentences above tells us that in English we may use a preposition or omit it when speaking of the time when something happened. The Latin sentences show that **ablative of time when** always omits the preposition. The second set of sentences shows that in English we always use a preposition to express **ablative of time in or within which,** but in Latin the preposition is always omitted.

The third set of sentences illustrates Latin **accusative of time how long.** In English do we use a preposition to express this idea?

Clement: Sometimes yes and sometimes no.

Magister: In Latin do we use a preposition? And what case do we use?

Clement: No preposition. The case is accusative instead of ablative.

Magister: The fourth set of sentences illustrates the **accusative of distance how far,** which is expressed without a preposition in both languages. In Latin, distance is expressed with the accusative case and no preposition. In the last two sentences there are cardinal numbers with no case endings. You should recall that cardinal numbers are indeclinable except for *one, two, three,* and *one thousand.* Activities F, G, and H give practice with ablative and accusative cases to express time and place. Activity I reviews the use and omission of prepositions in Latin sentences. Activity J is based on the information about Greek and Roman deities in Activity E and in this box.

Roman and Greek Myths

- The genitive form of *Iuppiter* is *Iovis.* Therefore all its case forms except the nominative begin *Iov-.* Later the initial letter *I* became *J.*

- The Greek word **Hades** is defined as "the abode or habitation of the dead." This definition indicates that the Greeks believed that people lived somewhere after death. In Greek and Roman mythology, the **Elysian Fields** were the place where heroes and people of noble character went after death. **Tartarus** was the place where wicked people went to pay for their crimes against the gods. The penalty for one such wicked man, Sisyphus, was the requirement that he forever roll a huge stone up a hill and it would forever roll back down the hill. Another wicked man, **Tantalus,** was forever hungry and thirsty. Fruit grew right above his head but just out of reach. Water flowed at his feet, but when he stooped to drink, it receded so that he could not reach it. Our word *tantalize* means to keep pleasant things just out of reach.

  In Roman mythology **Pluto,** one of the three major gods, ruled over the abode of the dead. **Neptune** ruled over the sea, and **Jupiter** ruled over the sky.

Activities F, G, H, I, J

Can you (1) translate from Latin to English and from English to Latin some sentences that express agent, means, place, time, and distance; and (2) identify some deities and myths of the ancient Greeks and Romans?

Derivatives

Magister: Activities G through J contain several words which you have not been asked to memorize. However, you will probably be able to remember their meanings from English derivatives. Here are a few examples.

- *occidental,* western *(occidēns)*
- *oriental,* eastern *(oriēns)*
- *furtive,* like a thief *(fūr)*
- *mortal,* being subject to death *(mors)*
- *martial,* related to war (Mars, god of war)
- *lunar,* pertaining to the moon *(lūna)*
- *solar,* pertaining to the sun *(sōl)*
- *celestial,* pertaining to the heavens *(caelum/coelum)*
- *merchant,* one who buys and sells *(mercātor)*
- *bellicose,* warlike *(bellum)*

Magister: In the last main section of this chapter, you reviewed the prepositions *ā/ab, dē, ē/ex,* and *ad.* These are among the many Latin prepositions that have become prefixes in English. Can you name four English words, each containing one of these prefixes—a different prefix in each word?

Paul: How about *absent, describe, exit,* and *adjective?*

Magister: Excellent. Based on the meaning of *ā* or *ab,* where is a person who is *absent* from a meeting?

Flora: He is away.

Magister: What does it mean to *describe* something?

Sylvia: You write or tell about it.

Magister: Yes. "About" is one of the meanings of *dē.* Another meaning is "from or down from." Can you think of a derivative in which *de* means "down from"?

Mark: How about *descend?*

Magister: Yes. Remember the irregular verb *eō?* The form *it* means "he goes." In the derivative *exit,* where does he go?

Timothy: He goes out.

Magister: Yes. This verb is used in directions for a play, telling an actor when to leave the stage. We also have an English noun spelled *exit,* from the noun *exitus.* It names a place where people may go out. In Latin what case is always used with *ā/ab, dē,* and *ē/ex?* And what case is used with *ad?*

341

Lydia: The ablative case with the first three and the accusative case with *ad.*

Magister: Very good. What does *ad* mean?

Clement: It means "to or toward or near."

Magister: What does the Latin verb *iaciō* mean?

Gloria: It means "to throw."

Magister: Right. Put the meanings of the prefix and the root together and you get *adjective.* Actually the root is a participle *iactus, -a, -um,* the fourth principal part of the verb. The *a* in the participle became an *e* (which takes less time to say) when the prefix was added and the word became longer. So the word means "thrown toward or near to." An *adjective,* then, is a word "thrown near to something." What part of speech is an adjective usually "thrown near to"?

Clara: Near to a noun.

Magister: Often the final consonant of a preposition changes when the preposition becomes a prefix. We call such spelling changes **assimilation.** The *x* in *ex* and the *d* in *ad* are examples of consonants that change by assimilation. This fact explains the double consonants in many words. Latin prefixes are attached to both Latin and non-Latin root words.

Here are a few words made by combining *ex* or *ad* with root words: *effort, effect, essay; appoint, allocate, announce, arrive, assimilate.* One of these is made from a Latin root word that you should recognize. What Latin prefix and root word are combined to make the word *assimilate?*

Rex: *Ad* and *similis.*

Magister: Correct. It is a verb that means "to make similar to." To assimilate the spelling of a prefix is to make the last letter of a prefix similar in sound to the first letter of a root word. Notice that the definitions of this and other such words read backwards: the meaning of the root and then the meaning of the prefix ("to make similar + to"). Activities K, L, and M provide practice in determining the meaning of English words from their Latin origins. You will be reviewing verbs that have occurred in this chapter and in previous chapters.

Activities K, L, M

Essential Information

Grammar terms

- objective complement
- participles: future active, future passive; stems of participles
- ablative of place from which
- ablative of place where; locative case
- ablative of time in or within which
- ablative of time when
- accusative of distance how far
- accusative of place to which
- accusative of time how long

Derivative term

- Assimilation

History terms

- Second Triumvirate: Octavian Caesar, Mark Antony, Marcus Lepidus

Mythological terms

- Hades, Elysian Fields, Tartarus
- Tantalus
- Pluto, Neptune, Jupiter (Zeus)

Participles

- See page 336 for the forms and translations of the future active and future passive participles.

Vocabulary

- You are responsible for the vocabulary words listed on page 334.
- Here are the new words that were used in the activities.

Nouns	Mercurius, -iī/-ī, *m.,* Roman messenger god
Apollo, -inis, *m.,* Roman god of the sun	Neptunus, -ī, *m.,* Roman god of the sea
Diana, -ae, *f.,* Roman goddess of the moon	Plūtō, -ōnis, *m.,* Roman god of the underworld
Iuppiter, Iovis, *m.,* Jupiter, supreme Roman god, god of the sky	āla, -ae, *f.,* wing
Mars, Martis, *m.,* Roman god of war	fraudātor, -ōris, *m.,* deceiver
	fūr, fūris, *c.,* thief

habitātiō, -iōnis, *f.,* house, abode

lūna, -ae, *f.,* moon

mensis, -is, *m.,* month

mercātor, -ōris, *m.,* merchant

mīlle passuum, *n.,* a thousand of paces, a mile

mortālis, -is, *c.,* a person; subject to death

nuntius, iī/ī, *m.,* messenger; message

saeculum, -ī, *n.,* age, century

servus, -ī, *m.,* slave

sōl, sōlis, *m.,* sun

solea, -ae, *f.,* sandal

spatium, -iī/ī, *n.,* space, distance

viātor, -ōris, *m.,* traveler

Adjective

mortuus, -a, -um, dead

Verbs

fraudō (1), to deceive

gerō, gerere, gessī, gestus, -a, -um, to wear, to bear or carry

LEGENDA VI

Legenda

This Legenda differs from the previous Legendas. Instead of reading paragraphs, you will read word comparisons that show some of the changes that have taken place when Latin words became English derivatives.

During this year of Latin study, you have probably already added many words to your English vocabulary and have come to understand more thoroughly many English words that were already in your vocabulary. The comparisons below show the process by which many derivatives have come into our language. In Section A you will see how some English nouns have come from fourth principal parts of Latin verbs (participles). In Section B you will see a variety of other patterns of derivation from Latin verbs.

The meanings of some derivatives changed somewhat from the meaning of their Latin origins. However, seeing the relationship between the English nouns and the original Latin verbs can help you in three ways: (1) by making the meanings of some English derivatives clearer, (2) by introducing you to some new English words, and (3) by making the meanings of the Latin words easier to remember.

Some of the Latin verbs given in the two sections below are made by adding or by changing prefixes. The verbs on which these prefixes have been added or changed are words that you have already worked with. They should be familiar to you because they are related to common English derivatives. The prefix changes do not affect the processes of derivation involved.

Remember that the letter *i* is a consonant when it is between two vowels or before a vowel at the beginning of a root word. In late Roman and early Medieval times, the Latin consonant *i* was changed to *j*.

Read or write, according to your teacher's instructions, each complete comparison in Sections A and B.

Dīcenda

Section A

Each item contains two pairs of words. The first pair is a Latin participle and an English noun that developed from it. The second pair asks you for the English noun that completes a similar pair. Read the comparison(s) aloud for your teacher or write them, according to your teacher's instructions. For example, *appellātus* is to *appellation* as *audītus* is to *audition*.

1. appellātus : appellation :: audītus : _____
2. ascēnsus : ascension :: inclūsus : _____
3. audītus : audition :: cogitātus : _____
4. celebrātus : celebration :: exclāmātus : _____
5. coniunctus : conjunction :: conscriptus : _____
6. constructus : construction :: contentus : _____
7. conventus : convention :: correctus : _____
8. creātus : creation :: dēstructus : _____
9. descriptus : description :: possessus : _____
10. dictus : diction :: rēductus : _____
11. ēdūcātus : education :: reiectus : _____
12. exsultātus (exultātus) : exultation :: inceptus : _____
13. inluminātus : illumination :: intentus : _____
14. invāsus : invasion :: līberātus : _____
15. inventus : invention :: mansus : _____
16. laudātus : laudation :: missus : _____
17. mūtātus : mutation :: nāvigātus : _____
18. sessus : session :: suffōcātus : _____
19. terminātus: termination :: transitus : _____
20. vīsus : vision :: vocātus : _____

Section B

In this section each English noun comes from the second or the fourth principal part of a Latin verb. Each pair or group of pairs illustrates a different pattern of derivation. Note (1) whether the form of each Latin verb is the second or fourth principal part and (2) what change took place to make the English word. Then say aloud or write the English noun that completes the second pair of words. You may not recall having seen or heard this word, and you may wish to add to your own vocabulary any words that you discover. You can do this by listing them and then watching or listening for them in context.

In the process of derivation, often the Latin diphthong *ae* has shortened to an *e*.

1. ambulāre : ambulance :: resurgere : _____
2. cadere : cadence :: stāre : _____
3. praevalēre : prevalence :: crēdere : _____
4. scīre : science :: audīre : _____
5. currere : current :: dīligere : _____
6. repellere : repellent :: resurgere : _____
7. servāre : servant :: celebrāre : _____
8. praevalēre : prevalent :: convenīre : _____
9. dērīdēre : deride :: scrībere : _____
10. inscrībere : inscribe :: construere : _____
11. invādēre : invade :: resurgere : _____
12. dēfendere : defend :: revertere : _____
13. debitus : debit :: actus : _____
14. factus : fact :: digestus : _____
15. habitus : habit :: conscriptus : _____
16. dēfensus : defense :: status : _____
17. suffōcātus : suffocate :: terminātus : _____
18. captus : captive :: cūrātus : _____
19. apertus : aperture :: captus : _____
20. datus : dative :: fūgitus : _____
21. ostensus : ostensive :: repulsus : _____
22. derīsus : derisive :: cursus : _____

Appendix A

Paradigms

NOUNS

	FIRST				SECOND			
	Feminine		**F. Irregular**		**Masculine**		**M. Irregular**	
	Sing.	Pl.	Sing.	Pl.	Sing.	Pl.	Sing.	Pl.
Nom.	fīli*a*	fīli*ae*	de*a*	de*ae*	amīc*us*	amīc*ī*	de*us*	de*ī*, d*ū*, d*ī*
Gen.	fīli*ae*	fīli*ārum*	de*ae*	de*ārum*	amīc*ī*	amīc*ōrum*	de*ī*	de*ōrum*, de*um*
Dat.	fīli*ae*	fīli*īs*	de*ae*	de*ābus*	amīc*ō*	amīc*īs*	de*ō*	de*īs*, di*īs*, d*īs*
Acc.	fīli*am*	fīli*ās*	de*am*	de*ās*	amīc*um*	amīc*ōs*	de*um*	de*ōs*
Abl.	fīli*ā*	fīli*īs*	de*ā*	de*ābus*	amīc*ō*	amīc*īs*	de*ō*	de*īs*, di*īs*, d*īs*
Voc.					amīc*e*	amīc*ī*		

- A few first-declension nouns are masculine: for example, *agricola, nauta, poēta, prophēta.*
- The genitive of an i-stem second-declension noun such as *fīlius* is either *fīliī* or *fīlī.*
- The vocative case differs from the nominative case *only* in second-declension masculine singular nouns that end in *-us.* The vocative inflection for these nouns, including those that end in *-ius,* is *-e.*

SECOND					
Masculine				**Neuter**	
	Sing.	Pl.	Sing.	Pl.	Sing.	Pl.

	Sing.	Pl.	Sing.	Pl.	Sing.	Pl.
Nom.	puer	puer*ī*	liber	libr*ī*	regn*um*	regn*a*
Gen.	puer*ī*	puer*ōrum*	libr*ī*	libr*ōrum*	regn*ī*	regn*ōrum*
Dat.	puer*ō*	puer*īs*	libr*ō*	libr*īs*	regn*ō*	regn*īs*
Acc.	puer*um*	puer*ōs*	libr*um*	libr*ōs*	regn*um*	regn*a*
Abl.	puer*ō*	puer*īs*	libr*ō*	libr*īs*	regn*ō*	regn*īs*

THIRD						
Masculine/Feminine				**Neuter**		
	Sing.	Pl.	Sing.	Pl.	Sing.	Pl.
Nom.	dux	duc*ēs*	mater	matr*ēs*	carmen	carmin*a*
Gen.	duc*is*	duc*um*	matr*is*	matr*um*	carmin*is*	carmin*um*
Dat.	duc*ī*	duc*ibus*	matr*ī*	matr*ibus*	carmin*ī*	carmin*ibus*
Acc.	duc*em*	duc*ēs*	matr*em*	matr*ēs*	carmen	carmin*a*
Abl.	duc*e*	duc*ibus*	matr*e*	matr*ibus*	carmin*e*	carmin*ibus*

THIRD (i-stem)				
Feminine			**Neuter**	
	Sing.	Pl.	Sing.	Pl.
Nom.	ars	art*ēs*	mar*e*	mar*ia*
Gen.	art*is*	art*ium*	mar*is*	mar*ium*
Dat.	art*ī*	art*ibus*	mar*ī*	mar*ibus*
Acc.	art*em*	art*ēs*	mar*e*	mar*ia*
Abl.	art*e*	art*ibus*	mar*ī*	mar*ibus*

• In third and third i-stem declensions, masculine and feminine are identical. Neuter differs only in the ablative case singular and in the nominative and accusative cases plural.

	FOURTH				FIFTH			
	Masculine/Feminine		**Neuter**		**Masculine/Feminine**		**Feminine**	
	Sing.	Pl.	Sing.	Pl.	Sing.	Pl.	Sing.	Pl.
Nom.	senāt*us*	senāt*ūs*	corn*ū*	corn*ua*	di*ēs*	di*ēs*	sp*ēs*	sp*ēs*
Gen.	senāt*ūs*	senāt*uum*	corn*ūs*	corn*uum*	di*ēī*	di*ērum*	sp*eī*	sp*ērum*
Dat.	senāt*uī*	senāt*ibus*	corn*ū*	corn*ibus*	di*ēī*	di*ēbus*	sp*eī*	sp*ēbus*
Acc.	senāt*um*	senāt*ūs*	corn*ū*	corn*ua*	di*em*	di*ēs*	sp*em*	sp*ēs*
Abl.	senāt*ū*	senāt*ibus*	corn*ū*	corn*ibus*	di*ē*	di*ēbus*	sp*ē*	sp*ēbus*

- In fourth declension, masculine and feminine inflections are identical.
- Most fifth-declension nouns are feminine. *Dies* is masculine except when it refers to a particular day.
- Fifth-declension nouns of one syllable in the nominative singular have a short *e* in the genitive and dative singular forms.

ADJECTIVES

	FIRST-SECOND					
	Singular			**Plural**		
	M	F	N	M	F	N
Nom.	alt*us*	alt*a*	alt*um*	alt*ī*	alt*ae*	alt*a*
Gen.	alt*ī*	alt*ae*	alt*ī*	alt*ōrum*	alt*ārum*	alt*ōrum*
Dat.	alt*ō*	alt*ae*	alt*ō*		alt*īs*	
Acc.	alt*um*	alt*am*	alt*um*	alt*ōs*	alt*ās*	alt*a*
Abl.	alt*ō*	alt*ā*	alt*ō*		alt*īs*	

- Identical forms in all genders are listed only in the *feminine* or the *masculine/feminine* column.

THIRD						
Singular						
	Two-Termination		**Three-Termination**			**One-Termination**
	M/F	N	M	F	N	M/F
Nom.	grav*is*	grav*e*	celer	celer*is*	celer*e*	vetus
Gen.	grav*is*			celer*is*		veteris
Dat.	grav*ī*			celer*ī*		veter*ī*
Acc.	grav*em*	grav*e*	celer*em*	celer*em*	celer*e*	veter*em* (neuter: vetus)
Abl.	grav*ī̲*			celer*ī̲*		veter*ī*

Plural					
Plural					
	Two-Termination		**Three-Termination**		**One-Termination**
	M/F	N	M/F	N	M/F
Nom.	grav*ēs*	grav*ia*	celer*ēs*	celer*ia*	veter*ēs* (neuter: veter*a*)
Gen.	grav*ium*		celer*ium*		veter*um*
Dat.	grav*ibus*		celer*ibus*		veter*ibus*
Acc.	grav*ēs*	grav*ia*	celer*ēs*	celer*ia*	veter*ēs* (neuter: veter*a*)
Abl.	grav*ibus*		celer*ibus*		veter*ibus*

- Present participles, such as *potēns,* are one-termination adjectives. They have the letter *i* where it is underlined in the forms of *gravis* and *celer.* The ablative-case *-e* ending is used when the participle shows action or when it acts as a noun (*ā potente,* "by the powerful man").

Comparison of Adjectives

COMPARATIVE DEGREE			
Singular		**Plural**	
M/F	**N**	**M/F**	**N**
fortior	fort*ius*	fortiōr*ēs*	fortiōr*a*
fortiōr*is*		fortiōr*um*	
fortiōr*ī*		fortiōr*ibus*	
fortiōr*em*	fort*ius*	fortiōr*ēs*	fortiōr*a*
fortiōr*e*		fortiōr*ibus*	

- Superlative-degree adjectives are first-second declension adjectives; they are declined like *altus*. Examples are *altissimus,* a regular adjective, and *optimus,* an irregular adjective.

ADVERBS

- Many adjectives become adverbs as follows.

First-Second Declension		Third Declension	
Adj.	**Adv.**	**Adj.**	**Adv.**
pūr*us*	pūr*ē*	fort*is*, *-e*	fort*iter*
līb*er*	līb*erē*	fēlī*x*, *-īcis*	fēlī*citer*
pulch*er*	pulch*rē*	sapiēn*s*, *-entis*	sapi*enter*
		ac*er*	ac*riter*
		facil*is*	facil*e*

PRONOUNS

PERSONAL				
	First Person		**Second Person**	
	Sing.	Pl.	Sing.	Pl.
Nom.	ego	nōs	tū	vōs
Gen.	meī	nostrum/nostrī	tuī	vestrum/vestrī
Dat.	mihi	nōbīs	tibi	vōbīs
Acc.	mē	nōs	tē	vōs
Abl.	mē	nōbīs	tē	vōbīs

Third Person					
	Singular			**Plural**	
	M	F	N	M	F	N
Nom.	is	ea	id	eī	eae	ea
Gen.		eius		eōrum	eārum	eōrum
Dat.		eī			eīs	
Acc.	eum	eam	id	eōs	eās	ea
Abl.	eō	eā	eō		eīs	

- *Is, ea, id* is both a personal pronoun and a demonstrative pronoun. As a personal pronoun it is translated *he, she,* or *it;* as a demonstrative pronoun it is translated *this (man, woman,* or *thing).*

DEMONSTRATIVE					
hic, haec, hoc					
	Singular			**Plural**		
	M	F	N	M	F	N
Nom.	h*ic*	h*aec*	h*oc*	h*ī*	h*ae*	h*aec*
Gen.		h*uius*		h*ōrum*	h*ārum*	h*ōrum*
Dat.		h*uic*			h*īs*	
Acc.	h*unc*	h*anc*	h*oc*	h*ōs*	h*ās*	h*aec*
Abl.	h*ōc*	h*āc*	h*ōc*		h*īs*	

ille, illa, illud						
Nom.	ill*e*	ill*a*	ill*ud*	ill*ī*	ill*ae*	ill*a*
Gen.		ill*īus*		ill*ōrum*	ill*ārum*	ill*ōrum*
Dat.		ill*ī*			ill*īs*	
Acc.	ill*um*	ill*am*	ill*ud*	ill*ōs*	ill*ās*	ill*a*
Abl.	ill*ō*	ill*ā*	ill*ō*		ill*īs*	

- *Hic, haec, hoc* and *ille, illa, illud* and *iste, ista, istud* are demonstrative pronouns that are translated *this, that, that of yours*. They can also be translated as personal pronouns—*he, she, it*—or as demonstrative adjectives—*this (man), this (woman), this (thing of yours)*.

- The declension of *iste, ista, istud* is identical to that of *ille, illa, illud. Iste, ista, istud* often refers to someone or something unpleasant or disapproved.

VERBS

- Notice that for *first conjugation*, **bold** type shows tense signs, and ***bold italics*** show inflections for the person of the verb. For the *other conjugations*, **bold** type also shows tense signs; ***bold italics*** show (1) variations in the first-person singular inflections -*ō* and -*m,* and (2) the present perfect tense to highlight the special set of inflections (only in the active voice).

Synopsis of a Verb to Show Possible Translations (Example: to praise, using first person singular in all tenses)		
Tense	**Active**	**Passive**
Pres.	I praise, I am praising, I do praise	I am praised, I am being praised
Imperf.	I praised, I was praising, I did praise	I was praised, I was being praised
Fut.	I will (shall) praise	I will (shall) be praised
Pres. Perf.	I have praised, I praised	I have been praised, I was praised
Past Perf.	I had praised	I had been praised
Fut. Perf.	I will (shall) have praised	I will (shall) have been praised

First Conjugation

Indicative Mood

laudō, laud**ā**re, laud**āvī,** laud**ā**tus, to praise

Present			
Active		**Passive**	
laud**ō**	laudā***mus***	laud**or**	laudā***mur***
laudā***s***	laudā***tis***	laudā***ris***	laudā***minī***
laud**a*t***	laud**a*nt***	laudā***tur***	laud**a*ntur***

Imperfect			
laudā**ba*m***	laudā**bā*mus***	laudā**ba*r***	laudā**bā*mur***
laudā**bā*s***	laudā**bā*tis***	laudā**bā*ris***	laudā**bā*minī***
laudā**ba*t***	laudā**ba*nt***	laudā**bā*tur***	laudā**ba*ntur***

Future			
laudāb*ō*	laudāb*i*mus	laudāb*or*	laudāb*i*mur
laudāb*is*	laudāb*i*tis	laudāb*eris*	laudāb*imin*ī
laudāb*it*	laudāb*u*nt	laudāb*i*tur	laudāb*u*ntur

Present Perfect					
Active		**Passive**			
laudāv*ī*	laudāv*imus*	laudāt**us, -a, -um** {	su*m*	laudāt**ī, -ae, -a** {	su*mus*
laudāv*istī*	laudāv*istis*		es		es*tis*
laudāv*it*	laudāv*ērunt*		est		su*nt*

Past Perfect					
laudāv**era***m*	laudāv**erā***mus*	laudāt**us, -a, -um** {	era*m*	laudāt**ī, -ae, -a** {	erā*mus*
laudāv**erā***s*	laudāv**erā***tis*		erā*s*		erā*tis*
laudāv**era**t	laudāv**era**n*t*		era*t*		era*nt*

Future Perfect					
laudāv**er***ō*	laudāv**eri***mus*	laudāt**us, -a, -um** {	er*ō*	laudāt**ī, -ae, -a** {	eri*mus*
laudāv**eris**	laudāv**eri***tis*		eris		eri*tis*
laudāv**eri***t*	laudāv**eri**n*t*		eri*t*		eru*nt*

Imperative Mood

Active (praise)		Passive (be praised)	
laudā*ā*	laudā*te*	laudā*re*	laudā*minī*

Participles

	Active		Passive	
Pres.	laud**āns, -antis**	praising	[*lacking*]	
Perf.	[*lacking*]		laudāt**us, -a, -um**	(having been) praised
Fut.	laudātūr**us, -a, -um**	about to praise	laudand**us, -a, -um**	(necessary) to be praised

Second Conjugation

Indicative Mood

doceō, docēre, docuī, doctus, to teach

Present			
Active		**Passive**	
doceō	docēmus	doceor	docēmur
docēs	docētis	docēris	docēminī
docet	docent	docētur	docentur

Imperfect			
docēbam	docēbāmus	docēbar	docēbāmur
docēbās	docēbātis	docēbāris	docēbāminī
docēbat	docēbant	docēbātur	docēbantur

Future			
docēbō	docēbimus	docēbor	docēbimur
docēbis	docēbitis	docēberis	docēbiminī
docēbit	docēbunt	docēbitur	docēbuntur

Present Perfect					
Active			**Passive**		
docuī	docuimus	doctus, -a, -um {	sum	doctī, -ae, -a {	sumus
docuistī	docuistis		es		estis
docuit	docuērunt		est		sunt

Past Perfect					
docueram	docuerāmus	doctus, -a, -um {	eram	doctī, -ae, -a {	erāmus
docuerās	docuerātis		erās		erātis
docuerat	docuerant		erat		erant

Future Perfect					
docuerō	docuerimus		erō		erimus
docueris	docueritis	doctus, -a, -um {	eris	docti, -ae, -a {	eritis
docuerit	docuerint		erit		erunt

Imperative Mood

Active (teach)		Passive (be taught)	
docē	docēte	docēre	docēminī

Participles

	Active		Passive	
Pres.	docēns, -entis	teaching	[lacking]	
Perf.	[lacking]		doctus, -a, -um	having been taught
Fut.	doctūrus, -a, -um	about to teach	docendus, -a, -um	(necessary) to be taught

Third Conjugation

Indicative Mood

dūcō, **dūcere**, **dūxī**, **ductus, -a, -um**, to lead

Present			
Active		Passive	
dūcō	dūcimus	dūcor	dūcimur
dūcis	dūcitis	dūceris	dūciminī
dūcit	dūcunt	dūcitur	dūcuntur

Imperfect			
dūcēbam	dūcēbāmus	dūcēbar	dūcēbāmur
dūcēbās	dūcēbātis	dūcēbāris	dūcēbāminī
dūcēbat	dūcēbant	dūcēbātur	dūcēbantur

Future			
dūca*m*	dūcē*mus*	dūcar	dūcē*mur*
dūcē*s*	dūcē*tis*	dūcē*ris*	dūcē*mini*
dūce*t*	dūce*nt*	dūcē*tur*	dūce*ntur*

Present Perfect						
Active		**Passive**				
dūx*ī*	dūx*imus*	ductus, -a, -um	sum	ductī, -ae, -a	sumus	
dūx*istī*	dūx*istis*		es		estis	
dūx*it*	dūx*ērunt*		est		sunt	

Past Perfect						
dūx**era***m*	dūx**erā**mus	ductus, -a, -um	era*m*	ductī, -ae, -a	erāmus	
dūx**erā**s	dūx**erā**tis		erās		erātis	
dūx**era**t	dūx**era**nt		erat		erant	

Future Perfect						
dūx**er***ō*	dūx**eri**mus	ductus, -a, -um	er*ō*	ductī, -ae, -a	erimus	
dūx**eri**s	dūx**eri**tis		eris		eritis	
dūx**eri**t	dūx**eri**nt		erit		erunt	

Imperative Mood

Active (lead)		Passive (be led)	
dūc	dūci*te*	ducere	duci*minī*

Participles

	Active		Passive	
Pres.	dūcē*ns, -entis*	leading	[*lacking*]	
Perf.	[*lacking*]		duct*us, -a, -um*	(having been) led
Fut.	ductūr*us, -a, -um*	about to lead	ducend*us, -a, -um*	(necessary) to be led

Third -iō

Indicative Mood

faciō, <u>face</u>**re,** <u>fec</u>**ī,** <u>fac</u>**tus,** to make

Present			
Active		**Passive**	
faci**ō**	facimus	facior	facimur
facis	facitis	face<u>ris</u>	faciminī
facit	faciunt	facitur	faciuntur

Imperfect			
faciē**ba***m*	faciē**bā**mus	faciē**bar**	faciē**bā**mur
faciē**bā**s	faciē**bā**tis	faciē**bā**ris	faciē**bā**minī
faciē**bat**	faciē**bant**	faciē**bā**tur	faciē**bant**ur

Future			
facia*m*	faciē**mus**	faciar	faciē**mur**
faciē**s**	faciē**tis**	faciē**ris**	faciē**minī**
faciet	facient	faciē**tur**	facientur

Present Perfect					
Active		**Passive**			
fēc**ī**	fēc**imus**		su*m*		sumus
fēc**is***tī*	fēc**istis**	fact*us, -a, -um*	es	fact*ī, -ae, -a*	estis
fēc**i***t*	fēc**ērunt**		est		sunt

Past Perfect					
fēc**era***m*	fēc**erā**mus		era*m*		erāmus
fēc**erā**s	fēc**erā**tis	fact*us, -a, -um*	erās	fact*ī, -ae, -a*	erātis
fēc**erat**	fēc**erant**		erat		erant

Future Perfect							
fēcerō	fēcerimus			erō			erimus
fēceris	fēceritis	factus, -a, -um	{	eris	factī, -ae, -a	{	eritis
fēcerit	fēcerint			erit			erunt

Imperative Mood

Active (make)		Passive (be made)	
fac	facite	facere	faciminī

Participles

	Active		Passive	
Pres.	faciēns, -ientis	making	[lacking]	
Perf.	[lacking]		factus, -a, -um	(having been) made
Fut.	factūrus, -a, -um	about to make	faciendus, -a, -um	(necessary) to be made

Fourth Conjugation

Indicative Mood

audiō, audīre, audīvī, audītus, to hear

Present			
Active		**Passive**	
audi*ō*	audīmus	audior	audīmur
audīs	audītis	audīris	audīminī
audit	audiunt	audītur	audiuntur

Imperfect			
audiē**ba***m*	audiē**bā**mus	audiē**bar**	audiē**bā**mur
audiē**bā**s	audiē**bā**tis	audiē**bā**ris	audiē**bā**minī
audiē**bat**	audiē**bant**	audiē**bā**tur	audiē**bantur**

Future			
audi**a***m*	audi**ē**mus	audi**ar**	audi**ē**mur
audi**ē**s	audi**ē**tis	audi**ē**ris	audi**ē**minī
audi**et**	audi**ent**	audi**ē**tur	audi**entur**

Present Perfect					
Active		**Passive**			
audīv*ī*	audīv*imus*		sum		sumus
audīv*istī*	audīv*istis*	audītus, -a, -um	es	audītī, -ae, -a	estis
audīv*it*	audīv**ē***runt*		est		sunt

Past Perfect					
audīv**era***m*	audīv**erā**mus		era*m*		erāmus
audīv**erā**s	audīv**erā**tis	audītus, -a, -um	erās	audītī, -ae, -a	erātis
audīv**erat**	audīv**erant**		erat		erant

Future Perfect					
audīverō	audīverimus		erō		erimus
audīveris	audīveritis	audītus, -a, -um {	eris	audītī, -ae, -a {	eritis
audīverit	audīverint		erit		erunt

Imperative Mood

Active (hear)		Passive (be heard)	
audī	audīte	audīre	audīminī

Participles

	Active		Passive	
Pres.	audiēns, -entis	hearing	[lacking]	
Perf.	[lacking]		audītus, -a, -um	(having been) heard
Fut.	audītūrus -a, -um	about to hear	audiendus, -a, -um	(necessary) to be heard

IRREGULAR VERBS

Indicative Mood

sum, esse, fuī, to be

Present (51)		Imperfect		Future	
sum	sumus	eram	erāmus	erō	erimus
es	estis	erās	erātis	eris	eritis
est	sunt	erat	erant	erit	erunt

Present Perfect		Past Perfect		Future Perfect	
fuī	fuimus	fueram	fuerāmus	fuerō	fuerimus
fuistī	fuistis	fuerās	fuerātis	fueris	fueritis
fuit	fuērunt	fuerat	fuerant	fuerit	fuerint

Imperative Mood

Active Voice	
es (be)	es*te, esto*

Participles

Pres.	[*lacking*]	
Perf.	[*lacking*]	
Fut.	futūr**us, -a, -um,**	about to be, going to be

Indicative Mood

possum, po**sse,** potu**ī,** to be able

Present (57)		Imperfect		Future	
possu**m**	possumus	potera**m**	poterāmus	poter**ō**	poterimus
potes	potestis	poterās	poterātis	poteris	poteritis
potest	possunt	poterat	poterant	poterit	poterunt

Present Perfect		Past Perfect		Future Perfect	
potu**ī**	potu**imus**	potu**eram**	potu**erāmus**	potu**erō**	potu**erimus**
potu**istī**	potu**istis**	potu**erās**	potu**erātis**	potu**eris**	potu**eritis**
potu**it**	potu**ērunt**	potu**erat**	potu**erant**	potu**erit**	potu**erint**

Imperative Mood

Imperative forms are lacking.

Participle

Pres.	potē**ns,** -e**ntis**	being able, being powerful
Perf.	[*lacking*]	
Fut.	[*lacking*]	

Indicative Mood

eō, īre, iī/īvī, itūrus, to go

Present		Imperfect		Future	
eō	īmus	ībam	ībāmus	ībō	ībimus
īs	īts	ībās	ībātis	ībis	ībitis
it	eunt	ībat	ībant	ībit	ībunt

Present Perfect		Past Perfect		Future Perfect	
iī/īvī	iīmus/īvimus	ieram	ierāmus	ierō	ierimus
iistī/īvistī	iistis/īvistis	ierās	ierātis	ieris	ieritis
iit/īvit	iērunt/īvērunt	ierat	ierant	ierit	ierint

Imperative Mood

Active Voice	
ī	īte

Participles

	Active	Passive
Pres.	iēns, -euntis going	[*lacking*]
Pres. Perf.	[*lacking*]	itum Not used in this text
Fut.	itūrus, -a, -um going to go, about to go	[*lacking*]

Appendix B

The cardinal numbers from 1 through 100 are indeclinable, except for *ūnus, duo, trēs*. The plural of *mīlle* also has case inflections. (See Chapter 19 for these declensions.) The cardinal numbers from 200 to 2,000 have plural first-second declension adjective inflections. In the list below, the gender inflections are shown only for *ducentī, -ae, -a*.

All the ordinal numbers are regular first-second declension adjectives. To save space, the three gender forms are shown for *prīmus* only. Notice that when *decem* is part of another word, the spelling changes to *-decim*. Watch for other spelling adjustments in combined forms.

In Roman numerals, any letter to the right of a letter with a higher value is added to the preceding number (letter); a letter to the left of a letter with a higher value is subtracted.

Roman Numerals

Numerals

**Letter values: I = 1; V = 5; X = 10; L = 50; C = 100; D = 500; M = 1,000.
Lower case letters have the same values: i = 1; v = 5, etc.**

Number	Numeral	Cardinal	Ordinal
1	I	ūnus, -a, -um	prīmus, -a, -um
2	II	duo, duae, duo	secundus
3	III	trēs, tria	tertius
4	IV	quattuor	quārtus

5	V	quīnque	quīntus
6	VI	sex	sextus
7	VII	septem	septimus
8	VIII	octō	octāvus
9	IX *or* VIIII	novem	nōnus
10	X	decem	decimus
11	XI	ūndecim	ūndecimus
12	XII	duodecim	duodecimus
13	XIII	tredecim	tertius decimus
14	XIV or XIIII	quattuordecim	quārtus decimus
15	XV	quīndecim	quīntus decimus
16	XVI	sēdecim	sextus decimus
17	XVII	septendecim	septimus decimus
18	XVIII	duodēvīgintī	duodēvīcēsimus
19	XIX or XVIIII	ūndēvīgintī	ūndēvīcēsimus
20	XX	vīgintī	vīcēsimus
21	XXI	vīgintī (et) ūnus	vīcēsimus (et) prīmus
29	XXIX	ūndētrīgintā	ūndētrīcēsimus
30	XXX	trīgintā	trīcēsimus
40	XL or XXXX	quadrāgintā	quadrāgēsimus
50	L	quīnquāgintā	quīnquāgēsimus
60	LX	sexāgintā	sexāgēsimus
70	LXX	septuāgintā	septuāgēsimus
80	LXXX	octōgintā	octōgēsimus
90	XC or LXXXX	nōnāgintā	nōnāgēsimus
100	C	centum	centēsimus
101	CI	centum (et) ūnus	centēsimus prīmus
200	CC	ducentī, -ae, -a	ducentēsimus
300	CCC	trecentī	trecentēsimus
400	CD or CCCC	quadringentī	quadringentēsimus

500	D	quīngentī	quīngentēsimus
600	DC	sescentī	sescentēsimus
700	DCC	septingentī	septingentēsimus
800	DCCC	octingentī	octingentēsimus
900	CM or DCCCC	nōngentī	nōngentēsimus
1,000	M	mīlle	mīllēsimus
2,000	MM	duo mīlia	bis mīllēsimus

Appendix C

Functions of Noun Cases

Nominative case

- Subject: *Rōma* est magna. "<u>Rome</u> is large."
- Predicate noun: Rōma est magna *urbs.* "Rome is a large <u>city</u>."

Genitive case

- Causes one noun to modify another noun
- Can express several ideas, including the following:
  - Showing possession: liber *puerī*, "the <u>boy's</u> book"
  - Renaming of another noun: urbs *Rōmae,* "the city <u>of Rome</u>"
  - Specifying a noun: officium *dictātōris,* "office <u>of dictator</u>"
  - Showing part of a whole: finis *librī*, "the end <u>of the book</u>"

- Showing a quality of a noun: dux *virtūtis,* "a leader of courage"
- It is translated either by an apostrophe and an *s* or by an *of* phrase.

Dative case

- Indirect object: Rōmānī *ducī* honōrem dant. "The Romans give honor to the leader. / The Romans give the leader honor."
- With special adjectives: Lingua Latīna est similis *linguae Graecae.* "The Latin language is similar to the Greek language."

Accusative case

- Direct object: Rōmānī ducī *honōrem* dant. "The Romans give honor to the leader."
- Object of a preposition: Ad *urbem* vēnimus. "We came to the city."
- Distance how far (no preposition): Arborem *vigintī pedēs* altam vīdimus. "We saw a tree twenty feet tall." (The cardinal number *vigintī* does not have case forms.)
- Place to which (most nouns): Ad *urbem* vēnimus. "We came to the city." For the name of a city, no preposition is used. *Rōmam* vēnimus. "We came to Rome."
- Time how long (no preposition): *Decem diēs* in Rōmā erāmus. "We were in Rome (for) ten days." (*Decem* does not have case forms.)

Ablative case

- Object of preposition: De *Rōmā* legimus. "We are reading about Rome."
- Agent: Labor ā *patre meō* factus est. "The work was done by my father."
- Means (no preposition): *Stilō* scrībit. "He writes with a pencil."
- Place where: In *Americā* vīvimus. "We live in America." Before the name of a city, no preposition is used. *Rōmā* vīvunt. "They live in/at Rome." This use without a proposition is also called the locative case.
- Place from which (most nouns): Ab/Ex/Dē *urbe* mōvimus. "We moved from the city." Before the name of a city, no preposition is used. *Rōmā* movimus. "We moved from Rome." Before the nouns *domus,* "home," and *rūs,* "country," no preposition is used. *Domō nostrō* movimus. "We moved from our home." *Rūre* movimus. "We moved from the country."

- Time when (no preposition): In Rōmā *illō diē* erāmus. "We were in Rome (on) that day."
- Time within which (no preposition): Opus *hōrīs paucīs* confēcimus. "We finished the work within a few hours."

Vocative case

- Address (speaking to someone): It has the same form as the nominative case except for second-declension nouns that end in *-us/-ius: Marce,* lege sententiam hanc. "Marcus, read this sentence." *Lucī*, scīsne fabulam hanc? "Lucius, do you understand this story?" Often a vocative form is the first word of a sentence.

Appendix D

Pronunciation and Spelling

Letters in Latin words

- Latin has *no* silent letters.

Vowels

- The sounds of long and short vowels are the same except for the length of time each is held. Long vowels (those with a macron) are held approximately twice as long as short vowels.
- *a* = first *a* in *aha*
- *e* = *e* in *let*
- *i* = *i* in *it*

- *o* = *o* in *obey*
- *u* = *u* in *put,* <u>not</u> as in *cut*
- *ā* = second *a* in *aha* or the *a* in *father*
- *ē* = *e* in *they*
- *ī* = *i* in *machine*
- *ō* = *o* in *home*
- *ū* = *u* in *rude*

Macron rules (vowel length)

- The vowel *e* has a macron when it follows another vowel: *diēī.* It does not have a macron when it follows a consonant: *speī.*
- A vowel is *never* long when it precedes a final *m, r,* or *t* in an inflection and *almost never* when not in an inflection.
- A vowel is *never* long before *-nt.*
- A vowel is *always* long before *-ns.*

Diphthongs

- *ae* = *ai* as in *aisle*
- *au* = *ou* as in *out*
- *oe* = *oi* as in *oil*
- *ei* = *ei* as in *reign, they*
- *eu* = *eu* as in *neuter, few*
- *ui* = *we* or Latin *cui*

Consonants

- *c* = *k* in *cat,* not *s* in *city*
- The letter *u* is a consonant when combined with *g* and *q.*
  - *gu* = *gw* in *language*
  - *qu* = *kw* in *quick*
- *s* = *s* in *this,* not *s* in *these*

- *v* = *w* in *win*

- *x* = *ks* in *box*

- *r* should be trilled.

- *g* is always hard, as in *gun,* not as in *gem.* It is pronounced even in such words as *Gnaeus.*

- An *i* before a vowel at the beginning of a word is pronounced like the consonant *y;* it is sometimes spelled *j.* When a prefix is placed before this letter, it remains a consonant: *i*ustus, ini*u*stus or *j*ustus, in*j*ustus.

- When double consonants occur, such as *ll,* both letters are pronounced. Latin has no silent letters.

- The consonants *nc* blend (are in the same syllable) when followed by a third consonant, as in *sanctus.*

- The letters *ti* do not blend (re•sur•rec•ti•ōnis). Often in English *ti* blends to make the *sh* sound as in *resurrection.*

Latinized forms of Greek consonants

- *ch* = *k* + *a quick outbreathing,* as in *chorus* (transliteration of the single Greek letter χ)

- *ph* = *p* + *a quick outbreathing* as in *elephantus* <u>not</u> *f* (transliteration of the single Greek letter φ)

- *th* = *t* + *a quick outbreathing,* not as in *this, these* (transliteration of the Greek letter θ)

Consonant blends

- **Consonant blends** are consonants that are not separated when syllables are divided.

- *bs* = *ps* in *tops* (urbs)

- *sp* = *sp* in *spin* (spem)

- *gl* = *gl* as in *glass* (An•gli•cam)

- *gr* = *gr* as in *grass* (con•gres•sus)

- *gu* and *qu* (*See* "Consonants" above.)

- *sc* = *sk* in *school* (Vol•sci)

- *tr* = *tr* in *train* (pa•tri•a)

Syllable division

- Every syllable must contain a vowel or diphthong.
- Vowels in a diphthong blend and are not divided when syllables are divided: pa•tri•**ae**.
- Syllables are divided between two vowels unless the vowels form a diphthong: **me•u**s, **tu•u**s, ven**i•ō**. Vowels in a prefix or an inflection do not combine with other vowels to form a diphthong: for example, the letters *e* and *u* in *meus* are not a diphthong because *u* is part of the inflection *us*.
- Latin has no schwa. For example, in *Cornelius* the syllables *li•us* are pronounced separately (Cor•nē•li•us), not as in English (Cor•nēl•yus).
- A single consonant goes with the vowel that follows it: li•ber, La•tī•na.
- Two consonants are divided unless they form a blend: An•tō•ni•us, puel•la. (See the section called "Consonant blends" above.)
- A consonant blend goes with the vowel that follows it: pa•**tri**•a. For three consonants, the two that blend are kept together: sa**nc**•tus, An•**gli**•ca

Accent

- The **penult** is accented if it is long. It is long if it contains a long vowel (a•mī′cus), if it contains a diphthong (pa•tri•ae′que), or if it ends with a consonant (ae•ter′nus).
- The **ultima** (last syllable) is never accented.
- The **antepenult** (syllable before the penult) is accented if the penult is not long: An•tō′•ni•us, pa′tri•a.
- When an enclitic such as *-ne* or *-que* is added to a word, the accent is on the syllable just before the enclitic (the new penult) unless the new penult is short (mū•rem′•que, lin′•gua•ne).

Elision

- The genitive singular form of an i-stem noun is sometimes shortened by elision: for example, *fīliī* may be shortened to *fīlī*.
- The masculine nominative plural of i-stem nouns is always *-iī*. In these forms the *i* in the stem *never* elides with the *-ī* inflection. For example, the nominative plural of *fīlius* is always *fīliī*.

Appendix E

Translation Helps

Latin word order

- Generally transitive active verbs are at the end of the sentence.
- Generally linking words are in the same position as in English sentences. (However, the linking verb is often omitted and must be supplied in translation.)
- In questions that do not begin with an interrogative word such as an interrogative pronoun, the verb is often the first word and ends with the enclitic *-ne: Estne liber . . .?*
- Generally adjectives follow the nouns they modify.
- Adjectives that indicate size or number are usually considered emphatic and are placed before the nouns they modify.
- Prepositions sometimes appear within a prepositional phrase: *magna cum laude.*
- The preposition *cum* is often attached to a pronoun object: *tēcum, vōbīscum.*
- A word in a position other than the usual position receives emphasis.

English-to-Latin translation

- Latin has no words for *yes* and *no*. The word *ita,* "thus," or the phrase *ita vērē,* "thus truly," can be used for *yes;* and *minimē,* "by no means," can be used for *no.*

Latin-to-English translation

- Latin has no articles (*a, an, the*); these words should be added to make normal English sentences.

- If a sentence contains an intransitive verb such as *est* and no predicate noun or predicate adjective, the English expletive *there* may be supplied: *Lacus est in silvā* ("There is a lake in the forest.") However, in some contexts a better translation would be "The lake is in the forest." (Latin has no equivalent of the expletive *there.*)

- A sentence containing *nōn* usually requires an auxiliary in the translation: *Claudia linguam Germānam nōn dīcit.* "Claudia *does not* speak the German language."

- Generally, genitive-case nouns that name persons are translated with an apostrophe and *s,* and genitive-case nouns that do not name persons are translated with the *of* phrase. There are exceptions to these rules, such as *the father of the boy* (sometimes used instead of *the boy's father*) and *a day's work.*

- The subject of the verb is frequently omitted in Latin sentences. The verb ending and the context provide the subject if the Latin subject is omitted. For example, the translation of *sum* and *ego sum* is the same. The pronoun subject, as in *ego sum,* gives emphasis to the subject.

- Often the Latin equivalent of the *be* verb is omitted and needs to be supplied in English translation (as stated under "Latin word order" above).

- When the first word of a question ends with the enclitic *-ne,* an English auxiliary such as *is/are, do/does, have/has* is often needed in translation. The English subject comes between the auxiliary and the main verb: *Does he have the book?*

- An indirect object can be translated (1) by placing it before the direct object or (2) by putting it in a prepositional phrase beginning with *to* or *for.*

- Special adjectives such as *similis, amīcus,* and *fidēlis* should be translated by placing *to* before the dative-case noun that is used with the special adjective.

Appendix F

Roman History

Historical periods

Seven kings of Rome: 753-509 B.C.

Roman Republic: 509-27 B.C.

Roman Empire: 27 B.C.–A.D. 476

Byzantine Empire: A.D. 330-1453

Historical events

Pyrrhic victory (Greeks over Romans): 279 B.C.

First Punic War: 264-241 B.C.

Second Punic War: 218-201 B.C.

Third Punic War: 149-146 B.C.

Roman invasion of Britain: 54 B.C.

Reign of Octavius (Augustus) Caesar: 27 B.C.–A.D. 14

Approximate date of the completing of the Vulgate: A.D. 405

End of Roman occupation of Britain:
   (approximate date) A.D. 410

Beginning of Germanic invasions of Britain: A.D. 449

Norman French invasion of Britain (Norman Conquest): A.D. 1066

Appendix G

Mythology Terms

In parentheses are the names of the corresponding Greek or Roman deities.

See the Index for terms related to Roman history and legends.

Not all the terms in this list are mentioned in this text.

Apollo (both Roman and Greek), god of music and light, 23

Ares (Mars, Roman), god of war, 18, 23

Artemis (Diana, Roman), goddess of youth and the hunt, 23

Ceres (Demeter, Greek), goddess of grain, 15, 17, Lg V

Cronos (Saturn, Roman), father of Zeus

deities, gods and goddesses

Demeter (Ceres, Roman), goddess of grain, 15, 17, Lg V

Diana, (Artemis, Greek), goddess of youth and the hunt, 23

Elysian Fields (both Roman and Greek), home of the heroes of the lower world, 23

fabula, myth, 15, 23

Flora, goddess of flowers

Fortuna, goddess of fortune or luck; symbol, a wheel

Hades (Pluto, Roman), god of the entire lower world, 17, Lg V, 23

Hera (Juno, Roman), queen of the gods, goddess of marriage, 17, 18

Hermes (Mercury, Roman), god of trade and travel, 23

Hestia (Vesta, Roman), goddess of the hearth, 17

inferī, the dead ones; the abode of the dead, the lower world

Janus, god of good beginnings, god of doors; he carried a large key; he had two faces looking in opposite directions, 18

Appendix H

Borrowed Words and Phrases

Words and phrases listed with asterisks are used in the chapters named but are not discussed as loan words.

Words and phrases presented only in Activities are indicated with the abbreviation *Act.*

Loan words

animal, 2	Dives, 21	minimum, 22	plebs, 12
arbor, 7	extra, 21	minor, 22	quorum, 11
arena, 7	finis*, 12, 19	neuter, 8	senator, 6
audio, 2	Gemini, 11	nova*, 3, 12, 15, 20	via, 3
bonus, Act. 22	genus, 8	optimum, 22	victor, 3
Cincinnati, 12	labor, 21	opus, 8	Victoria*, 12
data, 2	major, 22	pastor, 3	video, 2
dictator, 12	maximum, 22	pauper, 21	

Loan phrases

a Deo lux nostra, Act. 13

a Deo et rege, Act. 13

a die, Act. 13

ab initio, Act. 13, 20

"Adeste Fideles," 2

ad finem, Act. 20

ad multos annos, Act. 13

ad patres, Act. 13

ad rem, Act. 13

adsum, Act. 13

ad verbum, Act. 13

Agnus Dei, Act. 13

alter ego, 15

anno Domini, 3

antebellum, Act. 13

antecibum, Act. 13

antelucem, Act. 13

ante meridiem (A.M.), 2

antemortem, Act. 13

ante-omnia, Act. 13

aqua pura, 7

arbor vitae, 3, 7

ars longa, vita brevis, Act. 13, 20

aut mors aut victoria, Act. 13

bona fide, 2, Act. 22

carpe diem, 19

cum grano salis, Act. 9

cum laude, 15

de novo, Act. 20

Dominus tecum, 15

Dominus vobiscum, 15

dum vita est spes est, Act. 9

E pluribus unum, 2

et cetera (etc.), 2, 3

ex libris, Act. 20

ex tempore, Act. 9, 20

id est (i.e.), Act. 20

Magna Charta / Magna Carta, 3

magna cum laude, 15

magnum bonum, Act. 9

magnum opus, Act. 9, 22

mea culpa, Act. 9

Pater noster, Act. 9

pater patriae, Act. 9

Pax Romana, 3

pax tecum, 15

pax vobiscum, 15

per diem, 3, Act. 9

postbellum, Act. 13

post meridiem (P.M.), 2

postmortem, Act. 13, 20

prima facie, Act. 20

quod vide (q.v.), Act. 20

rara avis, Act. 9, 19

summa cum laude, 15

terra firma, 2, 7

veritas vincit, Act. 9

Appendix I

Latin Songs

Most of these songs contain vocabulary and grammar that you have not learned. Even though you cannot translate all the songs, you can enjoy singing them. And as you sing them, you will discover the meanings of many unfamiliar words. Later, when you study new vocabulary and grammar, you will understand more of the words.

Jesus Amat Me Scio ("Jesus Loves Me")

> Jesus amat me scio,
> Verbum dicit mihi ita;
> Jesus liberos tenet
> Infirmi sunt, sed firmus est.
>
> Me Jesus amat, me Jesus amat,
> Me Jesus amat,
> Verbum dicit mihi ita.

Ago Gratias ("Thank You, Lord, for Saving My Soul")

> Ago gratias, servatus sum;
> Ago gratias, complevisti me;
> Ago gratias dando mihi
> Salutem magnam, divite, libere.

Quisque Dies Cum Jesu ("Every Day with Jesus Is Sweeter Than the Day Before")

Quisque dies cum Jesu est dulcior quam dies prior,
Quisque dies eum plus et plus amo.
Jesus me servat et tenet et is est quem expecto.
Quisque dies cum Jesu est dulcior quam dies prior.

Adeste Fideles ("O Come, All Ye Faithful," Portuguese Hymn, attributed to J. Reading, 1692)

Adeste, fideles, Laeti triumphantes;
Venite, venite in Bethlehem;
Natum videte Regem angelorum.

Chorus
   Venite adoremus, venite adoremus,
   Venite adoremus Dominum.

Cantet nunc Io! Chorus angelorum,
Cantet nunc aula caelestium,
Gloria, gloria in excelsis Deo!

Ergo qui natus Die hodierna,
Jesu, tibi sit gloria;
Patris aeterni Verbum caro factum!

Nox Silens, Sancta Nox

Nox silens, sancta nox,
Tota quies, clara luce;
Nunc parentes pervigilant;
Dive puer, tam tener et parve,
   Dormi in pace sacra,
   Dormi in pace sacra!

Nox silens, sancta nox,
Pastores adorant.
Glori(ae) ex stellis veniunt,
Angeli hallelujah cantant,
   Christus Salvator est,
   Christus Salvator est.

Gaudeamus Igitur

Medieval Student Song

1. Gau - de - a - mus i - gi - tur, Ju - ve - nes dum su - mus;
2. U - bi sunt, qui an - te nos In mun - do fu - e - re?
3. Vi - ta nos - tra bre - vis est Bre - vi fi - ni - e - tur,

Gau - de - a - mus i - gi - tur, Ju - ve - nes dum su - mus;
U - bi sunt, qui an - te nos In mun - do fu - e - re?
Vi - ta nos - tra bre - vis est Bre - vi fi - ni - e - tur,

Post ju - cun - dam ju - ven - tu - tem, Post mo - les - tam se - nec - tu - tem,
Tran - se - as ad su - pe - ros, A - be - as ad in - fe - ros,
Ve - nit mors ve - lo - ci - ter, Ra - pit nos a - tro - ci - ter,

Nos ha - be - bit hu - mus, Nos ha - be - bit hu - mus.
Quos si vis vi - de - re, Quos si vis vi - de - re.
Ne - mi - ni par - ce - tur, Ne - mi - ni par - ce - tur.

4. Alma mater floreat,
   Quæ nos educavit,
   Caros et commilitones,
   Dissitas in regiones
   Sparsos, congregavit.

5. Vivat et re publica
   Et qui illam regit,
   Vivat nostra civitas,
   Mæcenatum caritas,
   Quæ nos hic protegit.

Gaudeamus Igitur ("Let Us Rejoice Therefore")

This is a medieval university song. It expresses the Epicurean philosophy that there is no life after death, so the goal of life is pleasure. Similarly, many people today think only about their days on earth. Christians can see in this song the emptiness of life without Christ and its contrast with the joy, peace, and assurance of eternal life found in the Scriptures.

Translation

Let us rejoice therefore while we are young. (Repeat)
After pleasurable youth, after troublesome old age,
The ground will have us (Repeat).

Where are those who were before us in the world? (Repeat)
May you cross over to the ones above, may you go away to the ones below,
If you wish to see them, if you wish to see them.

Our life is short, it will end briefly. (Repeat)
Death comes quickly, it snatches us cruelly;
It will spare no one (Repeat).

Let the academy flourish, which has educated us. (Repeat)
It has brought together dear companions,
Now dispersed into scattered regions (Repeat).

Let both the republic live and he who rules it. (Repeat)
Let our city live; and this dear fellowship
Which has brought us together here (Repeat).

ECCE CAESAR ("Behold Caesar" to the tune of "O My Darling Clementine")

Ecce Caesar nunc triumphat qui subegit Galliam;
Civiumque multitudo celebrat victoriam.

Chorus
    Gaius Iulius Caesar noster,
    Imperator, pontifex.
    Primum praetor, deinde consul,
    Nunc dictator, moxque rex.

En victores procedentes, laeti floribus novis;
Magna praeda sunt potiti et captivi plurimis.

Legiones viam sacram totam complent strepitu,
Capitolinumque collem scandit Caesar in carru.

LEGIONES CAESARIS (to the tune of "One Little, Two Little, Three Little Indians")

Caesar habet unam legionem
Caesar habet unam legionem
Caesar habet unam legionem
Unam bonam legionem.

Unam, duas, tres legiones
Quattuor, quinque, sex legiones
Septem, octo, novem legiones
Decem bonas legiones.

Decem, novem, octo legiones
Septem, sex, quinque legiones
Quattuor, tres, duas legiones
Unam bonam legionem.

MICA, MICA, PARVA STELLA ("Twinkle, Twinkle, Little Star")

Mica, mica, parva stella,
Miror quaenam sis tam bella;
Super terra parva pendes,
Alba velut gemma splendes.

Chorus
   Mica, mica, parva stella,
   Miror quaenam sis tam bella.

Quando fervens sol discessit,
Qui die natōs lacessit,
Mox ostendis lumen purum,
Micans, micans per obscurum.

Tibi noctu qui vagatur
Ob scintullulam gratatur;
Ni micares tu, non sciret
Quas per vias errans iret.

Thalamos tu specularis
Et in alto iam versaris,
Neque dormis unam horam
Donec cernimus auroram.

NONNE DORMIS ("Are You Sleeping, Brother John?")

Nonne dormis, nonne dormis,
Frater mi, frater mi?
Mane mane tinnit, mane mane tinnit
Aes tintinnabuli, aes tintinnabuli.

DUC, DUC, REMOS DUC ("Row, Row, Row Your Boat")

Duc, duc, remos duc
Flumine secundo.
Vivitur, vivitur
Vivitur, vivitur
Velut in somnio.

TRES MURES! ("Three Blind Mice")

Tres mures! Tres mures!
En fugiunt! En fugiunt!
Nam omnes secuti sunt rusticam
Quae caudas cultello desecuit;
Sane facinus insolitissimum!
O tres mures!

Vocābulārium

Anglicum–Latīnum

- See Appendix G for names of deities and other mythological terms.
- See Vocābulārium Latīnum-Anglicum for complete information.
- See the Index and the Vocābulārium Latīnum-Anglicum for proper nouns and adjectives that are not included here.

able, potēns
abode, habitātiō
about, *adv.,* circā, quasi; *prep.,* ad, circa, circum, dē
above, *adv., prep.,* super; *adj.,* superus
accomplish, perficiō
acquaintance with, cognitiō
acquire, inveniō
across, trāns
act, *verb,* agō
administer, cūrō
admirable, praeclārus
advice, consilium
affair, rēs
affection, cāritās
after, post
afterwards, posteā
again, iterum
against, adversus, contrā, in
age, saeculum
agree, consentiō

agreement, pactiō
aid, auxilium
aim, aim at, intendō
alive, vīvus
all, omnis
allow, dō
alone, sōlus
along, per
also, etiam, quoque
always, semper
am, sum
among, in, inter
ancestor, parēns
ancient, antīquus, vetus
and, et, -que
anger, īra
anguish, dolor
animated, alacer
announce, dēnuntiō
another, alius
approximately, circum, circa; quasi
area governed, imperium

arena, See sand.
arise, exsistō/existō
arm, *verb,* armō
arms (weapons), *noun,* arma
army, exercitus
around (about), *adv., prep.,* circā, circum
art, ars
as, sīcut
as a reward for, pro
ascend, ascendō
ask, interrogō
assembly, conventus
at, ad
at first, prīmō
at night, noctū
at once, statim
at that place, illīc
attack, invādō
attention, cūra
audacious, audāx
away from, ā, ab

389

Vocābulārium

bad, malus
band of men, grex, manus
barn, horreum
battle, *noun,* proelium
be, sum
be able, possum
be alive, vīvō
be inactive, sedeō
be lost, pereō
be obligated, dēbeō
be very strong, be powerful
  praevaleō
be well, aveō salveō, valeō
bear, gerō
because, quia, quod
because of, per, propter
before, *adv.,* ante, prius; *prep.,* ante
begin, incipiō
beginning, initium, principium
behind, post
behold, *adv.,* ecce; *verb,* conspiciō
believe, crēdō
beseech, supplicō
besides, etiam, super
best, optimus
better, melior
between, inter
beyond, super
Bible, Scriptūra
bite, mordeō
bitter, acer
bold, audāx, superbus
book, liber
both . . . and, et . . . et
boundary, finis
boy, puer
brave, fortis
bread, pānis
breath, spiritus
bridge, pōns
brief, brevis
bring up, ēdūcō
brother, brother-in-law, frāter
bubble, bulla
build, *verb,* aedificiō, condō,
  construō

burn, *verb,* incendō
business, mercātus
but, sed
by, ā, ab
by no means, minimē
cake (small), crūstulum
call, appellō, clāmō, vocō
camp, *noun,* castra
capture, *verb,* capiō
care, cūra
care for, cūrō
carefree, secūrus
carry, gerō
Carthaginians, Poenī
cast out, ēiciō
cat, fēlēs
catch, *verb,* capiō
cause to rise, suscitō
celebrate, celebrō
century, saeculum
certain, certus
certainly, ita vērē
chain, catēna
change, *noun,* mūtātiō
change, *verb,* mūtō
chariot, carrus
chief magistrate, dictātor
child, puer
child (little), īnfāns
children, līberī
choke, suffōcō
choose, legō
choose out, dīligō
Christ, Christus, Rēx, Salvātor,
  Fīlius Deī, Dominus
Christian, *n., adj.,* Christiānus
circumstance, rēs
citadel, arx
citizen, cīvis
citizenship, cīvitās
city, cīvitās, urbs
civil, cīvilis
class, genus
clean, pūrus
clear, clārus, pūrus
climb up, ascendō, ēvādō

close, *verb,* terminō
colony, colōnia
come, veniō
come back, redeō, reveniō
come into existence, crēscō
come together, conveniō
come upon, inveniō
command, *noun,* imperium,
  mandātum
commander, dux
commander-in-chief, imperātor
common people, plebs, vulgus
complete, *verb,* perficiō
concern, cūra
concerning, dē
conquer, superō, vincō
conqueror, victor
consecrated, augustus
construct, construō
continuous, perpetuus
conversation, colloquium
cookie, crūstulum
Coriolanus, Gnaeus Martius
correct, *verb,* corrigō
council of elders, senātus
country, patria
courage, virtūs
courageous, audāx, fortis
cousin, frāter
cover, *verb,* contegō
crime, vitium
cross, *verb,* transeō
crowd, populus, vulgus
crown of oak leaves, quercus
cry aloud, clāmō
cure, *noun,* remedium
cut down, succidō
danger, perīculum
daring, audāx
daughter, fīlia
day, diēs
dead, mortuus
dearness, cāritās
death, mors
death, subject to, *adj.,* mortālis
deceit, dolus

deceive, fraudō
deceiver, fraudātor
declare war, dēnuntiō
decline, *noun,* dēminūtiō
decree, mandātum
deep, altus
deeper, altior
deepest, altissimus
defeat, *noun,* clādēs
defeat, *verb,* superō, vincō
defend, dēfendō
deity, deus, dea
delay, mora
delegate, lēgātus
deliverer, salvātor
demand, postulō
deputy, lēgātus
descendant, nepos
deserted, vastus
desire, *verb,* optō
desolate, vastus
despotism, dominātiō
destroy, dēstrūō
dictator, dictātor
die, obeō, pereō
dignified, augustus
disaster, clādēs
disciple, discipula, discipulus
discover, inveniō
dismal, tristis
display, *verb,* ostendō
distance, spatium
do, agō, faciō
dog, canis
door, ostium
down from, dē
draw, dūcō
drive (a chariot), agō
drive back, repellō
drown, suffōcō
during, per
each, quisque
ear, auris
earn, inveniō
earth, terra
easy, facilis

Egypt, Aegyptus
Egyptian, Aegyptius
either . . . or, aut . . . aut
elder, maior
elect, creō
elephant, elephantus
emperor, imperātor
empire, imperium
empty, vastus
encampment, castra
end, *noun,* fīnis
end, *verb,* terminō
enduring, dūrus
enemy, *noun, adj.,* inimīcus
English, Anglicus
enjoyment, frūctus
enormous, vastus
enroll, conscrībō
enter, intrō, invādō
entire, tōtus
entrance, ostium
entreaty, rogātiō
envious, invidus
envy, *verb,* invideō
equip for war, armō
error, peccātum
escape, ēvādō
establish, condō, constituō
esteem, *noun,* cāritās
esteem highly, *verb,* dīligō
eternal, aeternus
even, etiam
even as, sīcut
even now, adhūc
every, omnis
evil, malus
examination, investīgātiō
excellence, virtus
excellent, praeclārus
exist, sum
expectation, spēs
experienced in, vetus
eye, oculus
fable, fabula
face, *noun,* faciēs
fair, iustus

faithful, fidēlis
fall, cadō
fall under, succidō
fame, glōria
family, familia
famous, clārus
farewell, aveō, valeō
farm, ager
farmer, agricola
father, pater, parēns
Father, Pater
father of the family, paterfamiliās
fault, peccātum, vitium
favor, venia
favorable, fēlix
fear, *verb,* timeō
fearless, secūrus
feed, pascō
fetter, catēna
field, ager
fight, *noun,* pugna, proelium
fight, *verb,* pugnō
fill, repleō
finally, dēnique
find, inveniō
fire, ignis
first, *adj.,* prīmus
first *adv.,* prīmō
flame, flamma
flee, fugiō
fleet, classis
flight (take), fugiō
float, natō
flock, grex
flow down, dēfluō
flower, flōs
follower, sectātor
food, cibus
foolhardy, audāx
foolish, stultus
foot, pēs
for, pro
force, *noun,* vīs
foremost, prīmus
forest, silva
forgiveness, venia

former, ille, prior
fortress, arx
fortunate, fēlix
fortuneteller, prophēta
found (establish), condō
fountain, fōns
four, quattuor
fourteen, quattuordecim
France, Gallia
free, *adj.,* līber; *verb,* līberō
fresh, novus
friend, amīcus
friendly, amīcus
frighten, terreō
from, ā, ab; dē; ē, ex
fruit, frūctus
fruit of the earth, frūx
furnish, dō
Gallic, *adj.,* Gallicus
Gaul, *noun,* Gallia
gave, dedit
general, *noun,* dux
genuinely, vērē
girl, puella
give, dō
give (thanks), agō
give up, dedō
gives, dat
gloomy, tristis
glory, glōria
go, eō
go away, abeō, obeō
go back, redeō
go in, invādō
go over, transeō
go through, pereō
god, deus
God, Deus, Pater
goddess, dea
gold, aurum
good, bonus
good-bye, valē
good day! aveō (haveō), salveō
good morning! salvē
goodness, virtūs
goose, anser

gospel, evangelium
government, gūbernātiō
grace, grātia, venia
grain, frūmentum, frūctus
grand, grandis
granddaughter, nepōs
grandfather, avus, parēns
grandmother, avia, parēns
grandson, nepōs
grant, *verb,* dō
grapevine, vītis
gratitude, grātia
great, grandis, magnus
greater, maior
greatly, magnopere
Greece, Graecia
greedy, avārus
Greek, *noun, adj.,* Graecus
ground, terra
grow up, crescō
growing things, frūctus
guard, servō
guide, *noun,* dux
guile, dolus
had, habēbat
hand, manus
happy, fēlix
hard, dūrus
harsh, dūrus, iniustus
hasten, contendō, currō
hatred, inimīcitia, odium
haughty, superbus
have, habeō, possideō
he, is, hic, ille, iste
head of a household, dominus, paterfamiliās
hear, audiō
heart, cor
heaven, caelum/coelum
heavy, gravis
hello, salvē
help, *noun,* auxilium
help, *verb,* adiuvō
her own, suus
herd, grex
hers, eius, huius, illīus, istius

herself, *See* **himself.**
high, altus
higher, altior
highest, altissimus, suprēmus
himself, herself, itself, themselves, *reflex. pro.,* sē (suī, sibi, sē, sē) *intens. pro.,* ipse
his, eius, huius, illīus, istius
his own, suus
history, historia
hit, feriō
hitherto, adhūc
hold, habeō, possideō
hold out (offer), praebeō
Holy Spirit, Spiritus
home, domus
honesty, probitās
honor, *noun,* honor/honos
hope, *noun,* spēs
horse, equus
hostile, inimīcus
hour, hōra
house, domus, habitātiō
household, familia
however, autem
human being, homō
hurl, iaciō
husband, vir
husbandman, agricola
I, ego
if, sī
if not, nisi
ill-mannered, insolēns
illuminate, inluminō
immediately, statim
imperfection, vitium
important, grandis
in, in
in behalf of, pro
in the least, minimē
in the presence of, apud
increase, crescō
injustice, iniustitia
inscription, titulus
instruct, doceō
intend, intendō

into, in
investigation, investīgātiō
ire, īra
is, est
island, īnsula
Italian, Italius, Italicus
Italy, Italia
its, eius, huius, illīus, istīus
its own, suus
itself, *See* **himself.**
Jerome, Eusebius Hieronymus, monk who produced the Vulgate
join (together), coniungō
judge, iūdex
judicious, prūdēns
jump, jump in, into, on, insiliō
jump over, transiliō
just, iustus
just as, sīcut
justice, iustitia
keen, acer
keep, servō
kill, necō
kind, genus
kindle, incendō
kindness, grātia
king, rēx
King of kings, Rēx rēgum, Christus
kingdom, regnum
kneel, supplicō
know, sciō
knowledge of, cognitiō
label, titulus
labor, labor, opus
lake, lacus
lamb, agnus
land, terra
language, lingua, ōrātiō
large, magnus
larger, maior
largest, maximus
last, ultimus, suprēmus
Latin, Latīnus
latter, hic
laugh, *verb,* rīdeō
laugh at, inrīdeō

law, iūs, lēx
lawful, iustus
lead, dūcō
leader, dux, imperātor
leap, *verb,* exsiliō, insiliō
leap across, transiliō
leap up, exsiliō
learn, learn how, discō
least, minimus
leave, abeō
legend, fābula
less, minor
lessening, *noun,* dēminūtiō
liberator, salvātor
lie, *verb,* iaceō
life, vīta
lift up, levō
light, lūx
lightning, fulmen
like, *verb,* amō
little, parvus
little cake, crūstulum
live, *verb,* vīvō
lively, alacer
living, *adj.,* vīvus
long, longus
look!, *imper. verb,* ecce
lord, dominus
Lord, Christus, Dominus
loss, iactūra
loud noise, strīdor
love, *noun,* cāritās; *verb,* amō, dīligō
lower world, regions, inferī
majestic, augustus
make, creō, faciō
make full, repleō
make to rise, suscitō
man, homō, vir
manage, cūrō
mankind, mundus
manliness, virtus
many, multus (*pl. forms*)
Mark, Marcus
Martius, Gnaeus, Coriolanus
masses, vulgus

master, *noun,* dominus, magister
mastery, dominātiō
matron, mulier
matter, rēs
me, mē (**to/for me,** mihi)
meeting, conventus
merchant, mercātor
message, nuntius
messenger, nuntius
middle, *noun,* medium
midst, medium
mighty, potēns
mile, mille passuum
mindful, memor
mistress, magistra
mistress of the household, māterfamilias
mob, vulgus
money, pecūnia
month, mensis
moon, lūna
moreover, autem
mortal, *adj.,* mortālis
mother, māter, parēns
mother of the family, māterfamilias
mother's brother, avunculus
mountain, mōns
mouse, mūs
mouth, ōs
mouth of a river, ostium
move, *verb,* moveō
much, multus
multitude, populus, vulgus
my, meus
myth, fābula
name, *noun,* nōmen; *verb,* appellō
narrate, narrō
nation, gēns, populus
native land, patria
near, ad, circum, circā
neither, neuter
nephew, nepos
never, numquam
new, novus
niece, fīlia sorōris *or* fīlia frātris

night, nox
no, *adj.,* nullus; *adv.,* minimē
no one, no man, nēmō
nobleman, patricius
nobody, nēmō
noise (loud), strīdor
none, nullus
north, north wind, aquilō
nose, nāsus
not, nōn
not any, nullus
not at all, minimē
nothing, nihil
nourish, pascō
now, nunc
number, numerus
oak, oak tree, quercus
object, *noun,* rēs
offer, *verb,* dō, praebeō
often, saepe
old, antīquus, vetus
old person, senex
on, in
on account of, propter
on all sides, circum
once, aliquando
one, ūnus
only, sōlus
onto, in
open, aperiō
opposed to, opposite, adversus
oppressive, iniustus
or, aut
oration, ōrātiō
orator, ōrātor
order, *noun,* imperium, mandātum
other, alius
our, noster
out from, out of, ē, ex
outside, extrā
over (in space), per, super, trāns
overcome, superō
owe, dēbeō
own (one's, their), *adj.,* suus; *possessive pronoun form,* (his, hers, its), eius; (their), eārum, eōrum

pain, dolor
painful, acer
pardon, venia
parent, parēns
part, pars
pass over, trānseō
patient, patiēns
patrician, *adj., noun,* patricius
pay (a soldier's), stipendium
peace, pāx
pen, stilus
peninsula, paenīnsula
people, gēns, populus, vulgus
perceive, conspiciō
perform, faciō
peril, perīculum
perish, pereō
person, homō
person in the prime of life, iuvenis
pick, carpō
pig, porcus
place, *noun,* locus
place confidence in, *verb,* crēdō
plan, *noun,* consilium; *verb,* intendō
plebeian, *adj.,* plēbēius
plebeians, *collective noun,* plēbs
pluck, carpō
poem, carmen
poor, pauper
possess, possideō
power, domīnātiō, imperium, regnum, vīs
powerful, potēns, validus
praise, laudō
pray, supplicō
prepared, parātus
presently, mox
prevail, praevaleō
prince, rēx
promise, *noun,* prōmissiō
proper, iustus
prophet, prophēta
protect, servō
proud, superbus
provide, praebeō

prudent, memor
public, *noun,* populus, publicus, vulgus
Punic War, Punicum Bellum
pupil, discipula, discipulus
pure, pūrus
put together, condō
queen, rēgīna
quick, alacer, celer
quickly, rapidē
rabble, vulgus
rapid, celer
rapidly, rapidē
rash, audāx
read, legō
reality, vēritās
really, vērē
rear, *verb,* ēdūcō
reason, ratiō
recline, iaceō
rejoice, exsultō
relate, narrō
reliable, fidēlis
remain, maneō
remain fixed, sedeō
remarkable, praeclārus
remedy, remedium
remembering, *adj.,* memor
republic, rēs publica
request, *noun,* rōgātiō
require, postulō
rest, iaceō
restraint, catēna
resurrection, resurrectiō
return, *verb,* redeō, reveniō, revertō
rich, dīvēs
ridicule, *verb,* inrideō
right, *noun,* is (jūs)
right to command, *noun,* imperium
right hand, dextra
rise again, rise up, resurgō
rise, cause to, suscitō
rise up, exsurgō
river, flūmen
road, via
Roman, Rōmānus

rough in appearance, vastus
rude in appearance, insolēns, vastus
rule, *noun,* regnum
ruler, dominus, dux, rēx
run, *verb,* currō
sacred, sacer
sad, tristis
safe, secūrus, tūtus
sail, *verb,* nāvigō
salt, sāl
sand, harēna (*also* arēna)
sandal, solea
save, servō
savior, salvātor
Savior, Salvātor
say, dīcō
school, schola
sea, mare
search for, quaerō
second, secundus
secret, *adj.,* sēcrētus
secretly, clam
secure, secūrus
see, videō
seek, quaerō
seize, capiō, invādō
-self/selves, *See* **himself.**
senate, senātus
senator, senātor
send, mittō
send back, remittō
serve, ministrō
set fire to, incendō
set free, līberō
set right, corrigō
seven, septem
severe, gravis
shadow, umbra
she, ea, haec, illa, ista
shepherd, pastor
ship, navis
short, brevis
shout, *verb,* clāmō
show, *verb,* ostendō
shut in, *verb,* circumclūdō

silver, *noun,* argentum
similar, similar to, similis
sin, *noun,* peccātum
sing, cantō
sinner, peccātor
sister, soror
sit, sedeō
skill, ars
sky, caelum/coelum
slave, *noun,* servus
small, parvus
small bird, passer
smaller, minor
smallest, minimus
smite, feriō
snatch, capiō
soil, terra
soldier, mīles
sole, *adj.,* sōlus
sometimes, aliquando, interdum
son, fīlius
Son of God (Christ), Fīlius Deī
song, carmen
soon, mox
soothsayer, prophēta
sorrow, dolor
southern, austrālis
space, spatium
Spain, Hispānia
sparrow, passer
speak, dīcō
speaker, ōrātor
speech, ōrātiō
spirit, spiritus
spring, *noun,* fōns; *verb,* insiliō
squirrel, sciūrus
stand, *verb,* stō, adstō
stand by, adstō
state, cīvitās
steadfast, fīdēlis
still, adhūc, etiam
story, fābula
strangle, suffōcō
street, via
strength, vīs

stretch (in a particular direction), intendō
strike, *verb,* feriō
stroke of lightning, fulmen
strong, dūrus, fortis, validus
study, *noun,* cognitiō
stylus, stilus
subject to death, mortālis
successful, fēlix
suffocate, suffōcō
summer, aestās
sun, sōl
supply, praebeō
surrender, dedō
surround, circumclūdō
sweetheart, puella
swift, celer
swim, natō
take, capiō
take care of, cūrō
take flight, fugiō
tale, fābula
tallest, altissimus
teach, doceō
teacher (female), magistra
teacher (male), magister
tell, narrō
tenement house, īnsula
terrify, terreō
test, investīgātiō
thankful for, memor
thanks, grātia
that, is, ille, iste, quī
that one near, iste
their, eārum, eōrum
their own, suus
themselves, sē (suī, sibi)
then, mox, tum
there, illīc
therefore, igitur
thereupon, posteā, mox
thief, fūr
thing, rēs
things to be read, legenda
things to be said, spoken, dīcenda
think, cōgitō

third, tertius
thirteen, tredecim
this, hic
thoughtful, memor
thousand, mille
thousand paces (a mile), mille passuum
threaten, dēnuntiō
three, trēs
three hundred, trecentī
throng, vulgus
through, per
throw, throw out, ēiciō
thunderbolt, fulmen
thus far, adhūc
thus truly, ita vērē
tiller of soil, agricola
time, tempus, diēs
title, titulus
to, *prep.,* ad
today, hodiē
tongue, lingua
too, *adv.,* quoque
total, tōtus
toward, *prep.,* ad
towards (against), adversus, in
town, oppidum
trade, *noun,* mercātus
traveler, viātor
treaty, pactiō
tree, arbor
tribe, tribus
tribune, tribūnus
tribune of the plebs, tribūnus
 plēbis
triumph, *verb,* exsultō
triumvirate, triumvirātus
Trojan War, Bellum Troiānum
troop (of soldiers), grex, manus
true, vērus
truly, vērē
trunk (of a tree), truncus
trust *verb,* crēdō
truth, vēritās

turn back, revertō
twin, geminus
two, duo
uncle, patruus
under, *prep.,* sub
understand, sciō
unfair, iniustus
unfriendly, inimīcus
universe, mundus
unjust, iniustus
unless, nisi
unworthy, indignus
upon, in, super
uprightness, probitās
us, nōs **(to/for us,** nōbīs)
vast, vastus
verity, vēritās
very little, minimē
vice, vitium
victor, victor
victory, victōria
vine, vītis
virtue, virtūs
voice, vōx
wagon, carrus
wait upon, ministrō
walk, *verb,* ambulō
wall, mūrus
war, bellum
was, erat
watch over, servō
water, aqua
way, via
we, nōs
wealthy, dīvēs
weapons, arma
wear, gerō
well, bene
what, *interr. pro.,* quid
what kind of, quālis
when, *conj.,* cum, ubi; *interrog.*
 adv., ubi
where, *interrog. adv.,* ubi

which, *rel. pro., interrog. adj.,* quī,
 quae, quod; *interrog. pro.,* quis,
 quid
while, dum
who, *rel. pro., interrog. adj.,* quī,
 quae, quod
who, *interrog. pro.,* quis, quid
whole, totus
whom, quem **(to whom,** cui)
whose, cuius, quōrum, quārum
why, cūr
wife, mulier, uxor
will, *noun,* voluntās
wing, āla
winter, hiems
wish, *noun,* voluntās
wish, *verb,* optō
with, *prep.,* apud, cum
without, sine
wolf, lupus
woman, fēmina, mulier
woodpecker, pīcus
woods, silva
word, verbum
words (list of), vocābulārium
work, *noun,* labor, opus
world, mundus
worship, *verb,* adōrō
wound, *noun,* vulnus
wrath, īra
write, scrībō
writer, scrīptor
writing, scriptūra
writing instrument, stilus
year, annus
yes, ita vērē
yet, etiam
you, tū, vōs, **(to/for you)** tibi, nōbīs
young, iuvenis, novus
young person, iuvenis
young woman, puella
your, *sing.,* tuus; *pl.,* vester
youthful, iuvenis

Vocābulārium

Latīnum–Anglicum

- See also Mythological Terms in Appendix G and Roman Numerals in Appendix B.
- Chapter references
  - If more than one chapter number is listed, the final listed chapter often has more complete information.
  - If no chapter is listed, the word may be useful in the activities.
- Definitions
  - *enclitic,* a word that is always attached to the end of another word
  - *postpositive,* a word that is always placed after one or more words at the beginning of its clause
- Short forms
  - The number *(1)* stands for the principal parts of any regular first-conjugation verb *(-āre, -āvī, -ātus).*
  - The last principal part of a verb is an adjective (participle) having three gender forms (-us, -a, -um). Only the masculine form (-us) is given in the Vocābulārium.

Abbreviations

- *abl.,* ablative
- *acc.,* accusative
- *adj.,* adjective
- *adv.,* adverb
- *com.,* common (masc. or fem.) gender
- *conj.,* conjunction
- *coord.,* coordinating
- *correl.,* correlative
- *dat.,* dative
- *dem.,* demonstrative

- *e.g. (exemplum gratia),* for example
- *fem.,* feminine
- *gen.,* genitive
- *imper.,* imperative
- *indecl.,* indeclinable
- *indef.,* indefinite
- *intens.,* intensive
- *interj.,* interjection
- *interrog.,* interrogative
- *masc.,* masculine

- *neut.,* neuter
- *nom.,* nominative
- *pers.,* personal
- *pl.,* plural
- *prep.,* preposition
- *pro.,* pronoun
- *q.v. (quod vide),* "which see"
- *reflex.,* reflexive
- *rel.,* relative
- *sing.,* singular

ā, ab, *prep. with abl.,* from, away from; by 7

abeō, -īre, -iī/īvī, -itus, to go away, leave 18

acer, acris, acre, bitter, keen, painful 10

ad, *prep. with acc.,* to, towards; at, near; about 7, 20

adhūc, *adv.,* thus far, hitherto; still, even now 14

adiuvō -āre, -iūvī, -iūtus, to help 17

adōrō (1), to worship 15

adstō, -āre, -stitī, to stand, stand by 21

adversus or **adversum,** *prep. with acc.,* against, opposed to; towards, opposite 20

aedificiō (1), to build 13

Aegyptius, -a, -um, Egyptian

Aegyptius, -iī/ī, *masc.,* an Egyptian man

Aegyptus, -ī, *fem.,* Egypt 22

Aenēās, -ae, *masc.,* Trojan hero in Virgil's epic poem 7, Lg III

Aequī, -ōrum, *masc.,* Aequians, a tribe of people in central Italy 12

aestās, -tātis, *fem.,* summer Lg V

aeternus, -a, -um, eternal 6

ager, agrī, *masc.,* a field, farm 12

agnus, -ī, *masc.,* a lamb 6

agō, -ere, ēgī, actus, to act, do; to drive (as a chariot); to give (as thanks) 16

agricola, -ae, *masc.,* a farmer, tiller of fields, husbandman 5

āla, -ae, *fem.,* a wing 23

alacer, -cris, -cre, lively, quick, animated

Alba Longa, -ae, *fem.,* town in Latium that Ascanius, son of Aeneas, is said to have founded 11

aliquando, *adv.,* once, sometimes Lg V

alius, -a, -um, other, another 21

altior, -iōris, higher 22

altissimus, -a, -um, highest, tallest 20, 22

altus, -a, -um, high, deep 22

ambulō (1), to walk 7

amīcus, -a, -um, *used with the dat. case,* friendly 6

amīcus, -ī, *masc.,* friend 3

amō (1), to love, like 19 (Act. M)

Amūlius, -iī/ī, *masc.,* brother of Numitor (king of Alba Longa);

killer of Numitor and attempted killer of Romulus and Remus 11

Anglicus, -a, -um, English 2

annus, -ī, *masc.,* a year 13

anser, -eris, *masc.,* a goose 16

ante, *adv.,* before 20

ante, *prep. with acc.,* before 7

antīquus, -a, -um, old, ancient 10, 14

Antōnius, -iī/ī, *masc.,* a name (Antony or Anthony) 2

Antōnius, Marcus, -iī/ī, -ī, *masc.,* a member of the Second Triumvirate 23

aperiō, -īre, -uī, -pertus, to open 21

Apollo, -inis, *masc.,* Roman god of the sun 23

appellō (1), to name, call 21

Appia via, -ae, *fem.,* the Appian Way, a road from Rome to Capua 21

apud, *prep. with acc.,* with, in the presence of 19

aqua, -ae, *fem.,* water 7

aquilo, -ōnis, *masc.,* the north wind; the north 19

arbor, -oris, *fem.,* a tree 7

argentum, -ī, *neut.,* silver 17

arma, -ōrum, *neut. pl.,* weapons, arms 20

armō (1), to arm, equip for war 20

ars, artis, *fem.,* skill; art 10, 17

arx, arcis, *fem.,* a fortress, citadel 16

Ascānius, -iī/ī, *masc.,* son of Aeneas, the Trojan War hero who went to Italy Lg III

ascendō, -ere, -cendī, -census, to climb up, ascend 16

audāx, aūdācis, bold, daring, courageous; audacious, rash, foolhardy 10

audiō, -īre, -īvī, -ītus, to hear 14

augustus, -a, -um, consecrated, holy; majestic, dignified 7

Augustus, *See* **Caesar.**

auris, -is, *fem.,* an ear 17

aurum, -ī, *neut.,* gold 17

austrālis, -e, southern 17

aut, *conj.,* or; **aut . . . aut,** *correl. conj.,* either . . . or 3

autem, *postpositive conj.,* however, moreover 11

auxilium, -iī/ī, *neut.,* help, aid 19

avārus, -a, -um, greedy 21

aveō, (haveō) -ēre, *used only in imper. mood:* **avē, avēte,** to be blessed; Good day! or Farewell! 17

avia, -ae, *fem.,* a grandmother 13

avunculus, -ī, *masc.,* a mother's brother

avus, -ī, *masc.,* a grandfather 13

bellum, -ī, *neut.,* war 10, 17

Bellum Troiānum, -ī, *neut.,* Trojan War 9

bene, *adv.,* well 17

bonus, -a, -um (melior, optimus, *q.v.*)**,** good 5

brevis, -e, short 9, 10

Brūtus, Lucius Junius, -ī, -iī/ī, *masc.,* one of the first two consuls in the Roman republic 13

bulla, -ae, *fem.,* bubble 7

cadō, -ere, cecidī, casus, to fall 13

caelum, (coelum), -ī, *neut.,* the heaven, sky 17

Caesar, -sāris, *masc.,* a Roman family name 7, 23

Caesar, Augustus (Octavius), -aris, -ī (-iī/ī), *masc.,* a member of the Second Triumvirate, the first emperor of Rome 7, 23

Caesar, Julius, -aris, -iī/ī, *masc.,* a member of the First Triumvirate; also a general, consul, proconsul, and dictator in the late Roman republic 7, 22

canis, -is, *com.,* a dog 2

Cannae, -ārum, *fem.,* a town in southern Italy 19

cantō (1), to sing 15

capiō, -ere, cēpī, captus, to take, catch, capture, seize, snatch 2, Lg V

Capua, -ae, *fem.,* a town in central Italy 19

cāritas, -tātis, *fem.,* dearness, high price; affection, love, esteem 13

carmen, -inis, *neut.,* a song, poem 12, 21

carpō, -ere, carpsī, carptus, to pick, pluck Lg V

carrus, -ī, *masc.,* a wagon, chariot 7

Carthāginiensis, -e, pertaining to Carthage, Carthaginian 18

Carthāgō, -inis, *fem.,* the city of Carthage in North Africa 18

castra, -ōrum, *neut., pl. form, sing. meaning,* a camp, an encampment 3

catēna, -ae, *fem.,* a chain, fetter; a restraint 19

Catullus, Gaius Valerius, -ī, -iī/ī, *masc.,* a Roman lyric poet, 84 B.C.– 54 B.C. 7

celebrō (1), to celebrate 15

celer, -eris, -ere, swift, quick, rapid 10

Cerēs, Cereris, *fem.,* Roman goddess of grain, agriculture, mother of Proserpina Lg V, 21

certus, -a, -um, certain 22

Christiānus, -a, -um, Christian 1

Christiānus, -ī, *masc.,* a Christian man or boy 5, 8

Christus, -ī, *masc.,* Christ, King of kings 6

cibus, -ī, *masc.,* food 12, 15

Cicero, -ōnis, Marcus Tullius, -ī, -iī/ī, *masc.,* a famous Roman statesman, orator, and writer during the late Roman republic 7

Cincinnātus, -ī, *masc.,* a Roman patrician who was a farmer, dictator, then farmer again 12

circā, *adv.; prep. with acc.,* around; about, near 19

circum, *adv.; prep. with acc.,* around, on all sides; near 11

circumclūdō, -ere, -clūsī, -clūsus, to surround, shut in 20

cīvilis, -e, civil, relating to the state 22

cīvis, -is, *com.,* a citizen 20

cīvitās, -tātis, *fem.,* a state, city; citizenship 9, 20

clādēs, -is, *fem.,* a defeat, disaster 12

clam, *adv.,* secretly 20

clāmō (1), to call, shout, cry aloud 14

clārus, -a, -um, clear; famous 9, 17

classis, -is, *fem.,* a fleet 18

Claudia, -ae, *fem.,* a name 5

Claudius, -iī/ī, *masc.,* a name 5

Claudius, Appius, -iī/ī, -iī/ī , *masc.,* a Roman consul and decemvir in fifth century B.C. 21

coelum, *See* **caelum.**

cōgnitō (1), to think Lg I, 17

cognitiō, -ōnis, *fem.,* a study, knowledge of, acquaintance with Lg I

colloquium, -iī/-ī, *neut.,* a conversation, Lg II

colōnia, -ae, *fem.,* a colony 17

condō, -ere, -didī, -ditus, to put together, build; to found, establish 11, 20

coniungō, -ere, -iunxī, -iunctus, to join together 22

conscrībō, -ere, -scripsī, -scriptus, to enroll 22

consentiō, -īre, -sensī, -sensus, to agree 23

consilium, -iī/ī, *neut.,* plan, advice 14

conspiciō, -ere, -spexī, -spectus, to behold, perceive 21

Constantius I, -ī, *masc.,* Constantine I, Roman emperor A.D. 306-337 8

Constantīnopilis, -is, *fem.,* Constantinople, a city originally called Byzantium, renamed in A.D. 330 by Constantine; now called Istanbul 8

constituō, -ere, -stituī, -stitūtus, to establish 23

construō, -ere, -struxī, -structus, to construct, build 11, 15

contegō, -ere, -texī, -tectus, to cover 20

contendō, -ere, -tendī, -tentus, to hasten 19

contrā, *prep. with acc.,* against, opposite to 12

conveniō, -īre, -vēnī, -ventus, to come together 14

conventus, ūs, *masc.,* a meeting, an assembly 7

cor, cordis, *neut.,* a heart 6

Coriolānus, -ī, *masc.,* a legendary patrician army general who fought against the Volscians in the 5th-6th century B.C., also called Gnaeus Martius 12

Coriolī, -ōrum, *masc.,* a town of the Volscians in Latium 12

Cornēlia, -ae, *fem.,* a name 3

Cornēlius, -iī/ī, *masc.,* a Roman centurion mentioned in the New Testament; a name 3

cornū, cornūs, *neut.,* a horn, as of an animal 9

corrigō, -ere, -rēxī, -rectus, to correct, set right 21

Crassus, Marcus Licinius (Dives), -ī, -ī, -iī/ī, *masc.,* a general in the Roman republic, a member of the First Triumvirate 22

crēdō, -ere, -didī, -ditus, to trust, believe, place confidence in 16

creō (1), to make; to elect 21 (Act. L)

crescō, -ere, crēvī, crētus, to come into existence, grow up, increase 11, 20, Lg V

crustulum, -ī, *neut.,* a small cake, cookie 12, 16

cuius, cui, whose, of whom; to/for whom 4, 6, 10, 18, 19, 20

cuiusque, *See* **quisque.**

cum, *conj.,* when

cum, *prep. with abl.,* with 7

cūr, *interrog. adv.,* why 13

cūra, -ae, *fem.,* care, concern, attention 11, 16

cūrō (1), to care for; to administer, manage, take care of 11

currō, -ere, cucurrī, cursus, to run, hasten 7

dat, gives 6, 15

dē, *prep. with abl.,* down from, away from, from; concerning, about 7

dea, -ae, a goddess 15

dēbeō, -ēre, -uī, itus, to owe, be obligated 16

decem, *indecl. number,* ten 18

decimus, -a, -um, tenth 18

dedit, gave, have given 6, 10, 12

dedō, -ere, dedidī, deditus, to give up, surrender 20

dēfendō, -ere, dēfendī, dēfensus, to defend 2

deī, -ōrum, *masc.,* gods and goddesses, deities 15

dēfluō, -ere, -fluxī, to flow down 10, 15

Demeter, Greek goddess of grain, mother of Persephone

dēminūtiō, -ōnis, *fem.,* a decline, lessening 22

dēnique, *adv.,* finally 12

dēnuntiō (1), to announce, threaten; to declare [war] 20

dēstruō, -ere, -struxī, -structus, to destroy 20

deus, -ī, *masc., nom. pl.,* **deī, diī,** *or* **dī;** *gen. pl.,* **deōrum** *or* **deum;** *dat. and abl. pl.,* **deīs, diīs,** *or* **dīs,** a (false) god, a deity 15

Deus, -ī, *masc.,* God 3

dextra, also **dextera,** *fem.,* the right hand 21

Diana, -ae, *fem.,* Roman goddess of the moon 23

dīcenda, *neut., pl.,* things to be said or spoken Lg I

dīcō, -ere, dīxī, dictus, to say, speak 2

dictātor, -ōris, *masc.,* dictator, chief magistrate 12

diēs, diēī, *masc.,* day (as opposed to night); a period of twenty-four hours; *fem.,* a fixed date, a particular day 4, 19

dīligō, -ere, -lēxī, -lectus, to choose out; to love, esteem highly 2

discipula, -ae, *fem.,* female pupil, disciple 3

discipulus, -ī, *masc.,* a male pupil, disciple 3

discō, -ere, didicī, to learn, learn how 2, 19

dīvēs, -itis, rich, wealthy 21

divitiae, -ārum, *fem.,* riches 22

dō, dare, dedī, datus, to give, grant; to offer, furnish, allow; to put 6, 15

doceō, -ēre, -cuī, -ctus, to teach, instruct 2

dolor, -ōris, *masc.,* sorrow, pain, anguish Lg V

dolus, -ī, *masc.,* deceit, guile 21

dominātiō, -iōnis, *fem.,* mastery, irresponsible power, despotism 18

dominus, -ī, *masc.,* a head of a household; master, lord, ruler 4

Dominus, -ī, *masc.,* the Lord, Christ 4

domus, -ūs, *fem.,* a house, home 19

dūcō, -ere, dūxī, ductus, to lead, draw 3, 19

dum, *conj.,* while 20

duo, duae, duo, two 13, 18, 19

dūrus, -a, -um, hard, harsh; strong, enduring 8

dux, ducis, *masc.,* a guide, leader, ruler, military commander, general 6

ē, ex, *prep. with abl.,* out from, from 7

ea, she 16

eārum, their *(fem.);* **eōrum,** their *(masc., neut.)* 16

ecce, *interj.,* behold 17, 19

ēdūcō (1), to bring up, rear 21

ego, *pers. pro.,* I 5, 15

ēiciō, -ere, -iēcī, iectus, to throw out, cast out 21

eius, his, her/hers, its 13, 14, 16

elephantus, -ī, *masc.,* an elephant 2

eō, īre, īvī/iī, itūrus, to go 19

Epirus, -ī, *fem.,* a region in northwest Greece 17

equus, -ī, *masc.,* a horse 2

erat, was 8

erit, will be 9

ergo, *adv.,* therefore 21

est, is 1

et, *coord. conj.,* and; **et . . . et,** *correl. conj.,* both . . . and 21

etiam, *conj.,* still, yet; also, besides; even 9

Etrūria, -ae, *fem.,* a district in northwest Italy 13

Etruscus, -a, -um, pertaining to or belonging to Etruria 13

Etruscus, -ī, *masc.,* an Etruscan man 13

eum, him 13

Eurōpa, -ae, *fem.,* Europe 7

ēvādō, -ere, -sī, -sus, to come out, climb up, escape 11

evangelium, -iī/ī, *neut.,* the gospel 20

ex, ē, *prep. with abl.,* out from, out of, from 7

exercitus, -ūs, *masc.,* an army 10, 12

exsiliō, -īre, -uī, to leap, leap up 21

exsistō, also **existō, -ere, -stitī, -sistus,** to arise 22

exsultō, also **exultō, (1),** to rejoice, triumph 16

exsurgō, -ere, -surrexī, to rise up 21

extrā, *prep. with acc.,* outside 21

Fabius, Quintus, -iī/ī, -ī, *masc.,* Quintus Fabius Maximus, Cunctator (the Delayer), a Roman opponent of Hannibal in the Second Punic War 19

fābula, -ae, *fem.,* a tale, legend, story, myth 12, 15

faciēs, -ēī, *fem.,* a face 20

facilis, -e, easy 10

faciō, -ere, fēcī, factus, to make, do, perform 13

fāma, -ae, *f.,* rumor, reputation, fame

familia, -ae, *fem.,* an entire household including family members and family servants or slaves 13

fēles, -is, *fem.,* a cat 2

fēlix, -līcis, fortunate, favorable; successful, happy 10

fēmina, -ae, *fem.,* a woman 13

feriō, -īre, -īvī, -ītus, to strike, hit, smite 19

fīdēlis, -e, *used with the dat. case,* faithful, reliable, steadfast 6

fīlia, -ae, *fem.,* a daughter 5, 11, 13

fīlia sorōris *or* **fīlia frātris,** *fem.,* a niece 13

fīlius, -iī/ī, *masc.,* a son 4, 13

Fīlius, -iī/ī, *masc.,* the Son of God, Christ 4

fīnis, -is, *masc. (sometimes fem.),* the/an end 12, 19

flamma, -ae, *fem.,* a flame 20

flōs, -ōris, *masc.,* a flower Lg V

flūmen, -minis, *neut.,* a river 11

fōns, fontis, *masc.,* a spring, fountain 10

fortis, -e, strong, brave, courageous 10

frāter, -tris, *masc.,* a brother; sometimes a cousin or brother-in-law 11, 13

fraudātor, -ōris, *masc.,* a deceiver 23

fraudō (1), to deceive 23

frūctus, -ūs, *masc.,* fruit 17

frūmentum, -ī, *neut.,* grain, growing things Lg V

frūx, frūgis, *fem.,* fruit of the earth Lg V

fugiō, -ere, fūgī, fūgitus, to flee, take flight 16

fulmen, -minis, *neut.,* a stroke of lightning, a thunderbolt 19

fūr, fūris, *com.,* a thief 23

Gallia, -ae, *fem.,* the area now called France and neighboring territory 22

Gallus, -ī, *masc.,* a Gaul, member of a Gallic tribe in Europe 16

geminus, -a, -um, twin, double 11, Lg III

geminus, -ī, *masc.,* a twin 11, Lg III

gēns, gentis, *fem.,* a people, nation 17

genus, -neris, *neut.,* kind, class 8

Germānia, -ae, *fem.,* Germany 4

Germānus, -a, -um, German 2

gerō, gerere, gessī, gestus, to wear; to bear or carry 23

glōria, -ae, *fem.,* glory, fame 4

Glōria, -ae, *fem.,* a name 4

Graecī, -ōrum, *masc.,* Greeks 9

Graecia, -ae, *fem.,* Greece 7

Graecus, -a, -um, Greek, pertaining to Greece or the Greek people 9

grandis, -e, great, grand, important 19

grātia, -ae, *fem.,* grace, kindness; gratitude, thanks 6

gravis, -e, heavy; severe 10

grex, gregis, *masc.,* a herd, flock; a troop or band (as of soldiers) 3

gūbernātiō, -iōnis, *fem.,* government 21

habēbat, had 8

habeō, -ēre, -buī, -bitus, to have, hold 2

habitātiō, -iōnis, *fem.,* a house, an abode 23

Hamilcar, -caris, *masc.,* a Carthaginian general in the First Punic War, father of Hannibal 19

Hannibal, -balis, *masc.,* son of Hamilcar Barca and leader of the Carthaginian army in the Second Punic War 19

harēna, -ae, *also* **arēna,** *fem.,* sand 7

Hasdrubal, -balis, *masc.,* name of several Carthaginian generals: (1) brother of Hannibal, (2) brother-in-law of Hannibal, (3) cavalry commander at Cannae, and (4) general who was forced to surrender Carthage at the end of the Third Punic War 19, 20

hic, haec, hoc, *dem. pro.,* this; he, she, it; *dem. adj.,* this; **ille . . . hic,** the former . . . the latter 1, 21

hiems, -emis, *fem.,* winter Lg V

Hispānia, -ae, *fem.,* Spain 9

historia, -ae, *fem.,* history 6

hodiē, *adv.,* today 14

homo, -minis, *masc.,* a human being, person, man 17

honos, also **honor, -nōris,** *masc.,* honor 6, 8

hōra, -ae, *fem.,* an hour 19

Horātius, -iī/ī, a hero in the early Roman republic 13; Horace, a famous Roman lyric poet in the late republic 7

horreum, -ī, *neut.,* a barn 16

huius, his, hers, its 21

iaceō, -ēre, -cuī, to lie (flat or resting), rest, recline 7

iaciō, -ere, -iēcī, -iactus, to throw, hurl 21

iactūra, -ae, *fem.,* a loss 18

id, it 16

igitur, *adv., (often a postpositive)* therefore 18

ignis, -is, *masc.,* fire 20

ille, illa, illud, *dem. pro.,* that one; he, she, it; *dem. adj.,* that; **ille . . . hic,** the former . . . the latter 1, 21

illīc, *adv.,* there, at that place 22

illīus, his, her/hers, its 21

imperātor, -tōris, *masc.,* a leader, commander-in-chief of the army, emperor 9

imperium, -iī/ī, *neut.,* a command, an order; power or right to command; area governed, empire 8

in, *prep. with abl.,* in, on, among 7

in, *prep. with acc.,* into, onto, upon, against, towards 7

incendō, -ere, -cendī, -census, to kindle, set fire to, burn 13, 15

incipiō, -ere, -cēpī, -ceptus, to begin 16

indignus, -a, -um, unworthy 12 (Act. H)

infāns, -antis, *com.,* a little child 13

inferī, -ōrum, *masc.,* the lower regions of the earth, the lower world Lg V

inimīcitia, -ae, *fem.,* hatred 23

inimīcus, -a, -um, unfriendly, hostile 12

inimīcus, -ī, *masc.,* an enemy 10, 12

initium, -iī/ī, *neut.,* the/a beginning 6, 8

iniūstitia, -ae, (injustitia), *fem.,* injustice 21

iniūstus, -a, -um, (injustus), unjust, unfair; harsh, oppressive 10 (Act. M), 12 (Act. K)

inlūminō (1), to illuminate 17

inrideō, -ēre, -rīsī, rīsus, to laugh at, ridicule 14

insiliō, -silīre, -siluī, to leap, spring, or jump in, into, on 7, 15

insolēns, -entis, rude, ill-mannered 20

īnsula, -ae, *fem.,* an island; a tenement house 7

intendō, -ere, -tendī, intentus, to stretch in a particular direction, aim; intend, plan, aim at 11

inter, *prep. with acc.,* between, among 18

interdum, sometimes 8

interrogō (1), to ask 14

intrō (1), to enter 21

invādō, -ere, -vāsī, -vāsus, to go in, enter; to attack; to seize 19

inveniō, -venīre, vēnī, -ventus, to come upon, find, discover; to acquire, earn 2, 15

investīgātiō, -tiōnis, *fem.,* an examination, investigation 8

invideō, -ēre, -vīdī, -vīsus, envy 22

invidus, -a, -um, envious

ipse, ipsa, ipsum, *intens. pro.,* himself, herself, itself

īra, -ae, *fem.,* wrath, anger, ire 7

is, ea, id, *pers. pro.; dem. pro.,* he, she, it; this; that 14, 16

iste, ista, istud, *dem. pro.,* that (man, woman, thing) near you, often expressing disapproval of the one indicated 21

Ītalia, -ae, *fem.,* Italy 3, 7

Ītalius or **Ītalicus, -a, -um,** Italian 16, 17

ita vērē, thus truly, certainly, yes 8

iterum, *adv.,* again, a second time 10, 20

Iūdaea, -ae (Jūdaea, -ae), *fem.,* Judea, Palestine, the country of the Jews

iūdex, -dicis, *masc.,* a judge 10

Iulius, -iī/ī (Julius, -iī/ī), *masc.,* a name (Julius)

Iūnō, -ōnis (Jūnō, -ōnis), *fem.,* a Roman goddess, a wife of Jupiter 15

Iuppiter, Iovis (Juppiter, Jovis), *masc.,* Jupiter, Roman god of the earth and sky 15, 17

iūs, iūris (jūs, jūris), *neut.,* right, law 8

iustitia, -ae, (justitia, -ae), *fem.,* justice 10 (Act. M), 21 (Act. E)

iustus, -a, -um, (justus, -a, -um), just, fair; lawful, proper 10

Iustus, -ī, (Justus, -ī), *masc.,* Justus, a name

iuvenis, -e, (juvenis, -e), young, youthful 10

iuvenis, -is, (juvenis, -e), *com.,* a young man or woman, a person in the prime of life 11

Jerome (Latin name, **Eusebius Hieronymus**), a fourth-century monk who produced the Latin Vulgate 5, 6

labor, -ōris, *masc.,* labor, work 21

lacus, -ūs, *masc.,* a lake 7

Lars Porsena, -tis, -ae, *masc.,* a sixth-century king of Etruria who besieged Rome in an attempt to return Tarquin the Proud to the throne 13

Latīnī, -ōrum, *masc.,* the people of Latium 11

Latium, -iī/ī, *neut.,* the district of Italy in which Rome is located 1

Latīnus, -a, -um, Latin 1

Latīnus, -ī, *masc.,* a man from Latium

laudō (1), to praise 19

Lāvinium, -iī/ī, *neut.,* town in Italy that, according to legend, was founded by Aeneas Lg III

lēgātus, -a, -um, *masc.,* a delegate, deputy 20

legenda, -ōrum, *neut.,* things to be read 15

legō, -ere, lēgī, lectus, to read; to choose 6, 15

Lepidus, Marcus Aemilius, -ī, -ī, -iī/ī, *masc.,* a member of the Second Triumvirate 23

levō (1), to lift up 21

lēx, lēgis, *fem.,* law 10

līber, -era, -erum, free 9

liber, -brī, *masc.,* a book 1

līberātor, -ōris, *masc.,* a liberator

līberī, -ōrum, *masc. (pl. only),* children 13

līberō (1), to set free 20

lingua, -ae, *fem.,* a language, tongue 1

Līvius, -iī/ī, *masc.,* Livy (59 B.C.–A.D. 17), author of *Ab Urbe Condita,* a history of Rome 12, Lg III

locus, -ī, *masc. in sing.; neut. in pl.,* place 16

longus, -a, -um, long 8

Lucius, -iī/ī, *masc.,* a name (Lucius or Luke) 4

lūna, -ae, *fem.,* the moon 18, 23

lupus, -ī, *masc.,* a wolf 2

lūx, lūcis, *fem.,* light 5

Macedonia, -ae, *fem.,* an ancient kingdom north of Thessaly 20

magister, -trī, *masc.,* a male teacher; master 3, 4

magistra, -ae, *fem.,* a female teacher; mistress 3, 4

magnopere, *adv.,* greatly 13

magnus, -a, -um, great, large 4

Maia, -ae, *fem.,* one of Jupiter's wives, for whom the month of May was named 18

Maior, the Elder 19

maior, maius (major, majus), larger, greater 15, 19

malus, -a, -um, bad, evil 18

mandātum, -ī, *neut.,* a command, order, decree Lg V

maneō, -ēre, mansī, mansus, to remain 16, 20

manus, -ūs, *fem.,* a hand; a band of men, troop of soldiers 17

Marcus, -ī, *masc.,* a name (Marcus or Mark) 2

mare, -is, *neut.,* a/the sea 18

Marius, -iī/ī, *masc.,* a military leader who was a rival of Sulla 22

Mars, Martis, *masc.,* Roman god of war 23

Martius, Gnaeus, -iī/ī, -ī, *masc.,* a patrician, later called Coriolanus, *q.v.* 12

māter, -tris, *fem.,* a mother 11, 13

māterfamilias, mātrisfamiliae, *fem. (sometimes written as two words),* the mother of the family, mistress of the household 13

maximus, -a, -um, largest, very large; great, very great 21, 22

medium, -ī, *neut.,* the middle, midst 21

melior, -ius, better 22

memor, *gen.* **memoris,** mindful, remembering; thankful; thoughtful, prudent 11 (Act. K)

mensis, -is, *masc.,* a month 18, 23

mercātor, -ōris, *masc.,* a merchant 23

mercātus, -ūs, *masc.,* trade, business 23

Mercurius, -iī/ī, *masc.,* Roman messenger god 23

meus, -a, -um, my 1

mihi, to/for me 6

mīles, -itis, *masc.,* a soldier 16

mille, *pl.* **milia,** a thousand 18, 19

mille passuum, *neut.,* a thousand [of] paces, a mile 23

minimē, *adv.,* not at all, by no means; very little, not in the least 19 (Act. A)

minimus, -a, -um, smallest, very small 22

ministrō (1), to serve, wait upon 19

minor, minus, smaller, less 15, 19

Minor, the Younger 19

mittō, -ere, mīsī, missus, to send 20

mōns, montis, *masc.,* a mountain 7, 21

mora, -ae, *fem.,* a delay 7

mordeō, -ēre, momordī, morsus, to bite 7, 15

mors, mortis, *fem.,* death 11

mortālis, -e, subject to death 13, 23

mortālis, -is, *com.,* one who is subject to death, a person 23

mortuus, -a, -um, dead Lg V, 23

moveō, -ēre, mōvī, mōtus, to move 21

mox, *adv.,* soon, presently; then, thereupon 11

mulier, -eris, *fem.,* a woman, wife, matron 13

multus, -a, -um, much; *pl.,* many 8, 17

mundus, -ī, *masc.,* the world, the universe; mankind 5

mūrus, -ī, *masc.,* a wall, especially a wall around a city 11

mūs, mūris, *com.,* a mouse 2

mūtātiō, -iōnis, *fem.,* a change 13, 21

mūtō (1), to change 20

narrō (1), to tell, relate, narrate 10, 14

nāsus, -ī, *masc.,* a nose 17

natō, -āre, to swim, float 7

nāvigō (1), to sail 20

navis, -is, *fem.,* a ship 20

-ne, *an enclitic, affixed to the first word of an interrogative sentence, often changing a statement to a "yes/no" question* 1, 2, 3

necō (1), to kill 11

nēmō, nēminis, *com., irregular,* nobody, no one, no man 7, 10

nepos, -ōtis, *masc., fem.,* a grandson or granddaughter, descendant; nephew 13

Neptūnus, -ī, *masc.,* Roman god of the sea, 15, 21, 23

neuter, -tra, -trum, neither one nor the other; neither masculine nor feminine 8

nihil (nil), *neut., indecl.,* nothing 12

nisi, *conj.,* if not, unless 17

nōbīs, to/for us 6, 15

noctū, also **nocte,** *adv.,* at night (from **nox, noctis**) 16

nōmen, -minis, *neut.,* a name 4

nōn, *adv.,* not 2

nōnne, *adv. + enclitic, indicating the beginning of a question that has the expected answer "yes"* 1, 2

nōnus, -a, -um, ninth 18

nōs, we, us 15

noster, -tra, -trum, our 6, 7

novem, *indecl. number,* nine 18

novus, -a, -um, new, fresh, young 3, 15

nox, noctis, *fem.,* night. *See* **noctū.**

nullus, -a, -um, no, none 13

numerus, -ī, *masc.,* a number 13

Numitor, -ōris, *masc.,* a king of Alba Longa, grandfather of Romulus and Remus; killed by his brother Amulius 11

numquam, *adv.,* never

nunc, *adv.,* now 6, 10

nuntius, iī/ī, *masc.,* a messenger; a message 23

obeō, -īre, -īvī, -itus, to go away; to die 21

Octāvius, -iī/ī, *masc.,* a name (Octavius or Octavian) 7

octāvus, -a, -um, eighth 18

octo, *indecl. number,* eight 18

oculus, -ī, *masc.,* the/an eye 17

odium, -iī/ī, *neut.,* hatred 19

omnis, -e, all, every 10

oppidum, -ī, *neut.,* a town 12

optimus, -a, -um, best, very good 22

optō (1), to wish, desire 21

opus, operis, *neut.,* work, labor 8

ōrātiō, -iōnis, *fem.,* speech, language; a speech, oration 6

ōrātor, -ōris, *masc.,* a speaker, orator 23

ōs, ōris, *neut.,* the/a mouth 17

ostendō, -ere, -tendī, -tentus/tensus, to show, display 4

ostium, -iī/ī, *neut.,* a door, entrance; the mouth (as of a river) 8

pactiō, -iōnis, *fem.,* a treaty, agreement 20

paenīnsula, -ae, *fem.,* a peninsula 16, 17

Palestīna, -ae, a country at the far eastern edge of the Mediterranean Sea inhabited by the Jews; the birthplace of Christ 5

pānis, -is, *masc.,* bread 5

parātus, -a, -um, prepared 19

parēns, -entis, *com.,* a parent, father, mother; a grandfather, ancestor 13

parvus, -a, -um, little, small 8

pars, partis, *fem.,* a part 14

pāscō, -ere, pāvī, pastus, to feed, lead to pasture; to nourish 2

passer, -eris, *masc.,* a sparrow, small bird 20

pastor, -tōris, *masc.,* shepherd 3

pater, -tris, *masc.,* a father 5, 13

Pater, -tris, *masc.,* the Father (God) 5

paterfamilias, patrisfamiliae, *masc. (sometimes written as two words),* the father of a family, head of a household 13

patiēns (*gen.,* **-entis**), patient 10

patria, -ae, *fem.,* a country, native land 2

patricius, -a, -um, patrician, belonging to the nobility 12

patricius, -iī/ī, *masc.,* a patrician, nobleman 12

patruus, -ī, *masc.,* an uncle 13 (Act. A)

Paulus, -ī, *masc.,* a name (Paul) 4

pauper, -eris, poor, not wealthy 21

pāx, pācis, *fem.,* peace 6

peccātor, -tōris, *masc.,* a sinner 4

peccātum, -ī, *neut.,* an error, fault, sin 8

pecūnia, -ae, *fem.,* money 6

peior, -ius (*comparative degree of* malus), worse 22

per, *prep. with acc.,* through, along, during, because of 7

pereō, -īre, -iī/īvī, -itus, to go through, be lost, die, perish 19

perficiō, -ere, -fēcī, fectus, to accomplish, complete 23

perīculum, -ī, *neut.,* danger 13

perpetuus, -a, -um, continuous, uninterrupted 16

pēs, pedis, *masc.,* foot 17

pessimus, -a, -um (*superlative degree of* malus), worst, very bad 22

pīcus, -ī, *masc.,* a woodpecker 11

Pīlātus, Pontius, -ī, -iī/ī, *masc.,* the Roman governor of Judea when Christ was crucified 4

plēbēius, -a, -um, belonging to the plebeian class, plebeian 12

plēbēs, -ēī, *fem., collective noun,* the plebeian class, the common people

plēbs, plēbis, *fem., collective noun (used with a sing. verb),* the plebeians, the common people

plūrimus, -a, -um, most, very many 22

plūs, plūris, more 22

Plūto, -ōnis, *masc.,* Pluto, king of the lower world 15, 21, 23

Poenī, -ōrum, *masc.,* the Carthaginians 18

Poenus, -a, -um or **Poeniceus, -a, -um,** Carthaginian 18

Pompēiī, *masc. pl.,* a town in Italy that was destroyed by the volcano Vesuvius in A.D. 79 22

Pompēius, Gnaeus, -iī/ī, -ī, *masc.,* Pompey the Great, general in the late Roman republic 22

pōns, pontis, *masc.,* a bridge 13

populus, -ī, *masc., collective (used with a sing. verb),* a people, a nation; the people, the public; crowd, multitude (includes both patricians and plebeians) 5

porcus, -ī, *masc.,* a pig 2

Porsena, (Porsenna) -ae, Lars, Lartis, *masc.,* a king in Etruria 13

possideō, -ēre, -sēdī, -sessus, to possess, have, hold 21 (Act. A)

possum, posse, potuī, to be able 16

post, *prep. with acc.,* after, behind 7

posteā, *adv.,* afterwards, thereupon 13, Lg V

postulō (1), to demand, require 20

potēns (*gen.,* **-entis**), able, powerful, mighty 10

praebeō, -ēre, -uī, -itus, to offer, hold out; to provide, supply 6

praeclārus, -a, -um, remarkable, admirable, excellent 21

praevaleō, -valēre, -valuī, to be very strong or powerful, to prevail 10, 15

prīmō, *adv.,* first, at first 8

prīmus, -a, -um, first, foremost 9, 18

principium, -iī/ī, *neut.,* a/the beginning 16

prior, -ius, former 22

prius, *adv.,* before 18

pro, *prep. with abl.,* as a reward for; in behalf of, for 22

probitās, -tātis, *fem.,* honesty, uprightness 20

proelium, -iī/ī, *neut.,* a battle, fight 16

prōmissiō, -iōnis, *fem.,* a promise 20

prophēta, -ae, *masc.,* a prophet; soothsayer, fortuneteller 5

propter, *prep. with acc.,* on account of, because of 16

Proserpina, -ae, *fem.,* Roman goddess of the lower world, daughter of Ceres Lg V

prūdēns, (*gen.,* **-entis**), wise, prudent, judicious 10

publicus, -a, -um, public 8

puella, -ae, *fem.,* a girl, young woman, sweetheart 12, 13

puer, puerī, *masc.,* a boy, child 2, 13

pugna, -ae, *fem.,* a fight, battle 21 (Act. J)

pugnō (1), to fight 12

Punicum Bellum Prīmum, -ī; -ī; -us, -a, -um (Secundum; Tertium), *neut.,* three wars fought between Rome and Carthage 18, 19, 20

Pūnicus, -a, -um, Carthaginian 18

pūrus, -a, -um, clean, pure 10

Pyrrhus, -ī, *masc.,* king of Epirus 319-272 B.C., who defeated the Romans but suffered enormous losses 17

quae, who, which 17, 18, 19, 20

quaecumque, *indef. pro.,* whatsoever 21

quaerō, -ere, quaesīvī, -sītus, to seek, search for 19

quālis, -e, what kind of, what sort of 10

quārtus, -a, -um, fourth 18

quārtus decimus, -a, -um, fourteenth

quasi, *adv.,* approximately, about 19

quattuor, *indecl. number,* four 18

quattuordecim, *indecl. number,* fourteen

-que, *enclitic conj., (usually attached to the second of two joined words, e.g.,* senatus populusque Romanus *or* SPQR, *"Roman Senate and People"; for two joined phrases or clauses, usually attached to the first word of the second part),* and 5

quem, *interrog. pro.,* whom

quercus, -ūs, *fem.,* oak, oak tree; crown of oak leaves awarded for saving a life in war 6

quī, quae, quod, *interrog. adj.,* who, what/which, 20. *See also* 11, 13, 18, 20.

quī, quae, quod, *rel. pron.,* who, which/that 19, 20

quia, *conj.,* because 17

quibus, whom, which 12, 18, 20

quid, *See* **quis.**

quindecim, *indecl. number,* fifteen

quinque, *indecl. number,* five 18

quīntus, -a, -um, fifth 18

Quīntus, -ī, *masc.,* a name 2

quīntus decimus, fifteenth

quis, quid, *interrog. pro.,* who, what 20

quisque, quidque, *pro. and adj.,* each one; each 22

quod, *pro., See* **quī, quae, quod.**

quod, *conj.,* because 17

quoque, *adv., (placed after the word it emphasizes)* also, too 1, 4, 5, 9, 11

quōrum, of whom, of which 11

rapidē, *adv.,* rapidly, quickly 16

ratiō, -iōnis, *fem.,* reason 20

redeō, -īre, -iī, īvī, -itus, to return, go back, come back 15

rēgīna, -ae, *fem.,* a/the queen Lg V

rēgnum, -ī, *neut.,* a kingdom; power; unrestrained rule 11

regō, -ere, rexī, rectus, to guide, direct; to rule, govern

Regulus, Attilus, -ī -ī, *masc.,* Roman general in the First Punic War who was captured by the Carthaginians 20

remedium, -iī/ī, *neut.,* a remedy, cure 7

remittō, -ere, remīsī, remissus, to send back Lg V

Remus, -ī, *masc.,* Remus, the twin brother of Romulus 11, Lg III

repellō, -ere, reppulī, repulsus, to drive back 16

repleō, -ēre, -ēvī, -ētus, to fill, make full 21

rēs, reī, *fem.,* a thing, object, affair, matter, circumstance 8

rēs publica, reī publicae, *fem.,* the republic 8

resurgō, -ere, -surrexī, -surrectus, to rise again 18

resurrectiō, -iōnis, *fem.,* a/the resurrection, a rising again from the dead 5

reveniō, -īre, -vēnī, -ventus, to come back, return 13

revertō, -ere, -vertī, to turn back, return 17, 19

rēx, rēgis, *masc.,* a king, ruler, prince 4

Rēx, Rēgis, *masc.,* Christ, the King of kings 4

Rhea Silvia, -ae, -ae, *fem.,* the daughter of King Numitor, mother of Romulus and Remus 11

Rhodanus, -ī, *masc.,* Rhone, a river in Gaul (now Switzerland and France) 7 (Act. F)

rīdeō, -ēre, rīsī, rīsus, to laugh 11, 15

rogātiō, -iōnis, *fem.,* a request, an entreaty 22

Rōma, -ae, *fem.,* Rome (the city, the republic, or the empire) 2

Rōmānus, -a, -um, Roman, pertaining to Rome or a person of Rome 2

Rōmānus, -ī, *masc.,* a Roman man or boy

Rōmulus, -ī, *masc.,* a grandson of King Numitor, legendary founder of Rome, twin brother of Remus 11, Lg III

Rubicō, -ōnis, *masc.,* the Rubicon River, a small river in northern Italy 22

sacer, -cra, -crum, sacred 16

Sabīnī, -ōrum, *masc.,* a tribe of people who lived north of the Latins 11

saeculum, -ī, *neut.,* an age, a century 23

saepe, *adv.,* often 9

sāl, salis, *masc.,* salt 20

salvātor, -tōris, *masc.,* a savior, liberator 4

Salvātor, -tōris, *masc.,* the Savior, Christ 4

salveō, -ēre, to be well; (*in the imperative mood*) Good day! Good morning! Hello! 1, 17

schola, -ae, *fem.,* a school 1

sciō, -īre, scīvī/sciī, scītus, to know, understand 15

Scīpio Maior, -iōnis, -iōris, *masc.,* Scipio the Elder, a Roman general in the Second Punic War 19

Scīpio Minor, -iōnis, -ōris, *masc.,* Scipio the Younger, a Roman general in the Second Punic War 19

sciūrus, -ī, *masc.,* a squirrel 7

scrībō, -ere, scrīpsī, scrīptus, to write 9, 15

scrīptor, -tōris, *masc.,* a writer 9

scrīptūra, -ae, *fem.,* a writing

Scrīptūra, -ae, *fem.,* Scripture, the Bible 6

sē, (*from* **suī**), *reflex. pro.,* herself, itself, himself, themselves 20, 22

sēcrētus, -a, -um, secret 16 (Act. M), 19 (Act. L)

sectātor, -ōris, *masc.,* a follower 21

secundus, -a, -um, second 18

Secundus, -ī, *masc.,* a name 4

secūrus, -a, -um, free from care, fearless; carefree; safe, secure 13

sed, *conj.,* but 17

sēdecim, *indecl. number,* sixteen

sedeō, -ēre, sēdī, sessus, to sit, be inactive; to remain fixed 7

semper, *adv.,* always 16, 21

Seneca, -ae, *masc.,* a Stoic philosopher and writer in the first century A.D. 7

senātor, -tōris, *masc.,* a senator 6

senātus, -ūs, *masc.,* a/the senate, council of elders 4

senex, senis, *com.,* an old man or woman, old person 20

septem, *indecl. number,* seven 13, 18

septendecim, *indecl. number,* seventeen

septimus, -a, -um, seventh 18

septimus decimus, seventeenth

servō (1), to watch over, protect, guard; to keep, save 11

servus, -ī, *masc.,* a slave 23

sex, *indecl. number,* six 18

sextus, -a, -um, sixth 18

sextus decimus, -a, -um, sixteenth

sī, *conj.,* if 17

Sicilia, -ae, *fem.,* Sicily, an island at the end of the Italian peninsula 18

sīcut, *adv.,* as, just as, even as 19, 20

silva, -ae, *fem.,* a forest, woods 4, 7

Silvia, Rhea, -ae -ae, *fem.,* the daughter of King Numitor, mother of Romulus and Remus 11, Lg III

similis, -e *(used with the dat. case),* similar, similar to 6

sine, *prep. with abl.,* without 7

sōl, sōlis, *masc.,* the sun 18, 23

solea, -ae, *fem.,* a sandal 23

sōlus, -a, -um, alone, only, sole 13

soror, -ōris, *fem.,* a sister 13

spatium, -iī/ī, *neut.,* space, distance 23

spēs, speī, *fem.,* hope, expectation 4

spiritus, -ūs, *masc.,* a spirit; a breathing or gentle blowing (of air), breath

Spiritus, -ūs, *masc.,* the Spirit, Holy Spirit 5

statim, *adv.,* at once, immediately 20

stilus, -ī, *masc.,* a stylus, pen, writing instrument 1

stipendium, -iī/ī, *neut.,* a soldier's pay 22

stō, stāre, stetī, status, to stand, stand still, remain standing 7, 15

strīdor, -dōris, *masc.,* a noise, loud noise 16

stultus, -a, -um, foolish 12 (Act. H)

sub, *prep. with abl. and acc.,* under 9

succīdō, -ere, -cidī, to cut down 13, 15

suffōcō (1), to strangle, choke, suffocate, drown 21

suī, *reflex. pro.,* of himself, herself, itself, themselves. *See also* **suus** *and* **sē.**

Sulla, -ae, *masc.,* a Roman general and dictator who fought against Marius 22

sum, esse, fuī, futūrus, to be, to exist 5, 16, 21

summus, -a, -um, highest, very high 22. *See also* **suprēmus, -a, –um.**

sunt, they are 11

super, *adv.,* over, above, besides; *prep. with abl.,* over, above, besides, beyond; *prep. with acc.,* over, above, upon 13

superbus, -a, -um, haughty, proud, bold 11, 20

superior, -ius, higher 22

superō (1), to overcome, conquer, defeat

superus, -a, -um, above 11, 22

supplicō (1), to kneel, beseech, pray 15

suprēmus, -a, -um, last 22. *See also* **summus, -a, -um.**

suscitō (1), to cause to rise, make to rise 19

suus, -a, -um, *reflex. adj.,* his own, her own, its own, their own 13, 19

Syria, ae, *fem.,* Syria, a country in southwestern Asia

Tarquinius Superbus, -iī/ī -ī, Tarquin the Proud, the last of the seven kings of Rome; was expelled from Rome 11

Tarsus, -ī, *fem.,* chief town of Cilicia (in Asia Minor)

tempus, -oris, *neut.,* time 6, 8

Terentia, -ae, *fem.,* a name, Cicero's wife 5

terminō (1), to close, end 22

terra, -ae, *fem.,* earth, soil, land 7

terreō, -ēre, terruī, territus, to frighten, terrify 17

tertius, -a, -um, third

tertius decimus, -a, -um, thirteenth

Tiber, -beris *(acc.,* **-berim),** *masc.,* a river near Rome 6

tibi, to/for you 6

timeō, -ēre, timuī, to fear 2

titulus, -ī, *masc.,* an inscription, label, title 12

tōtus, -a, -um, total, whole, entire 20 (Act. M), 21 (Act. E)

trāns, *prep. with acc.,* across, over 7

transeō, -īre, -iī, -itus, to go over, cross, pass over 19

transiliō, -īre, -siluī, to leap across, jump over 11, 15

trecentī, *indecl. number,* three hundred

tredecim, *indecl. number,* thirteen

trēs, tria, three 18

tribūnus, -ī, *masc.,* a tribune; one of several kinds of Roman officials, a magistrate 12

tribūnus plebis, -ī -is, *masc.,* a tribune who represented the plebeian class of people 12

tribus, -ūs, *fem.,* a tribe 19

triginta septem, *indecl. number,* thirty-seven

triginta trēs, *indecl. number,* thirty-three

tristis, -e, sad, gloomy, dismal 10

triumvir, -virī, *masc.,* one of three members of a board of commissioners; one of three chief magistrates

triumvirātus, -ūs, *masc.,* a triumvirate, group of three triumvirs; the office of a triumvir 22

Triumvirātus Prīmus, -ūs/ī, the First Triumvirate 22

Triumvirātus Secundus, -ūs/ī, the Second Triumvirate 22

Trōia, -ae, *fem.,* Troy, an ancient city in Asia Minor Lg III

Trōiānus, -a, -um, Trojan, pertaining to Troy or the people of Troy Lg III

Trōianus, -ī, *masc.,* a Trojan man

truncus, -ī, *masc.,* a trunk (of a tree) 2

tū, *pers. pro.,* you 14, 15
Tullia, -ae, *fem.,* a name 5
Tullius, -iī/ī, *masc.,* a name
tum, *adv.,* then 7, 16
tutus, -a, -um, safe 16
tuus, -a, -um, your (*sing.*) 1, 8
Tyrus (-os), -ī, *fem.,* a city of Phoenicia, where Carthage had a colony 18
ubi, *interrog. adv.,* where, when 7, 9, 16
ultimus, -a, -um, last 23
umbra, -ae, *fem.,* shadow 7
ūndecim, *indecl. number,* eleven
ūndecimus, -a, -um, eleventh
ūndēvīcēsimus, -a, -um, nineteenth
ūndēvigintī, *indecl. number,* nineteen
ūnus, -a, -um, one 5, 18, 19
urbs, urbis, *fem.,* a city 2
uxor, -ōris, *fem.,* a wife 13
valeō, -ēre, to be well; (*in imper. mood*) Farewell! Good-bye! 1, 17
validus, -a, -um, strong, powerful 20
vastus, -a, -um, empty, deserted, desolate; vast, enormous; rough or rude in appearance 8
venia, -ae, *fem.,* pardon, forgiveness; grace, favor 6
veniō, -īre, vēnī, ventus, to come 13, 15
verbum, -ī, *neut.,* a word 5
vērē, *adv.,* truly, really, genuinely 5

vēritās, -tātis, *fem.,* truth, verity, reality 5
vērus, -a, -um, true 5
Vesta, -ae, *fem.,* Roman goddess of the hearth 15
vester, -stra, -strum, your (*pl.*) 15
Vesuvius, -iī/ī, *masc.,* a volcano in Italy 22
vetus (*gen.,* **veteris**), old, ancient; experienced in 10
via, -ae, *fem.,* a way, road, street 4
viātor, -ōris, *masc.,* a traveler 23
vicēsimus, -a, -um, twentieth 19
victor, -tōris, *masc.,* a victor, conqueror 4
victōria, -ae, *fem.,* a victory 12
videō, -ēre, vīdī, vīsus, to see 17
vigintī, *indecl. number,* twenty 19
vincō, -ere, vīcī, victus, to conquer, defeat 13, 17
vir, virī, *masc.,* a man, husband 12, 13
Virgilius (Vergilius), P. Maro, -iī/ī, -ōnis, *masc.,* a Roman poet of the first century B.C., writer of the *Aeneid* 7
virtūs, -tūtis, *fem.,* manliness, courage; virtue, goodness, excellence 7
vīs, *irregular noun* (*acc.,* **vim,** *abl.,* **vī**), (*pl.,* **virēs, virium**), *fem.,* strength, force, power 20
vīta, -ae, *fem.,* life, a/the life 4
vitium, -iī/ī, *neut.,* a fault, imperfection; crime, vice 7, 8

vītis, -is, *fem.,* a vine, grapevine 5
vīvō, -ere, vīxī, victus, to live, be alive 8, 20
vīvus, -a, -um, living, alive 5, 8
vocābulārium, -iī/ī, *neut.* (*Medieval Latin*), words
vocō (1), to call 15
Volscī, ōrum, *masc.,* the Volscians, a tribe of people in Latium, to whom Coriolanus went when he left Rome 12
voluntās, -tātis, *fem.,* a wish; will 16
vōs, (*pl. of* **tū** *and* **tē**), you 15
vōx, vōcis, *fem.,* a voice 21
Vulgāta, -ae, *fem.,* the Vulgate, a translation of the Bible into Latin for the common people who did not know Greek and Hebrew 6, Lg IV
vulgus, -ī, *neut.,* a multitude, mass, throng (of persons or animals); the common people, the public; crowd, rabble, mob (suggesting contempt) 6
vulnus, -neris, *neut.,* a wound 19
Zama, -ae, *fem.,* an ancient town in northern Africa 19
Zēno or **Zēnōnis,** *masc.,* (1) a Greek philosopher, founder of the Stoic school of philosophy; (2) a later Greek philosopher of the Epicurean school, teacher of Cicero 7

Index

- The numbers indicate the chapters. Nearly every item can be located in the Essential Information section, in bold type, in a section title, or in a box.
- Items found only in the activities are not included.
- Mythological terms are not included. See Vocābulārium (E-L and L-E) and Appendix G for these.

Index

Photo Credits

The following agencies and individuals have furnished materials to meet the photographic needs of this textbook. We wish to express our gratitude to them for their important contribution.

Cartography & Graphics
George R. Collins
Corbis
Corbis-Bettmann
Creation Science Foundation, Ltd, Australia
Dr. Stewart Custer
Grace Collins Hargis
Information Service, Rome
Metropolitan Museum of Art
Miriam Mitchem
William L. Nelson
Photo Disc, Inc.
Larry Pryor
Unusual Films
West Point Museum

Cover
Unusual Films (top left); Miriam Mitchem (bottom left); Photo Disc, Inc. (middle right, background); Creation Science Foundation, Ltd, Australia (bottom right)

Title Page
Photo Disc, Inc. (background)

Chapter 2
Corbis 17

Chapter 3
Photo Disc, Inc. 28

Chapter 5
Corbis 60

Chapter 7
Corbis-Bettmann 82; Corbis 90

Chapter 8
Metropolitan Museum of Art 95; Unusual Films, courtesy of Larry Pryor 96-97